Price Theory in Action

A Book of Readings

Fourth Edition

Price Theory in Action

A Book of Readings
Fourth Edition

Edited by

Donald Stevenson Watson
George Washington University

Malcolm Getz
Vanderbilt University

Prospect Heights, Illinois

For more information about this book, write or call:

Waveland Press, Inc.
P.O. Box 400
Prospect Heights, Illinois 60070
(312) 634-0081

1987 reissued by Waveland Press, Inc. Third printing.

ISBN 0-88133-263-1

Printed in the United States of America.

Contents

Preface

Price theory is in action in many a national policy issue, in the operation of most social institutions, and in nearly everyone's life every day. This collection of readings is chosen to illustrate that action. Actual demand curves are examined; elasticity coefficients are calculated; cost curves are inspected. Most of the readings apply the basic ideas of microeconomics. Some of the readings explore the edges of microeconomics without going beyond topics normally discussed in intermediate courses. Just a few report some statistics. The Siegfried and Eisenberg essay on the demand for minor league baseball explains some basic statistics in simple terms that may help students understand some subsequent readings.

Articles dealing with energy are among the most topical here. The deregulation of gas and oil and the federal program of investment in synthetic fuels are discussed in three selections. The topic of deregulation comes up in articles on the airlines, trucking, railroads, utilities, banking, and the stock market. The future of the minimum wage is also a lively subject.

Several of the essays can be called classics. Cookenboo's investigation of cost relationships for pipelines is important and easily understood. The essays on the elasticity of demand for steel and durables are brief and insightful.

Some of the essays will extend the understanding of students. Kwoka's essay on market shares makes clear the importance of the distribution of firm size. Qualls's essay explores the issue of profit maximization with some interesting evidence. Gruen uses ideas concerning risk in estimating the demand for gambling. Other essays offer critiques of some common presumptions of microeconomics, as for example, Kindleberger's essay on quantity adjustment.

Among the more entertaining readings are Manne's essay on parking lots, the *Business Week* essay on the cereals industry, and Hanke's discussion of the demand for water.

The editing consists of condensation. Each author's main lines of analysis are presented with details and most footnotes being deleted. The originals should be available in most college libraries where microeconomics is taught. We are especially grateful to the authors and publishers who have allowed their works to appear here. Editing sometimes results in shifts in emphasis or omission of ancillary themes. We accept responsibility for such changes.

D. S. W.
M. G.

Price Theory in Action

A Book of Readings
Fourth Edition

Part One

The demand curve of standard theory is a smooth and continuous line on the page of a textbook or on a blackboard diagram. This demand curve declares an assumed relation between prices and quantities, all other variables (such as buyers' incomes) being held constant. The curve's position and shape also convey information about price elasticity of demand.

What about demand in real life? The best way to find out about this is to look at statistical estimates of demand functions. The selections to follow give examples of such estimates; the empirical materials on demand are drawn from what is now a large body of knowledge. The statistical estimates produce quantitative relationships between prices and amounts, as well as between variations in buyers' incomes and the corresponding amounts purchased. The estimating procedures usually also yield numerical values for both price elasticities and income elasticities.

One of the principal uses of statistical estimates of demand is in forecasting. Let us suppose Congress decides to raise or lower the excise tax on a product such as passenger automobiles. What will happen to revenue with the new tax? With a good empirical study of the demand for autos, the United States Treasury ought to be able to make a fairly reliable forecast of the probable change in tax revenue. Business firms also can use statistical studies of demand in making sales forecasts. The drawback here, however, is that the studies always cover industry demand—the demand for the automobiles, the steel, the meat, the refrigerators, the new houses, etc. produced by all of the firms in each of the industries. The demand for what any one firm has to sell depends critically upon the prices charged by the other competing firms. This fact makes it difficult or impossible to isolate, statistically, the demand for the output of a firm. But if any firms do indeed have good quantitative analyses of their own demands, they probably are wise, in their own interests, to guard the analyses as valuable business secrets. Nonetheless, the industry demand studies are useful, because a

Demand

firm can make a projection of industry sales, and if the firm believes that its market share is a constant, or nearly so, the firm can thus forecast its own sales.

It is not easy to conduct empirical analyses of demand and to come to dependable conclusions. Raw data on prices, quantities, incomes, and on other relevant matters are nearly always imperfect. They are likely to be meager or untrustworthy, or perversely and inextricably entangled with things the analyst wishes he could get rid of, such as hard-to-measure changes in the quality of the commodity being investigated. What the analyst has to do is to isolate the price-quantity relation and the income-quantity relation and to set them out in their pure forms, with every other variable locked up tightly in that well-known box—"other things being equal."

Even when much effort has gone into the measurement of the demand for a commodity, the results are not like those of a laboratory experiment—anyone has to agree with the results because if he repeated the experiment he would come to exactly the same conclusions. No, the measurement of demand results more often than not in conclusions that can be disputed, because the data are usually imperfect and because there is no one infallible method of analysis with just one interpretation. And conclusions are indeed disputed when something is at stake. This is well shown by the two selections on the demand for automobiles and by the two on the demand for steel. In fact, many of the best-known statistical studies of demand have been conducted for organizations (business firms or industries) with definite interests in having the findings come out in certain ways.

Demand functions can be measured from either or both of two kinds of data: time-series data or cross-section data. Time-series data are historical records, by months or years, of prices, quantities, incomes, and other variables. Cross-section data can be illustrated this way: Suppose the commodity is champagne. In one year, prices vary from state to state because of differences in taxes and in the markups in the various states that operate their own liquor stores. By comparing, for each state, per capita purchases with the different prices *in that one year,* the demand-price relation can be measured, provided of course that the other variables (incomes, tastes, prices of substitutes) can be satisfactorily handled.

The results from analysis of time-series data are likely to differ from those derived from cross-section data. Thus the same study can give more than one estimate of the coefficient of price elasticity. In fact, the more penetrating and the more sophisticated the statistical analysis, the more probable it is that the investigation will yield several estimates of a coefficient, each with its own little shade of meaning. This point is illustrated in the selection on the demand for durable goods.

It follows that numerical coefficients should not be taken literally—to the last digit after the decimal point. At best, they are good estimates. They are not exact measures. The reader is also warned to watch out for the minus sign for the coefficient of price elasticity. Sometimes it is there and sometimes it is not, even in the same selection. This inconsistency is normal in the literature.

1 Demand and supply in the presence of a price ceiling are used to analyze shortages of natural gas in the 1970s.

AN EXAMINATION OF REGULATION IN THE NATURAL GAS INDUSTRY

RONALD BRAEUTIGAM
Northwestern University

Natural gas is a clean burning fuel which presently supplies about one-third of the total United States energy requirement. It is the dominant energy source for domestic industry, and provides heat for about one-half the homes in America.

However, in recent years there has been a shortage of natural gas, particularly during heating seasons when the demand is highest. Since 1970 some users have simply not been able to purchase all the gas they desire at prices prevailing in the market. Importantly, this shortage has increased sharply over the last five years. The concern over the possibility of continued shortages is supported further by the observation that since 1968, as a nation we have consumed more natural gas than we have added to our proven reserves by discoveries of new fields and new extensions of existing ones.

For more than two decades prior to 1977, the Federal Power Commission regulated the prices at which producers could sell natural gas to pipelines in interstate commerce. The Commission tried to set these prices (called wellhead prices) at levels which were not "unreasonably" high and which at the same time ensured that "adequate" supplies of gas were available. At least throughout the 1970's it has not been possible for regulation to satisfy both objectives by controlling wellhead prices. Although wellhead price controls have been supplemented by other regulatory measures, the shortage has persisted.

With the signing of the Department of Energy Reorganization Act in August 1977, the control of wellhead prices was transferred to the new Department of Energy. The central issues raised by the natural gas shortage are whether the Department of Energy should continue to regulate interstate wellhead prices, and whether regulation should be extended to include wellhead prices sold into intrastate commerce as well as interstate commerce.

Reactions to the gas shortage have led to several suggested alternatives for wellhead price regulation. Some argue for stronger regulation, with an announced policy of very limited wellhead price increases over time. Others suggest that regulation should be continued for one reason or another, but that

---

Excerpted from U.S. Senate Committee on Governmental Affairs, "Study on Federal Regulation," Appendix to Volume VI, *Framework for Regulation,* December 1978.

more rapid price increases will be necessary to avert even more serious shortages in the future. Finally, there have been several proposals which argue for the deregulation of some or all wellhead prices.

Arguments have been raised through research to support each of these positions. Some of the research suggests rather strongly that it is not desirable to continue the present form of regulation. This research points out that the shortage will continue as long as regulated prices are all set below the levels which would be achieved in unregulated markets. In addition, producers will continue to sell gas into intrastate markets, which are largely unregulated, wherever they can. This will exacerbate the shortage in interstate markets. The deregulation arguments also point out that while consumers who are able to purchase gas at regulated prices find their purchasing power increased under present controls, there are potential users who must resort to alternative fuels because they cannot get gas. These users will generally have to pay relatively higher prices for an alternative fuel, perhaps prices even higher than they would have had to pay for gas had wellhead prices been unregulated. As a result, any estimate which attempts to measure the extent to which regulation redistributes income from producers to consumers by taking into account only those users who can actually get gas will overestimate (some argue, substantially) the real magnitude of the redistribution.

Those who argue for strengthened regulation point out that potentially large windfall profits (in the billions of dollars annually) would be bestowed on producers if wellhead prices were deregulated, and that consumers would pay additional billions of dollars for natural gas supplies each year. In particular they also argue that higher prices will not bring forth substantial increases in supplies of gas, perhaps even over a period of years. Some who favor strengthened regulation call for the extension of federal controls to intrastate markets, so that consumers in states which do not produce natural gas will not be at a disadvantage in their effort to obtain supplies, as is presently the case.

Those who support some form of deregulation of wellhead prices argue that in most gas producing areas there are a number of pipeline buyers, and even more producers, so that markets would probably be workably competitive with deregulation. They offer some empirical evidence to suggest that higher wellhead prices will lead to increased gas supplies, at least within a few years. They also point out that in order to eliminate the shortage, higher gas prices are required, particularly since other forms of energy are becoming increasingly costly. They contend that while the extension of federal controls to intrastate markets may redistribute some gas from intrastate to interstate commerce, an overall shortage will nevertheless exist, and will be worse as wellhead prices are held further below their market-clearing levels. It is also argued that the regulation of wellhead prices leads to a number of ways in which natural gas resources are misallocated, and that deregulation would largely eliminate these substantial misallocations.

Finally, there are some proposals which would deregulate so-called "new gas" prices, but continue to regulate prices for "old gas." There has been substantial debate over the appropriate definitions of new and old gas. New gas would include at least gas produced from fields discovered after some specified date. The most important question is whether newly discovered gas should be considered as new gas, even if the gas come from an old field, from which production was begun prior to the specified date. Since most additions to established reserves come from old fields, or extensions of old fields, the definitional question is a crucial one.

It is sometimes asserted that the alternative of deregulating only new gas wellhead prices will have all the advantages of total deregulation in terms of efficiently allocating resources, while preventing producers from earning windfall profits on old gas. This requires the imposition of two additional conditions. First, the time periods for which new and old gas are defined must not be changed once the proposal is in effect. Gas which is considered new at one time should not be reclassified as old at some later time. Second, a tax on the consumption of gas should be imposed so that the sum of the weighted average price of the gas stream plus the tax equals the price of new gas. These two conditions are needed to ensure that gas prices provide economically efficient signals to producers and consumers. . . .

Reserve Accumulation and Extraction

Since gas and oil are often found together, the incentives for exploration are affected by the prices for both crude oil and natural gas. These prices represent the revenues that can be derived from each barrel of oil and Mcf* of gas ultimately produced. At the same time, petroleum companies incur costs in exploration activities, and while the costs of exploration may be known, the prospects for actual discoveries of hydrocarbon reservoirs are quite uncertain. Producers therefore view exploration as a risky undertaking, and will have an incentive to explore if they believe that the potential revenues will cover the costs of exploration, development, and extraction, including the risk element.

Companies may choose to explore in the hope of extending the known boundaries of existing reservoirs by drilling wells near producing properties. This is called intensive drilling. They may also search in areas not near producing properties if data from seismological and geological surveys look promising. If an exploratory well is drilled for this purpose, it is characterized as extensive drilling.

If the exploration does result in the finding of gas deposits not previously established, then an attempt to estimate the volume of the deposits is made, using geological, geophysical, and engineering techniques. These estimates represent additions to reserves. Estimated total reserves may be adjusted as further information about the reservoir becomes available.

At the next stage of production, a company must decide if it is profitable to develop a proven gas reservoir in preparation for extraction. The attractiveness of development will depend on several things, including the quantity and quality

* million cubic feet

of gas, the properties of the reservoir, and again, the wellhead price. The properties of the reservoir include among other things the porosity of the rock (the amount of porous space in the reservoir), the permeability (which measures how well the porous spaces are connected so that gas can flow to producing wells), the reservoir pressure (higher pressures generally facilitate production), and reservoir depth (it is generally more costly to produce from deeper reservoirs). A company which has previously decided to explore for gas may not find development worthwhile even if gas is discovered, because some of the actual properties of the reservoir are not known until after further drilling takes place.

If a field is developed, then a decision must be made about rates of extraction. Some states impose limits on rates of extraction, and even within these guidelines a firm must make a technological assessment about extraction rates. In many cases if extraction is too rapid, damage to the rock formation near the well bore may result, making future extraction quite difficult. These technological considerations, including the actual cost of the extraction process, will be weighed against wellhead prices to determine the rate of production. As a volume of gas is extracted, total reserves will be reduced by that volume. The gas will then be sold to pipelines at the wellhead price. The contracts between producers and pipelines will typically be for a long term (from five to twenty years). A contract will dedicate production from reserves for delivery into certain pipelines. The pipelines, in turn, transport the gas to their own customers.

The Demand for Gas

Residential, commercial, and industrial users of gas take into account several factors in deciding how much gas they would like to purchase. For many of these customers there are alternative fuels, including various types of oil, coal, liquid natural gas, synthetic natural gas, and imported gas. The prices of these alternative fuels will be considered relative to the price and availability of gas delivered from field markets.

Industrial users will usually be able to obtain their gas directly from a pipeline, and will therefore pay a wholesale price which includes the wellhead price of gas and a charge for transportation by the pipeline. Most residential and commercial users obtain their gas through public utilities which act as local distributors. These customers pay a retail price which includes the wholesale price and a charge by the utility for the local distribution service.

The quantities of gas which residential, commercial, and industrial customers together wish to purchase at existing prices comprise the quantity of gas demanded.

The Forces and the Shortage

The effects of the forces at work in the production and consumption of natural gas can be illustrated using one of the most basic tools of economic analysis, supply and demand. In Fig. 1, S represents a supply schedule for gas. Faced with any prevailing price (e.g., p_1), producers will provide additional gas whenever the price (p_1) received for an additional Mcf exceeds the cost of producing the additional gas. At quantities less than $q_1{}^s$ this is the case. At quantities larger than $q_1{}^s$, the cost of producing additional gas exceeds the revenues which could be earned given p_1, and producers would find it profitable to cut back production to $q_1{}^s$. Thus, given any prevailing price, the supply schedule S shows how much gas producers would supply.

As shown in Fig. 1, S slopes upward, i.e., at higher prices, producers would offer more gas for sale. This corresponds to the discussion developed above. At higher wellhead prices, producers would find exploration profitable for prospects deemed too risky at lower prices. Producers would also find development of

FIGURE 1

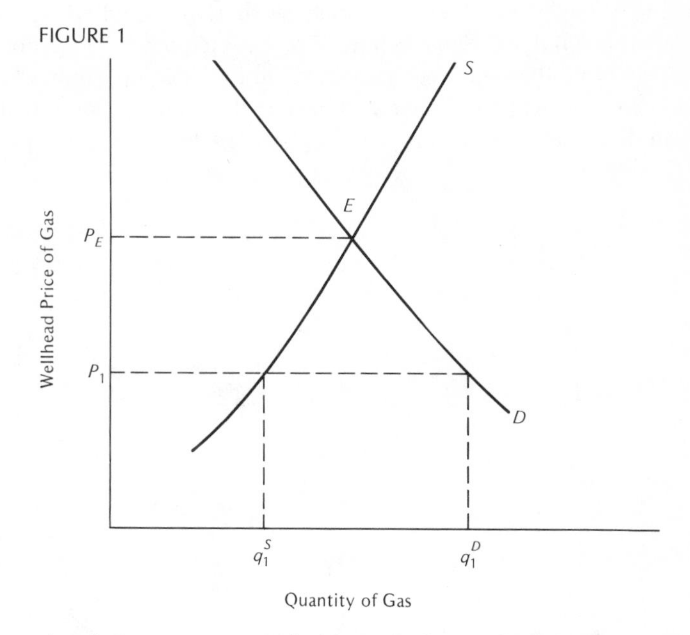

deeper and tighter reservoirs profitable at higher wellhead prices. All of this would lead to more reserves available for production at the higher prices.

The steepness of the slope of S is important. It is sometimes argued (particularly by those who favor continued regulation of wellhead prices) that S is very steep, i.e., that at higher prices producers would not offer much more gas than they would at lower prices. By others it is argued that the slope of S is not so steep, particularly if higher prices were allowed to prevail over a time period long enough (e.g., a few years) so that producers could respond by increased exploration and development. In other words, in the long run, S might not be very steep, although in the short run S might be quite steep since producers cannot succeed in discovering and developing new fields in response to price changes over only a few months. The responsiveness of quantity produced to changes in price is an empirical question.

The demand schedule for natural gas is represented by the curve labeled D in Fig. 1. At any wellhead price (e.g., p_1) the quantity which consumers would be willing to purchase is represented by the quantity on D corresponding to p_1 (q_1^D in the example). Given the prices of other fuels, consumers can be expected to purchase less gas as the price of gas rises. For example, if the price of gas rises and the price of fuel oil remains unchanged, some consumers may find it cheaper to switch from gas to fuel oil. A higher gas price may lead other consumers to cut back on their gas consumption, even though they do not substitute other fuels for gas. These effects mean that the demand schedule will have a negative slope, as shown in Fig. 1.

At point E in Fig. 1 the market is said to "clear," since the quantity demanded equals the quantity supplied. At a price below p_E, the quantity demanded will exceed the quantity supplied. In other words, if regulators were to set a wellhead price such as p_1 (below p_E), then a resulting gas shortage would be expected. If the regulation holding the wellhead price at p_1 were removed, those consumers willing to pay more than p_1 to get gas would bid the price up. Only when the price has risen to p_E will consumers stop bidding the price up, for at that price can all consumers who are willing to pay p_E or more for gas actually purchase it. . . .

2 Here is a close examination of one segment of air travel. Short-haul air service has close substitutes that strongly influence its demand. The speed, the frequency, and the timing of flights also help to determine the volume of short-haul air traffic. Professor Eads finds that although this form of travel is in general price-inelastic, some of its submarkets are in fact sensitive to changes in fares. The following excerpts from Professor Eads's book omit much statistical data and almost all references to sources.

THE DEMAND FOR SHORT-HAUL AIR SERVICE

GEORGE EADS
The George Washington University

The Total Demand for Passenger Transportation

Much of the current research on the demand for travel suggests that it is a mistake to consider in isolation the demand for any single mode of transportation, such as air travel. A classic hypothesis is that total travel between any two points increases in proportion to the product of the populations in the two cities and decreases in proportion to the square of the distance between them. Additional influences on total travel are assumed to include such factors as the cost of travel and the frequency and quality of service. Increases in the population of either locality, or improvements in the quality of the transportation network linking them, serve to increase travel. Similarly, reductions in the cost of service (including both ticket price and travel time, with the latter reflecting the opportunity cost of a traveler's time) are assumed to have a stimulating effect on travel.

More complex models . . . suggest that the choice of travel mode is determined solely by the characteristics of each relative to those of other modes. Examples of these characteristics are the price (again including the implicit value of the traveler's time), frequency, and timing of the service. Travelers are assumed to have no inherent preference for any one mode of travel. Taken together, these models indicate that an attempt to determine the factors affecting the demand for air travel solely as a function of such variables as the price of air travel, its frequency, and so on, must proceed under a strong and somewhat unrealistic *ceteris paribus* assumption concerning all other travel modes. Conclusions from studies of a single mode, therefore, should be interpreted with some caution. . . .

Excerpts from Chapter II in *The Local Service Airline Experiment,* by George Eads, Washington, D.C.: The Brookings Institution, 1972.

The Size of the Short-haul Air Travel Market

For present purposes, a *short-haul airline market* is defined as one that is less than five hundred miles in length, unless otherwise specified. In some studies, however, markets of more than three hundred miles are classified as medium-haul. Although the airplane generally is thought of as a means of long-distance transportation . . . the markets classified here as "short-haul" constitute a substantial portion of the total market for air transport.

In 1968 . . . the local service carriers originated 22 million passengers. Since in 1967, 92 percent of all local service carrier on-line originations were for trips of 400 miles or less, it seems that the locals carried only about half of the short-haul air passengers. Local carrier participation in many of the most lucrative short-haul markets, such as Boston–New York (190 miles, 2.4 million passengers), New York–Washington (216 miles, 1.9 million passengers), and Los Angeles–San Francisco (354 miles, 1.7 million passengers) was minimal. However, there were relatively dense markets in which the locals participated to a significant degree; two examples are Philadelphia–Pittsburgh (268 miles, 292,000 passengers in 1968), of which Allegheny Airlines carried about half, and Albany–New York (138 miles, 169,000 passengers), of which Mohawk Airlines carried 85 percent.

A Portrait of the Short-haul Air Traveler

The Census Bureau's *National Travel Survey*, together with relatively meager information made available by the carriers themselves, provides a portrait of the short-haul air traveler. More than half of all air travel is still for business reasons, though this proportion is declining. In 1967, 51 percent of all commercial air trips were made either for direct business purposes or to attend conventions. Business is the reason for at least as large a proportion of short-haul air travel. Surveys taken in the 1960–62 period by Ozark Air Lines showed that 80 percent of its passengers were traveling on business. A similar survey taken in 1961 by Central Airlines found that 56 percent of its passengers were traveling on either private or government business, and 16 percent were traveling under military orders.

These data refer to trips, not travelers, and this distinction is important. American Airlines, in a travel survey made in 1963, found that only 10 percent of its travelers took 57 percent of the airline trips. The median number of airline trips per year, per passenger responding to the Ozark survey, was about ten. Two-thirds of Ozark's passengers had traveled by air more than five times in the previous year; more than one-fourth had made between six and seventeen trips; another fourth had made between eighteen and sixty-five air trips; and about 11 percent had made more than sixty-five trips by air in the preceding year. One would assume that most of these frequent travelers were traveling for business purposes.

Although business is the predominant reason for short-haul air travel, most short-haul business travel is done by automobile. In 1967 only about 1 percent of all trips of less than 200 miles were made by air, while almost 95 percent were by automobile. The importance of air travel rises sharply as the length of trip increases; 12 percent of all trips in the 200–499-mile range were by air. Yet during 1967 the average length of on-line passenger trips for the local service carriers was only 227 miles, and 92 percent of local service on-line passenger originations were for trips of 400 miles or less. Ozark asked its passengers in 1960 how they would have traveled had Ozark's service been unavailable. Significantly, only 8.2 percent said they would not have made the trip. Automobile travel was the alternative for 40.2 percent; 37.1 percent said they would have taken a train; 6.9 percent designated private airplane; 6.1 percent would have ridden a bus; while 3.7 percent listed other means.

Thus, the average short-haul air traveler is likely to fly relatively frequently and to be traveling on business. He generally has alternative modes of transportation available to him. He chooses air travel presumably because of its relative cost, speed, and convenience; changes in these factors could be expected to affect his choice.

Factors Affecting the Demand for Short-haul Air Service

Perhaps the best statement of the problem faced by the local service carriers in attracting traffic was made by the CAB in its 1944 decision to create this class of air carriers:

> In connection with this relatively low traffic potential [of smaller cities] we believe it is desirable to emphasize constantly the fact that in attempting to develop this potential, local air carriers will be competing with the most highly developed rail and highway transportation systems in the world. The highway system not only provides a network of motor bus lines but also the roadway for the private automobile. We must assume that this vehicle will continue to carry the vast majority of all short-haul passengers, as in the past, and perhaps increase the proportion somewhat after the war. The further development of these surface systems will also be intensified with increased emphasis after the war, and they will also reap the benefits of technical developments and improvements. These systems have their greatest utility in short-haul services.
>
> The airplane, on the other hand, has had its greatest utility in the longer distance transportation market. In this market its outstanding characteristic of high speed gives it a great competitive advantage, and permits the fullest exploitation of its inherent characteristics. But this inherent competitive advantage diminishes sharply, with conventional type aircraft, as the length of the trip is reduced. Even in the long-haul market its speed advantage becomes less effective as the number of intermediate points at which landings must be made on each flight is increased.
>
> Thus, in going into the small-city, short-haul market, the airplane will be

faced with the most intense kind of competition, with its principal selling point, speed, greatly diminished in value. While it will still have advantages to offer, the differential in fare that it now appears will be necessary will counterbalance them to some extent. Five cents per mile, the figure generally considered as the prospective passenger fare, is approximately three times the average fare for motor bus transportation. In addition there are many other factors . . . which will affect the traffic potential, such as the distance between the airport and city center, the time of day at which service will be scheduled, the frequency and regularity of schedules, the mail departure requirements, the extent to which reservations will be necessary, and many other details which will vary according to the locality and the city size.

Price

It is generally believed that the price elasticity of demand for air travel varies with the length of trip and that demand is relatively inelastic for short-haul trips. This view is shared by the local carriers. Robert E. Peach, president of Mohawk Airlines, in testifying about the industry's problems before a congressional committee in 1966, said:

> It is our contention, based on 20 years of experience that a 5- to 10-percent reduction in short-haul fares will not stimulate traffic more than a minor amount—if at all—that short-haul air passengers are primarily business oriented. They respond not to a dollar or so fare reduction but [to] the frequency and timing of flight schedules, quality of reservations services, and the like.

In 1966, Mohawk's average revenue per passenger was $17.98. The average length of its passenger on-line trip was 222 miles. These two figures imply that Mohawk's "yield" (average revenue per revenue passenger-mile) was 8.10 cents. (The average yield for the local carriers as a whole during 1966 was 7.64 cents per revenue passenger-mile.) A 10 percent cut in Mohawk's average fare would have meant a saving to the passenger of only about $1.80, a fraction of the hourly salary of most businessmen. More significantly, the chief alternative mode of short-haul travel, the automobile, also costs about 8 cents a mile to operate. The average rate of reimbursement for automobile travel by companies is 8 cents a mile; and a rental car costs a flat daily rate of ten dollars or more, plus a mileage charge usually greater than 10 cents a mile, though this is offset to some extent by commercial discounts given by rental car agencies. Thus, most firms prefer that their executives and salesmen fly whenever any significant amount of time will be saved.

Gronau's work on the effect of travel time on the demand for passenger transportation emphasizes this point.[1] While these results should be treated with some caution, they do shed new light on this important topic. Gronau

[1] Reuben Gronau, *The Value of Time in Passenger Transportation: The Demand for Air Travel*, Occasional Paper 9 (Columbia University Press, for National Bureau of Economic Research, 1970). A critique of Gronau's work is provided in Philip K. Verleger, Jr., "A Point-to-Point Model of the Demand for Air Transportation" (Ph.D. thesis, Massachusetts Institute of Technology, 1971), pp. 36–48.

explicitly expanded the concept of travel cost to include what he refers to as the "price of travel time." Presumably this price reflects the opportunity cost of an individual's time. His results indicate that even when this price is presumed to be zero, for a single individual the automobile is a more expensive mode of transportation than the airplane for trips of more than 590 miles. As the "price of time" rises, the length of trip for which the automobile is the cheaper form of travel drops rapidly. At a price of time of only $4 an hour, the automobile is cheaper only for trips of less than 119 miles. However, increasing the price of time further does not serve to shorten appreciably the length of trip for which the automobile is the cheaper mode. Even at a price of travel time of $10 an hour, the switching distance is as high as 87 miles. Gronau's results are appreciably different if more than one person is making the trip. For a family of two adults and two children, the automobile is the cheapest mode for trips of 2,500 miles, even if the price of travel time for the family as a whole is approximately $4 an hour. Gronau, however, did not include the cost of food and lodging en route.

As for the switching distances between modes of public transportation, Gronau concludes that air travel saves no time at all relative to rail travel for trips of less than 135 miles. The public transportation modes in use for trips of less than 135 miles are rail (for higher-income passengers) and bus (for lower-income passengers).

For distances of more than 135 miles, air travel begins to cut sharply into the rail market, squeezing it out entirely at 176 miles. For trips of 176 miles or more, either air or bus is used. If a person's price of travel time is less than $4.70 an hour, he uses the bus for trips of up to 176 miles. If it is above that, he flies. The price of time necessary to induce a person to fly drops rapidly beyond 176 miles, becoming almost flat at about $2 an hour at 400 miles. Only if his price of travel time is less than $1 an hour will a person always take a bus rather than fly, regardless of the distance. . . .

The pricing policies actually followed by the airlines have supported the theory that short-haul air travel is relatively price inelastic. Until 1952, the fare per mile was virtually constant, regardless of trip length, and air fare changes were made on a percentage basis. In that year, however, there occurred the first of several "dollar-per-ticket" fare increases by the trunk carriers, which raised the per-mile fare for short trips relative to that for long ones. . . .

The belief by the local carriers that businessmen—their most important customers—are relatively insensitive to price has not blinded them to the price sensitivity of other significant groups in the public. The chronically low load factors (ratios of seats occupied to seats available) of the local airlines have led them to be among the most innovative in tailoring new fares to attract price-sensitive travelers while making sure that businessmen did not qualify for them. The locals have been strong supporters of the youth fare and have led in making it a purely price discriminatory device. While most of the trunks have required youths to accept a no-advance-reservations service in return for their discount, many of the locals have had full-reservation youth fares since the early 1960s. In order to tap the other end of the age spectrum, Mohawk introduced in 1961 a "golden-age" excursion fare, which offered a one-third discount on fares to men over 65 and women over 62 who paid a $5 membership fee and agreed to fly between midnight and 1 p.m.

In the fall of 1966 Frontier Airlines tried to introduce a special ladies' fare, which would have provided a 50 percent reduction for a fifteen-day round trip ticket usable throughout Frontier's system. Complaints by Western Air Lines, Northwest Airlines, and Trailways Bus System led the Board to disapprove the proposal as "unduly discriminatory." In 1967 Frontier reintroduced its proposal, this time reducing the discount to 40 percent and seeking to place the fare into effect for 3 months and then only on routes over which it did not compete with other air carriers. The proposal was again rejected. Frontier had originally proposed the ladies' fare when it found that only 20 percent of its passengers were women and that most women travel for personal rather than for business reasons. Frontier's president was quoted as saying: "This, in itself, presents an untapped source of personal travel without serious dilution of existing revenues. . . . Instead of being discriminatory, men as a class would benefit from this reduced fare, since the ladies' fare would generally be paid for by husbands or other relatives."

Another device with which the local carriers have attempted to tap price-sensitive submarkets is the off-peak fare. For example, the fact that such a high proportion of their customers are traveling on business has meant that the local carriers are subject to severe declines in traffic on weekends. In order to generate weekend traffic these carriers early adopted liberalized family plans that were applicable all week rather than, like the trunk-line family plans, only on weekdays. Some also adopted "weekends unlimited" fares that allow unlimited weekend travel on their systems for a flat charge.

The local carriers also have been leaders in promoting the use of standby fares that give substantial discounts to persons willing to come to the airport without a reservation on the chance that seats will be available. Furthermore, they have taken the lead in extending such fares to all passengers —not just young persons and military personnel.

The behavioral evidence concerning local service pricing policies is thus consistent with the statistical evidence and the a priori belief that a major portion of short-haul air travel—business travel—is relatively insensitive to price, but that traffic can be increased through price discrimination or other devices designed to tap price-sensitive, nonbusiness markets.

Improvements in Speed

It was argued above that when one takes into account the value a traveler places on his time, the airplane often is the cheapest mode of travel, even though the fare charged is usually higher than that of other modes of transportation. This suggests that, other things being equal, increasing the speed of air travel should increase the demand for this mode relative to that for other modes and should also have a positive impact on the total demand for travel.

The time spent in air travel consists of two parts: the time it takes to get to and from the air terminals and the time required for the actual flight, including that for intermediate stops and connections. For less than a certain distance (estimated by Gronau at 135 miles), an airplane saves no time relative to bus or rail. An example of this was indicated by a Mohawk Airlines executive in 1953. He observed that while a businessman seeking to go from downtown Buffalo to downtown Rochester, a distance of 55 miles, could fly between the two airports in only 28 minutes, the added time required to get to and from the airports raised the total travel time to 1.8 hours and reduced the average overall speed to only 37 miles an hour. In 1953 Mohawk was flying DC-3s, but . . . even if DC-9s had been used on the route, the problem would not have been alleviated. The time required to get an aircraft into the air and down again varies little with its speed, and for short flights it is this time and not the time spent at cruising speed that matters.

This also shows why the local carriers are particularly sensitive to such factors as air traffic congestion that tend to increase trip time. In 1968, the average local service hop of 130 miles required only 34 minutes. A delay of 15 minutes due to air traffic congestion at the hub terminal from which a flight originates would increase the total flight time by almost 50 percent and reduce the average airport-to-airport speed from 232 to 160 miles an hour. A delay of one hour, not uncommon today during peak traffic periods at New York, Chicago, or Washington, would lower the average speed to 84 miles an hour, not substantially faster than the speed attainable in an automobile on an interstate highway. The apparent success of the high-speed Metroliner on the 228-mile Washington–New York railroad run is further evidence that for short distances the fastest way to travel is not always by air.

Another factor that cuts down the inherent speed advantage of the airplane for short distances is the need to make intermediate stops. In 1968 the average local service passenger traveled 248 miles. Since the average length of hop was about 130 miles, this means that he was required to make one stop en route. Suppose that the passenger in question was traveling on a DC-9. A 250-mile nonstop flight on a DC-9 takes 42 minutes, which implies a speed of 357 miles an hour. A single 20-minute stop midway through the flight, that required no diversion from the original line of flight, would reduce the effective speed to about 210 miles an hour. These times do not include time spent traveling to and from the airports and are based on the assumption that a flight is ready to leave whenever the passenger desires.

If an airline were free to vary the type of flights it offered, it would offer nonstop flights whenever there was enough traffic. Intermediate stops would be made only if the additional traffic they provided more than made up for both the loss of passengers who chose other means of travel because of the lower quality of service offered and the additional operating cost incurred in making the stop. A carrier might choose to operate smaller, lower-cost equipment in a skip-stop pattern (landing at different intermediate points on each flight and thereby increasing the average stage length) if the improvement in service quality generated enough traffic. As will be seen below, the local carriers have not generally been free to make such scheduling decisions. The Board has placed restrictions of varying stringency on their scheduling in order to prevent trunk–local service competition in certain markets and to assure the provision of a certain minimum level of service to marginal communities. . . .

While air carriers operating in short-haul markets have been able to increase effective aircraft speeds by only a limited amount, improvements in other modes of transportation (generally excluding the railroads) have increased the average speed of their closest competitors. Since World War II the United States has undertaken massive federally financed road building, of which the Interstate Highway System is the main example. . . . The improvement in roads raised the average speed of automobiles and buses from 45.0 and 45.5 miles an hour, respectively in 1945 to 59.5 and 59.4 miles an hour in 1967. This represents an increase of about 33 percent since the end of World War II. In 1947 express bus service between New York City and Washington, D.C., was scheduled at 7.5 hours. In 1965 better roads and improved equipment brought the same trip down to 4 hours and 10 minutes. (In 1948 a nonstop DC-6 flight between New York [La Guardia Airport] and Washington was scheduled for 1 hour and 20 minutes. In 1968 the same flight was scheduled for 50 minutes [American Airlines, Boeing 727] to one hour [Eastern, DC-9], but actual elapsed times were running considerably longer due to congestion.). . . .

Frequency and Timing of Service

Another factor having an obvious impact on the demand for short-haul service is the frequency of the service provided. Of the 124 exclusively served local service stations where traffic fell off between 1968 and 1969, flight frequency had fallen at 101 of them. The average reduction in the number of flights per station per year was 11.1 percent, from 2,240 to 1,968. On an average, traffic at these stations dropped by 11.0 percent, from 16,802 in 1968 to 14,944 in 1969.

For a person using short-haul air transportation in getting to a final destination, high frequency makes it more likely that he can depart at a preferred time. For a person using short-haul air service to connect with a long-haul flight, high frequency means that airport waiting time will be minimized. In the area of frequency, short-haul air service faces its chief competition from the automobile—either owned or rented. Theoretically, the frequency of this travel mode is infinite. Put another way, the reciprocal of frequency—the mean expected time until the next departure—is zero. . . .

The experience of the air taxis has reinforced the belief that frequency of service is more important than ticket price in attracting traffic in short-haul markets where good travel alternatives exist. In almost every case the air taxis have emphasized frequency as the main selling point of their service. The example of Executive Airlines in the Boston/Augusta, Maine, market is illustrative. . . . Between 1960 and late 1966, Northeast Airlines, a trunkline, was the only carrier in the market. In the early 1960s Northeast cut its flight frequency by 30 percent. During the same period traffic fell by 40 percent. Between 1963 and 1965 Northeast restored its previous level of service, and traffic increased to above its former level. Executive Airlines entered the market in September 1966 using 20-seat De Havilland Twin Otters, while Northeast used 44-passenger Fairchild FH-227s. Between 1965 and 1967, weekly flight frequencies increased by 125 percent, and traffic rose by 143 percent. It should be noted that Northeast apparently benefited from the additional service provided by Executive, though it is not known how many persons flew one way on Northeast and the other on Executive. By 1969 Executive was attracting substantially more traffic than Northeast, in spite of the higher fares of the former.

While more frequent service improves the chances that a traveler will find a flight leaving at a convenient time, certain departure times during the day are obviously more generally desirable than others. Most airline executives agree that 8:30 a.m. and 5:30 p.m. are two such desirable times, and they schedule flights accordingly. A morning flight can get a businessman to his destination in time for a full day's work. A 5:30 p.m. flight allows him to get home without having to spend the night. . . .

A businessman can compensate for poor airline schedules by traveling by car. This is a solution, however, only for relatively short distances. Once the trip distance exceeds a few hundred miles, the travel time by car is so great that it pays the traveler to wait even for a flight at an inconvenient time.

The Short-haul Dilemma

This discussion has shown that while short-haul air travel is not totally insensitive to price and while certain segments of the market may indeed be quite price sensitive, the major portion of the market (which consists of business-related travel) appears to respond more to the frequency and overall quality of service than it does to direct monetary cost. Businessmen fly because by doing so they save time; but one of the major sources of time saving available to airlines—the use of faster equipment—has a limited effect on short-haul travel because of the fixed amount of time that must be spent in taxiing, landing and taking off, and climbing and descending, regardless of the aircraft used. Therefore, the best way a local service carrier can make its service more attractive in markets where good travel alternatives are available is to increase the frequency and improve the timing of its schedules. This creates a dilemma, however. A frequency of six round trips a day between two cities—one flight every two hours between 7:00 a.m. and 7:00 p.m.—which is not at all a high frequency of service, will (on the basis of a seven-day week) provide space for 1,200 passengers a day, or 437,000 passengers a year, if a 100-passenger DC-9-30 is used. The use of a Convair 580 would generate half this number of seats. If a 50 percent load factor were required for the service to be self-supporting, the two cities would have to exchange 110,000 air passengers a year to support even six round trips a day by Convairs. In 1967, however, only ten markets—Philadelphia–Pittsburgh, Philadelphia–Washington, New York–Syracuse, Albany–New York, Chicago–Milwaukee, Los Angeles–Las Vegas, Binghamton–New York, Chicago–Madison, Chicago–Peoria, and Champaign–Chicago—generated more than 100,000 passengers a year for local service carriers. The only possible way in which high frequency service can be offered, therefore, is with smaller aircraft. But if a 15-passenger Beech 99 turboprop is used in providing six round trips a day, a 50 percent breakeven load factor would require the city pair to generate 33,000 passengers a year, which is far fewer than the number required for the DC-9-30, but still considerably above the traffic exchanged by most local service city pairs. It is clear, therefore, that while the use of smaller aircraft can expand substantially the number of city pairs for which a frequent, convenient air service can be offered, the amount of traffic between most of the smaller communities and their major centers of commerce is so low that such a service cannot be supported by the revenues generated.

3

This selection is a condensation of part of the 1958 Report of the majority of the Senate Subcommittee on Antitrust and Monopoly. The subcommittee was popularly known as the Kefauver Committee, after the late Senator Estes Kefauver, Chairman of the Subcommittee. The report was written, after the subcommittee had held lengthy hearings, by the subcommittee's staff, which included professional economists.

The major theme of the Kefauver Committee's probing into the activities of the automobile and other industries was "administered prices," i.e., those prices established by business decision and subject to infrequent changes. Toward administered prices the attitude of the Kefauver Committee was more than faintly hostile.

The demand analysis in this selection also concentrates on price elasticity of demand. Competent scholars have not agreed on just what the coefficient is, and on how estimates of it should be interpreted. The subcommittee's report does its best to find merit in estimates of a high coefficient, so as to support the subcommittee's claim that the automobile industry, in its own interest, should lower prices.

This report was published before the Big Three began to produce compact cars. Notice the remark about "the virtual nonexistence of low-priced American makes."

THE DEMAND FOR AUTOMOBILES

SENATE SUBCOMMITTEE ON ANTITRUST AND MONOPOLY

It should be stressed at the outset that there is no one certain way of forecasting the demand for automobiles. The methods employed in estimating what demand will be range all the way from hunches to elaborate mathematical-statistical formulations. The state of knowledge and the quality of the underlying data are not such as to permit the conclusion that any one method is correct and all others invalid. After all, the demand for automobiles is an extremely complex phenomenon, influenced by many factors—income, price, quality, financing, and others. As compared to the enormous complexity of the problem, to say nothing of its importance, the amount of research that has been devoted to the analysis of demand is, by any standard, almost infinitesimal. In this chapter an attempt will be made to de-

---

Taken and adapted from "Chapter 6. The Demand for Automobiles," *Administered Prices: Automobiles.* Report, Together with Individual Views, of the Subcommittee on Antitrust and Monopoly of the Committee on the Judiciary, United States Senate. 85th Congress, 2nd Session. November 1, 1958 (Washington, D.C.: GPO, 1958), pp. 130–140, 142–148.

scribe briefly the nature of these various methods of forecasting—from the simplest to the most detailed.

Forecasting Methods

An example of the hunch method is provided by the forecasts of the automobile manufacturers, themselves, for 1958. It seems evident that they were expecting 1958 to be largely a repetition of the boom year of 1955. The most frequently cited reason for this optimistic viewpoint was the expectation that buyers of 1955 models, who by 1958 would have completed their payments, would again return to the market for a new car. That the buyer of a new car in 1955 could not reasonably have been expected to purchase a 1956 or 1957 model, while still in the process of making his payments, was generally conceded. But by 1958 even the buyers who had made their purchases on a 36-month contract would have had their 1955 models paid up. From this it was simply assumed that they would again become buyers in 1958, quite apart from the fact that automobiles appear to have a useful life of 13 years.

At a slightly higher conceptual level are projections based upon simple relationships assumed to exist between automobile sales and population or income. For example, according to the *Journal of Commerce*, Mr. R. S. McNamara, group vice president of Ford Motor Co.—

> sees a steady rise in gross national product of about 3 per cent a year, with auto population rising at the rate of about 1.5 million annually from the present level of slightly more than 50 million cars (August 12, 1957).

There is, in point of fact, a substantial body of thought which assumes the existence of a generally close relationship between changes in population and changes in economic activity in the economy as a whole and in its major components. Assumed here is a new type of Say's law: namely, that population (rather than production) creates its own demand.

Similar in conceptual simplicity are projections based upon relationships assumed to exist between automobile demand and income. The projections of income are themselves usually based on population, which leaves unanswered the question of whether a relationship actually does exist between population and income.

At a much higher conceptual level are inductive surveys, conducted through personal interviews of a scientifically selected sample, of consumer buying power and attitudes. Surveys of this type are conducted by the Survey Research Center of the University of Michigan under the direction of Dr. George Katona. Contrary to a point of view which regards price reductions in a period of declining demand as undesirable on the grounds that buyers, anticipating further price reductions, will hold off on their purchases, Dr. Katona has found that, in the eyes of consumers, price reductions are thought to be "to the good." If price declines are regarded as temporary, and if they are not accompanied by reductions in income, he said, they tend to stimulate demand.

On automobiles the Survey Center's studies indicated that the direction of consumer demand would be upward in 1955 and downward in 1958, and in each case of course they proved to be correct.

These surveys also shed light on the buying power and desires of various classes of consumers which constitute separate components of the automobile market, i.e., the "stratification" of the market. Thus it has been found not only that there is a sizable demand for a second car but that consumers do not want a large expensive model for their second car.

Studies of the Elasticity of Demand

The most complex type of analysis consists of studies of "the elasticity of demand." These studies have as their objective the measurement of the effect on sales of a given change in price or income. They employ elaborate mathematical formulas and are based on actual experience over long periods of time.

Although they represent the most comprehensive and carefully conceived approach to the problem, these studies are not without certain inherent limitations. For one thing they cannot be any better than the data on which they are based; and the basic data, which are almost invariably compiled for other purposes, usually have certain shortcomings that limit their usefulness for demand studies. Then, too, conditions must not be beyond the range of experience of the period in which the demand study is based. For example, in the base periods used in the various studies of elasticity of demand, a substantially greater range of cars with respect to price, quality, and style was available to buyers than is true today. Confronted with the recent upgrading of the "low-priced three" into the middle-price bracket and the virtual nonexistence of low-priced American makes, can the consumer be expected to react to a price reduction in the same manner as he did before this upgrading took place?

But because, with all their limitations, these studies represent the most objective and well-founded method of analysis, their techniques, underlying concepts, and results will be discussed at some length in this chapter.

Special Characteristics of Durable Goods

Obviously, new purchases of durable goods are typically smaller than ownership. This fact leads to a "magnification" of the effects of price, income, and other factors on new purchases as compared with their effects on ownership. Such magnification of effects has been subsumed under the technical phrase "acceleration." The way in which magnification or acceleration works can be illustrated by the following numerical example: Suppose the price elasticity of demand for automobile ownership is −0.6, i.e., a 10 per cent increase in price would have the effect of reducing ownership by 6 per cent. If the ownership of automobiles amounts to 24 million new car units and depreciation is 25 per cent per year, 6 million new cars will be purchased for replacement in the absence of any changes in price, income, or other factors affecting ownership. But if price increases by 10 per cent, consumers will, with an assumed price elasticity of −0.6, wish to reduce their ownership level by 6 per cent, or 1.44 million cars. They can do this by buying fewer than 6 million new cars. If the entire adjustment of ownership is made in 1 year, only 4.56 million new cars will be purchased. This represents a decline of 24 per cent in new car purchases. The elasticity of new car purchases with respect to price is thus −2.4, or 4 times the price elasticity of ownership.

The exact degree of magnification which takes place depends on two factors: (1) the annual rate of depreciation, and (2) the extent to which consumers make the full adjustment in their ownership level in any 1 year. This last factor is of special importance for durable goods in general, and automobiles in particular. In the above example it was assumed that consumers make full adjustment within a year. For various reasons, however, there may be delays so that full adjustment does not occur within a 1-year period. Thus consumers may be thought of as moving toward an "equilibrium" level of ownership but not attaining their goal in a 1-year period.

The causes of delays in downward adjustments are more difficult to disentangle, and indeed there are grounds for believing that such delays are much less pronounced than delays in upward adjustments. It is obvious that previous commitments of income do not place any restriction on the act of reducing a level of ownership. This can be accomplished regardless of whether one's income is committed in buying a TV or a refrigerator. The fact that consumers may have their income committed to the purchase of other items in no way keeps them from reducing their ownership of a durable good, if because of a decrease in income or increase in price they are motivated to do so. Insofar as transactions costs are concerned, it would seem that because no transactions costs are involved in not buying a car, transactions costs can have little or no effect in delaying downward adjustments in ownership.

The Statistical Studies

Six major studies have been made of the elasticity of demand for automobiles which utilize historical data; they are those of: (1) P. de Wolff,[1] (2) M. J. Farrell,[2] (3) C. F. Roos and V. von Szeliski,[3] (4) L. J. Atkinson,[4] (5) G. C.

[1] P. de Wolff, "The Demand for Passenger Cars in the United States," *Econometrica*, Vol. 6 (January 1938), pp. 113–129.
[2] M. J. Farrell, "The Demand for Motorcars in the United States," *Journal of the Royal Statistical Society*, Vol. 117, Series A (1954), pp. 171–193.
[3] C. F. Roos and Victor von Szeliski, "Factors Governing Changes in Domestic Automobile

Chow,[5] and (6) D. B. Suits.[6] Neither Mr. de Wolff's study nor Mr. Farrell's study lends itself to easy interpretation in terms of the price elasticity of demand for new cars. Chow and Suits testified before the subcommittee and their testimony will be discussed later. The studies by Roos and von Szeliski and Atkinson are based entirely on pre-World War II data, and are briefly summarized here.

In 1939 General Motors Corp. published Roos and von Szeliski's now classic study of automobile demand. Their study is long and quite complicated; however, they have provided a summary which is quoted in part:

> The concept of a variable maximum ownership level is of primary importance in the automobile industry because when car ownership is near the level of maximum ownership and a decrease in national income occurs, the effect is to make the market suddenly saturated. A consequence is the elimination of new-owner sales, and even the forcing of liquidation of part of the consumers' car stock. It is found by statistical analysis that a 1 per cent increase in supernumerary income (national income less direct taxes and necessary living cost) would raise the maximum ownership level by about 0.4 per cent. Income changes also affect replacement sales, and a 1 per cent increase in supernumerary income would increase replacement sales by about 1.2 per cent. The overall effect of income on total new-car sales, new owners as well as replacement, appears to be that a 1 per cent change in income causes a 2.5 per cent change in sales. When consumer car stocks approach the maximum ownership level and the quality of these stocks is high, new-car sales can be drastically lowered by moderate declines in income.
>
> The influence of price on replacement sales is such that with each 1 per cent increase in price, replacement sales tend to decrease by 0.74 per cent. The overall effect of price on combined new owners and replacement sales appears to be that a 1 per cent decrease in price increases sales by between 1 and 2 per cent, depending upon the degree of saturation of the market. A figure of 1.5 can be accepted as a fair average value of the elasticity of demand with respect to price under current conditions.

In an article on durable-goods demand published in April 1952, L. Jay Atkinson presents a brief statistical study of the demand for new passenger cars. He obtained a price elasticity of -1.4 and an income elasticity of $+2.5$. All the studies discussed in this chapter, with the exception of Atkinson's, rest, more or less, on the foundation that ownership is considered as basic, and new purchases are derived from ownership. His analysis relates new private passenger-car registrations per 1,000 households to 4 variables:

Demand," *The Dynamics of Automobile Demand* (New York: General Motors Corp., 1939), pp. 20–99.

[4] L. Jay Atkinson, "Consumer Markets for Durable Goods," *Survey of Current Business* (April 1952), pp. 19–24.

[5] Gregory C. Chow, *Demand for Automobiles in the United States* (Amsterdam: North Holland Publishing Co., 1957).

[6] Daniel B. Suits, "The Demand for New Automobiles in the United States, 1929–56," article to be published in the *Review of Economics and Statistics.* [Editor's note: The article was published in August 1958, Vol. XL, No. 3.]

(1) real disposable income per household in 1939 dollars, (2) percentage of current to preceding year real disposable income in 1939 dollars, (3) ratio of average retail price of new automobiles to the BLS Consumer Price Index, and (4) average scrappage age. For the period 1925–40, Atkinson's analysis explains 98 per cent of the variation in new-car purchases. Predictions based on his analysis for recent years in the postwar period are reasonably accurate.

The Statistical Investigation of Chow

The studies of Dr. Gregory C. Chow, of the Massachusetts Institute of Technology, and Dr. Daniel B. Suits, of the University of Michigan, have been singled out for more detailed discussion, principally on the grounds that they are the two most recent analyses and the only studies incorporating the post-World War II data.

Professor Chow finds the price elasticity for new-car sales to be −1.2 and the income elasticity to be +3.0. These elasticities are derived from the elasticities between ownership and price and income.

In obtaining his figure for total car ownership, Chow adjusts for age in the following manner:

> . . . the measure of automobile ownership really depends on how much the new car is worth as compared with the used cars, and I have observed the relative prices of automobiles of different age groups at one point in time.
>
> I have found that, historically, approximately 25 per cent is depreciated in a year, roughly speaking, so that if we count a new car as 1 unit, we will count a 1-year-old car as one 0.75 unit, and a 2-year-old car as 75 per cent of 75 per cent, or something like a half unit.

In his analysis, which covers the periods 1920–41 and 1948–53, Chow relates ownership per capita in this sense to the average price of all cars, new and used, deflated by a general price index, real disposable income per capita, and the ownership of automobiles the preceding year. He thus takes account of four of the major factors affecting the demand for any commodity: its price, the general price level, consumer income, and population. The way in which Chow has allowed for delays in adjustment assumes that such delays are the same, no matter in which direction the adjustment takes place. As indicated above, there are strong reasons for believing that the delays are less marked in a downward direction.

In describing his results on the income and price elasticities of the demand for ownership, Chow said:

> I have estimated that for every per cent increase in per capita income, automobile ownership would be increased by 1½ per cent.
>
> How about the effect of price? I have also estimated that for every per cent increase in price, there will be a 0.6 per cent drop in automobile ownership; it would decrease people's desire of ownership by 0.6 per cent.

Since he assumes that the ownership level depreciates at the rate of 25 per cent a year, the elasticities for new-car sales would be 4 times the ownership elasticities, or 2.4 for price and 6 for income. However, for the reasons described earlier (principally other commitments and transactions costs), he assumes that consumers do not fully adjust their level of ownership to changed prices and incomes within a 1-year period. He testified:

> The responses of 6 per cent to a 1 per cent change in income and 2.4 per cent to a 1 per cent change in price would result if the consumers adjusted their car ownership to the desired level at once. But they do not. Time elapses between decision and the act of purchasing. But more important is the cost involved in making a transaction. No one will change his car to a better one the moment his income increases, and to a cheaper one the moment his income drops. If he does that, he will be spending quite a bit of his time and money with the automobile dealers. I have found that about half of the desired change in ownership is achieved in 1 year. This means that a 1 per cent change in income, while raising the desired ownership by 1.5 per cent to be achieved in due course, will raise actual ownership only by 0.75 per cent in the current year. Therefore, the percentage response in sales within 1 year to a 1 per cent rise in income during that year will be only 3 per cent, and not 6. Similarly, the response of sales to price will only be 1.2 per cent, and not 2.4.

The Statistical Investigation of Suits

Dr. Suits' investigation concerns new purchases entirely, although the framework of his analysis does include elements which allow new-car purchases to depend indirectly on ownership. Suits' formulation is basically the same as Chow's, except that population is excluded entirely, some measure of credit terms is introduced, and ownership is treated in absolute numbers rather than in age-comparable units. His analysis covers the period 1929 through 1956, omitting the years 1942–48.

In view of the similarity in the formulation of Suits and Chow it is rather surprising that their statistical results turned out to be so different. Suits obtained a price elasticity of -0.6 and an income elasticity of $+4.2$ for new-car purchases. Thus his price elasticity is only half of that which Chow obtained and his income elasticity is nearly 40 per cent greater. The difference appears to be due largely to two factors: (*a*) the use of different price series and (*b*) a statistical procedure employed by Suits which has the effect of causing his analysis to ignore the 30 to 40 per cent of all cars not sold on credit.

Suits' use of data on average contract duration is unusual. Instead of using average contract duration as a separate variable in his analysis designed to explain year-to-year changes in new-car purchases, Suits divides real retail price by it and uses only the ratio of the two, i.e., he computes what he calls the "real monthly payment" and never introduces contract duration and price as separate variables. In the postwar period only some 50 to 70 per cent of all new automobiles purchased have been purchased on credit. Thus, to imply as Suits does that a variable representing the monthly payment for a new automobile is the only effective "price" variable is somewhat misleading because not all purchases of new cars are made on time. Retail price and contract duration should exert separable and possibly different effects on new-car demand.[7]

Summary Comparison of Statistical Findings

The investigation of the quantitative effect of price and income upon new automobile purchases is a complex and difficult subject, about which much more needs to be known. However, there is a substantial measure of agreement among the various authorities, as can be seen in Table 1.

Table 1 Summary Comparison of Several Studies of Automobile Demand

Study	*Elasticity of new purchases with respect to —*	
	Price	*Income*
Suits:		
1. As presented	−0.6	+4.2
2. As reworked by the subcommittee staff	−1.2	+3.9
Chow[a]	−1.2	+3.0
Roos and von Szeliski	−1.5	+2.5
Atkinson[a]	−1.4	+2.5

[a] Per capita basis.

Except for Suits' original analysis, the results presented in the table show price elasticities ranging between −1.2 and −1.5 and income elasticities ranging between +2.5 and +3.9. Because of the considerations which have been described above, a price elasticity of −1.2 appears to be a minimum estimate, particularly during a period of general economic decline.

[7] The objection can be put in slightly more precise, but also more technical form: By taking the ratio of real retail price to average contract duration in his analysis, Suits has restricted his results in such a way that the elasticity with respect to price, contract duration held constant, must turn out to be equal in magnitude to, but opposite in sign to, the elasticity with respect to contract duration, price held constant. Thus, in Suits' analysis, it is found that a 1 per cent increase in retail price results in a 0.6 per cent decrease in new-car purchases, and a 1 per cent increase in average contract duration results in a 0.6 per cent increase in new-car purchases. Thus, the effect of dividing retail price by contract duration may be to reduce the price elasticity so obtained.

Alternatives for the Future

As noted earlier, it has been found in studies of the elasticity of demand that changes in automobile sales can be largely explained by changes in two variables—income and price. The former is "exogenous" to the automobile industry in the sense that there is little that the automotive companies can do outside of the area of prices to raise the level of national and per capita income. The latter, however, is "endogenous" to the industry; it is within the power of the automobile producers to effect changes in their sales by changing their price. It is true that all of the studies have shown automobile sales to be more responsive to changes in income than to changes in price. But it is also true that, aside from the indirect effects on income of price-induced changes in production, material changes in income cannot be brought about by decisions of the automobile producers.

In appearing before the subcommittee, Dr. Chow presented a table (Table 2) which, using his elasticities of −1.2 for price and 3.0 for income, set forth in summary form the percentage change in automobile sales of given percentage changes in per capita income and relative price.[8] Again bearing in mind the sources of understatement in his procedure, an examination of the table suggests the range of alternative choices. Thus, if income remains the same, a 5 per cent increase in price would mean a 6 per cent decrease in annual purchases. If income fell by only 2 per cent, a 5 per cent price increase would mean a decline of 12 per cent. The combined effect of a 4 per cent decrease in income and a 5 per cent increase in price would approach the dimensions of a catastrophe—a decrease in purchases of 18 per cent.

On the other hand, if income were to remain unchanged, the automobile companies could increase sales 6 per cent by reducing price 5 per cent. A price decrease of this magnitude would offset a 2 per cent reduction in income. If income fell by 4 per cent and price remained unchanged, sales would drop by 12 per cent; but if price were reduced by 5 per cent the reduction in sales would be cut to 6 per cent. If income turned upward, rising by 4 per cent, the auto makers could sell 18 per cent more cars if they reduced their prices 5 per cent, but only 6 per cent more if they increased their prices by this amount.

In view of the possibility of increasing automobile sales through price reductions, the question arises as to why manufacturers do not utilize this avenue of recovery at the present time. The response of the automobile companies to this question is that they cannot lower prices and still maintain their present profit levels. The matter of overhead costs, discussed in the previous chapter, is important to an understanding of the manufacturers' position on price reduction.

[8] The price of automobiles adjusted by the Consumer Price Index.

Table 2 Percentage Changes in Annual Purchase of Automobiles Per Capita as Related to Percentage Changes in Income Per Capita and to Percentage Changes in the Relative Price of Automobiles

Percentage Change in Relative Price	*Percentage Change in Income (Per Capita in Constant Dollars)*						
	−8	−6	−4	−2	0	+2	+4
+10	−36	−30	−24	−18	−12	−6	0
+5	−30	−24	−18	−12	−6	0	6
0	−24	−18	−12	−6	0	6	12
−5	−18	−12	−6	0	6	12	18
−10	−12	−6	0	6	12	18	24
−15	−6	0	6	12	18	24	30
−20	0	6	12	18	24	30	36

It is recognized, of course, that a price reduction will decrease a company's net revenues unless the combined effects of increased sales and lower unit costs (as overhead is spread over the larger output) are sufficient to offset the adverse influence on profits of the price cuts themselves. Admittedly, the price elasticities of −1.2 or even −1.5 for the automobile industry are not high enough to insure this result. Thus, taking the industry as a whole, price cuts would in all probability reduce profits, given the present magnitude of overhead expense in the automobile industry. This is not to infer in any way that price reductions would not give an individual firm a greater share of the industry's total sales. As will be brought out later, cost-price relationships in the industry are now such as to invite the lesser members of the Big Three to follow a policy of price reductions which the largest producer could match only with some difficulty as long as it follows its present policy of making annual model changes.

The deceptively simple argument that high costs prevent any price reductions answers one question only to raise another: Why are costs so high? The explanation is to be found largely in the increase in overhead costs during recent years. As a result the major automobile producers now find themselves in a cul-de-sac of their own making. The overhead costs which make it so difficult to reduce prices in a period of low sales result in large part from the shift from price to nonprice competition discussed earlier in this report. It is ironic that in their efforts to avoid the rigors of price competition the automobile producers now find themselves in reduced circumstances largely as a result of the high cost of the very type of competition which they have embraced.

By their own testimony the three largest automobile companies now spend well over $1 billion a year in styling, engineering, and special tooling for their frequent model changes. With the addition of advertising expenditures, it appears that the Big Three are currently spending at least $1.2 billion to $1.3 billion a year to promote fictitious style obsolescence. It is by the reduction of these expenditures that General Motors and the other leading producers can serve both their own interests and those of the country. If the sums which they now spend on nonprice competition were reduced sufficiently, substantial price cuts could be made without sacrifice of total revenue or profits.

With the conservative estimate of elasticity of -1.2, a reduction in overhead costs sufficient to produce a 10 per cent price cut would provide the industry with total revenue slightly more than that which it could expect without the price reduction ($8.5 billion versus $8.4 billion). The reduction of revenue resulting from the price cut would be more than offset by the increase in the number of cars sold at the lower price. With more liberal estimates of elasticity, the increase in total revenue resulting from a price reduction would of course be even greater. Given an elasticity of -1.5, for example, a 5 per cent price cut would raise revenue by $200 million, and a 10 per cent cut would add $300 million to the revenue which would be received without the price change.

If the automobile manufacturers were to follow such a course of action, it would benefit their consumers, their suppliers and their labor force without injury to their own financial interests. The benefit to consumers is obvious. By adding 250,000 to more than 600,000 cars (depending on the size of the price reduction and the elasticity of demand) to the current output level, the price reductions would expand employment and act as a stimulus to industries which supply parts and materials to the automobile manufacturers. Since the price cuts are assumed to have been brought about by equivalent reductions in unit costs, the profit earned per car produced would not be affected. So long as average profits per car throughout the industry are now greater than zero, any increase in volume under the conditions outlined above would increase the total level of profits received by manufacturers over the level which they could earn before the price change.

4 The late Senator Dirksen wrote about 100 printed pages of dissenting comments on the majority Report of the Senate Subcommittee on Antitrust and Monopoly (see Selection 5). The Senator's specific comments were grouped under 12 points. This selection is from his Point 3, on price elasticity of demand.

THE PRICE ELASTICITY OF DEMAND FOR AUTOMOBILES

EVERETT MC KINLEY DIRKSEN
United States Senate

The position in the majority's report that the automobile industry does not use advanced economic and statistical research in determining the elasticity of demand for its products is erroneous and unfounded.

The subject of the probable elasticity of demand was injected into these hearings when Mr. Walter Reuther, president of the United Automobile Workers, suggested that automobile manufacturers could stimulate the sale of automobiles by reducing wholesale prices $100 per car.

Mr. Reuther's authority for the effect of price reductions on the demand for automobiles was Mr. Carl E. Fribley, a past president of the National Automobile Dealers' Association. In his prepared statement Mr. Reuther said:

> Fribley pointed to prewar pricing methods as ideal for the industry to follow this year.
>
> He said, "In the years before World War II when new model prices (were) held or reduced, the result was increased volume for manufacturer and dealer alike."

Mr. Yntema [Ford Motor Company] referred to Mr. Reuther's statement in his appearance before the subcommittee. He said:

> But Mr. Reuther asserts that this loss of profits would be largely offset by gains from our company's share of a 1-million-car increase in industry sales. What is the basis of this assertion? It is a statement by Mr. Carl E. Fribley, then head of the National Automobile Dealers Association, to the effect that if there had been no price increase on 1957 models, a million more units

Taken and adapted from "Individual Views of Senator Everett McKinley Dirksen," *Administered Prices: Automobiles.* Report, Together with Individual Views, of the Subcommittee on Antitrust and Monopoly of the Committee on the Judiciary, United States Senate. 85th Congress, 2nd Session, November 1, 1958 (Washington, D.C.: GPO, 1958), pp. 248, 249, 251, 252.

would have been sold. From this, Mr. Reuther has derived his assumption that a $100 reduction in car prices, about 4 per cent, would have increased sales by 16 per cent. This would indicate an elasticity of demand of minus 4.

Mr. Fribley was, I am sure, voicing his honest opinion. But his opinion is at odds with the serious, scholarly attempts to measure the elasticity of demand for automobiles.

These studies indicate a much smaller increase in units sold in response to a price reduction. They show that the elasticity of demand for new cars produced by the industry probably is in the minus 0.5 to minus 1.5 range—that is, only about 12 to 40 per cent as large as Mr. Reuther's interpretation of the Fribley guess.

The following colloquy took place:

Senator KEFAUVER. Mr. Yntema, turn back to the preceding page where you discuss Mr. Carl E. Fribley's statement. At the time Mr. Fribley made his statement that a $100 reduction in cars would increase the sale by 1 million cars or 16 per cent, he was the head of the National Automobile Dealers Association?

Mr. YNTEMA. That is correct, sir.

Senator KEFAUVER. Would you not think in that position that he would have a very good feel of the industry, a very good idea of sales possibilities?

Mr. YNTEMA. No, sir.

Senator KEFAUVER. You would not think so?

Mr. YNTEMA. We found generally that our dealers are not particularly well informed in judgments of this kind, and that by and large our own analyses are more reliable than the opinion that we get from the casual observation of a dealer.

A brief analysis of the staff's interpretation of the testimony by the marketing experts shows the futility of these proceedings. One study, by Prof. Gregory C. Chow, concludes that new-car sales tend to increase 1.2 per cent with a decrease of 1 per cent in new-car prices. The second, by Prof. Daniel R. Suits, indicates that unit sales would increase 0.6 per cent with a 1 per cent decrease in price. Both estimates fall between −0.6 and −1.5 per cent, the values suggested by Professor Suits and agreed to by Professor Chow as defining a range within which the true percentage response of unit sales to a 1 per cent price change would fall.

This agreement by two unbiased scholars is not enough for the staff. It has tried to move the range higher by attempting to discredit the data and concepts used by Professor Suits and by overlooking the deficiencies of Professor Chow's data and analysis. It has also suggested that the response of unit sales to a 1 per cent price change could be higher than 2 per cent despite the agreement of Professors Chow and Suits that a 1 per cent reduction in price would not increase sales by 2 per cent.

In actuality, the data used by Professor Chow are subject to as many questions as those of Professor Suits. The assertions in the majority's report concerning Professor Suits' concepts are, at best, naive. It has failed to cite the superiority of Professor Suits' method in considering year-to-year changes in the late 1950's. And the majority's report has completely overlooked the fact that a critical assumption made by Professor Chow in arriving at his estimated price elasticities (i.e., the percentage response of sales to a 1 per cent change in price) is contradicted by his own data.

Finally, the majority's report has not indicated that, conceptually, Professor Chow's elasticity measure is applicable only to the year in which the price change is made. Thereafter, if prices are maintained at a new lower price, sales will fall back in succeeding years to a level only 0.6 per cent, not 1.2 per cent, higher than those present prior to a 1 per cent price reduction. To maintain sales at the higher level, a further stimulus in the form of another price reduction is necessary. Professor Suits' elasticity measure of 0.6 per cent is not limited to the year of the price cut.

5 The steel industry has long had to suffer much, and occasionally stern, criticism for its pricing policies and practices. In the 1930's the industry was censured for failing to lower its prices and in the 1950's and 1960's for raising its prices too high. Unavoidably the price elasticity of demand for steel enters into the charges and countercharges.

Just before World War II, the Temporary National Economic Committee (TNEC) of Congress held long and much publicized hearings into the activities of the steel and other industries. Mr. Yntema, who was then Professor of Statistics at the University of Chicago, made a study of the demand for steel, a study destined to become a classic. This selection, a very small part of his testimony before the TNEC, begins in the midst of his discussion of the derived demand for steel. Notice that he saw no close substitutes for steel.

THE PRICE ELASTICITY OF DEMAND FOR STEEL

THEODORE O. YNTEMA

The demand for steel is derived from the demand for the services rendered by steel products, or, more directly, from the demand for the finished products themselves. A reduction in the price of steel, if passed on, will reduce the price of the finished product. In greater or less degree, this will increase the consumption of the product and, thus, the consumption of steel used in its manufacture. Furthermore, a reduction in the price of steel may perhaps increase the use of steel per unit of finished product. In each of these cases, however, the critical question is, how much?

The percentage decrease in the price of a finished product made possible by a reduction in the price of steel depends upon the proportion of the cost of steel to the value of the finished product. What is this proportion?

In the case of low-priced automobiles, the cost of steel is about 10 per cent of the delivered price. For a representative list of canned food products, the cost of tin plate per can varied from 3.4 to 13.9 per cent of the retail price of such food products. The cost of steel consumed by the railroads is estimated to average only about 5 per cent of the value of transportation services furnished by them. In the construction industry, steel costs range from 4 per cent of the total cost of a frame house to as much as 30 per cent

---

Taken and adapted from *Investigation of Concentration of Economic Power.* Hearings before the Temporary National Economic Committee. Congress of the United States. 76th Congress, 3rd Session. Part 26. Iron and Steel Industry. United States Steel Corporation Studies. Prices and Costs. January 1940 (Washington, D.C.: GPO, 1940), pp. 13592–13594.

of the total cost of a steel bridge. Extreme examples may be cited showing a very high or very low ratio of the cost of steel to the price of the finished product, but 10 per cent appears to be a reasonably typical proportion.

On this basis, a 10 per cent reduction in the price of steel would correspond to a 1 per cent reduction in the price of the finished product made from steel.

Since the elasticity of demand for the finished products of most steel-consuming industries is low, probably less than 1 or 2, a 1 per cent decrease in the price of the product would not increase the quantity sold by more than 1 or 2 per cent. If other conditions affecting demand and costs remain the same, a 10 per cent reduction in the price of steel would not increase the consumption of steel by more than 1 or 2 per cent through its effect upon the price of the finished product.

Price is generally not an important factor in the substitution of steel for other products. The physical characteristics of steel, especially its great tensile strength and durability in comparison with other materials, sharply limit the possible uses of substitutes. In the case of tin cans, there is some degree of substitutability between containers made of tin plate and those made of glass. Even in this case, however, numerous factors limit the possibility of substitution in response to price changes.

From the evidence, it is safe to conclude that the demand for steel is inelastic, that is, that a given percentage reduction in price will not bring about as large a percentage increase in the quantity sold. Although any such estimate is subject to a wide margin of error, it seems probable that the elasticity of demand for steel is not greater than 0.3 or 0.4, that is, that a 10 per cent reduction in price would not increase the quantity of steel sold by more than 3 or 4 per cent.

In concluding this part of our discussion, it should be pointed out that these estimates are based upon the assumption that other prices and other factors affecting the demand for steel remain the same.

Mr. BALLINGER. Dr. Yntema, how many industries did you analyze that use steel? I mean in testing this elasticity of demand?

Dr. YNTEMA. We analyzed in some detail these three to which I have referred.

Mr. BALLINGER. Representing about 40 per cent; the other 60 per cent you didn't look into?

Dr. YNTEMA. Yes; we investigated briefly the construction industry and found the problems there were so complicated that we were not prepared to submit a study of them to this committee.

Statistical analysis of the elasticity of demand for steel: The foregoing conclusions as to the elasticity of demand were tested by a separate statistical analysis of annual series of relevant economic data from 1919 to 1938. Production, shipments and bookings were respectively correlated with the factors deemed to exert a significant influence on the quantity of steel demanded. These factors were:

(1) The price of steel.
(2) Industrial production.
(3) Consumers' income.
(4) Industrial profits.
(5) A time-trend variable.

From four such correlations involving different combinations of these factors, it was found that a 1 per cent decrease in the price of steel (other factors remaining the same) would induce less than a 1 per cent increase in steel sales. Subsequent calculations in which mill net yields on shipments of steel, not available at the time of the original study, were used in lieu of published prices, confirmed these results. Although subject to considerable error, the best estimate of the elasticity of demand for steel indicated by this analysis is thought to be approximately 0.3 or 0.4.

These findings confirm our other estimates based on the study of the demand for steel by consuming industries, and indicate that changes in the level of steel prices cause smaller percentage changes in the opposite direction in the quantity of steel sold.

6 In 1958, the same Senate Subcommittee issued its report criticizing the steel industry, mainly for its pricing practices. But the Subcommittee had to face the belief that the demand for steel is inelastic, a belief fortified by Mr. Yntema's statistical estimates (Selection 7). Unwilling to place full credence in the belief, the Subcommittee thought that a few price reductions might demonstrate that the demand is more elastic than the steel companies believe.

PERHAPS STEEL'S PRICE ELASTICITY IS NOT LOW

SENATE SUBCOMMITTEE ON ANTITRUST AND MONOPOLY

It has long been the position of the steel companies, and apparently still is, that demand for the industry is highly inelastic; reductions in the price are thought to have little effect in increasing the demand for steel. This is the position taken before the subcommittee by the heads of the three steel companies who testified; this statement by Mr. Homer of Bethlehem Steel is a typical example:

> The second unwarranted assumption is that a decrease in the price of steel last July would have resulted in an increase in the demand for our steel products. This assumption overlooks one basic fact.
>
> The price of our steel is so low, about 7 cents a pound, that it accounts for a very small part of the cost incurred by our customers in producing finished products made from steel. Thus, a $5-a-ton reduction, say, in our steel prices last July would not have had any significant effect in increasing the sales by our customers of those finished products.

The steel companies are not without statistical support for their position. Thus, in an elaborate study of the elasticity of demand for steel, prepared by Dr. Theodore Yntema for the U. S. Steel Corp. and submitted to the TNEC, it was concluded that the demand for steel is very inelastic.

> This means that very large reductions in price would be necessary to effect significant increases in the volume of sales.

This finding may, however, oversimplify the problem as it exists today. For one thing, since the demand for steel is "derived," reaching the consumer through products made from steel, to know the elasticity of demand

---

Taken and adapted from *Administered Prices: Steel.* Report of the Committee on the Judiciary, United States Senate, made by its Subcommittee on Antitrust and Monopoly, together with Individual Views. 85th Congress. 2nd Session. March 13, 1958 (Washington, D.C.: GPO, 1958), pp. 63, 64.

for steel, it is necessary to know the aggregate elasticity of demand for the various consumer products in which it is ultimately incorporated. Such a body of knowledge of reasonable currency does not exist.

Then, too, it is virtually impossible to determine the relationship of the total cost of steel to the price of a finished consumer product. While crude estimates can be made, based upon such factors as the amount of steel embodied in a finished product, they ignore the amount of steel used by manufacturers of parts and components sold to the consumer industry; they ignore the amount of steel lost in the process of fabrication; and they ignore the indirect costs of steel affecting the product's prices, i. e., the cost of steel that enters into machines and equipment, into buildings, into transportation, etc., which in one way or another enter into the price of finished products.

One way by which the steel industry could make a contribution to knowledge on this subject would be by making a few price reductions. Except for a few nominal reductions, steel prices have moved in only one direction since 1938—upward. It is conceivable that the actual demand is more elastic than the steel companies believe, just as the elasticity of demand for automobiles proved to be considerably greater than was believed by the competitors of Henry Ford when he entered upon the scene with an extraordinarily low-priced car.

Finally, the price increases in steel serve to delimit the ability of the consuming industries, some of which may have relatively high elasticities of demand, to lower their prices. To the producers of finished goods, the constantly rising prices for steel exert an upward pressure on costs that may make it difficult for them to reduce prices, even if they were so inclined. It is conceivable that were they able to reduce their prices, their sales might increase to such an extent as to generate a significant increase in the demand for steel. But whether this might in fact prove to be the reality is something which is not likely to be known as long as the price of the basic material never registers a decline.

7 Most people (and, among them, those taking courses in economics) refuse to believe, so it often seems, that a higher price will curtail the use of water. But Professor Hanke shows clearly that the demand curve for water has a negative slope; it is not vertical. True enough, his factual inquiry is confined to Boulder, Colorado, where a higher price for water caused some consumers to substitute brown for green yards. Yet is there any reason to suppose that consumer response would be different elsewhere?

This selection should be read along with one that appears later in this volume. Selection 55 on "The Water Problem" deals with the larger economic issues of the supply of water.

THE DEMAND-PRICE RELATION FOR WATER

STEVE H. HANKE
Johns Hopkins University

. . . This paper focuses on the demand side of the market for water and presents an empirical analysis of the effects of changing from a flat rate price structure to a metered one. The basis for the study was the experience in Boulder, Colorado. . . .

Misconceptions of Urban Water Demand

The motivation for this investigation grew from the realization that water policies are frequently based on misconceptions concerning the nature of the demand for residential water. . . .

The Water Utility and Sources of Data

The data that were utilized in this study were derived from the experience of the water utility in Boulder, Colorado. Prior to 1961, the water utility managers relied exclusively on alterations in the city's water supply to meet shortages caused by increased demands. In 1961, however, a major change took place. The utility, in an attempt to meet impending water shortages, looked to the demand side of the market. Water meters were universally installed, and an incremental commodity charge of 35 cents per thousand gallons was adopted.

Adapted from Steve H. Hanke, "Demand for Water under Dynamic Conditions," *Water Resources Research*, Vol. 6, No. 5, pp. 1253–1260, October 1970, copyrighted by the American Geophysical Union.

A unique aspect of the following analyses is the time series data that were generated from this water metering experience. The data, while being unique, do have some shortcomings. The water use data for the flat rate period under investigation, 1955–1961, were available on an aggregate basis for the entire city. As a result, a sample of individual customers during this period could not be made. Commercial and industrial demands, which were metered, and public use and system leakages, which were estimated, were subtracted from total deliveries to yield a value for total residential use.

The water use data for the metered rate period under investigation, 1962–1968, were available on a considerably different basis from that for the flat rate interval. The metered data were restricted to those meter routes that were totally residential. The data were further constrained because sampling within this population could not be conducted. Since only aggregate data by meter route existed in most years, consumption for individual customers was not available for the entire period. Hence only data for entire meter routes containing residential customers could be constructed. Fourteen routes containing a total of 3086 customers met these criteria.

As a result of these constraints, the flat rate residential use data are not strictly comparable with the metered residential use data. The flat rate consumption is calculated on the basis of an average for the entire city, whereas the metered rate consumption is calculated for 14 routes within the city. . . .

Sprinkling Demands

Sprinkling consumption is the first segment of the residential water demand that will be analyzed. . . . The analysis compares the relationship between actual lawn irrigation and ideal sprinkling. The ideal use calculation includes such important variables as average irrigable area per dwelling unit, mean monthly temperature, monthly percent of daylight hours, effective rainfall, and an empirical monthly crop coefficient for grass. . . . The adjective 'ideal' does not imply an economic ideal or optimum but the minimum quantity of sprinkling water required to maintain the aesthetic quality of one's yard, its green appearance.

. . . Table 1 clearly demonstrates that the irrigation behavior of water consumers in Boulder was markedly altered by the installation of water meters. Notice that the general relationship between ideal and actual sprinkling is one in which the actual sprinkling is greater than the ideal under flat rates. Conversely, consumers reacted immediately to an incremental commodity charge with the actual sprinkling becoming less than the ideal. This marked alteration in relationships verifies that an increase in the incremental commodity charge for water reduces the quantity of water demanded. . . .

Let us turn our attention to the trends before and after metering, which heretofore have never been analyzed with continuous time series data. As mentioned earlier, a generally accepted hypothesis states that water meters will initially reduce the quantity of water consumed, but that their original impact will gradually wear off and consumers will begin consuming more water until a new equilibrium is reached at a level that approaches the original flat rate use. This hypothesis is refuted by the empirical findings of this study. Only two routes (37 and 79) show a slight recovery in the ratio of cumulative sprinkling use to ideal sprinkling after the initial impact of the incremental commodity charge. All other routes reflect falling ratios.

Table 1 Percentages of Average Actual Sprinkling to Average Ideal Sprinkling

Meter Routes	*Actual Sprinkling to Ideal Sprinkling, Flat Rate Period*	*Actual Sprinkling to Ideal Sprinkling, Metered Rate Period*
16, 18	128	78
37	175	72
53, 54	156	72
70, 71, 72	177	63
73, 75	175	97
74	175	102
76, 78	176	105
79	157	86

These results also imply extremely low income elasticities after the meters were installed, since incomes in Boulder have increased at a very rapid rate since metering. The decreasing use also implies an increasing price elasticity over time. . . .

Domestic Demands

Domestic (inside the house) use represents the other component of residential water demand. The conclusions with regard to this component are similar to, but more unexpected, a priori than those of sprinkling demand. The domestic consumption is reduced sharply upon the introduction of meters as people alter their activities in response to a positive water price. . . . The average use in the metered rate period for all of the routes being considered was 36% lower than in the flat rate period. The shift in demand can be observed in the southern routes in 1962 when all but route 79 were metered. This shift occurred in 1963 in the northern routes, since they were the last routes to be metered. The trends are similar to those derived for sprinkling use; domestic use does not start increasing after the initial drop in demand. As was the case with sprinkling, the implied income elasticities based on this time series data are extremely low.

The unexpected result of these time series data is that the shift in use is so sharp and of such great magnitude. This dramatic change implies much higher price elasticities for domestic use than have heretofore been calculated when cross-sectional data were employed. The reason for this disparity centers on the fact that the cross-sectional studies have used price–quantity relations for many price ranges, while the present study concentrates on the switch from flat to metered rates (a zero incremental price to a positive one). The large decrease in domestic consumption probably reflects a once-and-for-all change in use that accompanies the introduction of a positive incremental charge, and that decrease would not be observed if one moved incremental rates from one positive level to another.

A decrease in use of the magnitudes indicated above requires some explanation. These phenomena resulted from repairing leaks in the domestic plumbing systems and from altering basic consumption within the home, i.e., using a stopper or dishpan when washing dishes instead of using a constant flow. These types of changes are available only to a limited degree to consumers once they have made the first and most basic of alterations. Such significant responses of domestic demands to further increases in incremental commodity charges will probably not occur.

Conclusions

The responsiveness of domestic and sprinkling consumption to price changes has been measured for a local market for residential water by analyzing time series data of water use before and after water meter installation. The quantities of both domestic and sprinkling water demanded were markedly reduced by the introduction of a commodity charge. Moreover, residential water consumption in Boulder, Colorado, has remained at these lower levels since meter installation. Hence the results of this study substantiated the standard postulates of demand theory.

The implications of these results are significant. Forecasting models for the effective planning and development of water resources must incorporate the influences of pricing policies if efficient investment decisions are to be forthcoming. A greater emphasis must be placed upon the appropriate level and structure of commodity charges for residential water because pricing variations can induce large variations in water use patterns. . . .

8

This selection is from Professor Harberger's introduction to a group of econometric studies of the demand for durable goods. The demand studies mentioned in this selection are of nonfarm housing by Richard F. Muth, of household refrigerators by M. L. Burstein, of automobiles by Gregory C. Chow, and of farm tractors by Zvi Griliches.

THE DEMAND FOR DURABLE GOODS

ARNOLD C. HARBERGER
University of Chicago

In the growing mass of empirical demand studies, durable goods are poorly represented. Minor food items have been studied far more intensively than major durable items. The share of durable goods demand studies in the total of all demand studies is only a picayune fraction of the share of durable goods "consumption" in the national income. Yet a case could be made that the durables are actually deserving of a more than proportionate emphasis in our professional research effort. Durable goods, even in the United States, but more especially abroad, seem to have attracted excise taxation, tariff duties, quantitative trade controls, license fees, and other policy measures far out of proportion to their weight in the national output or expenditure. Housing is almost everywhere subject to a property tax, and the return on business capital to a corporation income tax as well. Durables demand, moreover, fluctuates so violently, in comparison with the demand for other sectors' products, that most modern theories give it a key role in causing and/or exacerbating business fluctuations.

Imperfections of Data

There can be little doubt that the paucity of durable goods demand studies is to be explained by the difficulty of making them rather than by any lack of interest in the quantitative relationships they seek to explore. The difficulties are, indeed, both substantial and numerous. In the first place, the data are far from ideal. Comparatively negligible errors are made in measuring wheat in bushels or salt or haddock or beef in pounds. It is quite another thing to measure housing by the number of dwelling units, refriger-

---

ators by the number of machines, or cars by the number of vehicles. At any point in time, great differences in quality exist among the major durables, and, furthermore, there are much greater changes in quality over time in the durables sector than in, say, the basic foods. Price data, too, tend to be shaky in the durables field. On the one hand, this is merely the counterpart of the quality problem on the quantity side: the market prices of dwelling units at any one time cover an enormous range, while the market prices of different bushels of wheat cluster narrowly about their mean. On the other hand, the price data suffer from a different problem in that for such items as automobiles and refrigerators the published prices tend to be manufacturers' suggested list prices, actual transactions prices being clouded from our view by such devices as trade-in allowances, cash discounts, and whatnot.

Stock Demand and Flow Demand

Second, durable goods studies face a set of problems peculiar to themselves, arising from the Hydra-headed nature of durables demand. At any point in time there is the demand for the ownership of houses, and also there is the demand for newly constructed dwellings. These two demands are obviously interrelated. The stock of houses on hand cannot be increased without new construction, and, indeed, new construction is necessary to maintain a given stock in the face of normal depreciation and natural disasters. But the precise nature of the interrelation is not clear. A desire on the part of the public to increase the stock of housing by 10 per cent can be accommodated by constructing all the added houses in a single year or by adding 1 per cent to the stock of housing each year for a ten-year period. And there are good reasons to doubt the obvious offhand reaction that the adjustment will be immediate. Not only does construction take time, but a major decision like the purchase of a new house is likely to be weighed carefully, and the alternatives well explored, before the move is finally made. Thus different patterns of change in the demand for new construction are consistent with given patterns of change in the demand for houseownership, depending on the speed of adjustment to changes in ownership demand. If adjustment is slow, of course, the possibility emerges of differences between the actual stock of housing and the "desired" stock, adding a further complication to the problem of estimating demand.

The problems associated with estimating "stock demand" (comparable to the demand for houseownership) as well as "flow demand" (comparable to the demand for newly constructed housing) are present throughout the durables area. Many of these problems arise from the inadequacies or unavailability of stock data. Only in the case of automobiles do we have really good information as to the size and composition of the available stock, year by year. For housing, our data on the number of dwelling units are fairly reliable, but we have only sketchy and sporadic information about the age and quality composition of the stock. For refrigerators, we do not even have information as to the number in use, year by year, let alone their distribution by age and quality. In such cases, it is necessary to build up a set of stock data by applying an assumed pattern of depreciation to the purchases of past years. Errors and inaccuracies are obviously introduced by this procedure, the more so in a case like refrigerators, where the market provides very little information on the pattern of depreciation.

We cannot get away from the problems of measuring the existing stock by focusing on "flow" demand, because of the crucial influence which the existing stock has on the rate of new purchases. For any given level of demand for the services provided by a durable, new purchases in a given period will be lower the higher is the level of services obtainable from the existing stock carried into the period. Moreover, it is not clear that the service yield obtainable from the existing stock can be measured easily. If cars of all ages really have the same service yield, the aggregate service yield of the existing stock of cars would be measured by their number; if, on the other hand, the service yield of individual cars is proportional to their value, the service yield of the stock would be measured by its aggregate value. We can get an indication of which of these two possible measures is more correct by looking at the pattern of depreciation. If cars tended to depreciate by a constant dollar amount per year, this would indicate that the service yield tended to be about the same for cars of different ages, and the "numbers" measure would be preferable. If, as appears to be in fact the case for cars, they tended to depreciate by a constant percentage of their value each year, the "aggregate value" would be the preferable measure of service yield. But either of these measures is at best only a rough approximation, not only because the depreciation pattern in any practical case will fit into neither mold precisely, but also because interest charges (actual or imputed), maintenance costs, and taxes are also components of what people pay for the use of a car for a period. Furthermore, maintenance costs can "substitute" for new purchases by raising the capacity of the existing stock: we cannot know precisely in advance how much service the stock carried into a year will yield in that year. Thus, even when the data on the depreciation pattern are good, as in the case of automobiles, we can in practice get only a measure of the stock which approximately captures what we seek. The situation is far worse in a case like refrigerators, where we must almost arbitrarily assume a depreciation pattern before we can generate any measure of stock at all.

Volatility of Demand

Finally, there are the problems associated with the comparatively great volatility of durable goods demand. Not only is it true that relatively small random shifts in stock demand lead, at least for a time, to much larger percentage shifts in flow demand but also, even when stock demand changes for some "systematic" reason, such as an income change, the pace at which this will be reflected in flow demand through altered purchases will vary from situation to situation. We can at best hope to capture the average effect of, say, a 5 per cent rise in income upon flow demand; the fact that the actual effect is sometimes greater and sometimes less than average operates to introduce an added "error component" into the relationship we estimate. The volatility of durables demand also raises questions as the "identifiability" of the relationships we try to measure. May not the relationship we measure between income and construction catch, in part, a causal connection which goes from swings in construction activity to resulting income movements, thus obscuring or at least blurring the "demand" relationship we seek, which runs from changes in income to resulting movements in construction? And may not shifts in durables demand *cause* price movements in the same direction, similarly blurring or obscuring the demand relationship by which price changes lead to quantity movements in the opposite direction?

All in all, the difficulties facing those who estimate durables demand are numerous and severe enough easily to explain why so few finished studies have emerged. They also, however, serve to warn both those who undertake and those who read studies in this field of the pitfalls along the way.

Expected Income

In the course of their experimentation with various series, all three studies of consumer durables test the effect of substituting Milton Friedman's "expected-income" variable for the more conventional disposable-income series. The expected-income series is intended to be an empirical approximation to the subjective concept of "normal" or "permanent" income. It is, in fact, a weighted moving average of disposable income, in which current income gets one-third of the total weight and past incomes get weights which decline progressively and roughly exponentially, income of nine years ago and earlier receiving zero weight. This variable was found to explain a larger percentage of the variation in total consumption than did disposable income or any of a large number of differently weighted moving averages which were tested by Friedman. The theoretical support for a variable of this type comes from the conjectures that consumption will conform to what the consumer considers his "normal" income to be rather than to the quite possibly transitory movements of his current income and that the consumer's view of his normal income position will be conditioned largely by his past experience and revised only gradually when current disposable income differs from its expected norm.

Muth's Study of Housing

The principal findings of Muth's study of housing are that the price and income elasticities of stock demand are probably in the neighborhood of unity (perhaps even greater), that the interest elasticity is substantial, and that the adjustment of the stock of housing to a change in the determinants of demand takes significantly more than a year. When it is assumed that the adjustment process is completed within a year, the price- and income-elasticity estimates are only in the neighborhood of 0.5. A substantially better explanation of variations in the stock of housing is obtained when the adjustment coefficient is estimated from the data. Muth's first equation yields price and income elasticities of stock demand of around 0.9 and an adjustment coefficient of around .33 (indicating that a third of the full adjustment to a given change typically occurs within a year). When disposable income is substituted for expected income, the estimated price and income elasticities remain about the same, but the adjustment coefficient is cut to about 15 per cent, and the explanatory power of the equation is reduced. Muth concludes from a series of experiments that Friedman's expected-income concept is superior to disposable income in explaining variations in new construction activity.

Muth then turns to an examination of the ratio of a rent index to the price of housing as a determinant of the rate of construction. Given the interest rate, construction varies directly with the ratio of rent to price, these two variables explaining some 70 per cent of the variation in the ratio of construction to the stock of housing. When, instead of the current ratio of rent to price, an "expected" ratio is used (based on a weighted moving average of current and past ratios), 85–95 per cent of the variance in construction relative to the existing stock of housing is explained.

The elasticity of demand for the stock of housing with respect to the interest rate is estimated at between −0.13 and −0.18. This suggests that a change in the interest rate from, say, 6 per cent to 4 per cent would ultimately lead to an increment of some 5 per cent in the nation's stock of housing. The initial response of construction would be more pronounced; the flow-demand elasticities of −0.80 and −0.95 imply that, in the initial year following the change in the interest rate, construction would be between a fourth and a third greater than it otherwise would have been.

Burstein's Study of Refrigerators

The key problems which determine the structure of Burstein's study of refrigerator demand are the related ones of price and quality. Quality has had a pronounced upward trend, making the problem of expressing "refrigeration" in equivalent units a serious one. Apart from the fact that we must solve the quality problem before we are able to obtain a time series of the price of equivalent units, price presents an additional difficulty in that most available data refer to "suggested list prices" rather than the average prices at which actual transactions took place. Burstein attacks these problems simultaneously by constructing a price index from Sears, Roebuck mail-order catalogue data. Sears's prices are actual transactions prices, uncolored by discounts or trade-ins, and external evidence suggests that they are reliable indicators of transactions prices for refrigerators in general. Burstein's index compares, in chain-link fashion, the prices of models with similar specifications in adjacent years. In each adjacent-year comparison quality is thus held constant; the quantity of "refrigeration" purchased by consumers, year by year, is then obtained by deflating the dollar volume of annual sales by the price index. Burstein next generates stock series, under several alternative assumptions as to the rate and pattern of depreciation, from the series on quantitites purchased.

The price-elasticity estimates of demand for the stock of refrigeration range from −1.07 to −2.06, and the income-elasticity estimates from 0.82 to 2.54. If the war years (data for which are more dubious) are excluded, the range of price-elasticity estimates is from −1.58 to −2.06 and that for income-elasticity estimates is from 1.23 to 1.64.

Though all the coefficients are highly significant statistically, the possibility exists that the price and income variables, both of which have strong trends, are in these regressions "explaining" a trendwise change in tastes. When trend is introduced as a separate variable, in addition to price and income, the price-elasticity estimate falls to around unity but remains highly significant. The income elasticity falls to 0.83 under the disposable-income variant and remains highly significant, but under the expected-income variant the income-elasticity estimate falls below 0.5 and becomes statistically insignificant.

Burstein also estimated equations in which a trend in tastes was imposed. When a "high" trend (implying an increase in per capita demand of over 300 per cent in twenty-four years) was imposed, estimated income elasticities ranged from 0.72 to 1.1, and estimated price elasticities from −1.19 to −1.58. With a "medium" trend (implying a 180 per cent increase over twenty-four years), income elasticities ranged from 0.97 to 1.57, and price elasticities from −1.32 to −1.87. When slow adjustment of actual to desired stock was allowed for, price elasticity was estimated at −1.4, income elasticity at 1.9, and the adjustment coefficient at .46.

The final section of Burstein's study uses cross-section data in an effort to gain further evidence on the income elasticity of demand for refrigeration. When the percentage changes in stock by state between 1940 and 1950 are related to the percentage changes in state incomes, a high estimate of income elasticity (over 2.0) emerges. When family budgets are used as the basis for estimating income elasticity, an estimate of around 0.7 results. This excludes freezers, which appear to have a higher income elasticity than refrigerators. Burstein's modest conclusions are that "the price elasticity is between −1.0 and −2.0 and, somewhat less conclusively, that the income elasticity is between 1.0 and 2.0."

Chow's Study of Automobiles

Chow's paper is an extension and further test of the model presented in his earlier study of automobile demand. Here the stock of automobiles is expressed in new-car equivalent units on the basis of the relative market prices of cars of different ages. On the assumption of instantaneous adjustment of actual to desired stock, Chow estimates the price elasticity to be between −0.6 and −1.1 and the income elasticity at from 1.5 to 1.7 under the disposable-income variant and at from 1.8 to 2.0 under the expected-income variant. The expected-income variant succeeds in explaining 90–95 per cent of the variance of the stock of cars, while the disposable-income variant explains 85–90 per cent.

When the possibility of slow adjustment of stock is allowed for, the estimated price elasticity of stock demand ranges around −0.7; the income elasticity, around 1.8.

The estimates were derived from data on the years 1921–53. The 1921–53 relations are then extrapolated to the 1954–57 period and appear to hold as well in this "forecast period" as they did in the observation period. A further extrapolation into the recession year 1958 turns out to be substantially above the actual figure, indicating the possibility that automobile demand shifted downward "autonomously" in that year. Chow also constructs a projection of automobile demand for the year 1968: according to his estimates, the normal annual demand for new cars in the United States will at that time be between 8.9 and 9.7 million units, if the relative price of cars remains unchanged.

Griliches' Study of Farm Tractors

In Griliches' study, the focus is shifted from consumer durables to a durable productive input. The demand for farm tractors is taken to depend on tractor prices relative to agricultural product prices, on the interest rate, and (in some variants) on other factor prices, on the stock of horses and mules on farms, on farmer's equity, and on a time trend. When instantaneous adjustment of actual to desired stock is assumed, the price elasticity of stock demand is estimated at −0.5, and the interest-rate elasticity at −4.9. When slow adjustment is allowed for, the estimates of price elasticity of stock demand come to exceed unity in absolute value, averaging around −1.5, and the estimates of interest elasticity come to exceed −5.0 in absolute value, averaging around −6.5. The adjustment coefficient is estimated to be about .17. The main variables affecting tractor demand appear to be the price of tractors relative to agricultural product prices and the interest rate. When the other variables listed above were tried, they turned out to be statistically insignificant. Relative price and the interest rate alone explain about 80 per cent of the variance in tractor stock; together with lagged tractor stock (in the slow-adjustment models), they explained about 99 per cent of this variance. When tractor purchases rather than tractor stock are taken as the variable to be explained, relative price, interest rate, and lagged tractor stock explain over 90 per cent of the variation (in purchases).

9 This essay is a very patient description of a statistical study of the demand for minor league baseball. Price, promotions, and the quality of play are found to be more strongly associated with attendance than advertising, winning, or income.

MEASURING AND FORECASTING DEMAND: A CASE STUDY OF BASEBALL ATTENDANCE

JOHN J. SIEGFRIED
JEFF D. EISENBERG
Vanderbilt University

Minor-league professional baseball teams have at least two obvious goals. First, they strive to develop and evaluate prospective major-league players. Second, they are concerned with the financial success of day-to-day team operations. Achievement of both goals can be financially rewarding to the team owners: (1) through the increased goodwill and future assistance from the parent major-league club, and (2) through current net profits from operations.

However, all of this hinges on the demand for minor-league baseball and thus on attendance at games. And yet, currently, there is no systematic compilation of the factors that determine attendance levels for minor-league baseball. This is despite the fact that in 1977 there were 124 U.S. and Canadian minor-league baseball teams, each making business decisions about the day-to-day operations of their clubs.

Better information about the factors that determine attendance levels and the relative effectiveness of alternative marketing strategies would greatly assist minor-league baseball teams in improving their financial stability and serving their respective communities. Such information would also aid them in evaluating the prospects for a team in a new city. Therefore, we have undertaken a systematic analysis to identify and determine the importance of various factors that may affect minor-league baseball attendance.

First, we applied the straightforward logic of economics to minor-league baseball in order to isolate the relevant information. Then we used data supplied by 27 different minor-league teams covering 86 separate seasons to statistically evaluate the inferences derived from our economic analysis. We found that the following factors influence attendance:

Average ticket prices.

Number of home dates.

Excerpted and reprinted by permission from *BUSINESS* Magazine. "Measuring and Forecasting Demand: A Case Study of Baseball Attendance," by John Siegfried and Jeff D. Eisenberg, January/February 1980, pp. 34–41. A more technical version appears in *The Atlantic Economic Journal*, 8 July 1980. Dr. Siegfried is an Associate Professor and Mr. Eisenberg was an undergraduate at Vanderbilt when this study was written.

Percent of the population that is black.

Longevity of the team.

Game excitement

Quality of play.

Merchandise and price promotional efforts.

In contrast, per capita income, winning record, and advertising appear to have little or no influence on attendance.

In addition to identifying the important factors determining attendance, we assessed the sensitivity of attendance to each factor. This information can be usefully applied by management to improve the financial success of a minor-league team. For example, our findings indicate an expected group of fans who will be drawn to the ball park by merchandise promotions (free merchandise such as bats, balls, caps, or T-shirts given away at games to all or a certain select group of fans) and by reduced-price promotions (ladies night, kids night, students night, senior citizens night, and so on, when all or a select group of fans are admitted to the ball park for less than the normal admission charge). We also determined that this group would not have attended another game in the absence of a promotion. This information plus cost data and the conditions of a promotional offer (e.g., the maximum number of fans eligible for the promotion) provide a way to determine how profitable a prospective additional promotion will be. . . .

Our estimates of the responsiveness of attendance to various factors determining the level of attendance at minor-league baseball games are strictly applicable only to the range of data employed in our analysis. Therefore, one should be cautious in drawing any conclusions for teams that are substantially above or below the average attendance of our sample (68,607 persons per season). In addition, the expected effect of each of the individual factors considered is applicable only near that factor's average, and strictly within the range of data values for that factor. The averages and ranges of each of the factors are reported in Exhibit 1; these should be consulted to ensure that the relationships are not applied to teams with factors having values extremely different from the teams in our sample.

Methodology and Data

The general theory of consumer demand for goods and services guided us in specifying factors that should influence minor-league baseball attendance. These fall into the general categories of price, income, availability and price of substitute recreation, consumer tastes, and population. Consumer preference for baseball and greater population obviously are expected to increase attendance. More and better recreational substitutes at reasonable prices can be expected to lessen the attendance at minor-league baseball games, as might an increase in the price of admission tickets to the games. The effect of income, however, is

Exhibit 1 Average and extreme values for minor-league baseball data: 86 seasons from 27 teams over 1973–1977

Item	*Units*	*Average**	*Minimum*	*Maximum*
Attendance	people	68,607	17,051	219,859
Population		348,514	42,179	1,109,882
Stadium capacity		5,509	1,300	24,000
Gaté receipts	dollars	$44,466.00	$6,950.00	$263,000.00
Average ticket price		0.60	0.08	1.69
Average available-seat price		1.32	.71	2.62
Per capita income		2,954.00	2,048.00	3,477.00
Newspaper advertising		1,757.00	0	12,776.00
Radio advertising		1,036.00	0	19,164.00
Television advertising		175.00	0	3,687.00
Other advertising		160.00	0	1,825.00
Black population	percent	7.7%	0.7%	52.1%
Games won		51.2	30.0	69.7
League level (percentage of team-seasons AAA or AA)		44.2	0	100.0
Reduced-price promotions (percentage of games)		33.8	0	75.4
Merchandise giveaway promotions (percentage of games)		14.0	0	100.0
Number of home dates	dates	52.9	26	69
Consecutive years in city	years	16.6	1	90
Home runs per game	home runs	0.53	0.09	1.26

Source: Authors' survey (see text for details) and U.S. Census of Population, 1970.
*Average = simple mean value for 86 team-seasons.

ambiguous. Although greater incomes may provide additional resources for consumers to spend on baseball tickets, increased incomes may also affect consumers' tastes and the availability of other alternatives. This could possibly lead to a decline in attendance if individuals with higher incomes have less preference for baseball or switch to substitute recreational activities.

Although logic can establish plausible relationships between each factor and attendance, it cannot help us in assessing the strength of the relationship. It is obviously important to a minor-league-baseball business manager to know whether a specific promotion will generate an additional 20 fans or an additional 2,000 fans; simply knowing that the promotion will generate *some* additional fans is insufficient. To evaluate this issue, we sent a questionnaire to each of 111 minor-league teams in operation at the end of the 1977 baseball season. There were 46 responses; 27 teams provided adequate data for at least one season. Since some teams provided satisfactory data for more than one season, we have a total of 86 different team-seasons represented in our sample. Of the 27 teams responding adequately, 4 were AAA-league teams, 8 were AA teams, 10 were A teams, and 5 were rookie-league teams. All of our data except population and income information are from the survey responses. The demographic data were collected from the U.S. Census of Population, 1970. Some team-performance information was obtained from *The Official Baseball Guide*, published by *The Sporting News*.

The statistical method we employed to estimate the responsiveness of attendance to each factor, or determinant, is called multiple linear regression analysis. This is a commonly used technique to identify the particular relationship between two variables, and is extensively employed in social science, medical, and business research.

Ideally, if we were to have a set of data to evaluate the relationship between minor-league baseball attendance and, say, ticket prices, we would include information from many different teams playing in identically sized cities, with identical income levels, having identical winning records, belonging to the same league, undertaking the same number of promotional efforts, and so on. Indeed, theoretically everything except ticket price and attendance would be the same for all teams. Then differences in attendance among teams could be logically attributed to differences in ticket prices, and a scatter diagram showing the relationship between price and attendance for each game would be helpful for assessing the relative responsiveness of attendance to changes in ticket prices.

Obviously, the real world cannot accommodate such an ideal research method. Therefore, statisticians have developed sophisticated techniques to accomplish this goal artificially. In our study, the multiple linear regression technique is used to "hold constant" all of the factors in the study, other than the one being examined, and to evaluate the relationship between the examined factor and attendance *independent of the level of anything else*. It does this for each factor, one at a time. The results, therefore, are a series of sets of relationships between each factor and attendance, which are estimated under the condition that all other factors are the same across all baseball seasons.

Multiple linear regression is a powerful statistical tool; however, it requires assumptions about the *way* that factors affect attendance. That is, if ticket prices were doubled, and if there were a decline in attendance of 1,000 people, would a second doubling of price generate a further decline of 1,000, or would the second price hike yield more or fewer than 1,000 fan defections?

The method we have used to estimate the effect of certain factors on attendance *relates percentage changes in the factors to percentage changes in attendance* and assumes that this responsiveness is similar across various levels of the factors and attendance. The most plausible alternative is to relate *unit* changes in the factors to *unit or percentage* changes in attendance. For technical reasons the second method (relating unit changes in the factor to percentage change in attendance) is used for assessing the impact of quality of play, advertising, and promotions.[1] . . .

Factors Affecting Attendance

The theoretical relationship of each factor to attendance is summarized in Exhibit 2 under the column "Expected Relationship." The actual relationship for our sample of 86 minor-league baseball seasons is reported in the column entitled "Coefficient." An example of the effect of a change in each of the determinants is provided in the last two columns of Exhibit 2. Details on how to interpret the coefficients are given in the previous section and in the notes in Exhibit 2.

Average Ticket Price: The average ticket price for the 86 baseball seasons in our sample is $.60, reflecting the fact that minor-league teams engage in many price promotions. This strategy may be sensible in view of (1) the objective of the teams to provide players with experience playing before large crowds, and, probably more important, (2) the fact that many teams own their own concession rights and may generate more revenues from concession sales than are lost by reduced ticket prices during promotional efforts.

The empirical results indicate that a 1% increase in price is likely to be accompanied by a .252 of 1% decrease in season attendance. For a team with an average ticket price of $.60 and average annual attendance of 68,607, this means that a price rise to $.66 would likely yield 1,729 fewer customers over the season. Although the actual price is not likely to be either $.60 or $.66 per year (since some people pay more and others pay less to gain admission), the analysis reflects the impact of any price changes that would increase the average ticket price. Therefore, a reduction in the number of tickets given away free could raise the average ticket price, and the impact would be fewer fans in attendance. Similarly, a rise in the average price could be accomplished by raising the regular price and continuing to give away the same number of tickets. Again, the analysis suggests that lower attendance will be the result, probably because some people will decide that the higher price of minor-league baseball attendance makes alternative recreational activities more attractive.

A coefficient of demand responsiveness to price that is smaller in absolute value than one indicates that price cuts will diminish total gate receipts, while

[1] The percentage-to-percentage relationship requires calculation of logarithms of the values of all variables as an intermediate step. The logarithm of zero does not exist. Consequently the percentage-to-percentage method cannot be employed for factors which are sometimes zero.

Exhibit 2 Statistical relationship between minor-league attendance and its determinants

			Effect for average team		
Determinant	*Expected relationship*	*Coefficient*	*Change in determinant*	*yields*	*Change in annual attendance*
1. Average ticket price	−	−.252*	+10.0%		− 1,729
2. Per capita income	±	+.398	+10.0%		+ 2,731
3. Percentage black population	−	−.096†	+10.0%		− 659
4. Number of home dates	+	+.462†	1.9% (1 date)		+ 602
5. Consecutive years in city	+	+.067†	+ 6.0% (1 year)		+ 276
6. Population	+	+.189*	+10.0%		+ 1,297
7. Percentage of games won	+	+.110	+10.0%		+ 755
8. Home runs per game	+	+.194†	+10.0%		+ 1,331
9. League level (AA or AAA = 1)		+.384*	0 to 1		+26,345
10. Reduced-price promotions (frequency)	±	+.007*	+ 1.9% (1 game)		+ 975
11. Merchandise promotions	+	+.012*	+ 1.9%		+ 1,568
12. Newspaper advertising	+	−.000	+$100		− 6
13. Radio advertising	+	−.000	+$100		− 70

* The results are statistically significant at the 99% confidence level. This means that data from at least 99 out of 100 of the conceivable samples of baseball seasons would reveal the same qualitative results as our findings. That is, in at least 99 out of 100 similar studies of the determinants of minor-league baseball attendance, the direction of the relationship (and whether it exists) would be the same as in this study.

† A statistical significance at the 95% confidence level; any relationship significant at the 99% level is also significant at the 95% level. Those factors that are not statistically significant cannot be said to be different from zero. Therefore, the appropriate interpretation of the coefficients on per capita income, percentage of games won, newspaper advertising, and radio advertising is that *those factors have no effect on attendance* in the minor leagues.

price increases will improve receipts. This is called "inelastic demand," which means that consumers do not respond very much to price changes. A 10% price rise from the average ticket price at the average attendance level (68,607) would increase revenues from ticket sales by 7.2%; a 10% price cut would diminish total gate receipts by 12.3%. Items that are a small part of consumers' budgets (e.g., salt or matches) and items that consumers consider to be necessities (medical care, coffee, cigarettes) usually have an inelastic demand. Also, goods

Key to column heads:

Expected relationship: If an increase in a determinant is expected to yield an increase in attendance, the relationship is indicated as positive (+). If an increase in a determinant is expected to yield a decrease in attendance, the relationship is indicated as negative (−). If there are conflicting expectations, both + and − are indicated.

Coefficient: For the first 8 determinants, the coefficient reports the *percentage* that attendance is expected to change as a result of a 1% change in the determinant, holding all other determinants fixed. For example, a 1% increase in the average ticket price (from $.60 to $.606 is expected to decrease attendance by .252 of 1% (0.00252 times 68,607, or 173 people) for a team with the average ticket price and average attendance. Similar calculations can be made for teams other than the average. For determinants 9 through 13, the coefficient reports the *percentage* that attendance is expected to change as a result of a one *unit* change in the determinant. For example, an additional 1% of games promoted is expected to yield .007 times 68,607, or 480 additional fans. Note that a 1 percentage-point increase in games promoted is less than 100 home dates per year. Therefore, realistic assessments of promotions need to be evaluated for percentage-point changes that reflect full games; for example, 1.9 percentage points represents a one-game increase for the average team that played 52.9 home dates per year.

Effect for average team: The last two columns of the table report the impact of a hypothetical change in each of the determinants of attendance. Most of the hypothetical determinants are either a 10% change or a one-game (1.9% for the typical team) change. For example, a 10% increase in the number of home runs per game (from .53 to .58 per game) is expected to yield an additional 1,331 fans over a season. A change in league level from either rookie or A to either AA or AAA is expected to yield an increase of 26,345 fans. Note that each of these changes is simulated under the assumption that all of the other determinants do not change. In reality, several factors may change simultaneously (e.g., a move of a team from one city to another would obviously change population, percentage of black population, per capita income, and years in city, among other things) and consequently the net impact of such a change would be the sum of the individual effects.

with relatively poor substitutes have an inelastic demand. In many smaller cities there may be relatively few alternative recreational opportunities competing for consumers' dollars.

Per Capita Income: Rising per capita income is normally expected to increase demand for a good or service. However, there has been speculation that baseball is one of the minority of goods and services whose demand decreases as incomes rise, since persons in less physically exerting occupations (who normally have higher incomes) may find the rather sedate pace of baseball less attractive and choose more exciting and diverse recreational opportunities. The statistical results reveal no association of per capita income with minor-league baseball attendance. If these alternative views of the effect of income on attendance are both valid, their quantitative effects must approximately cancel out each other. This contrasts with a study that found a negative impact of income on attendance for major-league baseball. It is likely that persons with increased incomes are able to purchase fewer alternative recreational services in the smaller cities of most minor-league baseball teams than they are in major-league cities, because the smaller cities have fewer alternatives available. Consequently, increased incomes in minor-league cities encourage fewer people to switch to alternative consumption goods.[2]

Percent Black Population: The same study of baseball demand also revealed a negative effect of black population on attendance. It was theorized that either of three hypotheses may be valid: (1) blacks have relatively less interest in baseball than whites; (2) prejudice by whites results in more than one white not attending for each additional black that attends a game; or (3) black population is correlated with undesirable stadium location and consequently we understate the price of attending a game.[3] In the minor-league cities of our sample the percentage of population that is black is considerably less than the nationwide average—an average of only 7.7% in our 86 observations, as opposed to a national average of about 11%. The statistical results reveal a minor negative effect of increased black population on baseball attendance, but the effect is very small. A 1% increase in black population is expected to yield only 66 fewer fans per season.

Number of Home Dates: Minor-league teams play different length schedules and have fairly flexible policies regarding making up games that were postponed due to inclement weather. As a result, the average number of home dates for our 86 team seasons was 52.9, but ranged from 26 to 69. Because attendance is obviously related to the number of games available, we consider home dates a determinant of attendance. Additional home dates should increase attendance, but less than proportionally. Additional games provide more opportunities for fans to attend, but many fans do not attend all of the games and can satisfy their total demand for attendance regardless of whether there are 26 or 69 home dates in a season. Therefore, additional games provide more opportunities only for those people who desire to attend a large number of games. The resulting response of +0.462 of 1% of attendance to a 1% increase in home dates is consistent with our prediction and statistically different from both zero and one (as we predicted). On the average, an increase of one home date is expected to

[2] Roger G. Noll, ed., *Government and the Sports Business* (Washington, D.C., Brookings, 1974), p. 121.
[3] Ibid.

yield an additional 602 fans per season, in contrast to the average game attendance of 1,297.

We also evaluated the form of price promotion known as a double-header—two consecutive games for the price of one. Although the major leagues have drastically reduced the number of scheduled double-headers, the minor leagues continue to schedule many of them. Usually they consist of two seven-inning games rather than one normal nine-inning game. One might expect greater attendance at such games because the price per game is nearly halved. On the other hand, there may be rapidly diminishing recreational benefits received from observing more than one game of baseball per day. Furthermore, much of the increased attendance at double-headers may simply be people switching their attendance from alternative single games. Statistical tests indicated that the number of double-headers had no perceptible effect on total season attendance when included in the estimates with the number of home dates. This means that it is not merely the *number of games* that has an impact on attendance; it is the number of *separate playing dates* that really counts. This finding is not surprising in view of the decision of the major leagues to reduce the frequency of double-headers in the last decade.

The more diverse goals of minor-league teams (especially in providing playing time for prospective major leaguers) and the financial returns from player development, as well as from gate attendance, can explain the persistence of the double-header in the minor leagues in spite of its apparent failure to increase attendance.

Consecutive Years in City: Longevity of a team in a city may reflect success. However, the *trend* of attendance over time can be either increasing or decreasing so long as its *level* is sufficiently high to ensure financial viability. The opportunity to cash in on the investment returns from earlier advertising and promotion and previous attendance indicates a positive relationship between attendance and the number of consecutive years in a single location. However, consumer satiation and the increase in competition from new recreational activities associated with growth in real incomes may make it difficult for teams to continue to hold their share of the recreational dollar over time. Finally, the novelty of a new team in a town is believed to cause a "honeymoon effect," which would yield relatively high attendance in the first few years a new team plays in a city.

Because of various conflicting views and the possibility that one of these effects may dominate in the early years and another as the team matures, we included this factor using a method to allow for different effects in the early and late stages of a team's life cycle. The results indicate that attendance increases with the age of a team. However, the impact is very small (survival through an additional season raised annual attendance by only 276 for the typical team). Furthermore, the positive impact may be an artifact of our method of estimation.

We compared the attendance of different teams with varying tenure in their respective cities. Teams that have remained in a single location for a long time probably have substantial enough attendance to remain financially viable. Of those teams new to their cities, some will succeed and some will fail. Thus, the average attendance, if related to time alone, may appear to increase when actually, if one evaluated only teams that were eventually successful, it would be declining over time.

Population: If income, tastes, prices, and other factors affect baseball attendance similarly, then teams playing in areas with greater population will enjoy greater attendance. However, larger cities also have more diverse recreational opportunities that compete with baseball. Therefore, we do not expect attendance to rise proportionally with population. The responsiveness of attendance with respect to a 1% increase in population is a .189% increase, which is statistically meaningful. A 10% increase in population for the average city in our sample (38,700 people) would likely increase attendance by about 1,300 per year.

Team Performance: One of the most persistent beliefs about the success of baseball teams is the notion that fans want to see a winner. In view of the apparent importance of team success, several alternative methods of measurement were examined. The current year's winning percentage was chosen in preference to place in the standings or previous year's winning percentage on the basis of ability to explain differences in attendance, since there is little conceptual basis on which to choose among them. None of the team-success measures were statistically meaningful. Apparently, a team's winning percentage is relatively unimportant in the minor leagues. Perhaps this is because fans believe that the minor baseball leagues' main role is to groom players for the parent club, and that when individual players excel, they are usually "called up" to a higher level of play. Consequently there is a self-equilibrating process, so that effort to generate a winning team in the long run has little effect. Furthermore, fans may be less likely to identify psychologically with a minor-league team (as they sometimes do with their favorite major-league team), and thus they may be less responsive to winning.

Game Excitement: We hypothesized that certain aspects of baseball games generate more utility to consumers than others. For example, greater physical activity is likely to be associated with higher attendance. Therefore, we evaluated both runs per game and home runs per game as measures of game activity. Home runs per game explained a greater share of the differences in attendance, as might be expected, since this is a partial measure of runs as well as one of the most exciting events in a baseball game. The responsiveness of attendance to home runs is positive and statistically meaningful. A 10% increase in home runs per season will probably mean an additional 1,331 fans. Minor-league baseball fans are evidently more responsive to scoring than to winning.

Quality of Play: The general quality of play reflects the physical skills of teams. Quality of play should improve as the level of the leagues increases. The study distinguishes teams in AAA and AA leagues from those in rookie and A leagues. Results indicate a large and statistically meaningful attendance response to quality of play. With no other changes (e.g., in population, winning record, or home dates), a team moving from the lower classification to the higher classification is expected to draw an additional 26,345 fans per year, a 38% increase for the average team.

Promotions: One of the most frequently employed discretionary measures that minor-league baseball teams use to induce greater attendance is game promotions. Many different types of promotions have been offered by teams, but all seem to fall into one of two general categories: (1) reduced-price promotions for games where everyone or a selected group is admitted to the game at less than the normal price—family night, student night, band night, ladies night, kids night, and so on; or (2) merchandise promotions for games where everyone or a selected group of fans receive certain merchandise, such as bats, balls, caps, beer, or pennants. The expectation is that these promotions will increase attendance. They have become very popular in the last several years. In our sample, almost half of the games were promoted in one way or another; for the 1977 season alone, 48.2% of games were promoted. Overall, 34% of the games were subject to some sort of price-reduction promotion, and 14% of the games were accompanied by merchandise promotions. Some teams—e.g., El Paso have gone so far as to offer a promotion at every one of their games.

Attendance at games on nights of promotions is usually much larger than attendance at other games. However, some of this additional attendance may be an illusion. Fans who plan to attend a fixed, relatively small number of games may choose to attend the promoted rather than the nonpromoted contests, thereby decreasing attendance at nonpromoted games while increasing attendance at promoted games. Therefore, over the season the net effect of promotions will be overstated by a simple comparison of average attendance at promoted games with average attendance at nonpromoted games. Our procedure for estimating the effectiveness of promotions provides controls for this problem by evaluating the sensitivity of *annual* attendance to an additional promotion date, rather than focusing on attendance at individual games.

The results indicate that promotions are effective attendance generators. For the average team with a season attendance of 68,607, an additional reduced-price promotion can be expected to yield at least 975 more fans per season, while an additional merchandise promotion is predicted to generate 1,568 extra fans over a season. Both of these estimated effects are statistically meaningful. For a team with an attendance of 200,000 per year, the effect of promotions would be about 2,842 fans per reduced-price game and 4,571 fans per merchandise promotion. The actual observed difference between promoted and nonpromoted games should exceed these estimates, since our predictions are for the net effect of a promotion over the entire season. These estimates also include the substitution of some customers from nonpromoted to promoted games as well as the spillovers to attendance at other games caused by interest generated from the promotions. In addition, part of the effect of price promotions is captured by the ticket price variable, since average ticket prices are measured as those actually paid, and a promotion will lower average ticket prices. Thus part of the fan response to price promotions is included in the estimated sensitivity of attendance to price. The promotions factor, therefore, represents the relative frequency and (inversely) intensity of price cuts. The results suggest that more modest price cuts spread over more games is a preferable strategy to relatively few, but deep, price cuts. The total effect of price promotions is the sum of the impact of the price *promotion* coefficient *plus* the impact of the price coefficient times the effect of the promotion on the average season ticket price. For example, if the price promotion at one game reduces average season price by about 1% (.6 of $.01), the price promotion would be expected to yield an additional 1,148 fans [(1.9 × .00748 × 68,607) + (.01 × .252 × 68.607)].

There are several reasons to exercise caution in interpreting these estimates. First, our measure of promotions is unfortunately primitive, since all promotions were valued equally. Obviously "key chain night" and "batting helmet night" have different values to consumers, as do fan-appreciation night (half-price tickets for everyone) and senior citizens night (half-price tickets for people over 65). Some promotions may have little value, in which case the extra attendance of an additional promotion, as estimated by our method, understates the average effect. Second, and perhaps more important, our statistical method does not permit us to separate the estimated effect of promotions on attendance from the reverse effect—namely, the impact of attendance on promotions. If extremely poor performance jolts teams into promoting, or if teams that are selling out most of their home games decide to forgo promotions (since promotions invariably reduce revenues), the observed correlation between promotions and attendance could be low or even negative.

Whether or not promotions are worthwhile depends on the cost of promotions relative to revenues. For example, if the typical team, drawing 68,607 fans per year, gave away a free cap to all children who came to a particular game accompanied by an adult, and caps cost the team $.50 each, the cost of the promotion would be at least $358 (average attendance of 1,297 plus incremental attendance of at least 1,568 times $.50 divided by 4). Additional revenues would be at least $941 ($.60 times 1,568). (This example assumes that children are one quarter of the attendance at the promoted game and that this corresponds roughly to their proportion of season attendance. The example also ignores the costs of administering the promotion.) Revenues would probably be substantially greater because it is likely that regular rather than discount prices would be charged during a merchandise promotion, and because the average price figure used in the projection reflects a weighting of regular and discount prices. In addition, to the extent that fans are diverted from other discount price games, or that fan interest expands attendance in subsequent seasons, revenues attributable to the promotion would be higher. In this hypothetical example the cap promotion appears to be profitable.

Similarly, the profitability reduced-price promotions could be estimated and would depend on the extent of the price reduction, the fraction of fans eligible for reduced prices, the extent of switching on the part of fans from regular-price to reduced-price games, and the attendance at subsequent games generated from the promotion.

Because the demand curve is inelastic, reduced prices for all fans will reduce total revenues. Therefore, it is more likely that reduced-price promotions will be discriminatory, directed at those groups of people who might otherwise not attend (e.g., senior citizens, Boy Scouts, ladies). This is the way in which most of the reduced-price promotions are actually implemented.

Advertising: In fact, minor-league baseball teams do very little advertising in comparison to the total media exposure that they usually receive. Since newspaper sports pages report extensively on the progress of minor-league baseball teams at no charge to the teams, and since local radio stations usually plug the team regularly, the impact of incremental advertising is quite low. Our study predicted that most minor-league baseball teams get sufficient "free" advertising via sports reporting, and that the impact of additional paid advertising is relatively insignificant. The statistical results support this prediction. Radio and newspaper advertising have no significant influence on total attendance.

It is possible that advertising may be effective only when it is employed in conjunction with some other strategy. For example, advertising directed toward informing the potential crowd that a promotion will be held at a particular game may be the mechanism through which advertising is effective. However, when this means of advertising effectiveness was tested using a special form of the multiple regression method, the results indicated no support for the theory.

Excluded Variables: Certain variables included in other studies of the demand for professional-sports attendance have been omitted here. Three of the more prominent ones include (1) stadium capacity, (2) weather, and (3) time. Seating capacity is sometimes included in attendance studies because it establishes an effective limit on attendance (although minor-league baseball teams frequently admit everyone who shows up to the ball park, seating them on the grass along the foul lines). But sell-outs are very infrequent in minor-league baseball. The average stadium capacity in our sample is 5,508, while average game attendance is only 1,297.

Weather variables are excluded for two reasons. First, although the weather might well influence attendance at baseball games, it will also affect involvement in alternative outdoor recreation activities. Thus it affects substitute recreation similarly and should have little differential impact on the demand for baseball attendance. Second, unlike football, baseball rain-outs (the most severe type of inclement weather during the baseball season) are rescheduled for a date later in the season. If the rain-outs are rescheduled as part of a double-header, and double-headers generate no greater attendance than single games, then rain-outs are treated in our model appropriately as a reduction in the number of home dates. The effect of sunny vs. cloudy weather is largely irrelevant because most games are played at night.

A 1973 study found that a time trend did not explain any of the differences in major-league baseball attendance over the period 1951–1969.[4] We included a time trend in our study for the years 1973 through 1977. Our findings were similar to those of the earlier study—no effect of time *apart from* the changes in other factors that occurred over time.

Conclusions

Overall our statistical study accounts for 80% of the variations in season attendance at minor-league baseball games for 27 teams over the 1973–1977 period. This compares very favorably with results from studies of the demand for other goods and services.

The results of our investigation of the determinants of the demand for minor-league baseball attendance are generally consistent with established economic doctrine. Attendance declines as price is raised; per capita income has little apparent effect on attendance, but the quality and excitement of play seem to be important to fans—indeed, more important than having a winning team. For example, the model predicts greater fan acceptance for a AAA team that hits lots of home runs, yet loses consistently, than for a winning rookie-league team that exhibits little slugging. Promotional efforts appear to be effective in generating attendance, although the cost information necessary to assess their net impact on profits is unavailable to us. Paid advertising seems to be wholly ineffective, which is probably due to the fact that so much "free" advertising occurs through sports reporting. If information is adequately spread by sports reporting, there appears to be no important role for paid advertising in minor-league baseball marketing.

The results of this study might be useful to the business managers of minor-league baseball teams. For those teams with attendance and determinants within the ranges of the data we employed, the coefficients can provide some guidance to the attendance payoff of alternative strategies such as ticket price changes, advertising, promotion, or even home runs. However, in order for this information to be used correctly, the extra costs of any such strategy must be assessed and weighed against the attendance benefits.

Our data were supplied by only 27 different teams. Applications of demand analysis to a more comprehensive set of data would improve the confidence we have in the results. Until such time as that occurs, the conclusions should be consumed only with a substantial side-order of caution. Finally, this study has completely ignored avenues of minor-league financial returns other than gate receipts, e.g., concession revenues and future returns for successful player development. When these other avenues interact with the options available to affect gate attendance, they, too, must be factored into the analysis.

[4] Henry G. Demmert, *The Economics of Professional Team Sports* (Lexington, Massachusetts, D.C. Heath, 1973), p. 69.

10 Race-track gambling is found to be sensitive to price and income just as demand theory predicts. The same statistical method used in selection 9 by Siegfried and Eisenberg is applied here to estimate price and income elasticities. The estimated demand relationship is used to determine the revenue maximizing take-out for state government.

AN INQUIRY INTO THE ECONOMICS OF RACETRACK GAMBLING

ARTHUR GRUEN
Tufts University

"All horseplayers die broke." [DAMON RUNYON]

In the face of mounting fiscal pressures state governments are looking increasingly to gambling as a source of revenue. If the sale of gambling is to provide revenues, however, it is important to understand the demand for this good in order to adopt the appropriate pricing mechanism. Standard economic theory posits a model where the quantity of a good consumed is negatively related to the price of the good if we fix tastes, income, and the prices of other goods. Such a concept is intuitively reasonable as well as useful in analyzing much of observed economic behavior. Does gambling have a price in this sense, and do consumers behave in the same rational framework so that this good fits the model?

In this paper I will examine the demand for horse-race wagering. Part I will present a model which attempts to systematically explain and predict the behavior of consumers who bet on horses. In Part II a demand equation for wagering will be estimated. From this the optimum price or rate of taxation can be derived so as to maximize the revenue received by both the state and the track.

I

The most obvious feature of gambling is the involvement of risk. In a landmark article on individual's reaction to risk, Friedman and Savage (1948, pp. 279–

Reprinted from "An Inquiry Into the Economics of Race-Track Gambling" by Arthur Gruen, *Journal of Political Economy,* Vol. 84, February 1976, pp. 169–177, by permission of The University of Chicago Press.

The author is grateful to Professor Thomas F. Cooley for his critical comments and encouragement with this project.

304) rationalized ostensibly inconsistent behavior (the same individual purchasing an insurance policy and a lottery ticket) by an application of orthodox utility analysis. By introducing decision theory (Raiffa 1968) we can extend this analysis to incorporate the direct participation of the bettor in horse-race wagering.

Let us approach this problem by considering a race with five horses and only win betting allowed. Assume bets are made as shown in table 1. The total amount bet is known as the "handle." The state and the track each receive a percentage commission, or "takeout," on the handle which is set by law. The remainder of the handle is returned to the bettors who picked the winning horse. If horse A should win and we assume a total commission of 10 percent, the winning bettors receive $135,000, which represents a profit of $85,000 or a return of $1.70 per dollar. Since bets are bought in $2.00 units the actual winnings would be $3.40 per bet. (The posted payoff would be $5.40, which includes the $2.00 which is returned to the bettor.) Each bet will affect the payoff, as payoffs are determined by the amount bet on each horse. Yet no

Table 1 Five-Horse Race with Win Bets

Horse	*Amount Bet* ($)
A	50,000
B	10,000
C	20,000
D	30,000
E	40,000
Total	150,000

single individual would expect his or her own bet to change the odds, and thus each bettor is a price taker in a perfectly competitive market. Actually, it is sufficient for the bettor to be confident that each payoff will fall within a predictable range in order to make a decision. The parimutual boards provide this information continuously to the bettor until the race begins.

The second bit of information required is the probability of each horse winning. The posted odds only reflect the collective wisdom of all individuals who bet on the race. It has no direct relationship to any "internal" probability. In fact, no such internal mathematical probability exists and the wagerers must determine for themselves the "true" odds.

The potential bettor can refuse to bet or bet on one or more of the five horses in the race. One can obtain the expected monetary value (EMV) of each option by multiplying each possible outcome by its probability and summing these products over all possible outcomes. The higher the expected monetary value of a given option the more bets the individual would be willing to make. This immediately follows from marginal utility analysis. A relative increase in the expected marginal utility per dollar of a given commodity will cause a redirection of expenditures to this commodity. In the limit, if an individual is 100 percent sure that a horse will win, all possible resources should be used to make bets. The crucial point is that bets are an increasing function of EMV. No assumptions about the nature of an individual's utility function or risk preference are required. Two cases are illustrated in figure 1.[1] The slopes are increasing due to the resource constraint of the individual. The risk seeker with an increasing marginal utility of income may be willing to bet even with a negative EMV. It is also perfectly consistent for the risk avoider to make a bet given a high enough EMV.

FIGURE 1

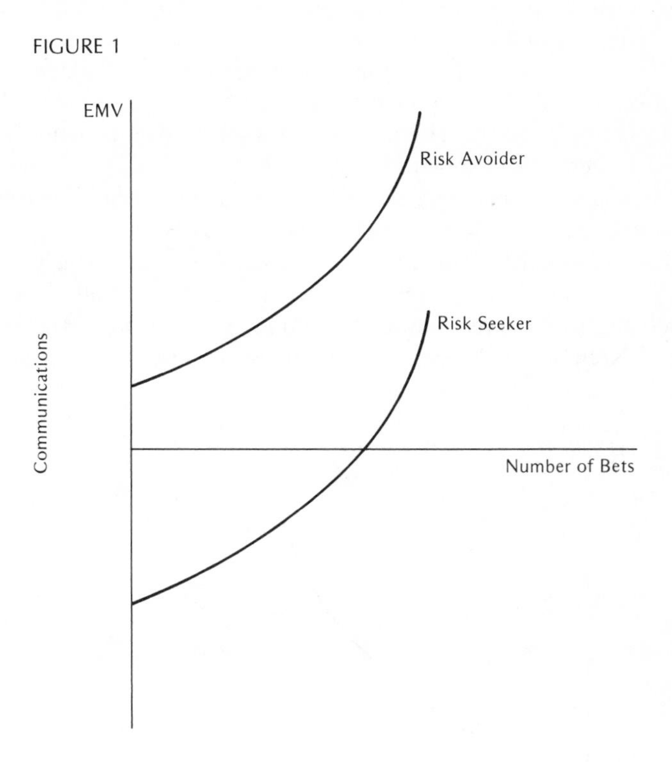

Let us assume that bettor 1 has analyzed the race and believes the probability of each horse winning is as shown in table 2. Given the probable payoffs with a 10 percent takeout, we can derive this bettor's EMV schedule. Let us assume for simplicity that both bettors have a linear utility function so that the relationship in figure 2 holds. This bettor would choose option 5 which has the

[1] This is implied by Rothschild and Stiglitz (1971, pp. 66–85).

Table 2 EMV Schedule of Bettor 1

Option	*Bet*	*Probability of Winning* (%)	*Payoff* ($)	EMV
1	No bet	0	0.00	.00
2	A	30	3.40	−.38
3	B	5	25.00	−.65
4	C	15	11.40	.01
5	D	25	7.00	.25
6	E	25	4.60	−.35

greatest value, and bet on horse D. Option 4 also has a positive EMV, and thus a bet on horse C would be made as well.

Bettor 2, however, has a different perception of the race and a different EMV schedule (see table 3). The highest expected monetary value is option 2, which indicates a bet on horse A. The next most feasible choice is option 1, which has a value of zero and represents no further betting.

Let us now assume that the takeout has been increased to 17 percent. The track now shares $25,500 with the state, and only $124,500 is returned to the bettors. This reduces the return on horse A to $1.49 per dollar which is rounded down to $1.40, and winnings become $2.80 on each bet instead of $3.40. The 18¢ which the bettor loses due to this rounding down process is known as "breakage." Nothing has happened to the horses themselves or to the relative

FIGURE 2

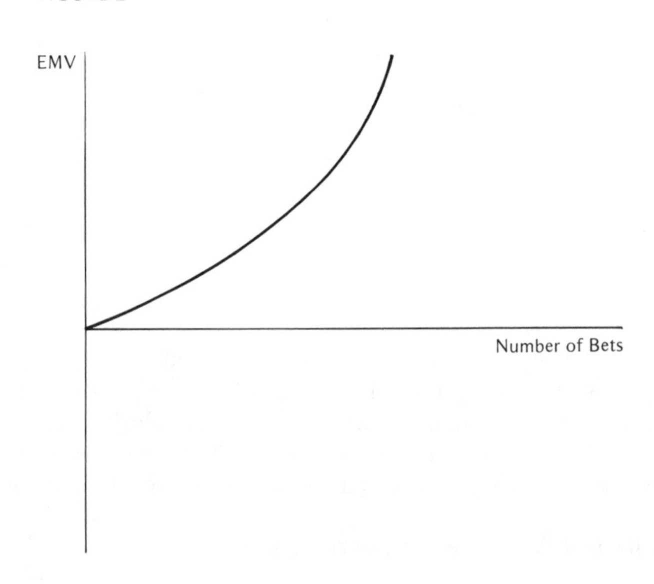

payoffs, and thus there is no reason for the bettors to alter their perceptions. The only change is the amount of the takeout. Since all payoffs are now 7 percent less, the relative odds remain the same.[2] Table 4 summarizes each bettor's new EMV schedules, given the same race but with a 17 percent takeout.

Table 3 EMV Schedule of Bettor 2

Option	*Bet*	*Probability of Winning* (%)	*Payoff* ($)	EMV
1	No bet	0	0.00	.00
2	A	40	3.40	.16
3	B	5	25.00	−.65
4	C	10	11.40	−.66
5	D	20	7.00	−.20
6	E	25	4.60	−.35

Thus an increase in the takeout, holding everything else constant, results in bettor 1 betting only on horse D while bettor 2 does not bet at all. The total number of bets, therefore, declines with an increase in the takeout. What is the nature of this takeout? If there were none, the total handle would be returned to the bettors, and our problem would reduce to mere redistribution of wealth. Its existence, however, ensures that bettors in the aggregate leave the track with less than when they came in. They thus pay a premium in order to participate. We have established theoretically that an increase in this premium while holding all other factors fixed will result in a decrease in the number of bets. Thus this premium serves the economic function of the purchase price of a bet which,

Table 4 New EMV Schedules

Bet	*Payoff with 17% Takeout* ($)	EMV *for Bettor* 1	EMV *for Bettor* 2
No bet	0.00	.00	.00
A	2.80	−.56	−.08
B	22.80	−.76	−.76
C	10.40	−.14	−.76
D	6.40	.10	−.32
E	4.20	−.45	−.45

[2] The rounding-down procedure may create minor distortions so that all payoffs might not be reduced by *exactly* the same percentage. The maximum amount of distortion, however, cannot exceed 20¢ per bet and is negligible.

like other commodities, has a downward-sloping demand curve. In the next section we shall test empirically this hypothesis and attempt to draw implications for optimum price policy.

II

The data to be used are the annual figures for Aqueduct Race Track and Belmont Park in New York City (*New York Racing Association Annual Report, 1940–1969*). The parimutual system was instituted in 1940, the first year explicit statistics were recorded, and our time series extends to 1969. A single location was chosen in order to correct as much as possible for tastes or customs, which may vary geographically. Furthermore, since the population and the volume wagered is so large relative to other locales, no single race or event is likely to distort the aggregate data and bias the results. New York, along with Florida and California, is a racing center, which means that the highest purses and the best horses are attracted to these tracks. No northeastern track can match New York in terms of quality of the product so the betting should not be affected by nearby competition. The racing year is divided into meets which are held alternately at Aqueduct and Belmont. The handle in the winter and spring meets can and does differ, therefore the New York Racing Association alternates the assignment of the meets from year to year so as not to systematically penalize one track. By using annual data we avoid problems of seasonal variation. The population sample is the area readily accessible to the two tracks: the five counties of New York City plus Nassau and Westchester Counties.

Our basic model postulates that the number of bets per race per capita is a function of the price of a wager plus real income per capita of the potential patrons. We do not include admission fees because these are more properly the nominal cost to the patron of enjoying the facilities and the spectacle of the track itself quite apart from the opportunity to gamble. The determination of the takeout is a political decision which the tracks are not free to alter in response to demand. We can also regard income per capita as an exogenous variable. Since the horse-racing industry is such a miniscule fraction of the economy of the New York Metropolitan area, changes in the income of this industry would have no noticeable effect on the total income of the region. Thus our explanatory variables are exogenous to the model and independent of each other.

The peripheral costs of racetrack betting such as fees, taxes, required attendance, and lack of credit make it the most expensive mode of gambling. For those individuals who already have chosen this alternative it is unlikely that small changes in these peripheral costs will affect the bettors. We therefore expect the potential substitution effect to be relatively constant over time. Off-track betting (OTB), on the other hand, would have a significant effect on on-track gambling. It is for this reason that our sample period stops before OTB was instituted. Gimic wagering (e.g., picking the first three horses in exact order) has the allure of huge payoffs and is designed to promote betting. Again our sample period stops before such bets were instituted. These factors can and should be incorporated into a forecasting model (Coate and Ross 1974), but this is beyond our present scope. The daily double has always been available and thus is a constant factor over the sample period.

In analysis of stock-market behavior mention inevitably is made of waves of optimisim or pessimism which affect stock prices above and beyond the strictly economic factors such as profits or price-earnings ratios. In gambling it is just as reasonable to assume that people will bet more if they are optimistic about the future and less if they are pessimistic. Part of this will be picked up by an increase in real per capita income, but bettors may be in a more expansive mood than can be explained by income alone. In a depression, of course, expectations of hardship may curtail spending by a greater amount than merely the effect of lowered income. There are several ways this phenomenon can be measured. One way is to consider national unemployment rates. Economists are generally agreed that unemployment rates lower than 4 percent (at least during this sample period) represent a full-employment economy. Use of a dummy variable during years of economic boom will pick up this effect of optimism while avoiding correlation with income. At the same time, it is reasonable to use a dummy variable from 1940–1944 to account for the depressing effect on consumption of rationing and wartime sacrifice. At no other time during the sample period did the national unemployment rate climb much over 7 percent.

Our variables are as follows:

BETS = Number of bets per race per capita or "quantity."[3]

P = Percentage of the handle which is not returned to the bettors. This consists of the state commission and the share to the track plus the breakage. In our analysis it is the "price" of the bet.

Y = income per capita deflated by the Consumer Price Index in 1967 dollars.

PES = 1, 1940–44, 0, otherwise; depression or pessimism factor.

OP = 1 when the unemployment rate is less than 4 percent, 0, otherwise; optimism or prosperity factor

A linear demand curve in all the variables yielded the best fit.[4]

[3] In the context of this model, each bet is a purchased commodity with a given price and *not* a dollar amount expended for the purchase of some other commodity. BETS are measured in real units and thus no deflation is needed.

[4] Since betting increases faster than income, Y^2 was tried for this equation. The results were similar, but this form was rejected because the degree of significance of the income variable was substantially reduced and the fit was not as good. Various other linear and nonlinear forms were also tried. The equation reported, however, proved to have the best fit and was most useful in determining an optimum price.

BETS

$$= .0226 - .1475X10^{-4}\ P + .4118X10^{-5}\ Y - .0087\ PES + .0019\ OP$$

t-statistic:

(5.18)	(4.93)	(7.81)	(5.70)	(3.49)

elasticity: (1.57) (.98)

R^2 (corrected) = .814 $F(4,25) = 32.66$

The income effect is positive, which indicates that bets are a normal good while the income elasticity of demand is higher than many might expect. The optimism and pessimism variables have the correct sign, and though it may be possible to find cleverer proxies these seem to serve adequately enough. The crux of our theory centers on the price variable which is found to be negative and significant. The theory predicted just this result, and it supports the view that a bet is like any other consumption good. We find further that not only do bettors react to price, but at the rates set by the state the demand is actually price elastic! Since there are so many substitute forms of entertainment even aside from gambling, on reflection this should not be too surprising a result. If this is the case, therefore, a decrease in the takeout should result in an increase in revenue. Since price is the percentage of each bet retained by the track and the state, maximizing the product of this percentage and the number of bets will maximize the total amount which both receive. Since we have a downward-sloping demand curve with respect to price, the price at which the elasticity of demand is unity will yield the maximum revenue. For example, let us consider 1969, the final year in our sample. We fix the curve for 1969 by setting

$$\begin{aligned} Y &= Y(1969) = 4722.22 \\ PES &= PES(1969) = 0 \\ OP &= OP(1969) = 1. \end{aligned}$$

Thus BETS = $.0439 - .1475X10^{-4}$ P which becomes P = 2976 − 67796 BETS. The point of unitary elasticity is at the midpoint of the demand curve so the optimum price is 14.88 percent. The actual takeout in 1969 was 17.16 percent. By enacting no other policy changes other than merely lowering the takeout by 2.28 percent the state and the track could have increased their net proceeds by $11,136,000.

Race-track wagering illustrates the fallacy of composition. While it is true that bettors in the aggregate are destined to lose, this does not imply that for any *single* bettor the act of gambling entails a probabilistic loss and is irrational. In fact we have demonstrated that those individuals who decide to go to the track and bet do indeed behave in a rational, price-elastic, utility-maximizing fashion. The failure of the state to realize this fact is costing it needed revenue. Each year the state can determine the takeout percentage for the coming year in order to maximize its potential revenue. All that is required are estimates of income. Thus we have devised a model where through mere price manipulation—virtually a costless procedure—we have a method for enriching both the profits of track owners, which should guarantee their cooperation, and the treasuries of state governments.

References

Coate, D., and Ross, G. "The Effect of Off-Track Betting in New York City on Revenues to the City and State Governments." *Nat. Tax J.* 27 (March 1974):63–69.

Friedman, M., and Savage, L. J. "The Utility Analysis of Choices Involving Risk." *J.P.E.* 56, no. 4 (August 1948):279–304.

New York Racing Association Annual Report. New York: New York Racing Assoc., 1940–69.

Raiffa, H. *Decision Analysis: Introductory Lectures on Choices under Uncertainty.* Reading, Mass.: Addison-Wesley, 1968.

Rothschild, M., and Stiglitz, J. E. "Increasing Risk II: Its Economic Consequences." *J. Econ. Theory* 5 (March 1971):66–85.

11 Kindleberger cites a variety of circumstances in which quantity, rather than price, adjusts when markets fail to clear. These situations suggest a limit to the role of prices.

QUANTITY AND PRICE, ESPECIALLY IN FINANCIAL MARKETS

C. P. KINDLEBERGER
Massachusetts Institute of Technology

The title of this lecture is very general, I am aware, and my credentials, such as they are, permit me to talk only about international economics on the one hand and European economic history on the other. But the train of thought that I propose to follow this evening, perhaps in a rather meandering fashion, was started by a remark of a practitioner in the foreign exchange market. I suggested that two devaluations and subsequent floating had probably destroyed the usefulness of the dollar as a vehicle currency for international lending, on the ground of exchange risk. "Not at all," this man said, "New York and the Eurodollar markets are the only financial markets in the world where one can borrow $250 million. And quantity is more important than price." Subsequently, I learned that a theorist colleague of mine was working on market clearing through changes in quantity rather than price, emphasizing uncertainty and at a rigorous mathematical level of microeconomics where I do not belong. And just a few weeks ago a student referred me to Chapter 2 of Axel Leijonhufvud's book on Keynes[1] which explores market clearing through quantity changes in its macroeconomic implications for a closed economy. At this stage my interest was fully aroused. In what follows I propose to follow Leijonhufvud's analysis for a short distance, and add microeconomic, monetary, and financial examples. . . .

Quantity and Price in Macroeconomics

Leijonhufvud's analysis starts with the Marshallian model of a single market for a perishable, that is, a nonstorable good such as fish, eggs, milk, or bread. It

[1] Axel Leijonhufvud, *On Keynesian Economics and the Economics of Keynes* (New York: Oxford University Press, 1958).

Excerpted from C. P. Kindleberger, "Quantity and Price, Especially in Financial Markets," *Quarterly Review of Economics and Business,* Vol. 15, Summer, 1975, pp. 7–19. This selection is an excerpt from the David Kinley Lecture at the University of Illinois in Urbana-Champaign, January 30, 1975.

is divided into stages. In the first stage, quantity is fixed and price is determined by the point on the demand curve corresponding to this quantity. In the short run, in contrast with the instantaneous solution, supply adjusts along an upward sloping supply curve until the intersection of demand and supply short-run schedules is reached. In the long run, the supply curve shifts as capital stock grows to lower unit costs and increasing output until long-run "normal profits" are reached. In this model the market clears initially through price, and then through both price and quantity adjustments. It is as if there were an auctioneer who shouts out prices until the market clears, with no transactions taking place at all until the auctioneer hears himself announcing a price at which the amounts sought and offered are equal. *Tâtonnement* as conceived by Walras or the recontracting of Edgeworth requires exploring the market through price changes before any quantities move.

The Keynesian analysis is altogether different. Price is initially a parameter, not a variable. When a man loses his job or a firm loses sales, the first reaction is not to lower the wage rate or goods prices to find a market-clearing price. On the contrary, they accept unemployment or lower quantities sold while they explore the market. The reason for this is uncertainty. The competitive market in which price moves instantly assumes perfect knowledge, which of course does not exist. In a world of uncertainty, instinct tells individuals, households, and firms that it is a mistake to lower price before ascertaining whether there are other opportunities at the existing price. Information is costly. In the long run it may be necessary to lower price or accept employment at the best known wage. The Keynesian revolution, however, according to Leijonhufvud, consisted in replacing the Marshallian model in which the market clears initially through price changes and only later through quantity adjustments, with one exactly opposite.

Quota Versus Tariff

The point is general. Let me first take one example from international economics and two from economic history. In the former case, our textbooks discuss the difference between a tariff and a quota, and state that they are in most respects equivalent. The tariff which alters price has price, trade, revenue, protection, consumption, redistribution, terms-of-trade, competition, income, and balance of payments effects, to limit ourselves to a few. A quota is equivalent in most of these respects, apart from the revenue effect and the indeterminacy of the terms of trade. If licenses to import under a quota are auctioned off by the government, moreover, the revenue and terms-of-trade effects are identical with a tariff. On what basis does a government then choose between a tariff and a quota?

Leave aside administrative complications which may assign tariff changes to the Congress and quotas to the executive branch of government, and turn to the 1930s when the French introduced quotas. They did so, it is clear in retrospect, because they were uncertain as to the shape abroad of the excess supply curve for wheat. There is, to be sure, an equivalent tariff for every quota, but it is not always clear what that tariff is. If the object of the exercise is to raise the price of wheat in France, a tariff of five francs a quintal may or may not achieve that result, depending upon the price elasticity of excess supply abroad. Australia might have zero elasticity for its excess supply of wheat down to a very low price at which it is better to feed it to animals than to sell it in export markets. If so, it is safer to establish a quantity of imports which will raise the price at home, and let the price abroad fall to where it will. Quotas were and are preferred to tariffs because of uncertainty as to how foreign suppliers will react to tariffs.

Quantity Versus Price in Economic History

But economic history supplies earlier examples of adjustment through quantity rather than price. I refer first to the practice of fixed prices, inscribed on price tags, in retail distribution. The French myth is that this was begun by Aristide Bouricault of the first Paris department store in the 1840s. The comparable American myth gives pride of place to R. H. Macy in Haverhill, Massachusetts, before he moved to and established a store in New York City. Both are wrong. Josiah Wedgwood in the 18th century practiced fixed, written prices on his wares, and the Quakers had been urging the policy since the 17th century. The Quakers' point was simple. They wanted to be able to send a child to the store to buy something without the risk that he would be cheated. The practice was not begun on a wide scale until the 19th century when scale of distribution outgrew the family. Before that time, family members set prices in bargaining with customers and could be relied upon, because of ties of consanguinity or marriage, to maximize family profit. When scale grew, this assurance evaporated. If an employee were permitted to haggle, in the Marshallian way, he might collude with a customer, possibly a member of his family, and sell goods too cheaply. Uncertainty made it desirable to fix prices in this short run. If they proved to be too high, it was possible to clear the market through January sales or bargain basements, but in the long run, not the short.

An earlier and perhaps even more telling example goes back to the 17th and 18th centuries. Goods were then sold at fairs. In some of them, orders were taken one year and the goods delivered a year later, as at the *Mustermesse* or sample fairs. But even in those where the actual goods arrived each year, many of the goods were taken home again. Jean-Baptiste Say, who asserted that supply created its own demand, with goods sold equal to goods bought, was wrong on two scores: the Keynesian one that goods might be sold for money, but a second one that the goods might not be sold at all but brought home. In his book on commerce and industry at Rouen and Le Havre,[2] Pierre Dardel provides a table for the 19th century which shows that the merchants bringing cloth to the fairs at Caen and Guilbray in Normandy never took home less than 14 percent of

[2] Pierre Dardel, *Commerce, industrie et navigation à Rouen et au Havre au XVIII*ᵉ *siecle* (Rouen: Société libre d'Emulation de la Seine-Maritime, 1966).

the cloth they took to market (1761) and in bad years took away more than half (51 percent at Caen in 1705 and 58 percent at Guilbray in 1781). Price did not adjust to clear the market.

Transactions Costs

Costs of information, transactions costs, and uncertainty argue for fixed prices and adjustments through quantity in more than one market. The Chicago School which believes in efficient markets and the use of price to clear them is sometimes mocked in a friendly way by the reductio ad absurdum of contemplating the auctioning off of seats in each train, bus, or trolley as it leaves the terminal, or even as it goes past a given street corner or station. Costs are sunk for the most part and marginal costs low. Fill the car up and let the market clear by price. But the absurdity of the system is revealed when one thinks of the housewives hanging on the telephone and waiting for the latest quotations on trolley cars to downtown department stores. Costs of information make it desirable to have a fixed price, even when it varies with the clock as in "Dimetime" for the Metropolitan Transit Authority in Greater Boston. Even this degree of flexibility in prices may be too much, in some circumstances. Eastern Airlines had an off-peak rate on the shuttle between Boston and New York for a time, in an effort to even out traffic flow. It will indicate how long ago this was when I say that the fare was $14 one way during commuting hours, and $12 off peak. The experiment was abandoned because of the difficulty of collecting extra fares from those in peak hours with off-peak tickets, and making refunds to passengers in the opposite situation. Transactions costs eventually induced the airline to return to a fixed-price system.

But the position is worse, I discovered just the other day. The practice of off-peak electricity pricing has been widely abandoned, and new installations are undertaken without provision for two rates: one standard and one for, say, heating hot water between midnight and breakfast as a means of evening the load factor through the 24 hours. The reason: transactions costs. Outages of varying length in electric distribution require the adjustment of timing devices on, say, water heaters if the system is to work as intended. But such adjustment is too expensive. As breaks in service for one or another reason occur, the initial heater clock may slide in time after two or three outages so that the hot water is produced during the evening hours, and even competes with summer air conditioning to accentuate rather than mitigate load peaking. High transactions costs call for abandonment of price adjustments.

Vertical Integration

. . . I should like to suggest the implications of information and transactions costs and uncertainty about market performance to the large corporation, frequently the multinational corporation. As I observe it, the larger corporations grow, the less willing they are to rely upon organized markets. There will be exceptions, of course, and the tendency is doubtless stronger in some industries than in others. But a major reason for vertical integration, forward to distribution and backward to supply, is the real, or at least perceived, danger of reliance on "uncertain" markets. Long-term contracts are a substitute for ownership of outlets or supplying units, but even these have to be renewed when their time runs out, and this introduces an element of uncertainty.

An executive of a petrochemical company told me once that his company was exploring for natural gas because when he mentioned to the president of an oil company with which he had a contract to supply gas feedstock that it might be useful to renew their contract then, before it had run out, the oil man said "Oh no, there is plenty of time." Since he knew that the oil company was going into the petrochemical business itself, he felt threatened and fearful that the supply might be cut off. Accordingly, he strove to get control of his own supply. Firms in the oil industry particularly like to be balanced: British Petroleum sought to acquire more outlets in the United States—buying portions of Sinclair and Sohio distribution facilities when the North Slope discovery in which it participated gave it an excess position in crude; and companies with outlets seek balance by searching for crude oil production. Oil companies own tankers and control others through 20-year contracts covering the lifetime of the ships because they hesitate to rely on the spot market or even the charter market for periods of time up to five years. Such companies want to be assured of their quantities of inputs and outlets, because of uncertainty not only of what future prices may be, but of whether they can get the quantities they need, at any price. The phenomenon is a result of imperfect competition and large scale. It is particularly found in continuous process industries with high costs for storage of bulky inventories. It leaves the residual free market highly volatile in price movements, for example, spot tank charters. A similar result can be found in what one would have thought was a competitively traded commodity, sugar. A large part of the world supply, perhaps as much as 80 percent, is traded in quantity-bound compartments—within the United States, the United Kingdom, the Common Market, and so on—leaving the free world market pathologically volatile.

The transition from large corporations to finance is easily made. In Japan, large conglomerates include with the trading company, the steel, oil, petrochemical, and machinery complex, a bank, a life insurance company, and a casualty company. Part of the reason is doubtless to provide a full range of services to their customers, but an important basis for the bank and insurance companies is to avoid dependence on the capital market for funds. There is more to this, to be sure, than I know, including governmental regulations which limit the amount of funds which the large complexes can invest from one subsidiary in another. It is of some modest historical interest that the owners of an early textile firm in New England in 1818, Lawrence, Lowell, Cabot, Jackson, Appleton, and the like, also constituted the Massachusetts Hospital Life Insurance Company to provide finance for the textile firm and obviate dependence on the banks and the capital markets.[3] . . .

[3] Glenn Porter and Harold C. Livesay, *Merchants and Manufacturers* (Baltimore: Johns Hopkins University Press, 1971), p. 64.

12 Professor Oi discusses the value consumers place on safety and considers alternative public policies for promoting safety.

SAFETY AT ANY PRICE?

WALTER OI
University of Rochester

Living is dangerous. We are reminded of this fact, from time to time, by stories about especially terrible accidents and diseases. An outbreak of legionnaires' disease can claim twenty-one lives, ruin a thriving hotel business, and spoil a city's bicentennial celebration. The collapse of an earthen dam, the crash of a jumbo jet, cotton dust in a textile plant, flammable pajamas, "high-rise" bicycles—all these are testimony to the hazards of living. An Upton Sinclair, Estes Kefauver, or Ralph Nader can bring about from one of these situations political actions intended to lower its human and financial costs.

The statistics are less sensational than grim news stories, but they allow us to quantify the magnitude of the problem. The most reliable data on fatalities reveal that 103,030 Americans were killed in accidents in 1975 (compared to 48,373 who were victims of homicides and suicides). The accidental death rate varies systematically with age, race, and sex, and is highest for young non-white males. Indeed, accidents are the leading cause of death for all persons under forty-five years of age. Injury statistics, though less reliable than statistics on deaths because they depend to some extent on self-assessments, reveal the pervasiveness of the accident problem. In 1972, Americans suffered 63.4 million injuries requiring either medical treatment or restricted activity for the victim or both. The injury frequency rate per 1,000 persons was 312 for all persons and 515 for young males. Accidents were responsible for nearly one-eighth of all hospital admissions (other than for maternity). According to the National Safety Council, the cost to the nation for accidents occurring in 1976 was some $52.8 billion. The toll is large whether measured by the economic costs to victims and property or by the human costs of pain and suffering.

Accident statistics are collected mainly in response to demands for information to aid in program planning and evaluation. Conceptually, the goals of accident research—to uncover the causes for disabling injuries and illnesses—should dictate the ways in which statistics are collected and analyzed, but all too often the opposite holds true: the direction of accident research is determined by the availability of data. Safety and health programs and policies have generated a substantial body of accident statistics. These give us some indication of the

---

Reprinted from Walter Oi, "Safety at Any Price?", *Regulation,* November/December 1977, pp. 16–23.

differences in risks associated with different activities and products. When these data are linked to the personal characteristics of the victims, we can also measure the variations in injury frequency rates as they relate to these personal characteristics.

Risks and Risk-Taking

No one—well, almost no one—voluntarily exposes himself to injury for the sheer joy of taking a risk. Given a sufficiently large and diverse population of individuals, there are, to be sure, some who contradict almost every generalization about human behavior. In the late 1950s, the Metropolitan Life Insurance Company studied the circumstances surrounding seventy-nine cases of accidental fatalities caused by firearms. In 40 percent of these cases, the death resulted from a silly action like pointing the gun at someone and saying "Bang! you're dead." What is perhaps more startling is that in 9 percent of the cases, the deceased had participated—and lost—in a game of Russian roulette. Perhaps I am ultraconservative, but hang-gliding and hydroplane-racing seem to be activities that are undertaken for the sheer joy of risk-taking. After calculating the risk levels for general aviation, one observer has concluded that flying in private planes could only be rationalized as "pure adventure." With enough people and enough dispersion in tastes, there will always be contrary individuals. In what follows, however, I shall look at the tendencies that are exhibited by the bulk of the population.

Accidents—like the slag that is produced along with the pig iron—are the unavoidable byproducts of production processes. The benefits that derive from the principal product or activity are sufficient to warrant incurring the contingent accident costs. Although most of us dislike exposing ourselves to risks of injury or death, we consciously do so in order to derive the benefits of the related activity or good. Thus, we do not always buy the safety ladder, we drive little Fords and Datsuns instead of brontosaurus tanks, and we live in the city.

In talking about accident risks, it is helpful to distinguish two related concepts of "risk," (1) exposure risks, which are explicitly linked to specific goods or specific activities (for example, the risk of hearing loss in a foundry) and (2) injury risks, which are the cumulative risks of injury over a given time period like a month or a year. An obvious safety principle can be stated in terms of these concepts:

> Each individual can achieve any level of perceived injury risk by choosing activities and goods with different exposure risks.

One is unlikely to be injured while in bed. Yet, although the evidence is shaky, it suggests that the hours spent at work are safer than the hours spent at home, at least for a majority of all employed persons. Exposure risks per hour vary widely across occupations, industries, and firms. Large firms are safer places to work than small firms. Data presented by Richard Thaler and Sherwin Rosen indicate that the risks of a fatal accident are twice as high for a taxi driver as for a truck driver. Guards, watchmen, and doorkeepers expose themselves to an accidental death risk that is fourteen times greater than that facing fishermen. Bureau of Labor Statistics data indicate that employment in refuse collection, stevedoring, drilling and tunneling, and logging is four to five times riskier than the average for all manufacturing and thirty to fifty times riskier than clerical employment.

The range of exposure risks is equally large for household and recreational activities of various kinds. One will be safer in a one-story house where there are no stairs, safer having someone else shovel your snow, and safer riding trains and buses than driving. By a suitable choice of activities and goods, a person can achieve any level of injury risk that he desires.

Assuming that individuals accurately assess exposure risks, how can we explain the stable and persistent differences in injury risks that are revealed by the accident statistics? If we return for a moment to the thesis that individuals engage in risky activities to get the benefits associated with these activities, we can discuss the question in terms of a hedonistic calculus of pleasures and pains. Individuals will pursue risky activities to the point where the marginal benefit of the principal activity is just equal to the marginal accident cost generated by the undesirable but possibly unavoidable byproduct—disabling accidents. The expected accident costs will depend on the chances of being injured and the cost if injured (which includes the medical bills, the losses in wages or salaries, compensation for pain and suffering or impairment, and so on). The benefits may be financial—as they are when a sandhog or an Air Force pilot gets a wage premium for engaging in high-risk activities. Or they may be in the form of the psychic utilitarian pleasures of, for example, skiing or driving one's own car. The assumption here is that individuals choose their portfolios of activities and goods to maximize the excess of benefits over accident costs. Persons who derive greater benefits from the activities or goods or who suffer lower accident costs in the event of an injury will undertake riskier activities. As a consequence, their injury rates will be higher.

The Role of Choice

The hypothesis that a person maximizes the difference between perceived benefits and perceived costs can be extended from the individual to other economic agents such as firms and employers. Employers do not intentionally maim their workers, nor do they intentionally market unnecessarily hazardous products. Accidents in the workplace involve not only added insurance premium costs for workers' compensation but also damage to property; moreover, excessively defective products may result in lawsuits and will surely depress future sales.

The individual actions of 200 million consumers, 90 million workers, and 10 million firms are expressed in markets that somehow produce an equilibrium pattern of accident risks. This pattern reflects millions of personal valuations of accident costs, of current safety technology and legal liability arrangements, and of the constraints imposed by safety and health regulations. Injury risk levels exhibit wide differences among groups of people—being, for example, substantially higher for males than for females. Among males, increasing age is associated with a lower injury rate but a higher accidental death rate. The reckless, nimble twenty-year-old is more likely than the older man to be hurt, but his youth and resiliency somehow keep him from being killed. It is not at all surprising to find that young men experience the highest injury rates. They are, after all, the ones who volunteer for the Marine Corps, supply most of our criminals, work at risky jobs, and ride motorcycles. Increasing wealth, urbanization, the changing composition of the labor force, and improvements in safety technology can all be expected to affect the pattern of changes in disabling injury rates over time. Indeed, U.S. historical statistics reveal that equilibrium risk levels have shifted downward over time—the accidental death rate, for example, having declined from 80 per 100,000 persons in 1930 to 56 per 100,000 in 1975.

Although we are safer today than we were a generation ago, social reformers can still point to situations which, in their view, constitute unreasonable risks and hazards. Books like Nader's *Unsafe at Any Speed* or Carsons's *The Silent Spring* have identified risks that appeared to call for government intervention. The Corvair was supposed to be unreasonably risky (1) because it inflicted substantial accident costs upon unsuspecting drivers and innocent third parties, (2) because insurance and legal liability arrangements did not fully compensate accident victims, and (3) because the risk could have been avoided by better design and quality control. In such cases as these, it is argued that, without government regulation, too many individuals are exposed to socially unacceptable risk levels because of information gaps, wrong incentives, and third party effects. It is also argued that unless we adopt appropriate social insurance and compensation schemes, the burden of accident costs will be inequitably distributed, being borne almost entirely by accident victims.

There is some evidence to indicate that people systematically underestimate risks, especially very small ones. Accidents happen to "the other guy." No amount of statistical evidence can ever persuade us that they can happen to ourselves. On the other end of the spectrum, loss of life or limb is of such awesome magnitude that people probably cannot gauge contingent accident costs—that is, the likelihood of an accident and the pattern of probable costs should it occur. The underestimation of the risks and of the contingent accident costs induces many individuals into working at unreasonably hazardous jobs and into buying dangerously shoddy products. But most of the evidence on this point is anecdotal, and our Russian roulette prototype assures us that we can always find exceptions to even the most reasonable rules. The anecdotes may concern such exceptions. More systematic studies suggest that people do have roughly accurate "guesstimates" about what are the high-risk activities. According to a Michigan Survey Research Center study of workers' attitudes, the workers' rankings of risky industries were closely correlated with rankings based on Bureau of Labor Statistics work injury rates.

An additional argument is that the accident toll is excessive because firms are provided with the wrong incentives. They allegedly will not adopt the best safety practices so long as accident costs can be shifted to unwary workers or passed along to helpless equipment manufacturers. (The present crisis in products liability illustrates the point: injured workers are circumventing workers' compensation by suing equipment manufacturers.) The counter argument holds that workers behave recklessly because they know that, in the remote chance of a truly serious injury, a benevolent society will pick up the medical bills and give them a subsistence income. Rules that provide the proper incentives to both firms and workers would surely promote greater safety. Some lessons can be learned from the trucking companies. The driver who owns his own rig is likely to take better care of it, thereby lowering maintenance costs. So most motor carriers now hire owner-operated rigs and provide plans that enable drivers to finance the purchase of their rigs.

Finally, accidents often involve what economists call externalities and what lawyers sometimes call third-party effects. The pollutants emitted by a pulp mill or the noise created by a supersonic jet are not matters that can be left entirely to the pulp mill and its workers or the airline and its customers. The risks to the health and hearing of other (third) parties must be taken into account. Residents of the Fox River Valley in Wisconsin have a legitimate interest in the output of kraft paper mills, and residents of the Borough of Queens a legitimate interest in the flight path of an SST landing at Kennedy Airport. If the Fox River is "too thin to walk on and too thick to drink" and the air above it too thick to breathe, that is important to society. If the sonic boom breaks windows and eardrums, that too is a matter of social concern.

The Valuation of Risks

Here we must pause to examine the question, what price are we willing to pay for more safety? Injury risks are not—like shoes, off-track-betting tickets, loquats, and visits to massage parlors—"goods" that can be produced, sold, and traded. Rather, they come packaged with power lawn mowers, coke bottles, and jobs in coal mines. But, as with other "mixed bags," the proportions of the components can be varied and we can impute a "price" to one component. These implicit "prices" for safety are reflected in markets. Wage premiums must be paid to attract workers to high-risk jobs, and sellers of the more hazardous types of cutting tools must accept lower prices for a package consisting of a cutting tool and a larger injury risk.

The willingness to pay for safety (higher prices for safer products or lower wages for safer jobs) depends on the probability of an accident and the cost inflicted by the accident. If an artificial limb were as good as a natural one, if there were working artificial eyes, if burned skin could be replaced, financial compensation could fully restore the "whole man." In this event, we could objectively calculate the accident costs and arrive at an optimal risk structure in which the cost of preventing accidents is equated, at the margin, with these objectively measured accident costs. The situation becomes a bit more complicated when the accidents involve truly nontraded goods like lives and limbs. Even here, market prices can be used to infer some implicit valuations of the contingent accident costs. Using data on wage differentials, Thaler and Rosen found that workers behaved as if they attached a value to life of $160,000 to $260,000. Robert S. Smith, using a slightly different body of data, came up with considerably higher implicit values of up to $1.5 million for a life. Some variation ought to be expected because human lives are not homogenous goods like bags of No. 2 wheat. The individuals who take the riskiest jobs are likely to be the ones who attach the lowest values to life and who incur the lowest accident costs if injured.

Let me come back to the idea of socially acceptable risks. In the Corvair case, three considerations entered into determining these:

(1) the size of the accident costs, which depends both on the probability that the untoward events will occur and the cost of these events;

(2) whether the accident costs are covered by existing insurance and liability arrangements; and

(3) the possibility of avoiding part of the risks by spending more on accident prevention.

If society can be persuaded that the accident costs which can be avoided by efforts at prevention exceed the accident prevention costs, then the risks are socially unacceptable. This is another way of stating the Calabresi rule—which says that accident risks are optimal when they minimize the sum of accident costs and accident prevention costs. (The restatement ignores distribution effects, or what Calabresi calls secondary accident avoidance costs. These include the compensation of victims and the legal and transaction costs of making these redistributions.) Determining which risks are socially acceptable thus turns on estimates of the accident costs and of accident prevention costs. If their sum can be reduced by public intervention, then the risks are socially unacceptable.

In situations involving "individual risks," I believe that personal valuations of accident costs should be used to judge whether risk levels are socially acceptable. With a given assessment of the risks and his personal estimate of the value of his life, my erstwhile colleague decides to go sailing. His friends hold a very different assessment of the risk and of the value of his life and argue that society would be better off by not letting him go. Should we invoke sanctions in this case? Indeed, most of the cases involving consumer product safety revolve about one of two alleged facts—(1) that consumers underestimate expected accident costs and buy unreasonably hazardous goods and (2) that manufacturers either do not know how to produce safer products or have no incentive to do so. As long as there are consumers and manufacturers who, because of ignorance, systematically underestimate the expected accident costs, the social reformer may conclude that many individual risks are unacceptably high even though consumers voluntarily choose to incur them.

Acceptable risk levels in situations involving "communal risks" tend to be far lower than for individual risks. Commercial jets must be considerably safer than executive jets. Richard Zeckhauser has argued that society will pay more for safety in a situation where there is one chance in 10,000 that ten lives will be lost than in a situation where there is one chance in 1,000 of losing one life. These arguments seem to appeal to the "public goods" nature of communal risks and to economies of scale in accident prevention. When the lives of 200 passengers are at stake, the aggregate sum that these passengers are prepared to pay to reduce their risk is large—indeed, it may be over 200 times larger than the sum the lone executive will pay. Further, the cost of lowering risk levels by enough to save one life is less in the case of the jumbo jets than in the case of executive jets.

My distinction between individual and communal risks differs from the distinction between voluntary and involuntary risks. I can voluntarily choose to live in a city with a nuclear power plant or to fly in a jumbo jet. But when I live in the nuclear city or fly in the giant plane, the risks that I confront are the same as the risks facing my neighbor or my fellow passenger. Insurance companies can assemble a portfolio of risks, so that premiums and claims balance out. But society's portfolio of accident risks is not diversified, and theory tells us that when we put all our eggs in one basket, we need the promise of a high return to justify carrying that basket to market If society is to be persuaded to invest in nondiversified portfolios of accident risks—as when a substantial part of the city could be destroyed by a nuclear explosion—it will demand a higher expected return, that is, a better chance of getting the eggs to market or, in this case, a lower possibility of a nuclear explosion.

The valuation of lives and disabling conditions may vary with the nature of the risk (whether voluntary or involuntary, individual or communal) or with the lives and injuries at stake. I recently read an analysis of OSHA's coke-oven standard where the estimated cost of complying with the standard was divided by the projected number of lives saved to arrive at a figure of $50 million in compliance costs to save each life. The author concluded that the standard was contrary to the public interest, given this high implicit value of a life saved. The funds required to comply with the standard would save many more lives if they were spent on highway safety, school crossings, and so on. In a study done at the University of Sussex in England, the authors pointed out that if they had applied to nuclear power plants the implicit life values revealed by safety programs in coal mining (an individual and quasi-voluntary risk), nuclear plants that had one explosion every three years would match the safety record of the coal mines. The "price" of safety may differ from one risk situation to another, but examination of the "implicit prices" helps to reveal just what more safety will cost.

Regulatory Approaches

Congress has identified various situations which, in its opinion, involve socially unacceptable risks calling for government regulation. Clean air, wholesome meat, unadulterated drugs, licensed doctors exemplify some of these. The agency that is charged with the responsibility for reducing risks and accident costs can follow any of several regulatory paths.

(1) The agency can produce and disseminate information. Products that might be unsafe or unhealthy could be certified and labeled (as cigarettes now are) rather than being banned from the market. Plants could be inspected and their compliance with specified safety standards publicized. Governments have almost universally rejected this informational path to safety. The National Commission on Product Safety asserted that consumer education has little if any impact on the accident toll. A very different story is told by A. P. Iskrant and P. V. Joliet in a study on crib deaths. When the dangers of putting plastic laundry bags in cribs were publicized by the Department of Health, Education, and Welfare, the reported number of suffocations in cribs fell sharply. More evidence is needed before we can judge the efficacy of the public production and distribution of safety and health information.

(2) The agency can impose penalties and fines to deter the creation of unsafe conditions and the manufacture of unsafe products. Robert S. Smith has proposed this path, which is usually associated with environmental protection, for occupational safety. According to his estimates, a tax of $2,000 per injury could be expected to reduce injury frequency rates by 8 to 12 percent. (To be sure, if the proceeds of this tax were paid to accident victims, counterproductive behavior might be encouraged—with workers feigning injuries to get compensation.) Smith's plan combines elements of "no-fault" insurance and self-insurance; its main weakness is that the injury taxes could be a source of great financial uncertainty for small firms.

(3) The agency can promulgate mandatory standards. The Occupational Safety and Health Administration (OSHA) and the Consumer Product Safety Commission (CPSC) were directed to follow this path to greater safety and health.

When OSHA was first established, it adopted some 1,700 standards that had been generated by industry self-regulation or mandated by state safety commissions. (When state standards varied, OSHA usually accepted the most stringent version.) Responsibility for creating new standards for the workplace was assigned to a separate organization, the National Institute for Occupational Safety and Health, which has devoted almost all its resources to the study of health hazards. The CPSC's task of producing safety standards has been considerably harder because there are fewer studies and fewer data on accidents associated with consumer products than on industrial accidents. The commission underwrote several projects intended to produce products standards—including projects on heavy soft-drink bottles and safe power lawn mowers. On the latter, the Cornell Aeronautical Laboratory recommended a model in which contact with the blade would not mangle one's hand, but very little was said about the way in which the blade cut grass. The standard that was proposed for lawn mowers in 1975 would have increased their price by more than $40—a fact that was highly publicized by the Council on Wage and Price Stability.

Standards, like laws, constrain individual behavior. If we insist that people obey the law, we must back up our insistence with enforcement, so it is not surprising that the largest part of OSHA's budget is allocated to "compliance." Inspectors must be trained and sent to examine work sites. If violations are found, citations must be issued. If the violation is serious and willful or deemed to present an imminent danger, plants can be closed or fines levied. But the fines are pitifully small. When compliance entails an added accident prevention cost of, say, $100,000 and the fine is only $100, a firm can afford up to 1,000 citations before the costs of noncompliance exceed the costs of compliance. But it must be remembered that there are over 1,700 standards and compliance with many of them requires far less than $100,000. In 1973, around 7 percent of all manufacturing establishments were inspected, and only 15 percent of that small number were found to be in compliance.

A Critique of Mandatory Standards

The main difficulty with the standards approach is that it fails to come to grips with the ways in which accidents and goods are jointly produced. In the accident research literature, accident "causes" are typically classified under three headings: the host, the accident agent, and the environment. Injuries on the ski slopes are "caused" by (1) the reckless actions and physical condition of the skier, (2) the design and condition of his ski equipment, and (3) the characteristics of the slope and the snow. One cannot prevent skiers from being reckless any more than one can enforce a standard that drivers keep their eyes on the road or that employees exercise "due care." In this context, we may note that the Occupational Safety and Health Act prescribes an employee's duties with respect to unsafe acts (Section 5b), but contains no provision for enforcing employee compliance. Contributory negligence used to be available as a defense for the employer, but this is no longer so. The courts appear to have embraced the position that workers are not responsible for wearing protective equipment. A boilermaker can receive compensation for loss of hearing, even if he was supplied with earmuffs and it is demonstrated that he refused to put them on.

The standards that are easiest to enforce are those pertaining to permanent fixtures—cabs on farm tractors, tensile strengths of cables, and irremovable safety guards. Housekeeping standards that call for clean floors are harder to enforce, unless inspectors are permanently stationed in the plant (as they are in the larger meatpacking plants—though under the United States Department of Agriculture, not the Occupational Safety and Health Administration).

Regardless of the difficulties of enforcement, the hardest problem comes in measuring the benefits of mandatory standards. It has generally been found that the actual reductions in injury rates or in lives lost from these standards tend to be far less than the reductions predicted. This is to be expected if people adjust their behavior to the greater built-in safety. Lester Lave and Warren Weber—and, more recently, Sam Peltzman—have argued this point. Seat belts, dual brakes, and collapsible steering columns make a car safer. But safer cars may tempt some people to drive faster, so that there is no change in the number of accidents. Peltzman's data show precisely this result. My examination of the before and after injury experience of the heavily inspected New York foundries indicated that safety codes had very little long-run impact on injury rates. Studies differ in their estimates of the effectiveness of mandatory standards. Most indicate reductions in injury frequency rates of 10 percent or less, and one or two studies find reductions of up to 25 percent. Unsafe acts by workers, temporary departures from safe work practices, the introduction of new employees to the assembly lines—all contribute to the firm's accident toll.

The heavy reliance on mandatory standards for safety in the workplace and for consumer products is not in the public interest, if that public interest is to minimize the sum of expected accident costs and accident prevention costs. The costs of administering the standards are high, when one properly counts the costs incurred by both the agency and the regulated firms. Moreover, the approach tends to be myopic in its view of the nature and causes of accidents. It fails to recognize the connection between built-in safety and risky actions, and it often neglects links between different risks. OSHA's performance over its first six years has not been impressive. The agency has made no systematic attempt to evaluate the effectiveness of its standards. The allocation of inspectors to plants seem to follow no rational pattern. One might contend that this is nothing more than growing pains, but it may be the approach that is wrong.

Safety and health are important economic issues. Some contend that the accident toll is an inevitable aspect of a modern industrial state in which goods and accidents are jointly produced. Jeffrey O'Connell, the leading advocate of elective no-fault insurance for almost everything (medical malpractice, defective power presses, workplace accidents, and so on) seems to embrace this position when he argues that the carnage will continue, that the frequency and severity of accidents cannot be significantly affected by government intervention. In his opinion, the important policy issue is how to compensate the victims. This is an extreme position. The other extreme is to hold that regulation can eliminate virtually all serious injuries and illnesses.

We can be safer and healthier if we are prepared to pay the price. Sometimes the price is apparent, as when we are told that it will be $300 more for the air bag in our 1979 Olds. At other times, the "price" may take the form of a foregone opportunity—the inability, for example, to buy a cheaper but possibly flammable pair of pajamas. Whether it direct or indirect, stated or implicit, there is always a "price" for reducing illness and accidents. When we or our elected representatives make decisions that are intended to improve our safety or health, it is important to recognize these "prices," so that we can weigh them against the benefits of lower expected illness or accident costs.

Do we want safety at any price? No—but when the price is less than the benefits we derive from more safety, we will pay that price.

Selected References

Calabresi, G. *The Costs of Accidents: A Legal and Economic Analysis.* New Haven, Connecticut: Yale University Press, 1970.

Iskrant, A. P., and Joliet, P. V. *Accidents and Homicides.* Cambridge, Massachusetts: Harvard University Press, 1968.

Lave, L., and Weber, W. "A Benefit-Cost Analysis of Auto Safety Features." *Applied Economics*, 1970, pp. 215–275.

Oi, W. Y. "On Evaluating the Effectiveness of the OSHA Inspection Program." Rochester, New York: University of Rochester, 1975. Prepared under U.S. Department of Labor, Contract No. L-72-86.

Peltzman, Sam. *Regulation of Automobile Safety.* Washington, D.C.: American Enterprise Institute, 1975.

Sinclair, T. C., Marstrand, P., and Newick, P. *Innovation and Human Risk.* University of Sussex: Science Policy Research Unit, 1974.

Smith, R. S. *The Occupational Safety and Health Act.* Washington, D.C.: American Enterprise Institute, 1976.

Starr, Chauncey, "Social Benefits vs. Technological Risks." *Science*, September 1969.

Thaler, R., and Rosen, S. "The Value of Saving a Life: Evidence from the Labor Market." In *Household Production and Consumption*, edited by N. E. Terleckyj. New York: Columbia University Press, 1976, pp. 265–297.

Zeckhauser, R. "Procedures for Valuing Lives." *Public Policy*, 1975, pp. 419–464.

Part Two

This part contains selections on profit and utility maximization and on the behavior of producers in the face of imperfect knowledge. The theory of the firm embraces, of course, other topics besides these. Several of the other parts of this book include materials on the behavior of the firm—production functions and cost functions, methods of cost calculation, and pricing decisions. In fact, some of the materials in Part Ten, "Efficiency in Government," are really extensions of the conventional theory of the firm.

The debate about profit maximization goes on and on. And it is an old subject of controversy, because economists long ago had to defend their use of this assumption about business behavior. Critics called the assumption a caricature; the "economic man," who always bought cheap and sold dear, became an object of as much aversion as ridicule. Despite this and the buffeting of later criticism, the profit-maximizing assumption continues to survive, owing to its simplicity, clarity, and to its obvious commonsense appeal. Since the end of World War II, the assumption has felt the impact of new forces. Because they pull in different directions, the forces have not moved the profit-maximizing assumption from the center of economic analysis. One of the new forces coming from the behavioral sciences is emphasis on men's levels of aspiration in reaching for goals. If they aim at satisfactory, rather than maximum, profits, their behavior is then the "satisficing" rather than the maximizing kind. Another new force in the postwar period is the growing and intense use in business of methods of rational decision making. Although operations research, managerial economics, and other new disciplines do not actually have to work with the profit-maximiz-

The Firm

ing assumption, they mostly do, and thus give the assumption a weight it would not otherwise possess. And linear programming is committed by its very nature to find solutions where something is minimized or maximized.

Marginal behavior, or marginalism, is an expression roughly synonymous with profit-maximizing and utility-maximizing behavior. When anyone or any organization behaves marginally, he or it adjusts a level of activity in such a way that the marginal gain is equal to the marginal cost or sacrifice. In that way an optimum is attained. Maximum profits are only one optimum, because consumers, people selling their productive services, and government agencies can also make the marginal adjustments that result in optimum solutions.

The word "marginal" can be a cause of trouble, because it is uttered every day with quite another meaning from the one it has in economics. In everyday speech, anything marginal is understood to be an inferior or doubtful thing. The true story is told of a young economist with a high position in the Department of Defense. The economist was briefing a group of senior generals in one of the Armed Services. He told them about the importance of economics as a way of thinking in achieving maximum military effectiveness from a given budget and in achieving any level of effectiveness at minimum cost. He went on to explain that optimum solutions are found by equating marginal effectiveness with marginal cost. While the economist was carefully expounding the significance of marginal analysis, one general became more impatient. He finally banged his fist on the table, stood up, and before he angrily stalked out, said to the economist, "I want you to know that in *my* command there are no marginal units."

13 Economists are paying increasing attention to business firms' maximization of utility functions. These functions include profits and other goals. Of course, if a firm has no goal other than profits, the maximization of utility coincides (under certainty) with the maximization of profits. Professor Johnson analyzes here utility functions containing profits and goals that embody social responsibilities.

UTILITY FUNCTIONS OF SOCIALLY RESPONSIBLE FIRMS

HAROLD L. JOHNSON
Emory University

The literature of firm theory abounds with multiple-goal models. Models positing complex objective functions for the firm underscore the theoretical versatility of conventional analytical tools and emphasize that the proverbial tool kit includes many rigorous alternatives to the profit-maximization construction.[1]

The multiple-goal models, moreover, can serve as analytical levers giving insight into the meaning of that "bewildering balderdash" called social responsibility of business. Many individuals find ideas of social responsibility and objectives in addition to profits not only dangerous but also highly conducive to hot air and nonsense. To espouse social responsibilities is regarded as dealing in the merchandise of empty sets or in terms devoid of meaning. Even as the least of evils, this concept is thought of simply as a public relations camouflage for sophisticated pursuit of profits. However, this concept or ideology can be interpreted in the vocabulary of economics. It can be framed in conventional terminology and diagrams, making it more tractable and open to appraisal.

The phenomenon of social responsibility, that is, the pursuit of particularized social goals in a business context, arises from two sources: one, through the actions of utility-maximizing entrepreneurs and, two, through the choices of consumers and suppliers who desire, along with commodities or monetary payments, the attainment of specific non-pecuniary results in

[1] For a survey and appraisal of the multiple-goal-model literature, see the following publication: Harold L. Johnson, "Graphic Analysis of Multiple Goal Firms: Development, Current Status and Critique" (Occasional Paper No. 5 [University Park: Center for Research, Pennsylvania State University, 1966]).

Taken, adapted, and reprinted from Harold L. Johnson, "Socially Responsible Firms: An Empty Box or a Universal Set?" *Journal of Business,* Vol. XXXIX, No. 3, July 1966, pp. 394–399, by permission of the University of Chicago Press.

commerce. In the first case, the firm really wants to be socially responsible, and in the second it learns that it pays to be so!

Looking first at the entrepreneurial definition, analytical advances point to an explanation in terms of optimization of a preference function containing non-profit variables derived from the mainstream of American values. Such preferences to be satisfied include aid to education, safe and pleasant working conditions, support of research, local charity, and employment of the handicapped. With this explanation, social responsibility exists if the general preference function of the enterpriser includes variables coinciding with what the American community regards as desirable.

FIGURE 1

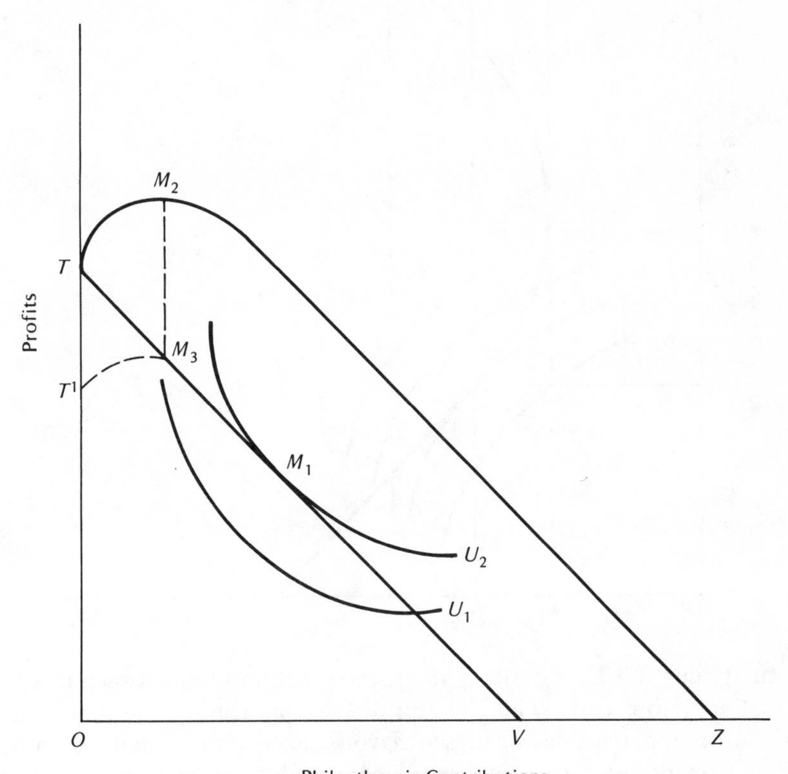

This interpretation can be illustrated graphically, as in Figure 1. Here profits and philanthropic contributions (to education, charity, or basic research) are plotted on the axes. The opportunity line TM_1V indicates a likely relationship between profits and charity. Of course, TM_1V is only one production frontier selected from a similarly shaped surface, with other factors of outlay and demand assumed bound by ceteris paribus. An enterpriser having a positive expense preference for charity, as shown by indifference curves U_1 and U_2, optimizes at M_1. He trades some profits for the satisfaction of being a philanthropic individual; a profit maximizer, on the other hand, finds his optimum at *T*. The diagram also indicates the general character of the second case of social responsibility, to which the discussion will turn in a moment.

Another graphic statement of the first explanation is depicted in Figure 2. This diagram, focusing on the layoff policies of business, contains an op-

FIGURE 2

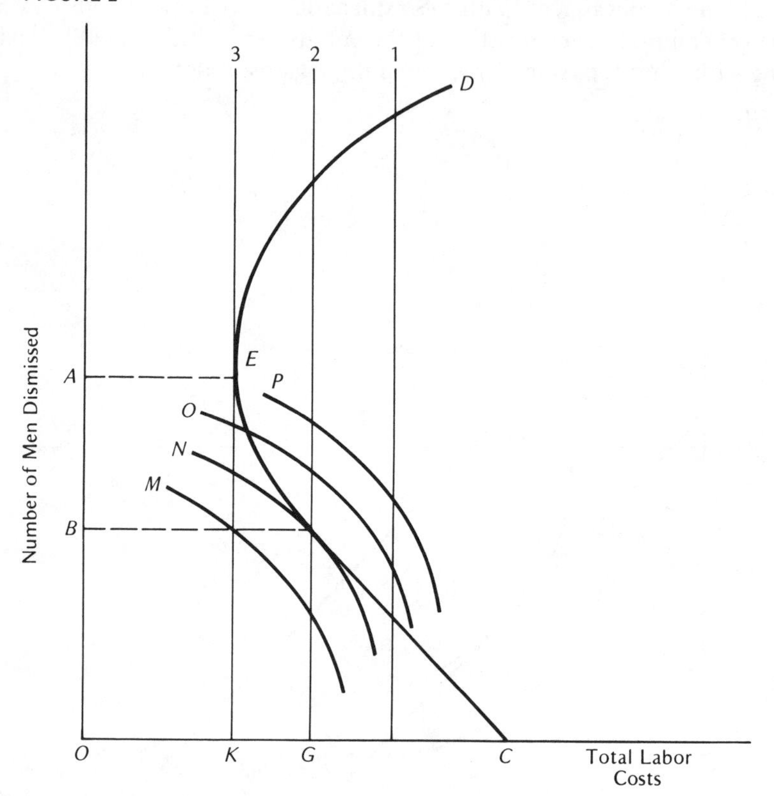

portunity line (*CED*) indicating an expected relationship between men dismissed and labor costs. The *ED* arm of the opportunity line reflects that with future repercussions of present layoffs taken into account, dismissals during a temporary decline in demand conceivably can be carried to excess. The hiring and training expenses involved with new employees and the necessity to maintain equipment pending a revival in the market suggest, for example, that the optimum number of workers to lay off in a slump is not the total company labor force!

An entrepreneur interested only in minimizing labor costs, as reflected in the numbered vertical indifference lines, has an optimum with *OA* layoffs and *OK* costs. Where layoffs and labor costs are *both* distasteful to the enterpriser, however, these can be characterized as "discommodities" in his preference system. Parenthetically, casual empiricism seems to reveal that many executives find quite unpleasant the task of laying off or firing people. In a discommodities situation, the indifference configuration is as depicted with the lettered utility map, an optimum being obtained with *OB* dismissals and *OG* costs. Fewer men are laid off, and labor expenses are higher. This latter solution undoubtedly fits what many would regard as responsible behavior.

The first case, based on an entrepreneurial taste for social responsibility, essentially places the responsible firm in a monopoly habitat where bonanza profits are available to be traded for satisfaction of non-profit goals. To complicate things, it should be noted that an enterpriser in pure competition may choose to "buy" charity or employee well-being with some of his normal profit dollars; however, market pressures undoubtedly foster a concentration on earnings in a competitive setting. But what, then, of the firm in competition where the entrepreneur cannot afford to indulge socially commendable preferences—or of the individual who seeks only the traditional goal of maximum profits? Even these entrepreneurs can be deemed responsible and held in highest social approbation, but only as related to the second case or interpretation.

To introduce the second interpretation, P. J. D. Wiles posits in the phrase "the standard of living includes a standard of working" that participants in a firm come partly as producers but also with the perspectives of consumers.[2] A consumer orientation is extended to the entrepreneur in other analyses as the entrepreneur seeks to optimize a mixed package of income, leisure, and easier work pressure. But the attractions of a proper standard of working also impress the owners of inputs; as an illustration, employees can be assumed interested in pleasant and safe working conditions and democratic supervisor-worker relations. These non-monetary aspects can be thought of as variables in their preference functions which must be satisfied to some degree for low-cost production in the firm. The enterpriser, mindful of the social environment in which he makes decisions, consequently finds acceptance of such policies the most profitable course of action.

Thus, activities generally considered as responsible, such as sharing the readjustment costs of employees faced with automation and plant closings, mutual adjustment of contracts between firms and suppliers, friendly and honest consumer relations, corporate charity, and public-service television programs, can be viewed as sophisticated efforts at long-run profit maximization. Enterprisers in this interpretation do socially desirable things not because of a positive preference for them but because American society threatens with lower profits if they do not. They can be characterized as *expedient* adherents to responsibility in contrast with *genuine* adherents who have positive preferences for such policies. In the second case, employees, suppliers, dealers. customers, and the community at large act as custodians

[2] *Price Cost and Output* (Oxford: Basil Blackwell, 1961), p. 196.

of social values, so to speak, via non-monetary aspects introduced into market transactions.

Diagrammatic illustration of the second explanation can also be presented. Returning to Figure 1, the opportunity line TM_2Z assumes that contemporary American culture lauds a generous giver; that is, even a profit-maximizer finds it advantageous to support to some degree "good" causes. An enterpriser unconcerned about charity while interested in profits —but at the same time confronted by consumers and owners of inputs who are favorably impressed with business contributions—finds that it pays to be somewhat generous. He optimizes at M_2 as the social environment operating through the market prompts him to act in a desired way.

Actually, the rising path from T to M_2 would be likely only for firms who were innovators of charity programs. As other firms pursue profits through business philanthropy, the opportunity surface could be expected to shift to the shape where TM_1V is a typical contour line. When all firms give to United Appeal, for example, none may obtain profits from such a policy. Furthermore, the innovating firm, finding itself at M_3 after all enterprises have imitated its strategy, could not expect to return to T. With American social norms blessing business philanthropy, or with customers and owners of inputs still favorably impressed with such outlays, the opportunity line confronting the firm eliminating its charity contributions most likely would be patterned after T^1M_3V. Thus, the final equilibrium position is M_3, with some gifts made to charity even by the profit-maximizer.

With these interpretations now before us, what comments and conclusions follow? One useful insight from the second case is that the emphasis of organization theory upon multiple participants in an organization is not in fundamental conflict with the conventional economic understanding of the relationships between the firm and customers or owners of inputs. The organization-theory statement that the continual bargaining between participants gives content to organizational goals, and thereby to behavior, is quite similar to the traditional picture of continual interplay in the market between the firm and factors. Economists have long recognized that payments to factors include both monetary and non-monetary elements. The chief difference is that the conventional understanding supposes that the total bargaining process is coordinated through a vision of profit maximization held by the entrepreneur. Organization theory, on the other hand, assumes firm goals either to be an amorphous, unstructured collection or, as in the case of Williamson and Marris, to represent the objectives of managers subject to constraints introduced by other participants. In the language of neoclassical economics, however, the firm can be assumed to meet diverse non-monetary dimensions of input and customer relations, through programs often labeled responsible, in order to maximize the present value of future profit streams and of the good-will element of company assets.

It is evident, further, that introducing social responsibility in the ways suggested here maintains the basic flavor and approach of economics. It does not substitute, for example, a vague altruism for the self-interest organizing principle of economics. Entrepreneurs or managers are still seen as self-seeking even in constructions where philanthropic urges, public reputation, and employee or supplier well-being are variables in the goal set to be optimized. With the second explanation, the enterpriser is a profit-maximizer prompted to behave in responsible ways because owners of inputs or consumers acting through the market require that he do so. Moreover, these interpretations keep intact the rationality assumption of theory, for with them the entrepreneur is presumed to move efficiently toward the goals he seeks. The "Type I good guy" gratifying his tastes for non-pecuniary income is assumed to organize his behavior effectively to do so, while the "Type II good guy" does what must be done to maximize his profits restricted by varied monetary and non-monetary constraints introduced by different participants in the enterprise.

This analysis, additionally, carries the provocative implication that the philosophy of social responsibility, instead of standing as an empty nonsense box, may be a somewhat overly full proposition! A great many firms may qualify for such a badge of social merit. To be sure, not all enterprises in the contemporary American economy fall under the utility-maximization definition; but the second interpretation may produce a virtually universal set. Thus, all enterprises with reasonably stable supplies of inputs and consumers over time may be presumed to be meeting the non-monetary constraints of suppliers and consumers. To apply with a twist Stigler's viable firm concept, the enterprise that lasts in the market must be at least minimally responsible. Along with efficiency or market power as requisites for survivorship, this note proposes a successful sensitivity to the diverse non-monetary demands of input owners, consumers, and society at large.

If, as it seems, most firms can be accommodated under the rubric "socially responsible" by one interpretation or another, this concept is of little model-building value to the investigator of business behavior—however valuable to the formulation of an apology for business. If everyone or everything falls in a certain analytical category, then only truism and tautology are the payoffs. The student of business behavior, consequently, can explore more fruitfully the two subsets or cases of the concept by probing analytically and empirically the activities of entrepreneurs optimizing complex objective functions as well as those of sophisticated profit-maximizers. For example, significant work may be possible in ascertaining empirically the actual distribution of firms by industries over these responsibility cases and in analyzing with greater sophistication the differences in behavior, if any, that exist among firms in these two categories.

14 One of the tests of an assumption is its usefulness in predicting behavior. Do businessmen follow those courses of action that are consistent with the desire to maximize profits? In this selection Dr. Enke discusses this problem, stressing decision-making under uncertainty. He argues that although businessmen *wish* to maximize profits, they do not *know* how to do so because they have no clear-cut ways for estimating the probabilities of future outcomes. Thus the assumption is not useful for short-run analyses. But then Dr. Enke goes on to say that for the prediction of business behavior in the long run, the profit-maximizing assumption is a good one.

ON MAXIMIZING PROFITS

STEPHEN ENKE
Center for Advanced Studies,
General Electric Company

One of the main potential uses of value theory to the economist is as a predictive aid. This is particularly so when, as is so often the case, the economist is concerned with public policy. He wants to employ value theory to predict the average effect of this or that autonomous event—and especially of actual or proposed government actions—upon the prices, outputs, employment, etc., of some industrial or regional class of firms.

It is the contention of this paper that it is quite unreasonable to suppose that each firm acts to maximize profits. The explanation of this unreasonableness is not simple ignorance of the logic of profit-maximizing theories or the practical impossibility of knowing all the relevant functions of the moment and relating them to one another. It is also that, in the face of future uncertainty, the profit-maximizing motive does not provide the entrepreneur with a single and unequivocal criterion for selecting one policy from among the alternatives open to him. The desire to maximize profits does not constitute a clear and unique behavior prescription; consequently, the economist cannot make individual-firm predictions in the short run. In the long run, however, if firms are in active competition with one another rather than constituting a number of isolated monopolies, natural selection will tend to permit the survival of only those firms that either through good

---

Taken and adapted from Stephen Enke, "On Maximizing Profits: A Distinction between Chamberlin and Robinson," *American Economic Review*, Vol. XLI, September 1951, No. 4, pp. 566–569, 571–573, 577, 578. Among the sections of the article omitted here are those containing comments on the theories of E. H. Chamberlin (*The Theory of Monopolistic Competition*, 1933) and of Joan Robinson (*The Economics of Imperfect Competition*, 1933). Reproduced by permission.

luck or great skill have managed, almost or completely, to optimize their position and earn the normal profits necessary for survival. In these instances the economist can make aggregate predictions *as if* each and every firm knew how to secure maximum long-run profits.

On Predicting Individual Firm Behavior in the Short Run

The fundamental difficulty is that a desire to maximize profits does not provide the entrepreneur with an action prescription. He does not know how he should act just because he knows he wishes to secure maximum profits. When the future outcomes of present decisions are uncertain, motivation does not constitute a criterion for each entrepreneur.[1]

An extreme gambling example may help to clarify the distinction between motivation and criterion. One gambler might be given a hundred dollars and told to make a single bet at a roulette table and "maximize profits"; another player might similarly be given one hundred dollars, but be told to "maximize losses." If they are obedient, both gamblers will play a number rather than a color because, if they are ever to secure the maximum profits and maximum losses that they respectively seek, the longest odds provide profits or losses at the highest rate; if they both played a color, they would be acting in a manner inconsistent with their instructions. Actually, both gamblers might play the same number without disobeying their instructions. Of course, if the gamblers had previously determined that 17 won more often than any other number, and 21 less often than any other number, then the profits-maximizing gambler should play 17 and the loss-maximizing gambler should play 21.[2]

Unless people have beliefs concerning the likelihood of certain future events occurring, a specific motivation cannot provide them with a criterion for selecting one alternative over another. The economist cannot predict how an individual entrepreneur will act if the economist does not know the entrepreneur's assessments of future probabilities. This difficulty is only partly mitigated when all entrepreneurs and all economists have perfect knowledge of the frequencies with which different events have occurred in the past; after all, in our changing economies, almost everyone senses that the past is an unreliable and uncertain guide to the future.

Even if an economist does know an entrepreneur's view of the future, the

[1] For the purposes of this article, and in order to avoid unnecessary controversy, let us stipulate that the goal of entrepreneurs is maximum profits in the above sense, and not social esteem, personal power, or a quiet life. If a firm has the choice of *A* or *B* actions, and it "knows" *A* will *always* occasion more profits than *B*, it will be assumed to elect the former policy. Let us assume that entrepreneurs possess electronic computers and are therefore capable of going through all calculations of the kind described in textbooks.

[2] This statement implies that the past frequency distribution can hardly be attributed to chance and that there are no reasons to suppose that the roulette table has recently been adjusted.

economist can not normally predict the entrepreneur's decisions, because rational behavior is ambiguous when the entrepreneur is uncertain regarding the future. In reality each possible decision does of course have a unique outcome—but very few entrepreneurs probably assume a single possible outcome for each policy. If an entrepreneur is of a contemplative nature, he may assign various probabilities to different profit outcomes for each alternative policy. If he does not do this, no external observer can hope to predict the actions of a particular entrepreneur. However, even if he does do this, there are grave difficulties.

Long-Run Viability Analysis

It does not follow, because an economist cannot predict individual firm behavior in the short run, that he can never predict aggregate firm behavior in the long run. The greater the intensity of inter-firm rivalry, the more competent is the economist to make long-run predictions of aggregate firm behavior. Perhaps, under certain circumstances, we can predict *as if* firms do in fact maximize profits by consciously equating marginal costs and marginal revenues.

A firm's survival depends usually upon its ability to escape negative profits. If there is no competition, a great many policies—all "good" but only one "best"—will permit an isolated monopoly to survive; the fact that such a firm exists is no reason for supposing that it is securing maximum profits. However, if there is intense competition, all policies save the "best" may result in negative profits, and in time elimination; then firms that survive must, through some combination of good luck or good management, have happened upon optimum policies. If environmental conditions are such that surviving and competing firms earn zero profits, we can often assume that they are securing maximum profits: it may then be justifiable to pretend that these firms cleverly and deliberately equated marginal revenue and marginal costs in all the various dimensions. However, this "as if" approach can only be validly used for the special case of intense competition in the long run.

Unfortunately, as is well known, long-run equilibrium is in practice never attained. The processes of long-run adjustment are always being interrupted, before their work has been completed, by some new autonomous event. This has important repercussions. It means that maximum possible profits of the moment may be far in excess of zero profits. It means that the essential condition of continued survival becomes the earning not of maximum profits (including the case of zero profits), but of zero or positive profits (including submaximum profits). Moreover, it means that the firms that exist at any moment will include both those that are destined to survive and those that are not. Hence the economist cannot proceed to predict actual aggregate behavior, even for those firms that will survive, as if each one arranged its affairs according to the precepts of marginal analysis. If the environment is changing rapidly and unexpectedly, some poorly managed firms will survive and some well managed firms will expire.

Nevertheless, long-run forces are always at work, even if long-run equilibrium is never quite attained. These long-run forces of adjustment operate in the main through the effect of altered conditions of survival and the births and deaths of firms. In most trades and industries, a considerable number of firms are born and die each year, and the existing population of firms in any locality adjusts in time to the current possibilities of survival.[3]

Consequently, so long as competition is sufficiently intense that zero profits *would* result in the long run, the economist can probably detect the direction in which average adjustments will proceed. He can predict directions of change, if he is willing to overlook the variance of individual behavior, *as if* firms always maximize profits in the end. However, he must supplement this marginal analysis with viability analysis or he may reach false conclusions.

In predicting the consequences of some environmental change, such as a new tax, subsidy, or technology, the economist can only adopt the *as if* approach, and employ marginal analysis, if there is intense competition. However, he can then employ viability analysis also; he can consider the altered conditions of survival that will now, through natural selection, affect the character of firms existing in the future. Will large firms now have a better or poorer chance of survival relative to small firms? Will firms that employ skilled labor now have a poorer chance against firms that employ unskilled labor? A consideration of these questions will indicate whether firms of the future are likely to be larger and employ more skilled labor. The character of the prediction may be the same whether the marginal analysis or the viability analysis is employed, and so the issue may seem rather immaterial; however, the language of the former method seems pedagogically and scientifically inferior because it attributes a quite unreasonable degree of omniscience and prescience to entrepreneurs.[4]

A Note on the Uses of Marginal Analysis

If an entrepreneur knew all relevant facts and functions with certainty, and also possessed sufficient computational ability, a careful equating of the proper marginal values would always secure him maximum profits. Moreover, marginal analysis would be essential for indicating what facts and relationships had first to be ascertained, estimated, or assumed. The orthodox theory of the firm, granted perfect knowledge of present and future, com-

[3] One often fails to appreciate the extent of business fatalities due to preoccupation with the successes of existing firms; such myopia might be lessened if more periodicals bore such doleful names as *Death* or *Misfortune*.

[4] How many students—especially the more sensible and independently minded—have not objected to the notion that firms do maximize profits? They seem to understand the survival approach far more readily. It is the author's opinion that economics teachers will do well to combine viability and marginal analyses—the survival and "as if" approaches—in the lecture hall.

prises a set of logical propositions which are in themselves irrefutable. The real question, in view of the actual uncertainty of the future, relates to their applicability.

As a matter of fact, a corporation economist, but not a government economist, should use marginal analysis even when dealing with problems involving the uncertain future. Once he has decided what future values to assume, for important variables and functions, he should introduce them into the formulae dictated by marginal analysis. Having made his assumptions, he needs marginal analysis to show what policies can yield what it is hoped will be maximum profits. If retrospect reveals that the realized profits are submaximum, and that other policies would have been more profitable, that will not be the fault of marginal analysis but of the disproved assumptions that were employed.

The whole situation is somewhat perplexing. As we have seen, the assumption that firms seek maximum profits does not enable the economist to predict the behavior of an individual firm. However, the fact that few if any firms ever do secure maximum profits does not mean that managers should never employ marginal analysis. Quite the contrary appears to be the case. Marginal analysis, given a set of expectations, will tend to give the greatest possible profits if the future confirms the expectations. Insofar as the future can be dimly sensed, the use of marginal analysis should increase firm profits more often than not.

Marginal analysis of unique future assumptions, that is the logic of profits maximizing, should be stressed even more in Business Administration than in Economics.

15

The remarkable thing about this article, in a prominent weekly news magazine devoted to business, is that it should have appeared at all. Perhaps its newsworthiness came from the novelty that the word "marginalism" had, still has, in much of the business community. The behavior described is unexceptional. Businessmen have always made similar kinds of decisions in paying close attention to their profits.

The expression "load factor" in the second paragraph means the ratio of seats occupied by revenue passengers to the total number of seats available. Thus if 30 passengers ride a plane with 50 seats, the load factor for that trip is 60 (per cent). At some average load factor per month, per year, etc., an airline breaks even. Observation of the load factor is a quick way to follow an airline's current profitability.

MARGINALISM IN THE AIR

BUSINESS WEEK

Continental Air Lines, Inc., last year [1962] filled only half the available seats on its Boeing 707 jet flights, a record some 15 percentage points worse than the national average.

By eliminating just a few runs—less than 5%—Continental could have raised its average load considerably. Some of its flights frequently carry as few as 30 passengers on the 120-seat plane. But the improved load factor would have meant reduced profits.

For Continental bolsters its corporate profits by deliberately running extra flights that aren't expected to do more than return their out-of-pocket costs—plus a little profit. Such marginal flights are an integral part of the over-all operating philosophy that has brought small, Denver-based Continental—tenth among the 11 trunk carriers—through the bumpy postwar period with only one loss year.

This philosophy leans heavily on marginal analysis. And the line leans heavily on Chris F. Whelan, vice-president in charge of economic planning, to translate marginalism into hard, dollars-and-cents decisions.

Getting management to accept and apply the marginal concept probably is the chief contribution any economist can make to his company. Put most

---

Taken and adapted from "Airline takes the Marginal Route," *Business Week,* April 20, 1963, pp. 111, 112, 114. Reprinted from the April 20, 1963 issue of *Business Week* by special permission, simply, marginalists maintain that a company should undertake any activity that adds more to revenues than it does to costs—and not limit itself to those activities whose returns equal average or "fully allocated" costs.

The approach, of course, can be applied to virtually any business, not just to air transportation. It can be used in consumer finance, for instance, where the question may be whether to make more loans—including more bad loans—if this will increase net profit. Similarly, in advertising, the decision may rest on how much extra business a dollar's worth of additional advertising will bring in, rather than pegging the advertising budget to a percentage of sales—and, in insurance, where setting high interest rates to discourage policy loans may actually damage profits by causing policyholders to borrow elsewhere.

Whelan finds all such cases wholly analogous to his run of problems, where he seeks to keep his company's eye trained on the big objective: net profit.

He is a genially gruff, shirt-sleeves kind of airline veteran, who resembles more a sales-manager type than an economist. This facet of his personality helps him "sell" ideas internally that might otherwise be brushed off as merely theoretical or too abstruse.

Last summer, Whelan politely chewed out a group of operational researchers at an international conference in Rome for being incomprehensible. "You have failed to educate the users of your talents to the potential you offer," he said. "Your studies, analyses, and reports are couched in tables that sales, operations, and maintenance personnel cannot comprehend."

In any complex business, there's likely to be a big difference between the costs of each company activity as it's carried on the accounting books and the marginal or "true" costs that can determine whether or not the activity should be undertaken.

The difficulty comes in applying the simple "textbook" marginal concept to specific decisions. If the economist is unwilling to make some bold simplifications, the job of determining "true" marginal costs may be highly complex, time-wasting, and too expensive. But even a rough application of marginal principles may come closer to the right answer for business decision-makers than an analysis based on precise average-cost data.

Proving that this is so demands economists who can break the crust of corporate habits and show concretely why the typical manager's response—that nobody ever made a profit without meeting all costs—is misleading and can reduce profits. To be sure, the whole business cannot make a profit unless average costs are met; but covering average costs should not determine whether any particular activity should be undertaken. For this would unduly restrict corporate decisions and cause managements to forgo opportunities for extra gains.

Management overhead at Continental is pared to the bone, so Whelan often is thrown such diverse problems as soothing a ruffled city council or planning the specifications for the plane the line will want to fly in 1970. But the biggest slice of his time goes to schedule planning—and it is here that the marginal concept comes most sharply into focus.

Whelan's approach is this: He considers that the bulk of his scheduled flights have to return at least their fully allocated costs. Overhead, depreciation, insurance are very real expenses and must be covered. The out-of-pocket approach comes into play, says Whelan, only after the line's basic schedule has been set.

"Then you go a step farther," he says, and see if adding more flights will contribute to the corporate net. Similarly, if he's thinking of dropping a flight with a disappointing record, he puts it under the marginal microscope: "If your revenues are going to be more than your out-of-pocket costs, you should keep the flight on."

By "out-of-pocket costs" Whelan means just that: the actual dollars that Continental has to pay out to run a flight. He gets the figure not by applying hypothetical equations but by circulating a proposed schedule to every operating department concerned and finding out just what extra expenses it will entail. If a ground crew already on duty can service the plane, the flight isn't charged a penny of their salary expense. There may even be some costs eliminated in running the flight; they won't need men to roll the plane to a hangar, for instance, if it flies on to another stop.

Most of these extra flights, of course, are run at off-beat hours, mainly late at night. At times, though, Continental discovers that the hours aren't so unpopular after all. A pair of night coach flights on the Houston-San Antonio-El Paso-Phoenix-Los Angeles leg, added on a marginal basis, have turned out to be so successful that they are now more than covering fully allocated costs.

Whelan uses an alternative cost analysis closely allied with the marginal concept in drawing up schedules. For instance on his 11:11 p.m. flight from Colorado Springs to Denver and a 5:20 a.m. flight the other way, Continental uses Viscounts that, though they carry some cargo, often go without a single passenger. But the net cost of these flights is less than would be the rent for overnight hangar space for the Viscount at Colorado Springs.

And there's more than one absolute-loss flight scheduled solely to bring passengers to a connecting Continental long-haul flight; even when the loss on the feeder service is considered a cost on the long-haul service, the line makes a net profit on the trip.

Continental's data handling system produces weekly reports on each flight, with revenues measured against both out-of-pocket and fully allocated costs. Whelan uses these to give each flight a careful analysis at least once a quarter. But those added on a marginal basis get the fine-tooth-comb treatment monthly.

The business on these flights tends to be useful as a leading indicator, Whelan finds, since the off-peak traffic is more than normally sensitive to economic trends and will fall off sooner than that on the popular-hour flights. When he sees the night coach flights turning in consistently poor showings, it's a clue to lower his projections for the rest of the schedule.

Marginal Analysis in a Nutshell

Problem:	Shall Continental run an extra daily flight from City X to City Y?	
The Facts:	Fully-allocated costs of this flight..........	$4,500
	Out-of-pocket costs of this flight..........	$2,000
	Flight should gross......................	$3,100
Decision:	Run the flight. It will add $1,110 to net profit — because it will add $3,100 to revenues and only $2,000 to costs. Overhead and other costs, totaling $2,500 [$4,500 minus $2,000], would be incurred whether the flight is run or not. Therefore, fully-allocated or "average" costs of $4,500 are not relevant to this business decision. It's the out-of-pocket or "marginal" costs that count.	

There are times, though, when the decisions dictated by the most expert marginal analysis seem silly at best, and downright costly at worst. For example, Continental will have two planes converging at the same time on Municipal Airport in Kansas City, when the new schedules take effect.

This is expensive because, normally, Continental doesn't have the facilities in K.C. to service two planes at once; the line will have to lease an extra fuel truck and hire three new hands—at a total monthly cost of $1,800.

But, when Whelan started pushing around proposed departure times in other cities to avoid the double landing, it began to look as though passengers switching to competitive flights leaving at choicer hours, would lose Continental $10,000 worth of business each month. The two flights will be on the ground in K.C. at the same time.

Part Three

The literature on price theory displays many a diagram on production and costs. Isoquants, marginal product curves, short-run and long-run cost curves all help to expound the theory. But what do these things actually look like? What are the findings of empirical investigations? Until the postwar period and except for agricultural commodities, very few empirical studies had been made. Many are now available, although vast areas of factual ignorance continue to exist. No attempt is made here to give a balanced view of the state of current empirical knowledge. Nor are the selections on production and cost functions necessarily representative in any sense. They have been chosen either for their interest or for their relevance to persistent problems of economic policy.

The materials here on short-run cost curves are comparatively brief. No great mystery surrounds short-run cost curves. Both the practical businessman and the economist agree that average costs (fixed plus variable) per unit must decline over a considerable range of output; the businessman sees the spread of the overhead over more units, whereas the economist sees the alterations in the proportions of the fixed and variable inputs. The early empirical studies of short-run cost curves showed that, even though total costs per unit decline as output expands, average variable costs and marginal costs are constant, or close to it, over a wide range of output. It has become common in analytical work to make the corresponding assumption, that constant proportional returns exist

Production Functions and Cost Functions

over a range of output and that therefore AVC = MC. The intellectual and practical success of linear programming has added further justification for the assumption.

A problem on the way to full understanding of the short-run cost curve is its minimum point and why the output corresponding to that point is the "capacity" output of the firm. Two selections touch upon this matter.

One of the great problems of price theory has to do with the shape of the long-run cost curve. Why must it too be U-shaped? Is there just one minimum-cost, or optimum, size of plant? Or is the curve flat, or nearly so, over a wide range of plant sizes?

The answers to these questions are important, because the answers are the bases of important beliefs. The widely prevalent faith in the greater efficiency of big business and the less common skepticism about that efficiency rest for the most part on differing views of the shapes of long-run cost curves. The wisdom of the antitrust laws in maintaining competition and thus, for example, in preventing certain kinds of mergers must depend in part on a vision of long-run cost curves that reach their minimum point or points before firm size becomes gigantic.

Some of the selections in other parts of this book also go into the subject of costs. Marginal costs are discussed in Parts Seven, Eight, and Ten.

16 This selection gives a clear and vivid view of the production functions and cost functions for oil pipe lines. Having one variable or else two of them, the simple production function of conventional theory can hardly impress anyone with an aura of reality. For oil pipe lines, however, only two variables—pipe diameter and horsepower—are enough to explain nearly everything. The isoquant diagram with these two variables is both elegant and remarkable in its resemblance to the diagram of abstract theory. On top of that, Dr. Cookenboo gives another diagram with just one variable input, thus providing a refreshing substitute for the venerable illustration of the farmer who can produce more with more hired men.

Observe that pipe lines have *throughput* rather than output. Instead of the usual two, this analysis has three runs—long, intermediate, and short. Long-run average costs are the minimum costs for optimum combinations of all variables, the important ones being pipe diameters, horsepower, and pumping stations. Intermediate-run average costs are the costs per barrel of carrying quantities larger than design throughput through a pipe of given diameter by adding more pumping stations and horsepower. Short-run average costs are those of carrying quantities of oil smaller than the design throughput.

PRODUCTION AND COST FUNCTIONS FOR OIL PIPE LINES

LESLIE COOKENBOO, JR.
Standard Oil Company (N.J.)

The pipe-line costs computed for this study were determined primarily by the method of engineering estimation, not by the use of actual historical costs. Where engineering estimation is feasible for cost studies it should be used, since actual costs may be subject to any number of erratic variations arising from construction or operating conditions unique to particular cases. In the case of the majority of the cost items, the process of computation involved a physical determination of the amount of equipment or services required, followed by the pricing of this amount from current price quotations furnished by suppliers and/or pipe-line companies. In some cases where particular items did not readily lend themselves to a priori engineering estimation, it was necessary to use historical costs.

Production Function

In order to determine costs by engineering estimation, it is necessary to compute an "engineering production function" relating the factors of production (the goods and services used to produce a product) and output. Such a function shows the possible combinations of the factors of production which can be used to produce various levels of output.

A basic choice between two "factors of production" exists in the determination of the optimum line diameter for carrying any particular throughput. A given size of line may be used for several different throughputs by applying different amounts of power (hydraulic horsepower) to the oil carried—the more horsepower, the more throughput (but less than proportionately more). Conversely, any given throughput can be achieved by the use of several possible sizes of lines with the proper amount of horsepower applied. There are, in short, variable physical proportions of these two basic factors of production, "line diameter" and "horsepower," which may be used to develop any given throughput. As a result, the management of a pipe-line company is forced to choose between several sizes of line when planning to develop a given throughput. Furthermore, the long-run cost of carrying crude oil might vary with throughput. Managements, then, not only have the option of several sizes of line for each throughput, they also may have the option of choosing throughputs having different costs per barrel. Other things being equal, a pipe-line company planning to build a line should select the cheapest combination of line diameter and horsepower for the throughput which can be carried at the least cost per barrel.

A production function relating line diameter, horsepower, and throughput can be derived for crude oil pipe lines. Indeed, many such functions could be derived, depending on the density and viscosity of the oil carried, the wall thickness of pipe used, and so forth. However, for the purposes of this monograph one function will suffice. A crude oil trunk pipe-line production function is shown in Figure 1.[1] This figure assumes a more or less typical Mid-Continent (60 SUS viscosity, 34° A.P.I. gravity) crude, ¼-inch pipe throughout the lines, lines 1000 miles in length with a 5 per cent terrain variation (giving 1050 miles of pipe), and no net gravity flow in the line (there may be hills as long as there are offsetting valleys). The production function covers throughputs of 50, 100, 200, 250, and 300 thousand barrels per day; this encompasses most of the range of throughputs for crude oil trunk lines which have yet been built. The curves in the figure show the amounts of horsepower required for the several line sizes which might be used for a given throughput; each curve applies to one of the throughputs listed. The line sizes used are 10¾, 12¾, 14, 16, 18, 20, 22, 24, 26, 30, and 32 inches (outside diameter) all having ¼-inch walls. This covers all line sizes used for recent crude trunk lines. (Standard line pipe is only available in these sizes in the 8–32-inch range.)

[1] Figure 1 has been simplified and redrawn by the editor of this book.

FIGURE 1

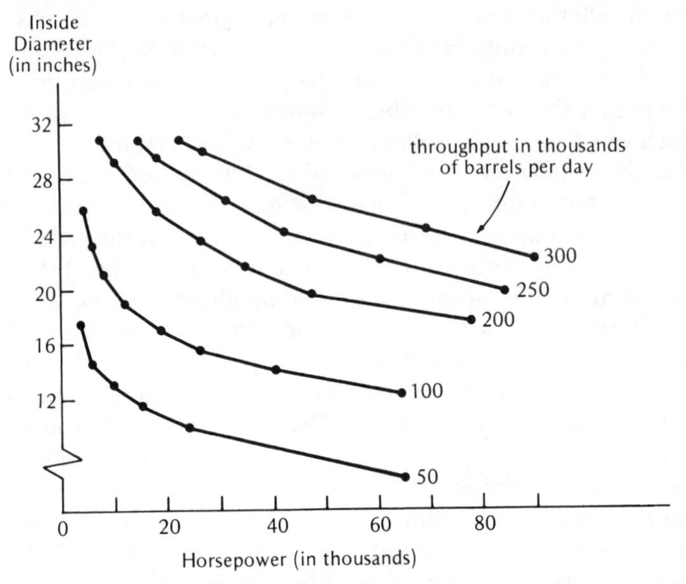

Figure 2[2] shows vertical cross sections of the production function drawn perpendicular to the line-diameter axis. These are intermediate-run physical productivity curves which show the amount of horsepower that must be used with any given line size for various throughputs. They are analogous to traditional physical productivity curves of economic theory. Such a physical productivity curve in the textbooks might show the amount of wheat that can be produced from an acre of land by the use of varying numbers of workers, where line diameter is equivalent to the fixed factor (land) and horsepower is more or less equivalent to the variable factor (labor). These curves are not, however, precisely equivalent to the traditional physical productivity curves, since the horsepower factor includes some capital equipment. When it is necessary to expand output over the designed capacity of the line, it is necessary to add more capital equipment as well as more labor. When throughput is decreased below the designed capacity, unnecessary capital equipment exists—equipment on which fixed costs are incurred. Hence, as was noted above, the designation "intermediate-run" instead of short-run.

It will be observed that these productivity curves exhibit decreasing returns (marginal and average) throughout the range of throughputs. That is, there is a less than proportionate increase in throughput for a given increase in horsepower in a particular size of line. This is a physical phenomenon deriving from the characteristics of liquid flow in pipes. Other things being

[2] Figure 2 has also been slightly simplified and redrawn by the editor.

FIGURE 2

Vertical Cross Section of Production Function:
Horsepower vs. Throughput –
Line Diameter Held Constant

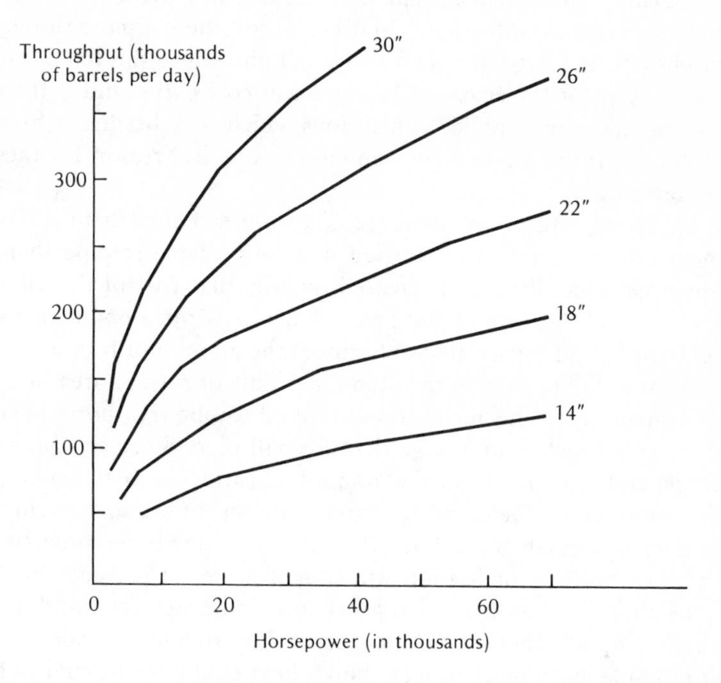

equal, this would mean that intermediate-run average costs attributable to horsepower should rise throughout the range of throughputs. (If the price of horsepower were constant and an addition to horsepower gave a less than proportionate increase in throughput, then the horsepower cost per barrel of throughput would rise.)

On the other hand, average costs attributable to line diameter will perforce fall throughout the range of throughputs for any given line size, since these costs are fixed in total. There are, then, offsetting forces at work, one tending to increasing average costs, the other to decreasing average costs. Whether aggregate average costs would rise, fall, or both, depends on the relative magnitudes of the horsepower and line diameter costs. In this case it will be seen that "U" shaped intermediate-run average cost curves result. That is, average costs fall at first, but then level off and rise as more and more horsepower is added to a given line. (The initial fall is accentuated by the fact that the price of horsepower falls somewhat as total horsepower used on a given line increases, thereby offsetting to some extent the decreasing physical returns.)

When horsepower is held constant and additional throughput is obtained by the use of more line-diameter (a long-run movement over the production function surface that is possible only when planning the line, not after the line is built), there are *increasing* physical returns (average and marginal) to scale. This means that the same amount of horsepower applied in a large-diameter line as in a small-diameter line will give a more than proportionate increase in throughput. In other words, there is more throughput per horsepower in a large line than in a small one. Since this relationship is the basic reason for the shape of the long-run cost curve, and is therefore the basis for the public policy conclusions which may be drawn from the long-run curve, it will be well to examine the physical reason for these increasing returns.

The increasing returns are attributable to the fact that there is less friction incurred per barrel of oil carried in a large-diameter pipe than in a small-diameter pipe. Friction is created by only that part of the oil which touches the inside surface of the pipe. Hence it is the amount of surface area per barrel of oil carried that determines the amount of friction per barrel of oil carried. There is more volume per unit of surface area in a large than in a small pipe. This means that more oil can be transported per unit of surface area touched in a large than a small pipe. Since the amount of friction generated depends on the amount of surface area touched, it follows that more oil can be carried per given amount of friction developed in a large than in a small pipe. Therefore, the horsepower required to overcome a given amount of friction will propel more oil per day through a large pipe than through a small pipe. The volume-area relationship is responsible for many other important technical economies of scale in industry, for example, economies of large tanks, heat containment, and so forth.

If the amounts of horsepower and line diameter used are increased in equal proportions, there would be a more than proportionate increase in throughput. This indicates that on an a priori basis it would be expected that long-run decreasing average costs would characterize pipe-line operation. Only if the price of one or both of the factors should increase sufficiently with the amount of the factor used to offset the increasing returns, would the long-run cost curve turn up. Actually, the price of horsepower decreases somewhat with the amount used, and the price of line diameter does not fluctuate sufficiently with the amount used to offset the physical relationship.

Costs

Pipe-line costs may be divided into three basic categories: (1) those variant with line diameter; (2) those variant with horsepower; (3) those variant only with throughput or length of line (a relatively small part of total cost). Since there is a choice for any given throughput among several possible combinations of line diameter and horsepower, to compute a long-run cost curve it is necessary to determine which of several possible combinations is least expensive for any throughput. This is done for each throughput by determining the total cost of each possible combination, on, say, an annual basis. That combination whose total cost is least for a given throughput is the optimum combination for that throughput. Note that it is only the costs of line diameter and horsepower which must be so manipulated, since the other costs are irrelevant to the choice of the optimum combination of these two. The other costs are, of course, incurred and cannot be ignored; but they do not influence the choice of the proper size line for a given throughput.

The principal items involved in the cost of line diameter are all represented by initial outlays made during the construction of the line. The most important line costs are the service costs of laying the line, and the material costs of steel, pipe coating, line block valves, corrosion protection, and so forth.

The principal items involved in the costs of horsepower are the annual expenditures for electric power and labor (and of less importance, maintenance) to operate the pumping stations. This category also includes the initial cost of the stations; this represents the most difficult, time-consuming part of a pipe-line cost computation (even though station costs are not too important in relation to total costs). The stations are semiautomatic, equipped with centrifugal pumps and electric motors. Stations pumping over 100,000 barrels per day are equipped with three full-size pumps and motors (one motor per pump) which together deliver the capacity throughput, and one half-size pump and motor. This provides flexibility of operation which would otherwise be unattainable with constant speed electric motors. Stations pumping less than 100,000 barrels per day utilize two full-size pumps and one half-size pump. The labor force required for such semiautomatic stations is two men per shift (regardless of the level of operation), unless the stations are very large; none used in this study was large enough to require extra operators. (In a semiautomatic pumping station the principal tasks of the operators are to watch the controls, shut off motor-operated valves when necessary, and maintain the equipment.)

The principal costs involved in the "other" category are the initial costs of (1) tankage (the lines in this study have 12.5 days' supply of storage capacity along the line), (2) surveying the right-of-way, (3) damages to terrain crossed, and (4) a communications system (here assumed to be a 12-channel microwave system). It should be noted that while these costs vary either with throughput or with length of line, they are *proportional* to either throughput or length of line as the case may be. There are no significant per-barrel costs of a pipe line which change with length. The only such costs are those of a central office force; these are inconsequential in relation to total. Hence, it is possible to state that costs per barrel-mile for a 1000-mile trunk line are representative of costs per barrel-mile of any trunk line (those, say, 75 or 100 miles in length and longer).

There are economies of scale (decreasing long-run average costs) throughout the range of throughputs covered. The analysis was only carried through 32-inch lines and 400,000 barrels per day. However, if larger lines could be had at a constant price per ton of steel (the only price per unit of material likely to change with larger amounts than those used), then the long-run average cost curve would fall even farther. On the other hand, pipe much larger than 34 or 36 inches might well require the creation of special pipe-making facilities and, consequently, might command a higher price per ton than the pipe sizes used in this study. In this case, the long-run average cost curve might turn up near, say, 500,000 barrels per day. In any event, the rate of decrease of the average cost curve has declined appreciably by the time a throughput of 400,000 barrels per day is reached. Consequently, the cost per barrel of carrying a throughput of 400,000 barrels per day is probably close to the minimum that can be achieved with present pipe-making facilities.

Short-run cost curves could be computed for any of the possible combinations of line diameter and horsepower. Each line would have a different short-run cost curve for each throughput it might carry. Building seven stations on an 18-inch line would yield one short-run curve. Building ten stations on an 18-inch line would yield another short-run curve. Building seven stations on a 20-inch line would yield yet another short-run curve—ad infinitum. To avoid the labor involved in computing short-run costs for every combination of line diameter and horsepower covered in the study (75 in all), two were computed: one for an 18-inch line carrying 100,000 barrels per day, another for a 30-inch line carrying 300,000 barrels per day.

Short-run average costs are always higher than intermediate-run average costs for throughputs less than the designed throughput (the short-run curve does not exist for higher throughputs, since pipe lines cannot be operated over the designed capacity without violating the safety factor). The significance of this is that a line built to carry 250,000 barrels per day will incur higher costs than necessary if it consistently carries 200,000 barrels per day. If it had been designed for 200,000 barrels per day, then the intermediate-run cost for 200,000 barrels per day would be the cost incurred. This figure is less than the short-run cost of 200,000 barrels per day on a line with a capacity of 250,000 barrels per day.

This may be made clear by discussing briefly the process of computation of short-run costs. The only significant cost of a pipe line that is not fixed once the line is built is the cost of electric power. If the line is run below capacity, as many workers are still needed; and, of course, the same number of stations and the same amount of pipe exists. The only significant saving is in power costs. In order to compute short-run costs one simply subtracts the cost of the appropriate amount of electric power which is saved when throughput is cut to various levels from the intermediate-run cost at the designed output. This figure must be higher than intermediate-run costs of lesser throughputs because these costs are computed upon the basis of the proper (smaller) number of stations for the smaller throughputs. It should be noted that a given cut in throughput means a more than proportionate saving in power requirements, since electric power requirements vary with horsepower requirements. Remember that it takes a more than proportionate increase in horsepower to get a given increase in throughput; conversely, a decrease in throughput means a more than proportionate decrease in horsepower required—and hence a more than proportionate decrease in electric power required.

Summary

The long-run average cost curve falls throughout the range of throughputs covered, and it would continue to fall indefinitely if larger pipe could be obtained without paying a premium price. However, the rate of decline of long-run costs per barrel has slowed considerably by the time a throughput of 400,000 barrels per day is reached. Intermediate-run curves are "U" shaped, but throughput can be increased appreciably over the designed level without increased per-barrel costs—especially in the case of large-diameter lines where the "U" is rather flat over wide ranges of throughputs.

Short-run costs are always greater than intermediate-run costs for a given line size. The only significant variable cost in pipe-line operation is the cost of power (or fuel).

It may be concluded from these cost curves that the economies of scale characteristic of the operation of pipe lines require that oil must be carried conglomerately in as large quantities as is possible in large-diameter line. This gives the least transportation costs obtainable—the optimum situation from the point of view of both the firm and society. Furthermore, pipe lines should not be run at throughputs appreciably below capacity; otherwise higher (short-run) costs per barrel will be incurred than need be. Finally, the capacity of a large line can be expanded appreciably without increasing average costs; indeed, *decreased* average costs can be obtained with moderate expansions.

17 Engineers usually seem to believe that substantial economies of scale are normal. Here is some evidence of economies of scale as engineers see them. Here too is a rule of thumb for measuring capital cost as capacity is expanded; this selection omits the quantitative evidence that can be adduced to support the rule. Dr. Moore is careful in his discussion of the rule of thumb. It applies to pieces of individual equipment and to plants in certain industries.

ENGINEERS' COST FUNCTIONS

FREDERICK T. MOORE
The RAND Corporation

Statistical evidence bearing on the existence of economies of scale in industry is, for the most part, sketchy and incomplete, although the logic of the economic and technical origins of such economies has been extensively developed. Reasons for this lack of statistical evidence are not hard to find; detailed cost studies of different sizes of plants are a *sine qua non* for analysis of the problem, yet such studies are difficult to obtain. Of necessity engineering information on technical possibilities for substitution among inputs must be combined with the mechanism of choice provided by economic calculations of cost. The number of combinations of inputs which may be considered feasible by the engineer is much greater than the number observed in operation and studied by the economist; yet changes in relative prices alone will change the range of economically feasible combinations.

In lieu of deriving production functions from technical data (which is what is actually required), engineers—and in particular chemical engineers—have experimented with various "rules of thumb" for estimating the capital cost of plants of different sizes or for estimating process equipment costs. One such rule of thumb which has found some acceptance is the ".6 factor" rule. The uses claimed and achieved for this rule will be summarized in a moment. Although the engineers do not seem to think of it as shedding light on economies of scale of plant, the rule can be so interpreted and will be discussed from that point of view.

The envelope cost curve usually serves as the vehicle for a discussion of economies of scale; the succession of plant short-run cost curves may trace out a smooth envelope curve or it may be scalloped in various ways. A discussion along this line overlooks the ways in which plant expansions actually

---

Reprinted by permission of the publishers from "Economies of Scale: Some Statistical Evidence," by Frederick T. Moore, *Quarterly Journal of Economics,* Vol. LXXVIII, No. 2, May 1959, pp. 232–236. Cambridge, Mass.: Harvard University Press.

take place, however. Expansions of capacity may occur through: the building of completely new plants at new locations; separate new productive facilities (multiple units) which utilize existing overhead facilities such as office buildings, laboratories, etc.; the addition of new productive facilities which are intermingled with the old (the case of "scrambled" facilities); conversions of plants or processes from one product to another; or the elimination of "bottleneck" areas in a plant (the case of "unbalanced" expansion).

In a copper smelter, capacity may be increased by lengthening or widening the reverbatory furnace by small increments (thus increasing its cubic content). This ability to increase the size of a capital input by small amounts exists for a fairly wide selection of industrial equipment; in fact the usefulness of the ".6 rule" is really predicated on this occurrence. It has been noted by engineers that the cost of an item is frequently related to its surface area, while the capacity of the item increases in accordance with its volume. For that reason alone economies in scale may be achieved.

In general it has been our experience in working with files of information on individual plant expansions in a number of industries that the complementary character of capital goods in a large expansion is quite marked. A large increase in capacity usually involves the plant in expenditures on all productive equipment, not just on selected items. This does not mean that fixed proportions are the rule; flexibility in the use of particular pieces of equipment is common. However, the isoquants probably tend to be more angular and less flat, as they would be in the case of easy substitution between inputs. Among other reasons, economies of scale arise because the proportions among inputs change as scale of plant changes, although the proportions are variable within certain limits.

The ".6 rule" derived by the engineers is a rough method of measuring increases in capital cost as capacity is expanded. Briefly stated, the rule says that the increase in cost is given by the increase in capacity raised to the .6 power. Symbolically,

$$C_2 = C_1 \left(\frac{X_2}{X_1}\right)^{.6}$$

Here C_1 and C_2 are the costs of two pieces of equipment and X_1 and X_2 are their respective capacities.[1] The rule has been adduced from the fact that for such items of equipment as tanks, gas holders, columns, compressors, etc., the cost is determined by the amount of materials used in enclosing a given volume, i.e., cost is a function of surface area, while capacity is directly related to the volume of the container. Consider a spherical container. The area varies as the volume to the 2/3 power, or in other language, cost varies as capacity to the 2/3 power. If the container is cylindrical, then,

[1] Editor's note: Suppose that C_1 is \$100,000 and that X_2 is twice the size of X_1. Then the formula with the "0.6 rule" gives approximately \$152,000 as C_2. That is to say, if capacity is increased by 100 per cent, cost goes up by just a little more than 50 per cent.

by the same analogy, cost varies as capacity to the .5 power, if the volume is increased by changes in diameter, and if the ratio of height to diameter is kept constant, cost varies as capacity to the 2/3 power. From a consideration of these factors, the .6 rule has been developed.

Originally the .6 rule was applied to individual pieces of equipment or processes. A reasonable argument can be made for its validity in those cases; however, the formula above cannot be indefinitely extrapolated. There are several reasons for this. In the first place an extrapolation may lead to sizes of equipment which are larger than the standard sizes available or in which stresses beyond the limits of the material are involved. Nelson points out that in building fractionating towers, an economical limit is reached at about 20-foot diameters since beyond that point very heavy beams are necessary in order to keep the trays level. Second, in some industries expansion takes place by a duplication of existing units rather than by an increase in their size, e.g., in aluminum reduction where several pot lines are constructed rather than enlarging individual pots.

The .6 rule when applied to complete plants runs into difficulties not encountered on individual equipment. Some expenditures are relatively fixed for large ranges of capacity, for example, the utilities system in the plant, the "overhead" facilities, plant transportation, instruments, etc. Complicated industrial machinery does not necessarily exhibit the same relationships between area (cost) and volume (capacity) as do simple structures like tanks and columns. Furthermore, for both items of equipment and complete plants, the gradations between sizes are not necessarily small.

In spite of these obvious limitations, estimates of the value of the formula have been made for a number of industries or products. These estimates are apt to be best for industries: (1) which are continuous-processes rather than batch-operation; (2) which are capital-intensive; and (3) in which a homogeneous, standardized product is produced, so that problems of product-mix do not intrude to muddy the definition of capacity. The industries which best meet these criteria are the chemical industries (including petroleum), cement, and the milling, smelting, refining, and rolling and drawing of metals. These are the industries for which statistical estimates have been made, and for which some explanation of economies of scale has been supplied.

18 Price theory defines a firm's capacity as its output when the firm is at the minimum point on the short-run average cost curve. But the word "capacity" suggests a maximum, such as the largest number of persons who can be squeezed into a room, or the maximum number the fire department will allow.

The McGraw-Hill Company collects and publishes data on percentage rates of capacity utilization in manufacturing industries. The companies providing the data set their own definitions of capacity, but in general they are said to follow the common sense definition of maximum output under normal work schedules. The relation of this definition to theory's minimum-cost definition is demonstrated in this selection.

UNIT COSTS AND PHYSICAL CAPACITY

DOUGLAS GREENWALD
Department of Economics,
McGraw-Hill Publishing Co., Inc.

Monday, May 14, 1962
CONGRESS OF THE UNITED STATES
SUBCOMMITTEE ON ECONOMIC STATISTICS
OF THE JOINT ECONOMIC COMMITTEE,
Washington, D.C.

The subcommittee met at 10 a.m., pursuant to call, in Room 6226, New Senate Office Building, Hon. William Proxmire (chairman of the subcommittee) presiding.

Present: Senator Proxmire.

Present also: James W. Knowles, staff economist.

Senator PROXMIRE. This morning the Subcommittee on Economic Statistics of the Joint Economic Committee begins hearings on the measurement of productive capacity. . . .

Mr. GREENWALD. According to the McGraw-Hill survey, manufacturers were operating at an average rate of 83 per cent of capacity at the end of 1961, compared with 81 per cent in September 1961, and 77 per cent in December 1960, and as high as 92 per cent at the end of 1955. Our current survey reported that manufacturers, on the average, preferred to operate at 90 per cent of capacity at the end of 1961. Earlier surveys indicated preferred

---

Taken and adapted from *Measures of Productive Capacity.* Hearings before the Subcommittee on Economic Statistics of the Joint Economic Committee, Congress of the United States. 87th Congress, 2nd Session. May 1962 (Washington, D.C.: GPO, 1962), p. 4.

rates of 89 per cent, 90 per cent, and 94 per cent at the end of 1954, 1956, and 1959, respectively.

Senator PROXMIRE. May I interrupt for just a minute?

Mr. GREENWALD. Surely.

Senator PROXMIRE. This puzzles me a little bit. Why would not manufacturers want to operate even closer to 100 per cent capacity?

By "preferred to operate," you are telling us they would express a preference for 89 per cent, 90 per cent, 94 per cent. They would prefer, for example, as far as the first figure is concerned, to operate at 89 per cent rather than 90 or 91, at 90 per cent instead of 92 per cent.

Why would they not prefer a full utilization?

Mr. GREENWALD. Well, just to clear up this: As the operating rate rises, you tend to use some inefficient capacity, and inefficient labor as well as more costly materials. So manufacturers prefer to operate at a less than 100 per cent rate.

Throughout our whole survey history, I think, only in the case of paper did we ever get an operating rate of 100 per cent reported for any industry.

Senator PROXMIRE. You mean to imply that in the capacity over 90, for example, or 94, or 89, in these various figures you have, the marginal cost is so great that additional production might be produced at less than a profit?

Mr. GREENWALD. That is right.

Senator PROXMIRE. Is that right? In other words, they have maximized their profits at these figures?

Mr. GREENWALD. That is right.

19 In 1962, Professor Klein gave the Joint Economic Committee much testimony, oral and written, on his quantitative studies of industrial capacity. This selection is from part of his oral testimony. Watch for the pardonable slip in theory that Senator Douglas makes. Observe too the splendid confusion between short-run and long-run cost curves. Such things easily occur in conversation.

MINIMUM COSTS AND CAPACITY

LAWRENCE R. KLEIN
University of Pennsylvania

Mr. KLEIN. Now, in one particular study that I undertook, I actually tried to estimate a cost function as an economist sees it for the electrical power industry. I determined the minimum point on this cost curve and compared it in terms of actual operation with the engineering estimates of capacity and actual operation, and I found that actual operations as a per cent of minimum average cost came very close to the engineering estimates of per cent of capacity utilization in the sample of electrical stations that I drew.

Senator PROXMIRE. I want to make sure I understand—minimum average cost?

Mr. KLEIN. Yes.

Senator PROXMIRE. Would that be the concept that McGraw-Hill has of 90 per cent?

Mr. KLEIN. Well, it probably is. It is stated to businessmen as the point of maximizing their return.

Senator PROXMIRE. Well, I think it would be quite different. For example, if you have a situation where you minimize your cost say 90 per cent operational capacity and your price for the particular product is 10, and your cost at the point goes down to 7, obviously, you can keep going until your costs come to 10 to maximize your profits. Now, it may take more input, but nevertheless, this is a different concept, minimizing your costs or maximizing your profits.

Mr. KLEIN. That is right. It is a different concept, but minimizing the costs is the academic economist's norm. We say if we had a competitive society, which is our theoretical norm, all sectors of the economy would be at minimum average cost. If they had such.

Senator PROXMIRE. I am glad to hear this notion. You are talking about

---

Taken and adapted from *Measures of Productive Capacity.* Hearings before the Subcommittee on Economic Statistics of the Joint Economic Committee, Congress of the United States. 87th Congress, 2nd Session. May 1962 (Washington, D.C.: GPO, 1962), pp. 61–63.

minimum average cost. That is what your measurement here is that you found correlated closely with your previous estimates of capacity.

Mr. KLEIN. With engineering estimates in the electrical field.

Senator PROXMIRE. Very good; that is very helpful.

Senator Paul H. DOUGLAS. Dr. Klein, I am somewhat struck by this comment of yours of minimum average total costs. Why not minimum marginal unit total costs?

Mr. KLEIN. Well, the reason we choose minimum average costs is that if the industries were in a competitive situation and if there was a long-run equilibrium established, it would be established at a minimum average cost and at the same point, we would have marginal costs equal to—

Senator DOUGLAS. As I recall, Professor Viner had an article on this subject in the Austrian Journal 30 years ago, so you agree that these two points are identical.

Mr. KLEIN. I do not say that minimum average costs and minimum marginal costs are at the same point, but I say in a competitive situation, the long-run equilibrium for all producing units would be to produce at minimum average cost. There would be a long-run equilibrium, with zero profits where profits are understood to be some excess return over and above the normal reward of management.

Now, this is a fairly abstract concept and very theoretical. Yet I think it is rather basic if we want to choose the kind of measure that we think ought to be our concept of capacity.

Senator PROXMIRE. I should think that a crucial measure in determining what capacity is would be where your marginal cost exceeds your revenue or your price, whatever you want to call it. You would keep operating up until the time that you would—the last unit that you produced, your cost would exceed your price and then you stop.

Mr. KLEIN. Well, you see, textbook economic theory says that you continue—

Senator PROXMIRE. Not economic theory; I am talking about what a businessman does if he has enough sense to really analyze exactly what is happening to what he is seeing and what his prices and his costs are?

Mr. KLEIN. That is right; and in the textbooks, it is expected that profits are maximized at the point where marginal revenue equals marginal costs. But that would be for a noncompetitive society if that point is to be different from minimum average cost. Marginal revenue and prices will be equal and also equal to—

Senator PROXMIRE. Oh, I see.

Mr. KLEIN. And also equal to minimum average cost in a competitive society.

Senator DOUGLAS. And you are assuming complete—free entrance of new firms into industry if there are pure profits to existing firms.

Mr. KLEIN. Yes. I think that this is an extremely valuable concept if we want to know what a national goal for capacity is to be, what a good set of outputs would be and what a realizable set of outputs would be for all different parts of the economy together.

20 The importance of economies of scale transcends the interest of the firm in striving for a profitable relation between revenues and costs. In his first paragraph, Professor Stigler refers to economies of scale as they bear upon the efficient organization of economic life.

Measurement of economies of scale is a difficult task. Professor Stigler discusses the difficulties and makes a strong case for the survivor principle, a technique of finding ranges of optimum sizes. Subsequent research has supported the validity of the survivor principle.

This selection omits the statistical materials on the steel, automobile, and oil refining industries. The conclusion is that long-run cost curves are typically flat over some range. The conclusion is consistent with the results of other postwar research.

THE SURVIVOR PRINCIPLE AND ECONOMIES OF SCALE

GEORGE J. STIGLER
University of Chicago

The theory of the economies of scale is the theory of the relationship between the scale of use of a properly chosen combination of all productive services and the rate of output of the enterprise. In its broadest formulation, this theory is a crucial element of the economic theory of social organization, for it underlies every question of market organization and the role (and locus) of governmental control over economic life. Let one ask himself how an economy would be organized if every economic activity were prohibitively inefficient upon alternately a small scale and a large scale, and the answer will convince him that here lies a basic element of the theory of economic organization.

The central thesis of this paper is that the determination of the optimum size is not difficult if one formalizes the logic that sensible men have always employed to judge efficient size. This technique, which I am old-fashioned enough to call the survivor technique, reveals the optimum size in terms of private costs—that is, in terms of the environment in which the enterprise finds itself. After discussing the technique, we turn to the question of how the forces governing optimum size may be isolated.

Taken and adapted from "The Economies of Scale." Reprinted with permission from *Journal of Law and Economics,* Vol. 1, October 1958, pp. 54–57, 70, 71.

The Survivor Principle

The optimum size (or range of sizes) of enterprises in an industry is now ascertained empirically by one of three methods. The first is that of direct comparison of actual costs of firms of different sizes; the second is the comparison of rates of return on investment; and the third is the calculation of probable costs of enterprises of different sizes in the light of technological information. All three methods are practically objectionable in demanding data which are usually unobtainable and seldom up-to-date. But this cannot be the root of their difficulties, for there is up-to-date information on many economic concepts which are complex and even basically incapable of precise measurement (such as income). The plain fact is that we have not demanded the data because we have been unable to specify what we wanted.

The comparisons of both actual costs and rates of return are strongly influenced by the valuations which are put on productive services, so that an enterprise which over or undervalues important productive services, will under or overstate its efficiency. Historical cost valuations of resources, which are most commonly available, are in principle irrelevant under changed conditions.

The technological studies of costs of different sizes of plant encounter equally formidable obstacles. These studies are compounded of some fairly precise (although not necessarily very relevant) technical information and some crude guesses on nontechnological aspects such as marketing costs, transportation rate changes, labor relations, etc.—that is, much of the problem is solved only in the unhappy sense of being delegated to a technologist. Even ideal results, moreover, do not tell us the optimum size of a firm in industry A in 1958, but rather the optimum size of new plants in the industry, on the assumption that the industry starts *de novo* or that only a small increment of investment is being made.

The survivor technique avoids both the problems of valuation of resources and the hypothetical nature of the technological studies. Its fundamental postulate is that the competition of different sizes of firms sifts out the more efficient enterprises. In the words of Mill, who long ago proposed the technique:

> Whether or not the advantages obtained by operating on a large-scale preponderate in any particular case over the more watchful attention, and greater regard to minor gains and losses usually found in small establishments, can be ascertained, in a state of free competition, by an unfailing test. . . . Wherever there are large and small establishments in the same business, that one of the two which in existing circumstances carries on the production at the greater advantage will be able to undersell the other.[1]

Mill was wrong only in suggesting that the technique was inapplicable under oligopoly, for even under oligopoly the drive of maximum profits will lead to the disappearance of relatively inefficient sizes of firms.

[1] *Principles of Political Economy*, p. 134 (Ashley ed.)

The survivor technique proceeds to solve the problem of determining the optimum firm size as follows: Classify the firms in an industry by size, and calculate the share of industry output coming from each class over time. If the share of a given class falls, it is relatively inefficient, and in general is more inefficient the more rapidly the share falls.

An efficient size of firm, on this argument, is one that meets any and all problems the entrepreneur actually faces: strained labor relations, rapid innovation, government regulation, unstable foreign markets, and what not. This is, of course, the decisive meaning of efficiency from the viewpoint of the enterprise. Of course, social efficiency may be a very different thing: the most efficient firm size may arise from possession of monopoly power, undesirable labor practices, discriminatory legislation, etc. The survivor technique is not directly applicable to the determination of the socially optimum size of enterprise, and we do not enter into this question. The socially optimum firm is fundamentally an ethical concept, and we question neither its importance nor its elusiveness.

Not only is the survivor technique more direct and simpler than the alternative techniques for the determination of the optimum size of firm, it is also more authoritative. Suppose that the cost, rate of return, and technological studies all find that in a given industry the optimum size of firm is one which produces 500 to 600 units per day, and that costs per unit are much higher if one goes far outside this range. Suppose also that most of the firms in the industry are three times as large, and that those firms which are in the 500 to 600 unit class are rapidly failing or growing to a larger size. Would we believe that the optimum size was 500 to 600 units? Clearly not: an optimum size that cannot survive in rivalry with other sizes is a contradiction, and some error, we would all say, has been made in the traditional studies. Implicitly all judgments on economies of scale have always been based directly upon, or at least verified by recourse to, the experience of survivorship.

This is not to say that the findings of the survivor technique are unequivocal. Entrepreneurs may make mistakes in their choice of firm size, and we must seek to eliminate the effects of such errors either by invoking large numbers of firms so errors tend to cancel or by utilizing time periods such that errors are revealed and corrected. Or the optimum size may be changing because of changes in factor prices or technology, so that perhaps the optimum size rises in one period and falls in another. This problem too calls for a close examination of the time periods which should be employed.

Conclusion

The survivor technique for determining the range of optimum sizes of a firm seems well adapted to lift the theory of economies of scale to a higher level of substantive content. Although it is prey to the usual frustrations of inadequate information, the determination of optimum sizes avoids the enormously difficult problem of valuing resources properly that is encountered by alternative methods.

Perhaps the most striking finding in our exploratory studies is that there is customarily a fairly wide range of optimum sizes—the long run marginal and average cost curves of the firm are customarily horizontal over a long range of sizes. This finding could be corroborated, I suspect, by a related investigation: if there were a unique optimum size in an industry, increases in demand would normally be met primarily by near proportional increases in the number of firms, but it appears that much of the increase is usually met by expansion of the existing firms.

21 Measurement of economies of scale is carried out in a different way in this selection. Professor Moroney finds that most manufacturing industries in the United States have constant returns to scale. Thus he too lends support to the thesis that long-run cost curves are likely to be close to the horizontal over a wide range of output.

ECONOMIES OF SCALE IN MANUFACTURING

JOHN R. MORONEY
Tulane University

The economies of scale is certainly one of the most interesting and important areas in economics. In pure theory, the existence of net internal economies for the firm is incompatible with competitive industry: if lower average costs of production are achievable by larger firms or plants in an industry, one would expect in unregulated industries an increase in the concentration of industry output. Accordingly, empirical answers to the following questions are basic in the theory of industrial organization: "Is there an optimum size plant or firm in any particular industry? And if so, how large?" If there is a more or less unique optimum entailing an output that is a relatively large fraction of total industry production, the achievement of technological efficiency requires an obviously different form of industrial organization (and perhaps of social control) than if there is a broad range of "optimum" sizes.

There are at least three potentially useful approaches for seeking answers to the above questions. First, one may use the "survivor technique," [see Selection 22] which involves the comparison of the size distribution of plants (or firms) in an industry at two or more points in time. The underlying theory is that changes in the distribution will indicate the optimum size (or range of size) because existing plants and new ones will tend toward that size (or range) having minimum average costs.

A second approach, apparently more controversial than the first, is to estimate statistical cost functions from available data.

The third approach, which is used here, is to estimate the parameters of a production function from value added, labor input, and capital input. Specifically, the parameters of Cobb-Douglas production functions are esti-

---

Written by the author especially for this volume, this selection is an adaptation of John R. Moroney, "Cobb-Douglas Production Functions and Returns to Scale in U. S. Manufacturing Industry," *Western Economic Journal*, Vol. VI, No. 1, December 1967, pp. 39–51. With permission of the Western Economic Association.

mated from cross-section statistics in U. S. two-digit manufacturing industries. Two-digit industries are broad industry groups, such as "food and beverages," "chemicals," "primary metals," and "transportation equipment." There are twenty such industry groups in the manufacturing sector of the United States. The object of this paper is to provide some evidence concerning the returns to scale in most of these broadly-classified industry groups.

1. Theoretical and Statistical Production Models

The general notion of a production function is theoretically important because it forms the technological basis of cost functions and the supply side of partial and general equilibrium models. For econometric purposes, however, the generalized production function must be given a specific mathematical form. Among the alternatives one might choose, the Cobb-Douglas production function has enjoyed a rich empirical history. Indeed, Douglas (originally Economics Professor and subsequently U.S. Senator) was able to identify nearly 40 different studies prior to 1948 that used the Cobb-Douglas model.[1] Since then, numerous studies in manufacturing, utilities, and agriculture have utilized the Cobb-Douglas function.

Assuming that a typical firm produces according to a Cobb-Douglas model and employs three productive factors, capital (X_1), production workers (X_2) and non-production workers (X_3), the mathematical relation describing the maximum output obtainable from the given inputs is

$$Y = \gamma X_1^{\beta_1} X_2^{\beta_2} X_3^{\beta_3}, \qquad (\gamma, \beta_1, \beta_2, \beta_3 > 0)$$

where Y is physical output, γ is an index of the firm's technology, and β_1, β_2, and β_3 are elasticities (or percentage changes) of output with respect to the separate inputs. Notice that if technological progress occurs, which allows the firm to produce more output with a given set of inputs, the equation is characterized by an increase in γ. But assuming that the state of technology is fixed (as it surely is during arbitrarily short intervals of time), the only way a firm can augment production is by increasing the employment of one or more of its inputs.

The above equation is characterized by a mathematical property, known as homogeneity, that permits a very convenient test for the nature of returns to scale. Formally, the function $Y = f(X_1, X_2, X_3)$ is homogeneous of degree r if $f(\lambda X_1, \lambda X_2, \lambda X_3) + \lambda^r f(X_1, X_2, X_3)$, where λ is an arbitrary positive constant. Imagine that the firm expands the employment of each of its inputs by some factor λ. By doing so, the output of the firm obtained from the λ-fold increase in inputs becomes

[1] Paul H. Douglas, "Are There Laws of Production?", *American Economic Review*, XXXVIII (March 1948), pp. 1–41.

$$\gamma(\lambda X_1)^{\beta_1}(\lambda X_2)^{\beta_2}(\lambda X_3)^{\beta_3} = (\lambda^{\beta_1+\beta_2+\beta_3})\gamma X_1^{\beta_1}X_2^{\beta_2}X_3^{\beta_3} = (\lambda^{\beta_1+\beta_2+\beta_3})Y.$$

Thus a λ-fold increase in all inputs, representing a λ-fold increase in the *scale of production*, gives rise to a $(\lambda\, \beta_1 + \beta_2 + \beta_3)$-fold increase in output. Consequently if $(\beta_1 + \beta_2 + \beta_3) = 1$, a given increase in all inputs produces an exactly equal increase in output. This is the case of *constant technological returns to scale*, and the production function is said to be *linearly homogeneous, or homogeneous of degree one*. Technologically, there are neither advantages of large scale nor disadvantages of small scale production in this case, because physical output varies in exactly the same proportion as the variation in inputs.

By contrast, suppose that $(\beta_1 + \beta_2 + \beta_3) = .9$, so the production function is homogeneous, but of degree less than one. Now a λ-fold increase in factor employment gives rise to a $(\lambda)^{.9}$-fold increase in physical output, and there are technological diseconomies of large scale production. This might occur (and surely does eventually) because the managerial patterns of production control become more complex (and inefficient) as the scale of production increases. To obtain some idea of the magnitude of the diseconomies involved, suppose a given plant and its volume of employment are both doubled in size ($\lambda = 2$). Then physical output increases by $(2^{.9}) = 1.87$. If money wage rates and costs of capital in the larger plant are the same as in the smaller, the average cost of production in the larger plant is about 7 per cent higher than in the smaller.[2] Of course the magnitude of the diseconomies increases as the scale of production increases.

Finally, suppose that $(\beta_1 + \beta_2 + \beta_3) = 1.1$, so the production function is homogeneous of degree greater than one. A λ-fold increase in scale now produces a $(\lambda)^{1.1}$-fold increase in physical output, and there are technological economies of scale. One could imagine that (among other things) specialization of labor and machines as the scale of production increases might make such economies possible. Assuming that $\lambda = 3$, tripling the scale of production increases output by the factor $(3)^{1.1} = 3.35$. Assuming that wage rates and costs of capital are identical in both sizes of plant, the average cost of production in the larger plant is about 10½ per cent less than in the smaller. If the production function is homogeneous of degree 1.1, very substantial cost advantages are achievable by enlarging the scale of production.

The problem of determining the returns to scale using a Cobb-Douglas model is to obtain statistical estimates of the parameters β_1, β_2, and β_3. In theory, this might appear to be simple enough: one could transform the production function to logarithms and estimate these parameters from the following multiple linear regression model:

[2] For example, suppose the smaller plant produces 100 units at a total cost of $200 per time period. The larger plant therefore produces 187 units at a total cost of $400 per period, so its average cost is about $2.14.

$$\log Y = \log \gamma + \beta_1 \log X_1 + \beta_2 \log X_2 + \beta_3 \log X_3 + u,$$

where u is a random disturbance. Nevertheless, this procedure is beset with numerous theoretical and statistical difficulties, and only four of these can be mentioned briefly here. At the purely theoretical level one must recognize that the production function is not an isolated relation, and that the observed statistical data are generated by (random or non-random) profit-maximizing or cost-minimizing decisions of the firm. Therefore it has sometimes been suggested that one should consider the entire set of factor employment decision equations in the estimation of the production function of the firm. Nonetheless, if one assumes that the firm makes its employment decisions in an effort to maximize *expected* profit (instead of a well-defined, numerical profit variable), the production function parameters can be estimated accurately by classical single-equation methods.[3]

A frequently-encountered statistical problem concerns the paucity of data: it has usually been impossible or impracticable to obtain an adequate number of observations on the input-output relations of an individual firm to estimate β_1, β_2, and β_3 using standard statistical methods. Consequently, one often has to *assume* that these *intrafirm* parameters are also constants *among* firms. Using this restriction, one may obtain estimates from a sample of observed input-output relations of several firms.

A related statistical difficulty is that the published production statistics frequently represent sample observations that are aggregated from several firms (or plants). Since different firms (or plants) in the same "industry" often manufacture products that are physically dissimilar, the only way to aggregate their outputs is to add the *monetary value* of these outputs. Thus one is required to use monetary values as surrogates for the ideal magnitudes of physical output (a problem known technically as "specification error"). Fortunately, however, as long as the product mix and prices of individual products do not vary substantially among firms, the use of monetary value of output yields tolerably reliable estimates of the parameters of interest.

A fourth problem concerns the measurement of input variables. Labor inputs normally do not present serious problems because labor services are usually recorded as man hours or man years of employment. Even so, difficulties arise if the *quality* of measured labor services differs within the sample. Sometimes, however, the magnitude of the qualitative differences are known so that adjustments in the observed labor services can be made. Capital inputs occasionally present more intractable problems. Capital is usually measured as asset values, and these are *stock* variables. It is often impossible to estimate the services yielded by these stocks during a specific time period; so if one must measure capital inputs by capital stocks, he may obtain a distorted estimate of capital services. A convenient property of the

[3] This point is elaborated in the original article from which this paper is condensed.

Cobb-Douglas model, however, is that as long as stock utilization rates are uniform within a sample, one obtains an accurate (unbiased) estimate of capital's output elasticity by using capital stocks.

II. Data and Parameter Estimates

The samples consist of cross-section observations on *value added*, gross book values of capital stock, production worker man-hours, and non-production worker man years in 1957 with states serving as units of observation. Samples are taken in each two-digit manufacturing industry with the exceptions of miscellaneous manufactures, a residual industry classification for products not classified elsewhere, and tobacco manufactures for which there is not a sufficiently large number of observations. Since the observations are taken from various states in a single year, it seems reasonable to assume that the level of technology is constant and uniform among states within each industry. Hence the complex problem of allocating the observed changes in output between improvements in technology and changes in factor employment is finessed. The specific model for which parameters are estimated is:

$$\log V = \log \gamma + \beta_1 \log X_1 + \beta_2 \log X_2 + \beta_3 \log X_3 + e,$$

where V is value added, X_1 is the gross capital stock, X_2 is production worker man hours, X_3 is non-production worker man years, and e is a random disturbance assumed to have constant variance and to be independently distributed about a mean of zero.

Regression results appear in Table 1. It is apparent that the Cobb-Douglas model fits the sample observations very closely. In every industry the coefficient of determination (which indicates the percentage of interstate variation in value added explained by interstate variation in factor employment) is .95 or higher, and in five industries R^2 exceeds .99.

In every industry except one (Rubber and Plastics) all estimated output elasticities are positive as expected. Most elasticities are estimated with acceptable precision, 39 of 54 being significantly different from zero.

Although this point is of only passing interest, several of the statistically significant output elasticities correspond very closely to the relative income share of their associated input. Since this identity between relative shares and output elasticities is expected theoretically only under purely competitive conditions in product and factor markets, discrepancies between the two could be attributable to market imperfections. In addition, the sampling errors of the estimated β's are substantial enough to warrant some random differences between output elasticities and relative shares even under hypothetically ideal (competitive) market conditions.

The main concern of this paper is the sum of output elasticities listed in column 6. It is striking that these sums are close to unity in most industries,

Table 1 Output Elasticities in Two-Digit Manufacturing Industries, 1957

Industry	*No. of Observations*	*Capital Elasticities* β_1 (S_{β_1})	*Prod. Worker Elasticities* β_2 (S_{β_2})	*Non-Prod. Worker Elasticities* β_3 (S_{β_3})	*Sum of Elasticities* $\beta_1 + \beta_2 + \beta_3$ ($S_{\beta_1+\beta_2+\beta_3}$)	R^2
20 Food and Beverages	41	.55529* (.12101)	.43882* (.12793)	.07610* (.03746)	1.07021** (.02128)	.9865
22 Textiles	21	.12065 (.17334)	.54881* (.21573)	.33462* (.08580)	1.00408 (.02365)	.9913
23 Apparel	24	.12762 (.08926)	.43705* (.08612)	.47654* (.09297)	1.04121 (.03741)	.9823
24 Lumber	23	.39170* (.09316)	.50391* (.12467)	.14533 (.10157)	1.04094 (.06014)	.9509
25 Furniture	22	.20458 (.15344)	.80154* (.18552)	.10263 (.07893)	1.10875** (.05082)	.9659
26 Paper and Pulp	30	.42054* (.04460)	.36666* (.09430)	.19723* (.07035)	.98443 (.01890)	.9902
27 Printing, etc.	17	.45900* (.05562)	.04543 (.17089)	.57413* (.19199)	1.07856** (.03168)	.9888
28 Chemicals	32	.20025* (.09879)	.55345* (.20996)	.33626* (.14650)	1.08996** (.03693)	.9701
29 Petroleum and Coal	17	.30783* (.11162)	.54621* (.22207)	.09309 (.16847)	.94713 (.04489)	.9826
30 Rubber and Plastics	16	.48071* (.10535)	1.03317* (.20567)	−.45754* (.14574)	1.05634 (.04139)	.9912
31 Leather	11	.07597 (.14921)	.44124* (.20105)	.52273 (.31491)	1.03994 (.03916)	.9897
32 Stone, Clay, etc.	26	.63167* (.10538)	.03165 (.22449)	.36592* (.20104)	1.02924 (.04543)	.9614
33 Primary Metals	29	.37146* (.10260)	.07734 (.18842)	.50881* (.16433)	.95761 (.03454)	.9693
34 Fabri. Metals	33	.15110* (.07426)	.51172* (.09379)	.36457* (.09204)	1.02739** (.01589)	.9947
35 Non-elec. Mach.	30	.40382* (.12827)	.22784 (.18375)	.38870* (.20542)	1.02036 (.03122)	.9804
36 Elec. Mach.	25	.36796* (.11869)	.42908* (.19225)	.22905* (.12937)	1.02609 (.03640)	.9832
37 Trans. Equip.	29	.23353* (.06969)	.74885* (.12572)	.04103 (.08809)	1.02341 (.03915)	.9719
38 Instruments	11	.20557 (.15204)	.81865* (.20592)	.01978 (.16806)	1.04420 (.02437)	.9969

* Significantly different from zero at $P \leq 0.05$ (one-tail test).
** Significantly greater than one at $P \leq 0.05$ (one-tail test).

ranging from a minimum of .94714 (petroleum and coal) to a maximum of 1.10875 (furniture). Since there are increasing, constant, or decreasing technological returns to scale according as $(\beta_1 + \beta_2 + \beta_3) \gtreqless 1$, it is important to test the hypothesis that the sum of output elasticities differs significantly from one. This hypothesis is tested using standard statistical methods, and it is found that only five of the industries display statistical evidence of economies of scale. One might imagine that these industries are systematically more capital-intensive than others. Yet such a relation is not apparent: the chemical industry and food and beverage industry rank 2 and 6 in capital-intensity (defined as book value of capital per man-year of total employment), but fabricated metals, printing, and furniture rank 9, 13, and 16 respectively. Inasmuch as the thirteen remaining industries do not display sums of output elasticities significantly different from one, the hypothesis of constant returns to scale is acceptable in them.

III. Conclusions

Direct production function estimates indicate that a large majority of U.S. manufacturing industries are characterized by constant returns to scale. The data from which these estimates are made are taken from a sample of establishments (plants) and aggregated for states. Thus the estimates are made from statistics that treat each state as though it were a homogeneous production unit.

One would attach more confidence to the inferences on economies of scale if in fact the average scale of the intrastate plants shows substantial variation. That is, one would hope that the state aggregates are derived from intrastate statistics for which the typical plant size varies from state to state. Actually there are significant differences in the average sizes of intrastate production units. Table 2 presents the mean, range, and standard deviation for the size distribution of the average size state plant by industry in 1958. Size is measured as value added per "average state plant," which in a particular industry is computed by dividing state value added by the number of plants in the state. The range is substantial in all industries, 9 of the 16 industries having largest "average state plants" more than ten times the size of the smallest "average state plants." Additional evidence concerning the dispersion in the size of "average state plants" is found by comparing the standard deviations with the means: in 11 of the 16 industries the mean is less than twice the standard deviation.

Substantial variation in the average size of intrastate production units coupled with the extremely good statistical fits of the regression equations indicate that variation across states in the average scale of production has practically no effect on economic efficiency. Consequently, the regression results are consistent with the hypothesis that there is a broad range of "optimal" plant size, and that in most industries there are constant technological returns to scale.

Table 2 Value Added in Smallest, Largest, and Industry Mean Size Average State Plants in Two-Digit Industries, 1958

Industry	*Value Added in Smallest Plant ($1000)*	*Value Added in Largest Plant ($1000)*	*Value Added in Mean-Size Plant ($1000)*	*Std. Dev. of Plant Size Dist.*
20 Food and Beverages	191.5	774.6	361.9	144.7
22 Textiles	203.4	2,277.9	827.1	534.6
23 Apparel	88.6	1,013.9	367.2	213.7
24 Lumber	40.6	201.1	85.8	45.1
25 Furniture	85.1	726.9	281.3	148.1
26 Paper and Pulp	360.7	5,156.9	1,693.3	1,202.8
27 Printing, etc.	134.7	321.5	214.1	24.7
28 Chemicals	365.7	6,414.3	1,410.0	1,168.0
29 Petroleum and Coal	299.1	5,046.7	1,986.4	1,329.4
30 Rubber and Plastics	203.7	6,452.7	1,304.1	1,462.6
31 Leather	202.0	1,475.9	725.0	310.5
32 Stone, Clay, etc.	156.2	575.5	335.8	118.9
33 Primary Metals	344.3	9,349.2	2,239.0	2,140.4
34 Fabricated Metals	167.1	645.0	387.5	136.7
35 Non-elec. Mach.	†	†	†	—
36 Elec. Mach.	†	†	†	—
37 Trans. Equip.	194.0	5,196.4	2,286.8	1,413.8
38 Instruments	148.0	1,528.5	840.3	380.7

† Plant sizes are not determinable since industries 35 and 36 are combined in reporting number of plants by state.

There seems to be a good deal of additional economic evidence to support the conclusion of predominantly constant returns to scale in U.S. manufacturing. Constant returns is of course consistent with the facts of widely-dispersed intraindustry size distributions of plants and firms reported in other recent studies. It is also consistent with the observation that expansion of industrial output often involves proportionate expansion of firms (or plants) of all sizes. During the early history of American manufacturing there were surely numerous sources of economies of scale. Evidence in this paper and elsewhere, however, indicates that by 1957 these economies had largely been realized in most industries. Thus it appears that by 1957 most industries produce according to constant returns to scale, and there are not technological reasons to expect increased concentration of production in these industries.

22 Conventional theory holds that the long-run curve is U-shaped. Application of the survivor principle to empirical data results in the finding, as the preceding selection shows, that many curves are L-shaped (or shaped like the letter J lying on its back). This selection marshals evidence to support the belief that the long-run cost curve for automobile assembly is also flat over a wide range, with American Motors at one end of the flat part and General Motors at the other.

The reader will remember, from Selection 5, that the Senate Subcommittee on Antitrust and Monopoly was strongly critical of the big three in the auto industry. This selection, which is from the same report, displays grudging admiration of General Motors' efficiency as a producer of automobiles.

But General Motors produces many other commodities besides automobiles. Whether or not the company is "too big" is a question not settled by looking at its position on the flat portion of the long-run cost curve for automobiles.

IS GENERAL MOTORS' SIZE AN OPTIMUM?

SENATE SUBCOMMITTEE ON ANTITRUST AND MONOPOLY

General Motors enjoys an enviable reputation both within and without the automotive industry as an efficient firm. It is not always clear whether what is being referred to is its business efficiency, i. e., its ability to show a high profit rate and steady earnings or its true economic efficiency, i. e., its ability to make the most economical use of resources and produce at the lowest possible unit cost. Its efficiency in the former sense is manifest from the most cursory inspection of its financial data. There seems to be a considerable body of opinion that it is a highly efficient firm in the latter sense as well. In the absence of unit cost data for the industry, it is certainly not the intention here to question this widely held impression. General Motors, it is conceded, is an efficient producer in both the business and economic sense of the term.

There is one aspect to this question of efficiency, however, which is open to scrutiny. To what extent can General Motors' position of dominance be traced back to the requirements of obtaining optimum plant efficiency? By the term "plant" is meant "a related complex of facilities for manufacturing components normally 'integrated' by the assembler and then assembling

---

Taken and adapted from Administered Prices: Automobiles. Report, Together with Individual Views of the Subcommittee on Antitrust and Monopoly of the Committee of the Judiciary, United States Senate. 85th Congress, 2nd Session. November 1, 1958 (Washington, D.C.: 1958), pp. 13–16.

them."[1] Principal among these components are engines and bodies. The question is, How large must such a plant complex be in order to obtain all, or at least virtually all, of the possible economies of production?

It should be emphasized at the outset that an analysis of this question will not provide the answer to the further and related question of whether the operation of several separate plant complexes under common ownership and control yields economies that are not to be secured if they were each to be operated as an independent enterprise. In short, what is to be examined here is optimum plant size, not the question of whether economies exist in the operation of plural productive units. That there are possibilities for obtaining economies of this latter type has long been recognized. At the same time, it has also long been recognized that these possibilities for economies may be offset, in full or in part, by diseconomies resulting from excessive bureaucracy, inertia, difficulties in working out the best scheduling of the component plants, etc. But whether and to what extent these economies exist in the automobile industry and whether and to what extent they may be offset by the attendant diseconomies are questions on which there are no bodies of data and accordingly will not be examined in this report.

On the question of the optimum size of plant, or plant-complex as it should more properly be termed in the automobile industry, there are two recent bodies of data. The first forms part of a study by Professor Joe S. Bain on the economies of scale. On the basis of new data obtained by questionnaire from the automobile companies, as well as other information, Professor Bain found that—

> In general, 300,000 units per annum is a low estimate of what is needed for productive efficiency in any one line; there are probable added advantages to 600,000 units.[2]

This represents from 5 to 10 per cent of the industry's national output.

According to Professor Bain, the requirements for size come more from the production of bodies and engines than from assembly: "In assembly alone, from 60,000 to 180,000 units per annum is considered optimal. . . ."[3] He presents evidence showing that bodies and engines are typically integrated by the assembler or otherwise manufactured to special designs so as not to be generally interchangeable with those used by other firms. It is the requirement of producing bodies and engines in the same plant-complex which is largely responsible for the increase from the 60,000 to 180,000 units needed for assembly alone to the estimate of 300,000 to 600,000 for the integrated operation.

These estimates would be excessive if it were feasible for a number of sep-

[1] Joe S. Bain, *Barriers to New Competition* (Cambridge: Harvard University Press, 1956), p. 244.

[2] *Ibid.*, p. 245.

[3] *Ibid.*, p. 245.

arate automobile companies to secure their bodies and engines from firms specializing in the production of those components. This is a pattern of production which did exist in former years, but now a sort of endless circle exists. As long as there are so few companies in the industry as is now the case, it is most unlikely that any firm venturing to specialize in the production of engines and bodies would have enough customers to make its operations profitable. And as long as such specialty firms do not exist, any automobile firm must perforce produce its own engines and bodies. Professor Bain's estimates may also prove to be excessive for future years, since he assumes as given the present state of technology. There are on the horizon new technological developments, e. g., the possible substitution of plastics for steel in the body and the possible replacement of the present internal combustion gasoline engine by an electric motor—both of which would probably tend to reduce the optimum size of plants.

The second source of information on this issue of optimum plant size is Mr. George Romney, president of American Motors Corp. Testifying before the subcommittee, Mr. Romney held that according to studies carried out by his company, the optimum output from an automobile assembly line is 62.5 cars per hour. The optimum balanced plant design would include 2 such assembly lines, and 1 machine and press line to produce major parts and components to feed the assembly line. On a single 8-hour-shift basis, this aggregate plant would produce 1,000 cars per day (62.5 r 2 r 8 q= 1,000). Assuming a 5-day week, and 180 to 220 days full operation per year, this plant would produce 180,000 to 220,000 cars annually. On a straight 2-shift basis the output would range from 360,000 to 440,000 cars per year. Mr. Romney stated:

> Our studies based on our own experience and that of our competitors is that optimum manufacturing conditions are achieved with a production rate of 62.5 cars per hour per assembly line. To absorb the desired machine-line and press-line rate, two final assembly lines would be required. Of course your press line and your machine line are the principal lines on which you depend for work leading up to subassemblies and the ultimate production of the car itself on the assembly line. This would result in production of 1,000 cars per shift.
>
> A company that can build between 180,000 and 220,000 cars a year on a 1-shift basis can make a very good profit and not take a back seat to anyone in the industry in production efficiency. On a 2-shift basis, annual production of 360,000 to 440,000 cars will achieve additional small economies, but beyond that volume only theoretical and insignificant reductions in manufacturing costs are possible. It is possible to be one of the best without being the biggest.
>
> . . . my point is that when you get up to 180,000 to 200,000 cars a year, the cost reduction flattens out, from a manufacturing cost standpoint, and from 360,000 to 400,000 on up it is a negligible thing.

Comparing American Motors Corp. to his larger rivals, Mr. Romney observed:

And Senator, they beat us in certain elements of cost and we beat them in certain elements of cost.

We know that in relationship to their average plants—and incidentally you cannot say that any one of those big corporations produces cars at a particular level of efficiency because you will find varying rates of efficiency as between their different plants. But taking their best and their worst, we beat them in a number of areas.

We have got more modern facilities than they have got in many areas. We are using more modern equipment in many areas than they are using.

Now they are using more modern (equipment) in some areas than we are using.

Our material handling costs are less. Our overhead costs are less. We assemble the car more efficiently than they do in the main.

Senator WILEY. Do they agree with that?

Mr. ROMNEY. I will say this to you. That they have been over in our plant studying those methods because one thing about the automobile business is that you do not refuse to permit a competitor to come in your plant and take a look at how you are doing things.

I think that is one of the fine things about the automobile industry, that there has been more than just a narrow approach.

We have had Big Three companies in our plants in the last 2 or 3 years studying some of these methods that we use that are more modern than theirs. We are more modern in painting our cars than many of their plants.

The estimates of Professor Bain (300,000 to 600,000) and of Mr. Romney (approximately 200,000 to 400,000) can thus be seen to be in the same general order of magnitude. If they are at all correct, the inevitable conclusion is that General Motors, with its annual output of around 3,000,000 cars, is from 5 to 10 times the size of the optimum size plant.

This, of course, does not mean that General Motors has passed the point of optimum plant efficiency. Reflecting its longstanding policy of decentralization, General Motors production is carried on by a number of separate divisions and a larger number of plants. The output during the 1957 model year of each of General Motors' automotive divisions is as follows:

Number of Cars Produced, Model Year 1957

Buick	405,000	Oldsmobile	384,000
Cadillac	147,000	Pontiac	334,000
Chevrolet	1,553,000		

What is surprising is the extent to which the output of General Motors' divisions, except two, falls within the general range of the Bain and Romney estimates. Cadillac's production falls below the estimate, and possibly, because of its quality, it is not mass-produced in quite the same way as are the other makes. The output of Chevrolet, alone, is substantially in excess of the estimates. But not even in the case of Chevrolet does the comparison of its output with the Bain and Romney estimates suggest that its unit costs would be lower if its output were less. Those estimates only had to do with the size necessary to attain optimum efficiency; they did not purport to indicate whether, once that point is reached, unit costs begin to rise or remain relatively constant. Moreover, Chevrolet's output, itself, is carried on in a number of plant-complexes, each of which may fall within the estimates.

But while these estimates, supported as they are by the actual showings of the Pontiac, Buick, and Oldsmobile divisions, do not in any way disprove the widely held impression that General Motors is an efficient producer, they do suggest that a comparable degree of efficiency in production can be attained by an enterprise well below the size of General Motors.

Part Four

It used to be said that the theory of pure competition is a nearly useless thing, because even if some parts of the American economy are like the model of pure competition, they are small and shrinking parts. But the theory of pure competition continues to demonstrate its usefulness. It serves to give a standard of economic efficiency; thus if ever the theory were somehow lost, it would have to be invented again. And even though the agricultural and other natural-resource industries no longer bulk so large in the American economy as they once did,

Competitive Pricing

they continue to be important for sufficiently obvious reasons. Mainly because of their simplicity, competitive models can be successfully used even where an essential feature of pure competition is lacking. This is well illustrated in Selection 53, which employs a competitive model to explain the contemporary shortages of scientists and engineers. These people are certainly not homogeneous. Far from it; but they can be treated as if they were alike in some kinds of analytical problems.

23

Here is a clear analysis of a system of competitive prices under the influences of well-intentioned price controls.

THE PRICING OF FOOD IN INDIA

ALI M. KHUSRO
Institute of Economic Growth, University of Delhi

Introduction

In economies where the degree of monetization of produce is small and where neither much of output is destined for nor much of input purchased from the market, there is a strong presumption about rigidities in people's response to the price mechanism. There is a presumption, that is to say, that demand patterns are rigidly fixed, that supply curves of output and inputs—land and labor—are inelastic (and some even backward-sloping), that marketed surpluses are inelastic or backward-bending, too, and that substitution of cheaper for dearer methods in production and consumption does not occur, or occurs much too sluggishly.

In very recent years, however, in India at any rate, a good deal of evidence has piled up to the contrary. Shifts in relative acreage under different crops seem to be adequately explained by relative crop price changes together with weather and one or two other factors. Production, not only of commercial nonfood crops but also of food crops, seems sensitive to prices. There is some evidence, too, of positive responses of marketed farm surpluses to price variations; and although controversy still exists, with supply responding positively, it is becoming increasingly difficult to maintain that marketed supply does not respond or responds negatively to prices.

Recent responses of Indian farmers to floor prices, controlled prices of output (foodgrains) and input (fertilizer, water, seeds, etc.) and price expectations—all derived from the pricing policies of government—further underline the price-sensitivity of farm people and the great force that price

---

Condensed slightly from Ali M. Khusro, "The Pricing of Food in India," *Quarterly Journal of Economics,* Vol. LXXXI, No. 2, May 1967, pp. 271–285.

mechanism is—even in a substantially nonmonetized set-up. It is clear that a small degree of monetization ought not to be confused with price-insensitivity.

The concern of the present study is with the pricing of foodgrains output in India and with the sensitivity of consumer demand and producers' supply to pricing policies. Knowing how iniquitous the price mechanism can be under circumstances of ignorance, immobilities, imperfect competition and income inequalities, one need not unduly eulogize it. But as pieces of evidence are piling up to the effect that the price mechanism is perhaps as compelling a force in the Indian economy as in any other, one might attempt to understand its working. It might well be that the harm done to Indian agriculture, in terms of destroying the incentive to produce more with better techniques and a more efficient combination of new and old inputs, emanates in a large measure from a lack of understanding of the price mechanism and the consequent adoption of false pricing policies.

Food and the Price Mechanism

For more than a decade now India's production of foodgrains has been growing at a trend rate of little more than 2½ per cent per year,[1] aside from vicissitudes of good and bad weather. Yearly population growth also is of that order so that this factor alone can absorb nearly all increments of foodgrains production—nearly, because of price and some other considerations. But since incomes per head grow, too, and tastes change towards superior cereals, home supplies at their current rate of growth become insufficient and prices rise. If yearly population growth is about 2½ per cent, per head real income grows each year by 3 per cent and the income-elasticity of demand for foodgrains (net of population changes) is 0.5, then it is most likely that consumer demand for foodgrains would rise by 4 per cent per year until these factors change. On this reckoning, consumer demand exceeds supplies at constant prices. But in such a situation, since prices actually rise, demand is somewhat restrained owing to a small negative value of the price-elasticity of demand. By the same fact of higher prices, supplies, other things being equal, actually ought to be somewhat greater.

At a very early stage of analysis it is best to get out of the way two simple but much-misunderstood ideas. In the first place, if the trend demand for food continually exceeds the trend home supply of food, no amount of rationing or buffer-stock operation or imports can stabilize food prices. Governments can keep on attempting to build up stocks: but the run on the stocks, having its origin in annual excesses of demand over supply, will con-

[1] The fitting of regression lines to food production data for the post-1951 planning era yields a growth rate of 3 to 4 per cent per year depending on the base and the terminal year(s) chosen. However, estimates of what might be called full-capacity growth, based on production changes from one peak year to another, yield figures no higher than 2½ per cent per year.

tinue and stocks will again and again tend to get exhausted. The medium-long-run concomitant of a short-run price stabilization policy is that the trend supply should overtake trend demand for food within a small number of years. The best thing to do to a shortage is to abolish it and the best price policy is an effective production policy. The long-run solution to the problem of rising food prices is not found within the boundaries of the theory of price control and rationing.

In the second place, it has to be recognized that the thing that eventually equilibrates demand and supply and abolishes shortages is the high price of food. Under conditions of severe shortages, consumers, of course, must be cushioned against high prices to the extent political, humanitarian and distributional considerations make it necessary. But, as will be demonstrated presently, with prices controlled at lower than equilibrium level, demand will always exceed supply (even if there is comprehensive urban rationing), production will remain depressed, government stocks will continually run down and shortages will perpetuate themselves. When the lesson has been learnt that high prices restrain consumer demand—however little—and simultaneously encourage production, equilibrium in food will emerge. It will not emerge until attention has been shifted from consumers *alone* to producers *as well.*

To turn now to the more immediate problem, Figure 1 sums up several aspects of the Indian food problem. *St*1, *St*2, and *St*3 are supply curves over time, depicting increases in supply of, say, 2½ per cent per annum. *dt*1, *dt*2 and *dt*3 are hypothetical demand curves over time if the only factor affecting demand were population growth of the same order per annum as supply. Prices, as shown by the intersection of these curves, would then be stable. But since incomes, etc., have been rising on top of population, the actual demand curve has been shifting rightwards or upwards—as seen by the position of *Dt*1, *Dt*2, *Dt*3—say at 4 per cent per annum. Prices then have been rising from *Pt*1 to *Pt*2, and to *Pt*3. These are prices in the primary markets—paid by the traders and received by the farmers. For simplicity, we merge the wholesale and the retail traders into just one category, the trader.

When at *t*3 the primary market is cleared at price *Pt*3, the traders get the supplies and adding their own margins of transport, storage, interest, insurance and profits, offer the grain in the retail market through a supply curve, *Sr*. The consumers offer a demand curve, *Dr*, and the market is cleared at price *Pr*.

But a retail price, *Pr*, may well be economically and politically unacceptable. The retail demand curve, *Dr*, is the aggregate of millions of individual demand curves of low income consumers like *Dl* and several high income consumers, *Dh*. At a retail price as high as *Pr*, the high income group would buy quantity *OH* but the low income consumers no more than *OL*, while the minimum nutritional requirement may well be *ON*. At price *Pr*, malnutrition and loss of efficiency on the one hand, and looting of grainshops, godowns and trucks on the other are some of the unwholesome possibilities.

So, on grounds of consumer welfare and distributional equity, the retail price is sought to be controlled by legislation, etc., at a level lower than *Pr* or food subsidies are given, say, in the shape of cheap grain in government-controlled fair-price shops. The effective consumer price is sought to be reduced, through controls, to *Pc*.

FIGURE 1

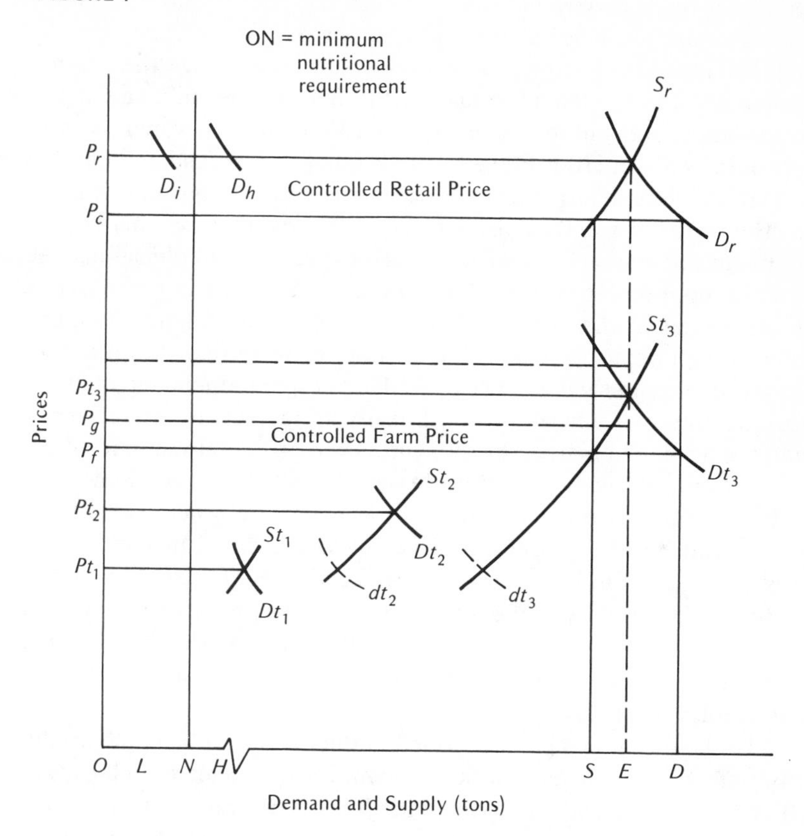

But if consumer price is lowered to *Pc*, the purchase price paid by the trader (and the government which also buys grain for counter-speculative as well as reserve stocks) would presumably have to be lowered to *Pf*, since the two prices are taken to be separated from each other by given margins. So a lower-than-equilibrium farm purchase price, *Pf*, is announced and made into a law. (To the statutorily controlled, below-the-equilibrium prices, *Pr* and *Pf*, if we add, on the same principles, a wholesale price, *Pw*, in the intermediate market, we get the kind of three-tiered price system which the government of India announced late in 1964 and sought to implement during 1965.)

Effects of Price Control

Now the theory of price control informs us that under these circumstances one of the three things, or a combination of them, would happen:

(a) Sellers (i.e., farmers in the primary markets and traders in the secondary and tertiary markets) would attempt to bypass controls and sell in the uncontrolled or black markets.

(b) Sellers (farmers) would increase their self-consumption of grain.

(c) If farmers could do neither of the above, or having done some of either one or both, they would submit to controls; but if they did, the effect on production might be adverse, unless other steps were taken.

(a) The immediate attempt all-round would be to dodge the controls in order to be able to take advantage of the free market price. Examples of this abound in India in recent times. From 1958 onwards, when the government of the state of Uttar Pradesh decreed that farmers and grain dealers in the markets should surrender half their stocks to the government at less than the market price, they began to boycott the established market places and conducted transactions outside market premises and official marketing hours. In more recent years, in Uttar Pradesh and elsewhere, the free market has moved to the farmer's door. There is some evidence, too, of the traders using farmers as their agents to store grain so that they may escape the official raids on their godowns, etc. The meager mopping-up of grains in raids, the failure of official buyers in nearly all markets to produce enough grain, the decline in market arrival figures even in a good year, are all symptoms of a shift of transactions outside the controlled market. Even more recently, in areas of serious shortages like Maharashtra, where the difference between controlled and free prices is very large, the farm families themselves are reported to have started taking headloads of grain directly to the consumers. The essence of the matter in all these cases is the boycott of the controlled price. Farmers and traders are all too aware that they are operating in sellers' markets; governmental policies, on the other hand, show a great deal less of such an awareness.

(b) To the extent it is possible to sell in the free market, people would do so; beyond this an increase in farm retentions for increased self-consumption is a very clear and easy possibility. Theory is again very clear on the point that if producers have the choice to consume or to sell their wares, an attempt to force controlled (lower) prices on them promotes self-consumption. Figure 2 illustrates this point.

AZ is a farmer's total output of foodgrains. He must retain some of it for family consumption and sell some for cash, to buy his basket of urban-industrial goods and to pay taxes and debts, if any. To begin with, he has strong preferences or a hard core of demand for some food retentions and some sales and the marginal utilities of both are high. But retaining more and more, as he moves on from *A* to *E* the marginal utility of retentions declines along the *RR*' curve. Similarly, as he sells more and more the marginal utility of income from sales at free market prices declines along the *SS'* curve. When *AE* output is retained and *EZ* sold, the two marginal utilities are equal and total utility (the area under the marginal utility curves, the area *ARDSZ*) is maximized.

FIGURE 2

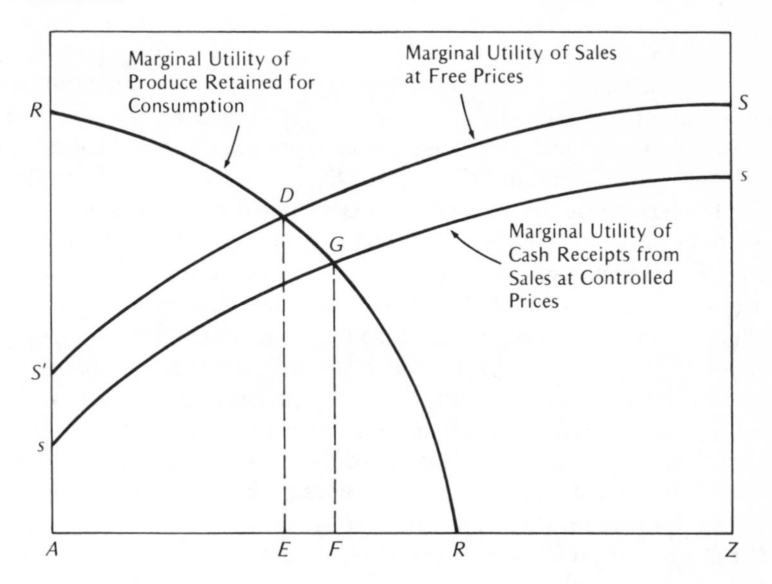

Now, if the farmer is obliged to sell at controlled prices, his cash receipts from each unit of output sold will be lower, and so will his marginal utility of each sale, as seen in the *ss'* curve. The point of equi-marginal utility of retentions and sales has shifted from *D* to *G*, so that a larger output, *AF*, is retained and a smaller output, *ZF*, is sold. Retentions have increased. So long as farmers have normal, forward-sloping, marketed supply curves, it is not necessary to assume that they will retain more only if they produce more: they will retain more, even out of a constant produce, if they get a lower price.[2]

(c) Having attempted to sell in the free market and having consumed somewhat more, it is possible, though it is not clear how,[3] that farmers

[2] In Figure 2 we assume separable utility, i.e., that marginal utility of sales is not dependent on marginal utility of retentions for consumption. The *ss'* curve should not be taken to run equidistant to the *SS'* curve. With a utility function $U(px)$, marginal utility of sales at any given price is a product of the marginal utility of the cash received from sales and the price at which sales are made. The marginal utility of sales at a higher price will be larger than that at a smaller price, if the rate of diminishing marginal utility of cash receipt is small, which may not be an improper assumption to make when new consumables are fast penetrating the rural sector.

might have to sell some grain in the controlled market. In that case, the average price—the weighted average of the two prices in the two markets—has decreased. In terms of Figure 2, their marginal utility curve would be somewhere between *SS* and *ss* and hence their retentions would have increased beyond *AE* though not as much as *AF*. But it is clear that total marketed surplus has decreased, by the sheer fact of price control, even though some grain deliveries at controlled prices have accrued to the procuring authority.

Aside from this adverse effect on marketed surplus, the effect on farm production, probably would be adverse too, as Figure 1 points out. If the equilibrium price is *Pt*3 and the controlled farm price, *Pf*, is lower, then, at *Pf*; not only is demand, *OD*, higher than equilibrium demand but supply, *OS*, is lower than equilibrium supply, *OE*. The very success of control in giving farmers a lower average price, causes some disincentives to invest and produce in the following season, so long as supply curves are normal. This is the reason why, unless a number of other things are done simultaneously, controls tend to perpetuate themselves, for they discourage supply (both production and marketing) as much as they encourage demand.

A policy of mere price control which starts with an immediate regard for urban consumers, tends to end, through depressing production and augmenting consumption, in an actual disregard for those very consumers in the long run. While production is discouraged, the thing to note is that excess food demand at controlled prices comes both from nonfarm consumers and from farmers (in their capacity as consumers).

It follows that no scheme of price control is worth the name which does not have a built-in objective of quantity control (rationing) in the short run and of increasing production in the long run. To be effective on the demand side price control has to be combined with rationing; to be effective on the supply side it must be combined with incentives to producers. There is a way, other than the methods practiced by the Ministry of Food and Agriculture or those advocated by the Price Commission, in which these combinations can perhaps be successfully achieved.

Rationing

From the peculiar fact that food producers can eat up their own produce and from the fact that a low market price might lead them to eat more, it follows that demand-restricting measures have to be applied as much to farmers as to nonfarm consumers, those 30 per cent or so of people who eat out of the marketed surplus. Policy has so far considered demand restriction on the latter but has assumed in too facile a manner that this is not possible

[3] Sometimes there is administrative pressure to sell. Farmers also wish to avoid the impression that they have not sold any grain at all in the established markets.

with the former. Quantitative rationing of farmers, of course, is not possible as experience in several controlled economies has again and again shown. But incentives, including price incentives, to consume less and deliver more grain are possible. This will be shown presently, but meanwhile a word about nonfarm rationing.

Policymakers have soft-pedalled rationing too long and left it in the realm of debate: should it take a statutory or an informal shape? Should it apply to all urban areas or to large cities alone? The war psychology and forecasts of poor 1965–66 crops have brought some urgency in the matter. But the basic issue is simple. Rationing, to be really effective, has to apply to the whole of the marketed surplus of major foodgrains and the whole of food imports which are consumed by some 30 per cent of the population. Since neither storage capacity of the public sector nor the administrative machinery permits the casting of the rationing net so wide, the second best solution is sought to be attempted by rationing of large cities through a system of extended fair-price shops, large imports and an attempted procurement of only 15 to 25 per cent of the marketed surplus. The remaining nonfarm population which eats out of the marketed surplus is expected to buy its food in the free market at the uncontrolled price, even though a statutorily restricted price is hopefully expected to prevail in that market. Such hopes are obviously unwarranted.

Now it is true that in India a strong consumer preference for home-grown as distinct from imported varieties of food (wheat) has led the high income consumers to go for the high-priced home varieties while the small man has generally been able to get cheap grain from the fair-price shops. The fair-price shop has, thus, in fact, become the instrument of some redistribution of real income and public criticism of food policy has been somewhat more restrained than it would otherwise be.

But now with more comprehensive rationing and commitment to provide rationed food to a wider section of the nonfarm population, the basic questions once again arise. The larger the net of rationing, the greater the need for procurement of supplies from the farm. But if a free market with a free price prevails alongside a controlled procurement price, why should the farmers sell in the controlled market? What will be the sanctions to force them to do so? And what safeguards will exist against an increase of farm consumption and a stagnation of food production?

Thus, from whatever angle we approach it, the real problem of Indian food policy is (in the short run):

(1) the restriction of nonfarm demand for food through comprehensive rationing;

(2) the restriction of farmers' demand for food;

(3) tempting the farmers to give up their boycott of the established markets and come back to them to sell openly so that the procuring authority can buy as much grain as it likes in order to run the rationing scheme; and (in the medium-long run)

(4) to press forward on increasing farm production.

The Right Combination of Food Policy Measures

Measures for increasing farm production are not discussed in this section, but the first three prime objectives can be achieved with the following combination of measures, as other combinations seem wasteful or incapable of achieving the ends.

(1) The procuring authority, hereafter called government, announces floor prices in advance of the sowing season, a condition not always fulfilled in the recent past, and stands ready to buy from farmers. Separate floor prices are announced for each major commodity and each major variety of a commodity. These prices are so fixed as to be (a) higher than a three-year average of the post-harvest low of farm prices; (b) higher than the average (paid-out) cost of production plus the cost of transport of any farmer whom it is intended to keep in production; and, (c) higher than (a) or (b) whichever is higher.

Floor prices, save in the case of specific areas, should make no separate allowances for high and low cost farmers, short or long transport distances and efficient or inefficient regions. Let the low cost farmers get a rent of efficiency, farmers bringing grain from nearby farms a rent of location and low cost or better endowed regions a rent of endowment. To do otherwise is to be inefficient.

Floor prices so designed, will revise minimum price expectations during harvest upwards and will lead to more investment, better crop planning and higher production. But what needs to be understood is that floor prices provide incentives only to those farmers who sell in the post-harvest season. To others who have storage and holding power and sell in off-season at a high price anyway, floors are no attraction. For them other measures are necessary.

(2) Floor prices should not be ceiling prices but should perform the function of a floor. When prices in the market rise above the floor the government buys, in whichever market it prefers, at the ruling price. There is no self-defeating attempt to buy at less than the market price. The difference between the price at which the farmer sells to the trader and that at which he is asked to sell to the government (or the Food Corporation) is abolished.

This brings the farmer back to the established markets without fear of a low price. Since marketed supply curves are forward-sloping, a higher average price now received by the farmer, increases marketed surpluses. The latent phenomenon of increased food consumption by farmers is avoided. Buying in markets with larger arrivals than before, the government procures larger supplies and moves towards a larger rationing scheme in urban areas and, indeed, larger price-stabilizing reserve and buffer stocks.

(3) But it might be feared that purchasing grain at higher than controlled farm prices would subsequently involve the government in selling grain at unnecessarily high and unpalatable consumer prices, or in giving consumers a large subsidy. A high cost purchase, it will be argued, would restrict the

government's ability to stabilize intermediate, wholesale, etc., markets through releasing grain from its stocks, since the release price must not involve the government in a loss.

But all these are paper tigers. To begin with, it must be conceded that even with an apparently high price purchase, by successfully buying more at the going market price, the physical problem of not having any grain to sell or store has been converted into a financial problem of subsidy and a possible money loss. But (a) this problem can be tackled at the monetary-fiscal level, or (b) need not arise at all.

The main clue lies in the fact that while a free market purchase looks like a high price purchase, in fact it can easily be made into a low cost purchase. A reputable and efficient civil servant or manager, sitting in a control room in a state headquarters or in the office of the Food Corporation of India, receives the telephone or the telegraph, etc., price quotations, say twice daily, for specified commodities from several dozen markets in the region. He conducts switch operations, much as a stockbroker does in national or world markets, ordering purchases in market *A* and stopping them in market *B*. A private trader operates only in one, two, or a few markets but the official operator, operating in fifty, ends up with a cheaper *average* purchase each day. Moreover, he is armed with better information, a large fleet of trucks, a possible monopoly of railway wagons and an efficient storage system: that is to say, he has scale economies all along the line. The government, if it wants, can thus procure grain cheaply and can afford to compete with the trade, provided it shows a respect for the market mechanism at points at which it is due.

(4) The government must not only buy aggressively but also conserve its stocks judiciously. A large storage capacity—possibly 6 million tons rather than the current 2 to 3 million tons—is a necessary condition, though by no means a sufficient one for judicious operation. But there is also the great need to realize that pipeline stocks of food are by no means the same thing as reserve stocks or antispeculative buffer stocks. It is true that stocks cannot be easily labeled and the difference is conceptual. Yet, the concept is very meaningful and provision ought to exist for all the three kinds of stocks. If the government stores in the beginning of the year and is obliged to sell towards the end of the year to meet consumer demand (this is how pipeline stocks are defined), there is no particular merit in holding the pipelines during the interim. The farmer and the trader can also do this. Government stocks—reserves and buffers—have to be over and above normal consumption requirements, if prices are to be stabilized, and these should be aggressively built up (a) through free market purchases, (b) through imports, and (c) through larger inventories if ever the country gets two consecutive good years. (Experience of the last fifteen years shows that whenever India gets two consecutive good years, above the trend line, prices tend to get stabilized. Probably it takes one good year to rebuild depleted inven-

tories and another one to meet consumer demand adequately without further price increases).

Until two good years occur, the other means of stock conservation are rationing and high prices of food, perhaps just below the limit of public tolerance.

(5) But we have seen that rationing in urban areas alone is not enough. A problem exists of reducing the farmers' recently enhanced grain consumption owing to fear of forced sale at controlled prices. The abolition of differential pricing would itself eliminate this excess consumption. But the other means of reducing or preventing farm consumption from rising are:

(a) making larger and newer inputs of production available to the farmers if they agree to deliver grain to the government by means of an advanced contract;

(b) giving input subsidies and tying the amount of subsidy to the quantity of grain delivered;

(c) supplying specific consumer goods to farmers against grain deliveries; and

(d) making land revenue progressive while generally increasing direct and indirect taxes on farmers so as to lead them to monetize a greater proportion of output and to prevent the terms of trade from moving unduly in their favor.

(6) A cause of serious inefficiency in the present food policy is the system of food zones. Zones are justified primarily on the grounds that they bottle up surplus areas, enable cheap procurement and subsequent distribution according to the needs of each region, with minimum transport cost. But these claims are more imaginary than real.

Zones cannot stand rigorous theoretical scrutiny. If the government purchases grain in surplus areas and transfers to the deficit regions exactly the amount which private trade would have done, its activity is unnecessary or redundant. If it transfers less or more, it is to be blamed squarely. In actual fact, attempts by the governments of surplus states to procure at less than market prices have led, as pointed out earlier, to the boycott of established markets and to an increase in farm consumption. Governments have thus procured and transferred much less than the market would have done in its attempt to equalize the profit of trade, and transport.

The fundamental, almost incontrovertible, economic argument against zones is that:

(a) by keeping producer prices in surplus areas lower than they would otherwise be, zones depress production in surplus areas (where precisely it ought to be encouraged for reasons of better endowment in respect of the particular grain in question);

(b) by keeping consumer prices in surplus areas lower than they would otherwise be, zones encourage consumption in these areas;

(c) by keeping consumer prices in deficit regions higher than they would be, zones depress consumption in these regions, hit the consumers here harder than is necessary and make for national disharmony; and

(d) by keeping producer prices in deficit areas higher than they would be, zones perpetuate production in regions badly endowed (for the commodity in question) and tie up resources precisely where these should not be tied up.

In any case the zonal scheme is a bundle of contradictions, meant to cushion the consumer rather than the producer in surplus states and geared more to politics than to economics, to votes than to prices. If a state has a surplus of food, that is due either to better endowment by nature or to the sturdiness of the sons of its soil. What have the consumers done in a surplus state that—in a single national unit—they should deserve better treatment than their brethren in deficit states? Be that as it may, zones cannot last long. Owing to built-in inefficiencies, as one surplus state after another embraces a deficit, there will be enough deficit states in the country to vote for an abolition of zones. But India has shown sufficient realism in the recent past not to wait till the bitter end and will probably drop the zonal policy before that time.

24 Arrow and Kalt discuss the efficiency gains and equity consequences of decontrol of oil prices.

WHY OIL PRICES SHOULD BE DECONTROLLED

KENNETH J. ARROW
JOSEPH P. KALT
Stanford University and Harvard University

Policy-makers currently face major decisions on petroleum pricing and have an important opportunity to rethink the direction of U.S. energy policy. Present oil price control regulations are scheduled to expire in October 1981; and in June 1979 the Carter administration began to phase out price ceilings so as to bring about a gradual transition to decontrol. It remains to be seen whether Congress will block gradual decontrol and extend price regulation past 1981. Nevertheless, if these decisions are to be made rationally, policy-makers must be clear on the issues involved.

There are two basic kinds of issues raised by the prospect of decontrol. Because federal price regulation forbids crude oil producers from selling their output at market prices and because it forestalls much of the prospective transfer of wealth from domestic users to domestic producers portended by the rising world oil prices of the 1970s, issues of fairness (or equity) arise in the debate over policy. And because the constraints placed on this prospective transfer themselves distort energy use and production decisions, issues of efficiency inevitably arise as well.

Oil price regulations in fact impose a net efficiency loss on the U.S. economy. Consequently, the crucial question is whether the gains in efficiency from decontrol outweigh any equity losses. On the basis of explicit measurement and comparison, we conclude that the answer to this question is yes. Oil prices should be decontrolled.

The Costs of Controls

Demand-Side Inefficiency

Domestic crude oil price controls prevent much of the increase in the wealth of crude oil producers that would accompany an increase in domestic prices to

---

Reprinted from Kenneth J. Arrow and Joseph P. Kalt, "Safety at Any Price," *Regulation*, September/October 1979, pp. 13–17. Professor Arrow received the 1972 Noble Memorial Award in Economic Science.

world levels. An estimate of this potential wealth increase can be found by calculating the difference between the revenues that would be generated in the absence of controls and the actual revenues on controlled output. Assuming that domestic regulation has had no effect on the "uncontrolled" world price for crude oil, these "transfers" were running at a pace of roughly $17 billion in May 1979 (that is, immediately before the administration's first gradual steps toward decontrol). These billions of dollars represent a windfall to *users* of crude oil—including large refiners, small refiners, and ultimate consumers, both industrial and individual. The division of the windfall among these groups depends on the impact of a complicated set of regulations called entitlements.

Obviously, the prospect of any transfer of $17 billion a year would induce interest-group competition. The entitlements program is an outcome of such competition and is the mechanism that determines the eventual ownership of the windfall gains arising under crude oil price controls. Essentially, the program taxes away these gains and redistributes them as subsidies for the expansion of refinery output. Since the supplies of crude oil available for such expansion primarily consist of imported oil, the entitlements program subsidizes the use of foreign oil. This subsidy, which varies with the gap between the world price of oil and the domestic weighted average price, averaged $2.35 per barrel over 1975–78 and was $2.44 in May 1979.

Now, as far as the nation's economy is concerned, efficient use of crude oil requires that the price paid by the nation to acquire a barrel of crude oil not exceed the value consumers place on the contribution of that crude oil to the refined products they desire. The present inefficiency arises because, with the entitlements subsidy, refiners see the cost of crude oil to themselves as something less than the amount actually paid to foreign suppliers. Consequently, they use too much crude oil—too much in the sense that the country hands over resources to foreign oil sellers which are more valuable than the goods produced by having additional crude oil for refining. Assuming (as the evidence suggests) a 1 percent reduction in the price of crude oil induces refiners to increase use of crude oil by one-half of 1 percent within the year of the price reduction, then (based on May 1979 data) domestic refiners use about 375 million extra barrels of imported crude oil per year as a result of the entitlements subsidy—though, of course, these entitlements-induced expenditures produce goods of some value to the intermediate and ultimate consumers of crude oil. Our calculations show a gain of $13.2 billion a year to crude oil users, at a cost of $13.7 billion a year. The net loss—in demand-side efficiency—is thus $500 million a year.

Supply-Side Inefficiency

Federal regulation of domestic petroleum prices not only induces overconsumption of crude oil in the United States. It also causes underproduction, and this results in a net loss to the economy.

Efficiency in crude oil production requires that, for a given level of demand, the total cost of acquiring oil from both foreign and domestic sources be as low as possible. When the alternative to domestic oil is imported oil bought at the world price, efficiency requires the production of all domestic crude oil that can be had at a cost not exceeding the price of foreign oil. If the cost of an incremental unit of output of domestic oil is greater than the price of imported oil, the nation could save by replacing domestic output with imported oil. Conversely, if the cost of an incremental unit of output of domestic oil is less than the price of imported oil, we would save by importing less and producing more. It makes little sense to hand over, say, $19 to foreign oil producers for a barrel of crude oil if a comparable barrel can be acquired domestically for, say, $13.

Federal price controls violate the criteria for efficiency in oil production. Ceilings on the prices that can be paid for so-called lower- and upper-tier crude oil discourage producers from taking full advantage of sources of supply with production costs greater than those ceilings—even though there are, among these, sources that could produce oil at a cost below the price of imported oil.

What are the supply-side costs of crude oil price controls? Assuming (somewhat conservatively) that a 1 percent increase in price causes a one-tenth of 1 percent increase in production from existing wells, the cost of discouraging production from existing supply sources is about $800 million a year. Assuming that production from newly developed wells shows a one-half of a percent increase in response to a 1 percent increase in price, the cost of discouraging the development of new supply sources is about $1.2 billion.

The total $2 billion estimate of the annual supply-side costs of controls is likely to be an underestimate if price controls have increased the uncertainty of investors who develop new supply sources. Though newly producing oil properties qualify for upper-tier prices today, there is no guarantee they will tomorrow. Indeed, since 1971, domestic crude oil prices have been subject to no less than eight pricing schemes. If the developers of new supply sources expect to be able to sell their output at the *average* domestic price (about $11) rather than the upper-tier price (about $13), the supply-side costs are on the order of $4 billion a year.

The supply-side costs of controls are also likely to be underestimated—as are the demand-side costs—if there are unmeasured costs of overdependence on foreign crude oil that petroleum users do not take into account when buying on world markets. Such costs—from the threats to national security or macroeconomic stability posed by import dependence—make the real cost of each barrel of imported oil higher than the real price paid on world markets. A $1.00 per barrel "overdependence" cost would raise the sum of the annual supply- and demand-side efficiency costs by more than $1 billion.

To summarize, even if we do not complicate things with considerations of investor uncertainty or import overdependence, the sum of the supply-side costs ($2 billion) and the demand-side costs ($0.5 billion) of petroleum price controls appears to be at least $2.5 billion a year. Inclusion of the complications which have been mentioned could double this estimate. And this is not all.

Other Costs

Private-sector costs of carrying out the administrative duties and obligations created by current regulations may be as much as $500 million annually, not counting the costs created by regulatory distortions in business transactions and competitive behavior. The *federal* administrative burden of regulation (paid for, of course, by the taxpayers) may be approaching $200 million annually. More subtle costs arise from the unambiguous support given OPEC by discouraging domestic production and subsidizing imports. And, finally, the inflexibility and inefficiency of current policies magnify the difficulties of adjusting to sudden shocks in world energy prices and supplies.

Winners and Losers under Controls

Recognition of the costs of controls is not in itself a sufficient base for major policy change. While removing the controls would avoid current inefficiencies, it would also have unavoidable "distributional" consequences—that is, it would redistribute income among the citizens of the United States. This raises the issue of fairness (or equity).

The windfall gains that accrue to crude oil producers as a result of rising oil prices are windfall losses to crude oil consumers. Of course, petroleum may be consumed either directly or indirectly. While automobile drivers and homeowners, for example, are direct consumers of gasoline and heating oil, they are by no means the only consumers adversely affected by higher oil prices. Industrial, commercial, and transportation-sector buyers of energy also face higher oil prices, which raise production costs and thus raise prices of goods and services or reduce stockholder wealth in these sectors.

The burden of rising prices on the users of petroleum induces reductions in the "energy-intensiveness" of production processes and consumption patterns. Firms, industries, and sectors of the economy most able to make these reductions over time enjoy relative competitive advantages. Final consumers most able to make such reductions find their real incomes relatively less vulnerable to erosion. Indeed, over the long run, the severest burden of rising energy prices must fall on those users whose behavior is least responsive to price changes. This is particularly pertinent to one group—crude oil refiners.

Reduction of consumer demand in response to rising oil prices tends to leave current refining capacity underutilized and to discourage industry expansion. Moreover, the depressing effect of rising prices on the quantity of petroleum products demanded tends to prevent the industry from passing on to consumers the full amount of any crude oil price increases. These effects decrease the value of refiners' assets. Thus, much of the burden of crude oil price increases rests on the owners (stockholders) of oil refineries rather than on final consumers.

Needless to say, the users of crude oil, whether refiners or consumers, do not welcome increases in oil prices. It is to be expected that they will use whatever political influence they have to prevent, forestall, or otherwise avoid the distributional effects of those increases. The ensuing political struggle should not, however, be naively represented as a contest between "consumers" and "the oil companies"—an oversimplification that ignores the fundamental divergence of interests between oil companies that are primarily refiners and oil companies that are primarily crude oil producers. While raising the specter of a monolithic oil lobby has value as a tactic of political debate, it obscures the more subtle reality.

The removal of crude oil price controls would benefit producers by about $19 billion annually. Of this, $17 billion would arise from the ability to sell current production levels at world prices and $2 billion would arise as a net gain on the additional output induced by decontrol (that is, from the removal of the supply-side inefficiency). Of the $17 billion withheld from producers on currently controlled oil, $3.3 billion is used to find such special programs as the grants made under the Small Refiner Bias, $13.2 billion goes to crude oil users through the entitlements subsidy, and $0.5 billion (as we saw in our discussion of demand-side inefficiency) is wasted. Crude oil users include both refiners and consumers, and their division of the $13.2 billion transfer is not self-evident. Since the entitlements subsidy lowers (incremental) refining costs and encourages an expansion of the domestic refining industry, it therefore lowers the price of refined petroleum products—but not by the full amount of the entitlements transfer.

The upward pressure of refinery expansion on production costs other than crude oil costs and the negative relationship between price and demand for petroleum products prevent a full pass-through. The most generous assumption we can make without being totally at odds with available evidence is that approximately 55 percent of the entitlements subsidy is passed through to consumers. At 55 percent, consumers capture approximately $7.3 billion. Refiners retain $5.9 billion. When the impacts of special programs such as the grants to small refiners are added to those of the entitlements subsidy, the net gains of consumers and refiners are approximately $8 billion and $8.5 billion a year, respectively.

Fairness and Decontrol

If we believe any efficiency-improving policy change is fair, then obviously decontrol should be supported. And if we believe that voluntarism in exchange—that is, the freedom of the individual—is the relevant criterion for fairness (or equity), we should also support decontrol.

These views of fairness, however, seem to be side issues in the current debate where the most commonly invoked notion of equity concerns the effects of decontrol on the poor. Other things being equal, it is taken as given in the debate that a more equal distribution of income is better than a less equal distribution of income.

The egalitarian policy-maker who is concerned about the distribution of income and who would like to redistribute toward the lower end of the income scale faces a trade-off between fairness and efficiency. This trade-off arises because the implicit or explicit taxes on the rich (or "non-poor") needed to accomplish a redistribution tend to discourage income-generating investment and employment. A policy that redistributes income downward, but reduces the size of the total economic pie (so that the amount taken from the rich is greater than the amount delivered to the poor), should be supported only if the value assigned by the policy-maker to the dollars transferred to the poor exceeds the value assigned by the policy-maker to the dollars lost by the rich.

To make this sort of comparison, a decision must be made as to how much weight should be given to rich and poor. In our calculations here, we have assumed that the contribution of an extra dollar of income to the well-being of the recipient is inversely proportional to the recipient's present income. Thus, for example, it would be half as worthwhile to give a dollar to someone earning $20,000 a year as to someone earning $10,000. In keeping with available evidence, we have assumed that the consumption of energy is roughly proportional to income. We have also assumed that dollar transfers to or from industries are transfers to or from the stockholders of those industries. Consequently, redistributions among industries have no effect on fairness, the position of stockholders in the income distribution tending to be much the same from industry to industry.

The key empirical fact in analyzing the fairness of decontrol is that the distribution of stock ownership is very different from the distribution of income. If indeed, as we assume, the stockholders in petroleum-related companies are much like stockholders in general, then the percentage of stock held (by market value) in such companies varies positively with family income. In fact, given our weighting system, the distribution of stockholders implies that a dollar given to a typical petroleum product consumer has roughly twice the "equity value" of a dollar given to a typical stockholder in a crude oil producing firm. Thus, decontrol would certainly have a reverse Robin Hood effect: it would take from those whose income is weighted relatively heavily and give to those whose income is weighted relatively lightly.

As noted, about $8 billion would be transferred from users of petroleum products to stockholders of crude oil producing companies. Part of this $8 billion, of course, is a transfer from some corporations (for example, industrial users) to other corporations (producers). We estimate that the intercorporate transfer is about $0.6 billion, leaving a net consumer-to-producer transfer of $7.4 billion. Of this, 48 percent is taken back by taxes (federal income, state income, and severance). If these tax revenues produce benefits which, like energy consumption, are approximately proportional to income, a net transfer of $3.8 billion rmains. Thus, with crude oil producers given only half of the weight given to consumers, decontrol has a net fairness (or equity) cost of $1.9 billion.

This is probably a high estimate. Consumers bear a significant portion of the costs stemming from administrative burdens, support for OPEC pricing, impairment of U.S. ability to adjust to outside shocks, and overdependence on foreign oil. These costs, as we noted, are difficult to measure, but they are certainly large. If we take only the estimated $500 million current private and administrative compliance costs, and if we assume that three-fourths of these are passed directly to consumers, our estimated equity cost of decontrol declines from $1.9 billion to $1.5 billion. Similarly, if even one-half of the budget of about $200 million that is allocated to petroleum regulation could be freed by decontrol and applied to other programs, with benefits distributed roughly in proportion to income, the equity cost estimate would be reduced to $1.4 billion. Of the costs of current policies that are not readily measurable—impairment of macroeconomic adjustment, alteration of normal business practices in the petroleum industry, national security problems from increased dependence on foreign crude—it is fair to conclude that many fall on the general public, and perhaps disproportionately on those with relatively low incomes.

Comparing Gains and Losses under Decontrol

Forced to place dollar figures on the overall equity cost of decontrol—that is, its unfavorable consequences for the distribution of wealth—we come up with something like $1.4 billion as a generous but not unreasonable estimate. The conservative estimates of supply- and demand-side gains amount to approximately $2.5 billion. Less conservative estimates would raise this closer to $4.5 billion. Certainly, an efficiency gain in the range of $2.5 to $3.5 billion (scaling down our upper limit) is unlikely to be too high. But this estimate of benefits cannot be directly compared to the $1.4 billion equity cost without specifying who it is that would receive the benefits. If all of the efficiency gain goes to producers, for example, this gain would have an equity value of one-half of the efficiency improvement.

In fact, the net supply- and demand-side gains from decontrol would accrue to producers. If we maintain our assumptions about taxes on producers and the use of tax revenues, a portion of the producer gains would be channeled back to consumers and the $2.5 to $3.5 billion efficiency gain from decontrol would have a net equity value of $1.9 to $2.6 billion. This exceeds the $1.4 billion equity cost of decontrol. Of course, from the egalitarian point of view, a windfall profits tax (with revenues used to offset the distributional effects of decontrol) would increase overall equity still more than decontrol by itself; but the point here is that decontrol, even without such a tax, would have benefits that exceed its costs.

In short, our analysis indicates that, even with standards of social justice that find the prospective transfer of income from consumers to producers highly inequitable, the efficiency gains from decontrol are dominant. Consequently, with full cognizance of the distributional implications, we recommend deregulation of domestic petroleum prices. The nation quite simply pays too great a price for trying to maintain income patterns in their pre-OPEC status and trying to forestall the adjustment to a present and future of rising energy prices.

25 Joskow and Pindyck argue against direct government subsidies of synthetic fuels on efficiency grounds. An important issue is the choice of discount rate to be used in evaluating alternatives.

SYNTHETIC FUELS: SHOULD THE GOVERNMENT SUBSIDIZE NON-CONVENTIONAL ENERGY SUPPLIES?

PAUL L. JOSKOW
ROBERT S. PINDYCK
Massachusetts Institute of Technology

The centerpiece of President Carter's energy policy is a program of massive subsidies to hasten the commercial development of synthetic fuels and other "non-conventional" energy supplies. While the ultimate size of the effort will be determined by the Congress, the administration has proposed spending over $100 billion in the next decade, and views the program as its major instrument for bridging the growing gap between our consumption and production of energy.

The particular sources of energy likely to be most heavily subsidized by this program include oil from shale rock and gas and liquid fuel from coal, but subsidies will also be allocated to solar energy, biomass, wind power, and other technologies. Producing energy from these sources does not require fundamental new scientific or technological advances. Shale oil was first produced in Britain in the 1850s, and gaseous and liquid hydrocarbons were produced from coal in Germany during World War II and are being produced today in South Africa. But energy from these sources is often called nonconventional because it is not at present being produced or consumed in significant quantities in the United States or, for that matter, almost anywhere else. The reason is quite simple—these sources of energy are extremely expensive. It is difficult to say just how much more expensive they are than conventional energy supplies, but estimates we have examined put them at twice the cost, on a thermal-equivalent basis.

Of course, as conventional energy supplies become increasingly scarce and their prices rise, shale oil, gasified coal, solar energy, and a variety of other nonconventional sources may become commercially viable, and in fact may eventually displace conventional oil and natural gas as major fuels. When that day will dawn is difficult to predict. But if, as the Carter administration argues,

---

Reprinted from Paul L. Joskow and Robert S. Pindyck, "Synthetic Fuels," *Regulation,* September/October 1979, pp. 18–24, 43.

it will be in the next decade, why is it that we do not already observe the private sector gearing up to produce these sources of energy in the absence of federal subsidies? More important, is it desirable to spend billions of tax dollars to subsidize these sources of energy sufficiently to make them economically attractive to producers and consumers? At a time when there is growing pressure to limit government spending in areas like health, education, and the environment, are these subsidies to specific energy supply technologies really in the public interest?

The Plan for Government Involvement

In the President's proposal for an Energy Security Corporation to support the commercial development of nonconventional energy, as in alternative plans, government subsidies take a variety of forms. First among these are direct subsidies to reduce the cost and increase the profitability of new energy technologies. The most common form of direct subsidy is the use of government revenues to finance part or even all of the construction of "demonstration plants" for nonconventional energy—a demonstration plant being a production facility at (or close to) commercial scale whose construction provides a way of finding out the actual cost and operating characteristics of each technology. This information is useful more for evaluating the "commercial" possibilities of a specific technology than for obtaining basic or applied scientific knowledge.

Outside of the military and space programs (where commercial viability is not an issue), the government has traditionally focused its R&D expenditures on financing basic and applied scientific research, leaving industrial development and commercialization to the private sector where both the benefits and costs of expenditures can be most effectively balanced. But it is now argued that, without direct government subsidies to finance the construction of demonstration plants, private firms will face too much uncertainty to allow them to make the "correct" investments.

Of course any new technology involves uncertainty and requires an investment in learning—problems long recognized in our patent system. Private investors are normally willing to undertake such projects when the expected rewards from success are greater than the expected losses from failure. Yet we are now being told that, for nonconventional energy, the government should bear much of the cost and the risk because the private sector is unwilling to do so. We have not, however, been told why it should be necessary for the taxpayer to bear these costs if these technologies are in fact "good bets."

Tax credits are another form of proposed subsidy, though one that is somewhat less direct. If the production of a particular form of energy is at all profitable in the long run, tax credits will obviously increase the aftertax profitability. And even if a particular project is *never* profitable, tax credits may have the effect of reducing the overall tax burden to the companies, and thus making the new technology more attractive. The energy tax credits specified in the President's plan are substantially those contained in last year's unsuccessful energy tax bill. They include a $3 per barrel credit for oil from shale and tar sands, a 50¢ per mcf credit for geopressurized methane and for any gas from a nonconventional source, and residential credits for home insulation and expenditures on solar and wind energy.

Loan guarantees, likewise an indirect form of subsidy, are also part of the President's plan. Because shale oil and coal gasification and liquefaction projects have large capital requirements, debt-financing costs are a major component of total cost. By reducing the riskiness of loans, loan guarantees reduce financing costs. What this form of subsidy costs the public is difficult to measure, since that depends on the number and sizes of loans that default. An extensive program combined with a high default rate could be very costly.

We have gathered and evaluated cost data for several nonconventional energy sources and have found only limited prospects for profitability. To put it simply, at least for the next several years, conventional sources are likely to be cheaper than nonconventional sources (for specific data, see Saman Majd, "Financial Analysis of Non-Conventional Energy Technologies," MIT Energy Laboratory). It is therefore not surprising that the private sector has not been particularly interested in developing these sources without the government subsidies; indeed their development is probably not an efficient use of society's scarce resources. It does not make sense to invest large sums of money in projects that do not appear to be economical, unless it can be shown that there are good reasons why the decisions made by the private sector are inconsistent with the public interest. We must always remember to ask the question: if energy producers and consumers, who are in the best position to assess the commercial value of alternative energy supplies, are not interested in attempting commercial development, why should the taxpayer overrule their decisions and—what is worse—pay for doing so?

The Rationale for Subsidies

Two basic arguments are made in favor of government participation in the development of nonconventional energy supplies. The first says that the United States is becoming more and more dependent on imported energy from sources that are increasingly insecure and that we can reduce this dependence by accelerating the production of new domestic energy supplies. There is no question that U.S. dependence on imported energy is increasing as the gap between our energy consumption and our domestic energy production continues to grow. The issue, however, is whether there are more efficient means of bridging the consumption-production gap that would end up costing the American public less.

The second argument says that projects to produce these energy sources are of a special nature that makes it difficult or impossible for them to be undertaken by the private sector without government assistance. Moreover, the administration claims that the special nature of these technologies is such that government participation in their commercialization will be needed even when energy prices are higher. Proponents of this view usually point to the fact that commercialization of these technologies typically involves large capital expenditures and, in some cases, considerable risk, so that private firms would be unwilling or unable to raise the necessary capital and make the necessary investments. In effect, it is argued that there are significant market imperfections which make nonconventional technology *look* unprofitable to private firms, even though its social value is considerable, and that it is these imperfections which justify intervention.

Here we examine these two arguments in some detail to determine whether they do indeed justify the kinds of programs the Carter administration is now proposing. We also present what we think is the proper role of the government in the commercialization of non-conventional energy supplies—first in the context of an ideal, or "first-best," energy policy, and then in the context of a "second-best" energy policy operating under the kinds of political constraints that are likely to exist in the near future.

New Energy Technologies as a Substitute for Imports

Before we consider whether the subsidization of nonconventional energy supplies is a desirable way of reducing the gap between domestic energy consumption and production, we should be clear on just why that gap exists. For the last several years, U.S. energy policy has kept the domestic price of energy well below the world level. Maintaining an artificially low price for consumers—and domestic producers—has stimulated energy demand and, at the same time, reduced domestic production. Some 4 to 6 million barrels per day of our current 8 or 9 million barrels per day of oil imports can be traced directly to recent policies that have kept domestic energy prices far below world market levels. (See article by R. Hall and R. Pindyck in *The Public Interest*, Spring 1977.)

Two principal policies have been used to maintain a low domestic price of energy. One is the crude oil price controls entitlement program, which taxes the domestic production of oil (by holding its price below the refiner's price) and uses the proceeds of the tax to subsidize imports (thereby reducing the cost of high-priced imported oil to the refiner). This has had the effect of keeping the average price of crude oil to U.S. producers about 50 percent below the world price—and has had the interesting side effect of putting the U.S. government in the business of subsidizing oil imports from OPEC.

The second policy is the regulation of the wellhead price of natural gas, which has held natural gas prices far below the world market level for many years, producing domestic shortages even before the 1973 oil embargo. The Natural Gas Act of 1978 represents a major step in correcting this policy, although gas prices will not reach free market levels for several years.

Now the administration, in its synfuel proposals, is asking taxpayers to finance the difference between the high cost of producing non-conventional energy in the United States and the low price consumers will be asked to pay. But Americans will be much worse off with higher taxes than with higher energy prices. Individuals can choose to avoid paying higher energy prices by limiting their consumption, but they have no choice about the taxes they must pay. The proposed "commercialization" program will force consumers to pay a good portion of the high cost of energy indirectly, through their taxes. As a result, there will be little incentive to conserve, so consumption will rise while production falls. A growing tax burden will then be required to finance a growing amount of subsidized production.

Rather than subsidize nonconventional energy, it would be better to purchase oil and natural gas at home and from abroad at world market prices. Offering government subsidies of one kind or another to developers of new energy forms means requiring the nation to pay much more for energy than is necessary—which is exactly what government policy should avoid.

A counter argument sometimes raised is that the development of more expensive non-conventioinal energy should be accelerated today so that lower-cost conventional energy can be saved for future generations. But this argument ignores the time value of money—which makes it cheaper for us to consume low-cost supplies now, in 1979/80, and higher-cost supplies then, in the future. As conventional oil and natural gas reserves are gradually depleted, the market prices of these resources will rise, so that eventually we will shift to higher-cost resources such as shale oil, gasified coal, and solar energy. To reverse this order of use by accelerating the commercialization of non-conventional supplies would only impose an unnecessary cost on the American public.

New Energy Sources and Market Imperfections

We have argued that if a new energy technology does not appear profitable to the private sector, its development may well not be an efficient use of society's scarce resources. But in some cases there may be significant market imperfections that make the technology *appear* unprofitable to private firms, even though its true social value is quite high. It is only in such a case that some type of government intervention might be desirable.

Those who advocate government intervention more often point directly or indirectly to one or more alleged failures of the market. Here we examine those alleged failures that have attracted the most attention.

Energy Price Imperfections

As we have pointed out, government regulation has kept most energy prices below their true marginal social cost. But it is prevailing or expected market prices on which private firms base their decisions about the profitability of new energy technologies.

Government price regulation has therefore created an important disincentive to investments in new energy technologies. It may be that such investments are "justified" by a complete analysis of the costs and benefits to the U.S. economy, even though private firms do not find them attractive in the face of regulated energy prices that do not reflect the true social costs of additional consumption to the U.S. economy. Since energy prices are "too low," we cannot expect the private market to provide the proper signals on new sources of supply.

While price regulation clearly leads to an important market imperfection, it is an artificial one created by the government's own actions. To set things right the government can either eliminate the source of the problem by allowing energy prices to rise to replacement cost, or it can try to "balance" the disincentives created by regulation with additional incentives in the form of subsidies to new technologies. We will explore this matter later on.

Discount Rates

It is sometimes contended that private firms, when making investment and planning decisions, use discount rates that are "too high" and that therefore bias their decisions away from capital-intensive projects like the commercialization of nonconventional energy supplies. There are essentially four reasons cited to explain why private discount rates tend to be higher than the "social" discount rates that should be used to properly evaluate the benefit of a project to society.

First, it is argued that social discount rates are lower than private discount rates because private agents do not value the well-being of future generations sufficiently. Using a lower social discount rate would lead us to shift expenditures towards more investment (and less consumption) today and more consumption tomorrow. (Alternatively, some have argued that we should impute a lower social discount rate in cost-benefit calculations so as to account for external economies or public goods characteristics that are not properly accounted for by private decision-makers.*

Second, it is argued that market interest rates ordinarily include some premium for the risk (or uncertainty) associated with the investment. This risk is reflected in (real and nominal) differences in the interest rates of risky and safe assets. Proponents of subsidies argue that such risk premiums would be unnecessary with government investment projects, since the government is so large and has so many projects over which it can diversify risk that its investments could be treated as being riskless. Government investment would therefore be evaluated at lower interest rates than those private firms use, reducing their apparent costs and making the investments more profitable from a "social" point of view.

Third, it is argued that corporate taxes distort discount rates, since the rate

* By "public goods characteristics" we refer in particular to the fact that once a "public good" exists (a highway, a dam, or a navy), it costs little or nothing for each additional user to gain its benefits—which, of course, makes cost allocation difficult.

of return on private projects must include a provision for the payment of income and other taxes. According to this argument, because the government does not have to pay taxes to itself, the social rate of discount would be lower than the private discount rate, making projects "socially profitable" even though they are unprofitable in the private market.

Finally, it is argued that the *social* returns from domestic energy projection are higher than the private returns. A reason given for this is that an increase in domestic production will lead to a reduction in imports, which in turn will lead to a reduction in the OPEC price.

For alternative energy sources, all four arguments are largely specious. Most of the historical discussion of social discounting has been conducted in the context of very large capital-intensive projects (such as dams), which have very long lifetimes as well as public goods characteristics and external economies, and which will be owned and operated by the government. But new energy technologies do not fit this bill.

There is also little evidence that private firms "overdiscount" the future, though this is a question not really subject to objective analysis. In any case, there is no reason to believe that such an effect would appear only in energy supply and demand decisions.

While it is true that government bonds will carry a lower interest rate than other bonds because bondholders always expect the government to pay up, this is risk reduction from the viewpoint of investors rather than from the viewpoint of society. If new energy technologies are inherently risky, there is little reason to believe that the government can make them any less so. Government only shifts risk from investors to taxpayers: it does not eliminate it.

It is true that the government might be in a better position to diversify risks than the private capital market when such extremely large amounts of capital are involved that the risks of default cannot be adequately absorbed by a single firm or a consortium of firms. But such situations are rare. The investments contemplated for most new energy technologies are not significantly larger than the amounts the energy industry has been able to raise in the past. Private firms have had little or no trouble in raising capital for projects like the Alaskan pipeline, liquefied-natural-gas tankers, oil refineries, and large chemical plants—projects whose capital requirements were of roughly the same magnitude as a shale-oil or coal-gasification plant. If there is a problem here it is not in the size of plant investment required.

The argument that taxes distort discount rates if likewise specious. The capital that might be used by the government to finance a project has an opportunity cost—that is, it is withdrawn from the private sector, thereby losing returns from private investments that would otherwise have been made and losing tax revenues that such investments might have generated. In short, the cost of obtaining funds for public investment projects is equal to the gross rate of return, including taxes, forgone by diverting this capital from the private sector to the public sector.

Finally, it is unlikely that a reduction of 2 or 3 million barrels per day of imports (in 1990) will significantly affect the OPEC price, since the United States simply does not have enough effective monopsony power as a buyer of OPEC oil. But even if it did, subsidizing particular synthetic fuels is surely not the most cost-effective way of reducing imports.

It is thus hard to be impressed by arguments that private decision-makers use a discount rate that is "too high." Let us therefore turn to the other arguments about market imperfections.

Capturing the Benefits of Technological Information

Considerable technological information might of course be forthcoming from greater R&D efforts. But—it is argued—because this information is difficult to keep private, the benefits will not all accrue to private investors, and thus private firms will tend to underinvest in R&D. Alternatively, greater patent protection might solve this problem but would be undesirable because of the distortion caused by the resulting monopoly power.

While this argument is generally true for R&D activities that produce basic scientific and technical knowledge, it is not applicable to the commercialization of new energy technologies. Commercialization is not basic research. Most new energy technologies that are candidates for huge subsidies are well understood. While there may be some uncertainty about their ultimate cost, the uncertainty is no greater than what is involved in many other ventures commonly undertaken by private firms. Thus, while a good case can be made for government funding of basic energy research activities, the argument does not apply to government funding for the industrial development and commercialization of alternative energy technologies.

Regulatory Uncertainty

The technological and economic risks of new energy technologies are likely to be overshadowed by uncertainties about environmental regulations. Environmental (and other public policy) controversies surrounding the Clinch River Breeder Reactor and the Barnwell Reprocessing Plant are examples of the kinds of problems potential investors fear.

Uncertainties over the ability to meet current and future environmental standards are present in many industrial investments, but are probably greater for such energy technologies as shale oil and coal gasification. These technologies raise new and different environmental questions, and to the extent that environmental standards may not be promulgated until the plants are operational, there may indeed be significantly greater regulatory uncertainty.

The environmental problems fall into three main areas: air quality, land, and water. Plant emissions and fugitive dust can cause air quality problems. Second, both the plants and mines needed for these coal technologies and the disposal of the spent shale may seriously scar the landscape. Indeed the use of the land for these plants may permanently destroy vegetation and wildlife and, as with

Appalachian coal-based synfuels, render agricultural and forest lands unsuitable for their original use, even with reclamation. Reclamation and revegetation would be even more difficult in areas of low precipitation. Finally, the development of these technologies raises concern over the adequacy of water supplies and the pollution of existing sources, since synthetic fuels production requires large quantities of water. In some regions this would mean a shortage of water for other uses (for example, agriculture). Discharge of pollutants into surface streams and leaching into underground sources are dealt with at the planning stage by designing the plants for "zero-discharge," involving recycling of spent water for use at the plant site. But whether the discharge will be quite "zero" at full-scale operation remains to be seen.

It has been argued that understanding and solving the environmental problems presented by new energy technologies may require the technology to operate for some period of time. While this would provide the information needed to draw up regulations, the technology may not be developed without clearly defined regulations because of the associated uncertainties. To the extent that this dilemma exists, the construction and operation of first-of-a-kind facilities may have "public goods" characteristics that would justify some form of government intervention. On the other hand, regulatory reform, leading to the removal of unnecessary, even counterproductive, regulations and to a clarification of the kinds of environmental standards likely to be enforced in the future, seems a better way of dealing with this kind of market imperfection.

The Proper Role for Government

If the President's proposals are adopted, subsidized nonconventional energy supplies will soon be relied upon to help close the growing gap between the consumption and production of energy in the United States. This would indeed be unfortunate. Most of the gap comes from price controls on crude oil, natural gas, and electricity, and it would be much more effective and much less costly to eliminate the regulation that produces the gap than to subsidize expensive energy substitutes for low-priced but nonavailable energy. Eliminating price controls would enable us to begin using nonconventional energy supplies as they become economically viable.

Of the various forms of market imperfections that are put forth as reasons for government intervention, the most real and most serious is uncertainty over future regulation. We have noted the existing uncertainty about future environmental constraints and regulations, but of even greater concern to the potential producer of new energy technology is uncertainty over future government *price* regulation.

The commercialization of shale oil, for example, is a risky venture. Indeed, if private firms do undertake it, they will do so only because they see a profit potential large enough to warrant the considerable risk. The fear of private firms, however, is that while they will be permitted to lose almost any amount of money, they will not be permitted to make almost any amount of money. Firms considering shale oil projects rightly worry that, if the world price of conventional oil rises considerably over the next decade so that a shale oil facility turns out to be an economic success, the government will then regulate the price of the shale oil, thereby reducing the profits that can be earned.

Private firms usually have no problem with downside risk as long as there is a commensurate potential for profit on the upside. The problem with nonconventional energy supplies is that firms are unwilling to take downside risk when they perceive a probable government ceiling on upside potential. It is therefore not surprising that these firms are asking for various forms of government subsidies to limit their downside risk. Once again, government subsidies are a costly and unnecessary alternative to dealing with the problem directly. The removal of price controls—and the guarantee that controls will not be imposed on the prices of nonconventional energy supplies produced by the private sector in the future—would eliminate the one form of market imperfection that is indeed significant and serious.

Decontrol of the current and future prices of energy supplies is the most important part of a "first-best" energy policy. This, together with a revision of those environmental regulations that are unnecessary and unreasonable and a clarification of environmental standards and regulations that would apply in the future, would permit private firms to develop new energy technologies at a socially optimal rate. There would then be little or no need for the government to subsidize the commercialization of these technologies. While we would hope to see continued government support for basic energy research, subsidies for the production of nonconventional energy supplies are no more warranted than subsidies for the production of sugar, tobacco, or peanuts.

It has been argued that the deregulation of domestic energy prices is politically impossible, at least over the next several years. Would this make government subsidies for new energy technologies desirable? That is, if we cannot have the "first-best," what role should the government play in the commercialization of these technologies as part of a "second-best" policy?

In this case, the government should use its limited resources to reduce the cost (or the risk) of producing nonconventional energy supplies, but should avoid determining the specific technologies to be developed. An especially attractive way to do this would be for the government to provide price guarantees or purchase agreements for broad categories of non-conventional energy supplies, rather than subsidizing specific demonstration plants or technologies directly. For example, the federal government might announce that it is willing to buy a million barrels per day (or the equivalent) of liquid or gaseous fuels produced from coal or shale at some fixed price above the current market price. But it should not itself pick a particular process or demonstration plant or get involved in technological decisions or production activities. Instead, it should provide an incentive for the private sector to pursue the development of the most cost-effective technologies.

It is private industry, not the government, that is in the best position to determine which new technologies are most economical and most promising, and to manage the commercialization of those technologies. In addition, private industry is much better able than government bureaucracies to drop a particular project should it turn out that the technology is not as promising as it appeared. By choosing to subsidize a project in a particular congressional district and creating a government bureaucracy to manage the project, we inevitably create a set of political forces that makes termination of the project very difficult. Nor is there any reason to believe that the personnel in government agencies are in a particularly good position to evaluate the many proposals always put forward when government subsidies become available.

We should never repeat the mistake made in our breeder reactor program by giving the government a primary role in choosing among programs or managing any particular program. By using broad price and purchase guarantees we can avoid committing ourselves to a technology that appears less and less desirable as time goes on.

To the extent that the government does participate in commercialization, its role should be strictly limited to the most efficient subsidization of alternative energy supplies in general, rather than particular technologies and programs. But we must recognize that this "second-best" policy will still be far more costly to the American public than the "first-best" policy, which largely eliminates the need for government participation in the production of energy in the first place.

26 The cobweb theorem is important for at least two reasons.One is that by introducing a lagged supply response, the theorem is a simple form of a genuinely dynamic theory. The other is that the theorem demonstrates that the mechanism of demand and supply does not always result in equilibrium.

When the cobweb theorem applies to annual crops, the cycles of prices and production are two-year cycles; every other year, the price is above equilibrium. Dr. Harlow finds a four-year cycle for hogs in the 1950's, even though it does not take two years to produce a hog.

THE HOG CYCLE AND THE COBWEB THEOREM

ARTHUR A. HARLOW

Bonneville Power Administration

There has been increasing awareness of a fairly regular four-year cycle for hogs in recent years, although the existence of a hog cycle has been recognized for over three-quarters of a century. The hog cycle may be described in terms of price or production. Production may be measured at the initial or final stage, i.e., pig crop or slaughter. This article examines the interrelationships among these three manifestations of the hog cycle—price, pig crop, and slaughter—and attempts to determine the suitability of the cobweb theorem as a theoretical framework for an explanation of the cycle.

The use of annual data in charting hog cycles may tend to obscure some responses of farmers to changing conditions because there are usually two farrowings per year. The typical practice is to breed sows in the fall to farrow in the spring about four months later. A large proportion of these sows farrow again the following fall. Most analysts have found that farmers make their basic decision as to the number of sows to farrow on a yearly basis, with some adjustment of fall farrowings in response to changed conditions.

The price of hogs depends upon demand as well as supply, and the demand for pork is affected by consumer income and the prices and supplies of competing meats.

On the supply side, there are many factors besides price which have an effect on the size of the pig crop. The price and supply of feed and the relative profitability of alternative uses of farmers' labor and feed are important factors in determining the number of sows farrowing. The number of pigs

---

Taken and adapted from "The Hog Cycle and the Cobweb Theorem," by Arthur A. Harlow, *Journal of Farm Economics*, Vol. XLII, No. 4, November 1960, pp. 842, 845–849, 852, 853. Reprinted by permission.

saved is influenced by weather, genetics, and production practices in addition to the number of sows farrowing. The number slaughtered differs from the size of the pig crop because of the number of gilts saved for breeding purposes and the number of deaths that occur between the counting of the pig crop and slaughter. Also, the supply of pork is determined by the average slaughter weight as well as the number slaughtered.

In order to obtain a four-year cycle in a model of the cobweb theorem, it was necessary to assume one-year lags between price and pig crop, and between pig crop and slaughter. These lags are somewhat longer than those expected from the physiological processes involved in hog production. The gestation period is slightly less than four months, pigs are weaned in about two months, and an additional four to six months are usually required for feeding to market weights. Using these approximate six-month lags between breeding and weaning and between weaning and slaughter, the resultant cycle would be two years instead of four years in length.

There are two main reasons for the existence of yearly lags. The first is the previously cited evidence that, at least in the past, farmers have tended to plan hog production on an annual basis. Whether this practice will continue with the changing technology of hog production is open to question. In the last two years, the size of the fall pig crop has not varied with the spring crop as closely as it usually has in the past decade.

The second reason is the statistical limitation imposed by the use of annual data. Their use requires that measurements be made in terms of years although the actual figures may vary considerably from a precise twelve months. The use of a calendar year instead of a marketing year also introduces predilection toward annual lags. The price of hogs when sows are bred in the fall affects the number of sows farrowing the following spring and the following fall. The actual lag between the price which influences farmers to breed more sows and the increased pig crop resulting from this decision may be as short as six months for the spring crop. However, the price occurs in one calendar year and the pig crop in the next so the lag between them becomes one year with this imprecise measurement. The actual lag between pig crop and slaughter is also considerably less than a year. But since all the fall crop and part of the spring crop are slaughtered the following year, annual slaughter figures tend to lag the annual pig crop by a year.

The actual data are surprisingly close to the theoretical model, especially since 1950. There have been two complete four-year cycles in the past eight years, and the relationships among the variables were as predicted by the model. Price preceded pig crop by one year, and slaughter followed the pig crop by a year. Prices were high when slaughter was low and vice versa. All three series rose two years, fell two years, then rose again two years and fell two years, as would be expected from the theoretical model.

Prior to 1950 the cycle was not as evident, although the interrelationships were similar. Pig crop led slaughter by a year except during the 1930's when drought and depression obscured the relationship, and the inverse price-slaughter relation held except during some of the war years when price controls were in effect. Hog production was influenced much more by the supply of corn in the prewar than in the postwar period because smaller stocks were carried over from year to year. The price support program and favorable weather in the postwar years have contributed to the development of relatively stable corn prices and the accumulation of large stocks of feed grains. In the prewar period, however, fluctuations in the corn supply due primarily to the weather tended to create random disturbances in the cycle and prevented its regular appearance.

Other discrepancies between the model and the actual figures arise because of the limitations of the statistical data which in many cases are estimates based on sample surveys. But in view of the simplifying assumptions which were made in the formulation of the model, the actual data fit the basic pattern surprisingly well.

Applicability of the Cobweb Theorem

The cobweb theorem has been discussed at various times as an explanation for the hog cycle, both in England and the United States. The relationship between price and supply hypothesized by the cobweb theorem can arise only if the time lag between a change in price and the resulting supply response is sufficient to create a relatively fixed supply for a given period. According to the theorem, a large supply and low price in one period will be followed by a small supply with an accompanying high price in the next period, which, in turn, will be followed in the succeeding period by a large supply and a low price, and so on. Assuming there are no external influences, these fluctuations will either increase or decrease in amplitude, or continue at the same level indefinitely depending upon the slopes of the demand and supply curves.

The application of the theorem depends upon the fulfillment of three conditions. (1) Producers plan for output in the next period on the basis of present prices. (2) Once production plans are made, they are unalterable until the following time period. (3) Price is determined by the available supply, i.e., price is set by the intersection of the demand curve with a vertical supply curve.

The production of hogs probably approximates these conditions as well as any agricultural commodity. Available evidence indicates that the extension of current prices is of major importance in future production plans. Production is essentially fixed once sows are bred, at least on the upward side. Farmers can decrease production by marketing bred sows although there is a considerable discount after the second month of pregnancy. There is some variation in marketing weights in response to price and other factors, but supply is relatively fixed in any given year.

A Four-Year Cycle from the Cobweb THeorem

The length of the cycle produced by the cobweb theorem depends upon the time required for a change in price to affect supply. The expectation of a two-year cycle in hogs may be due to the use of the technical lag in hog production while ignoring some of the other lags involved. The time required to produce an average pig, from breeding to slaughter, is approximately twelve months. Using this lag, the cobweb produces a two-year cycle. The lag involved in the cobweb theorem, however, is the lag between price and its effect on market supply which is not necessarily the lag between breeding and slaughter.

The lag between price and marketings has been longer than the one year between breeding and slaughter because of the lag between price and farmers' response to it. This latter lag is not determinate *a priori* because it depends largely upon producers' expectations. If farmers expect a price to continue in the future, they will respond to it; but if the price is thought to be only temporary, it will initiate little or no response. There is also a period of variable intensity of the effect of price. In other words, price during one year may have some effect on production decisions during the next two or three years in addition to its more pronounced effect in the immediately succeeding year. The fastest possible reaction from price to marketing is the one year required to produce a pig. Thus the two-year lag indicates that there is some lag between price and production response in addition to the lag between breeding and slaughter.

Various types of cycles can be produced by the cobweb theorem by using different supply and demand curves, initial positions and lags. Supply and demand curves plus the initial positions determine the shape and amplitude of a cycle, while the lag between price and marketings determines the cycle length. The cobweb theorem thus has sufficient flexibility to serve as a theoretical basis for a variety of cycles.

Summary

A four-year cycle in hogs has appeared in the last decade and has continued with surprising regularity. The interrelationships among price, pig crop, and slaughter could account for a cycle of this length if there were initial disequilibrium and no outside interference. However, outside influences are ever present and their effect is constantly changing, although they do not usually occur in regular cyclical patterns. This statement is especially true for the hog industry where the major exogenous factors are the price and supply of feed which, in turn, are affected by the weather. In recent years, favorable weather and the price support program have produced abundant feed supplies with relatively stable prices. The appearance of the present regular cycle in hogs while outside influences are comparatively stable would seem to indicate an inherent cyclical character within the industry.

The length of time required for reproduction and growth results in an inevitable lag in the response of agricultural commodities to changes in the factors which influence their production. The cobweb theorem is a theoretical tool which has been used as an explanation for cycles resulting from such lags in response. Using appropriate lags, the application of this theorem results in a four-year cycle for hogs instead of the two-year cycle its application usually produces. The cycle thus produced is similar to the one which was found to arise because of the interrelationships among price, pig crop, and slaughter. The similarity of the cycles produced by the two methods occurs because the interrelationships are determined by the nature of the hog industry which also determines the lag required for the application of the cobweb theorem. The cobweb theorem furnishes a more precise theoretical explanation of the cycle because it includes the demand and supply functions for the industry, which determine the amplitude of the cycle, as well as the lag in production response, which determines the cycle length.

Whether the cycle continues its present regularity depends upon the effects of outside influences and the extent to which producers' responses change. As producers become better informed about probable future hog prices, they will adjust production more according to outlook information. Increased reaction to anticipated prices rather than past prices will tend to dampen and shorten the cycle.

27

Peak-period prices may increase the efficiency of use of airports, and reduce apparent shortages.

USER CHARGES AND INCENTIVES FOR AIRPORT USE

SENATE COMMITTEE ON GOVERNMENTAL AFFAIRS

. . . Charges for the use of public facilities can lower use below what it otherwise would be, and can help allocate such facilities to the higher value uses. By doing so, charges can reduce emissions, pollution or other undesirable social effects and lower the cost of achieving social goals. The environment is one such "public facility" subject to "use and overuse" by polluters. The capacity of other public facilities, such as airports and highways, can also be overused. During rush hours the addition of extra vehicles to the road will increase delays for other traffic. In choosing whether to use a road during the peak hours, a driver will, in a sense, consider his personal benefits and costs, but will probably ignore the delaying effect on other vehicles.[1] Yet even small delays imposed on a sufficient number of other vehicles can cause substantial external cost and excessive highway congestion.

1. Charges to Cover Facility Cost Versus Incentives for Efficiency

A primary objective of user charges is to help defray the cost of construction and maintenance of public facilities. Charges may be based on frequency of use, or a flat fee may be set for access without regard to use. In general, the law allows fees to be charged provided that they are not excessive relative to actual costs. That reduces the effectiveness of charges in internalizing external effects. Certainly flat fees cannot effectively take account of those external costs which vary with use. It is equally true that basing user charges on the cost of facility construction necessarily excludes consideration of either the social values of the facilities or consequential external damages. Actual user charges would be either

[1] Suppose that the addition of an extra vehicle to the highway imposes one second delays on 10,000 other vehicles. The total delay imposed is 10,000 vehicle seconds. If the average vehicle has 1.5 riders then the delay would be 15,000 person seconds. At a $4.00 per hour value of time this would be worth about $16.33. Since driving on congested roads is aggravating the perceived value to drivers may be higher. The crowding will make accidents more likely and the resulting delay will increase fuel consumption and vehicle wear and tear. The total external cost of rush hour highway use may be much higher than the direct time costs imposed on driver and passengers.

Excerpted from U.S. Senate Committee on Governmental Affairs, "Study on Federal Regulation," Vol. VI, *Framework for Regulation,* December 1978. pp. 179–186.

higher or lower than the total cost including any incremental social damage caused by an activity. Thus, for facilities such as airports and highways, which are subject to heavy peak-load demands, flat user charges cannot correctly take account of the full social costs of use. These costs will vary according to the time and circumstance of the use. To efficiently ration facility use, charges must recognize at least some of these differences.

In some cases legal obstacles may prevent the use of charges to internalize external effects. For example, by Federal statute, airports must set user charges "which will make the airport as self-sustaining as possible," in order to qualify for Department of Transportation approval of airport development projects. Federal laws also prohibit EPA approval of sewage treatment construction grants unless the municipality has adopted or agrees to adopt user charges which require each receiver of service to pay a proportional share of the costs of operation and maintenance, including replacement. These costs may not be related to pollution damage.

2. Incentives for Efficient Use of Airports; User Charges, Subsidies, Regulation, and Alternatives

A system of charges for airport use, based on the actual costs of building and operating that facility, can lead to gross inefficiencies as well as apparent inequity. A plane landing at a busy time can inflict substantial costs on others by delaying their arrival. User charges based on airport costs do not reflect these very real external social costs. Certainly there is no incentive for operators of small planes to avoid peak hours, even when their use can significantly delay the arrival of commercial flights carrying hundreds of passengers. Such fees also do not encourage small planes to utilize less densely used but perhaps more distant airports. Instead the fee structure prompts use, and thus increases delay costs on travelers and the risk of accidents, by adding to congestion and complicating the tasks of air traffic controllers. In short, the flying situation is far more risky than it need be. Because such charges are an incentive for use, the resulting congestion heightens the perceived "need" for airports, thereby raising Federal subsidy costs and escalating potential environmental damages from increased airport construction.

3. The Effects of Improper Airport Pricing: Congestion Costs, Increased Subsidy Burden, and Exaggerated "Needs" for Costly Airport Capacity

The costs of incorrect pricing can be very large. For example, a RAND Corporation study found that the full costs, including delays imposed on other travelers, of an arrival during Kennedy airport's peak hour of 4 to 5 p.m. were over $2,000 for each air carrier commercial airline arrival and $1,800 per general aviation arrival. For La Guardia airport, the respective costs were approximately $960 and $520.[2] An analysis of delays at Washington National Airport in 1967 estimated that the increased delay imposed on others by an extra carrier operation was 14.3 minutes imposed on carriers and 7.3 minutes on general aviation. While the average air carrier landing fee was $10, at peak time the incremental delay costs were up to $139. When the airport was operating close to capacity, increasing general aviation movements by one per hour was estimated to reduce air carrier movements by 0.8 per hour, yet the landing fees paid by the smaller planes were less than 1/5th of the fees paid by larger aircraft. Landing fees, typically uniform over the day, are much below the real social costs of airport use at peak hours. In 1971 the landing charges per thousand pounds of gross aircraft weight (for air carriers) were $.73 at Chicago's O'Hare, $.09 at Kansas City, $.29 at Los Angeles, $.59 at Seattle, $.30 at JFK International and $1.03 at La Guardia.[3] For a 707 jet the landing fees were $75 at JFK and $258 at La Guardia.[4] While these airport fees may approximate social costs at normal times, they are much too low at the peak hours which travelers prefer.

Fees are also very low relative to the total flight cost, thus airlines are not encouraged to shift flights away from peak hours. In 1972 the out-of-pocket cost of flying a 707 jet from Los Angeles to New York was about $5,500, while the JFK landing fee was $75, or about 1.3 percent of the total.[5] By contrast, the social cost (including delays imposed on others) of a peak period air carrier landing at JFK was over 36 percent of total cost. Thus, the social costs of peak-time landings are sufficiently great to have a significant effect on scheduling were they reflected in landing fees. Also if those costs were reflected in fares, traffic would shift, as travelers selected less expensive departure times. As it is now, that is usually not a consideration in determining travel plans.

General aviation flights very significantly increase congestion problems by contributing substantial amounts of traffic. Such traffic amounted to 30 percent of all operations at La Guardia in 1968. Outside of New York, general aviation fees are very low (rarely over $15) and many airports levy no charge at all. A good portion of these flights could be shifted to other times or other airports without major costs.[6]

Failure to charge delay or congestion-related landing fees is not only inefficient, but are also questionable as a matter of equity: travelers on commercial flights and the general taxpayer must subsidize the general aviation flyer. Furthermore, general aviation flyers often gain only slightly from using congested public airports, rather than sometimes less conveniently located private facilities.

[2] A. Carlin and R. E. Park, "The Efficient Use of Airport Runway Capacity is a Time of Scarcity," Santa Monica, California: The RAND Corporation, Memorandum RM-5817-PA, 1969, exp. pp. 3–12.

[3] Peak-hour operations of O'Hare, Kennedy International, Washington National and La Guardia airports are affected by quotas administered by FAA's Airport Reservation Office, so use of the facilities is not on a simple "first-come, first-served" basis.

[4] Eckert, "Airports and Congestion." op. cit. (sic), p. 21.

[5] Ibid., p. 21.

[6] Ibid., p. 21, pp. 30–31. Some general aviation flights, including some trips of company executives, are undoubtedly of very high commercial value. Those involved would be willing to pay substantial amounts rather than be delayed or travel to a less well-situated airport.

Ross Eckert, an aviation expert at the University of Southern California, makes the essential point well:

> ". . . a cab from Palwaukee [a private airport outside of the city] to the northwest part of Chicago costs $7.50 more than a cab from O'Hare. If the time in the O'Hare stack is no greater than the extra time traveling from Palwaukee, the private flyer frequently lands at O'Hare and pays the $2.50 fee (single engine plane) rather than going to Palwaukee (where he can land free if he buys gas). Thus he imposes congestion costs on carrier flights of as much as $1,000 in order to save taxi fare. In addition, to relieve congestion at peak hours, extra capacity has been provided at O'Hare whose cost is well over $100 per flight removed. These are large prices to pay to save the private flyer or air taxi passenger $5.00 and a few moments time.[7]

Therefore, allowing such "equal access" at present landing fees causes a substantial transfer from air carriers and their passengers to general aviation flyers. It is also clear that low landing fees for general aviation flights decrease the demand for construction of privately owned airports, which could relieve congestion at public facilities.

In addition, Federal subsidy for airport construction lowers the amount which must be recovered in landing fees, and so exacerbates both overall congestion and the misallocation of general aviation flights to congested public airports. Even if a public airport has substantial "excess" capacity, so that congestion is not a significant problem, the excessively high demand for service by general aviation will inflate the observed "need" for public airport capacity. These "needs" are then treated as amounts of capacity which public subsidy should be designed to assure. But such "needs" should not be met at *any* cost. The cost to society of small decreases in air travel, or in shifting some air travelers to slightly less preferred times are not always significant; also substantial evidence demonstrates that travelers are sensitive to fares. Shifting passengers from peak hours would mean more airport capacity, lower resource costs to society, decreased subsidy burden on the general taxpayer, less environmental damage from airport construction, greater safety, and diminished noise at peak travel hours.

Several alternatives could alleviate congestion problems. An obvious alternative is greater airport capacity, a course that has been encouraged and funded by the Federal Aviation Administration. But that is very expensive, and can cause substantial noise and pollution problems. In 1969 offshore airports at a cost of over $6 billion each were proposed to lessen noise and pollution problems in New York and Los Angeles. One problem is that capacity "needs", which are a major justification for that expense, have been based on FAA standards as to acceptable delays at peak periods. This means that airport capacity is in part adjusted according to the demands of peak period travelers alone. The costs of the extra capacity, necessary only at peak times, are sustained by Federal and

[7] Ibid., pp. 24–25. Some of the general aviation flyers may place very high values on the convenience of using O'Hare. They will include some busy corporate executives, others on tight time schedules, some individuals to whom surface travel is particularly unpleasant or expensive, and flyers who enjoy using a large busy airport, or in the limit, actually enjoy waiting in the stack.

local governments as well as non-peak users who do not substantially benefit from that extra capacity. Further, the delay standard is not based on a comparison of the costs of congestion and the investment and other costs of increased capacity. As with pollution standards, and standards for flood protection, it is important to consider potential damages relative to control costs when setting standards.

4. Non-Price Methods for Dealing With Airport Congestion

An obvious way to handle airport congestion is to construct larger airport facilities. Several other alternatives have been considered. The FAA sets quotas on hourly operations at four high-density airports, including Kennedy, La Guardia, O'Hare and Washington National. A major purpose of the quotas—which involve separate classifications for air carrier, air taxis, and general aviation—is to restrict general aviation operations. Actual landing slots are allocated by bargaining among airlines in "scheduling conferences." However, although general aviation and air taxi flights may use vacant air carrier slots, the reverse is not true. This might be justified by an "equity" motivation to reserve at least some peak capacity for these users. All the same, the previously discussed evidence indicates that this use may be inefficient.

Direct regulation of airport use is still another option. The FAA controls Washington National and Dulles International Airports and has tried to shift flights in order to lessen congestion at the former and promote use of the latter. Flights of more than 650 miles from Washington are required to use Dulles. The policy has not been wholly successful. Because of National's more convenient location, airlines have scheduled flights from National to the West Coast with intermediate stops in order to meet the regulations. The problem is that the policy did not directly address the problem: excessive demand for scarce capacity at National.

In the past, Civil Aeronautics Board policies have aggravated problems of airport congestion. Fixed fares and entry prohibitions induced carriers to compete by offering additional flights, particularly at the more popular peak hours. The CAB, which has no statutory authority to restrict scheduling, has on occasion approved carrier agreements to reduce capacity. Such CAB sanctioned agreements are exempt from the anti-trust laws. Capacity agreements could lower peak-hour demands for airport capacity and moderate both congestion and the "need" for extra airport capacity. In order to achieve this potential the agreements would have to include all carriers. Otherwise, congestion might not be reduced and those outside the agreement might have strong incentives to offer additional flights at peak hours. However the CAB lacks authority to compel participation in such agreements. Moreover, capacity agreements are blunt instruments for dealing with congestion and excessive demands for airport capacity: they do not directly focus on the primary problem of excess demand at certain peak hours, and further may entail risks of substantial anticompetitive effects.

The CAB has also considered requiring that new route certificates stipulate the use of satellite airports rather than more congested central airports. Some new certificates did embody such restrictions, but at present the policy, though "active," is not effective. Carriers have not been enthusiastic about routes with such restrictions, in part because CAB fare policies have in the past prevented discounts on flights to less desirable airports. This may change as several carriers have proposed that they provide discount service out of Chicago's Midway Airport and discount fares are now encouraged by the CAB. All the same, such shifts would have a slow effect on congestion, since the policy has no direct effect on flights now certificated to serve congested airports.[8]

5. Price of Economic Incentive Methods for Dealing With Airport Congestion

Pricing mechanisms are an alternative to directly rationing use of facilities and do provide guidance on the areas where expansion is needed. Higher landing fees, based on estimated congestion costs, could be imposed at peak hours. Imposing even moderate fees would significantly reduce congestion by decreasing low value general aviation operations. For example, following the 1968 increase from $5 to $25 of the minimum small plane landing fee at New York airports, general aviation decreased by 40% during peak hours.[9] As previously noted, estimates of the full delay costs of operations at some large, congested airports far exceed the sum of $25. Yet imposing fees equal to full costs might not be politically acceptable. But, as the New York example suggests, making peak flights bear even a portion of the costs could have a substantial effect. Whatever pricing scheme is adopted vary by time of day, day of the week, and season.

For efficiency, fees should be designed to ration capacity and reduce congestion, not simply to cover airport costs. Setting fees at exactly efficient levels is impossible, thus—instead of trying for ideal results—fees might be set on a provisional basis and adjusted until delays reached levels considered safe and manageable. Congestion fees should be basically the same for all categories of flights at any given time. Thus, all users would have to bear at least part of the costs; with the result that of their actions, lower valued flights would shift to off-peak hours, and scheduling competition at peak periods would be moderated.

Rational allocation could also be achieved by using saleable or exchangeable landing rights. Airport authorities or regulatory agencies could determine allowable rates of operation at various peak congestion times. Once set, those operation levels could apply for some period of time. The rights could be sold by government to the highest bidder. To be sure, giving away the rights could lessen carrier resistance to raising the cost of operations. But, that may be objectionable as the users, and not the public, would capture the value of scarce airport resources. Selling the rights at auction would incidentally provide useful information about the value of operations at various times, the need for addi-

[8] Ross Eckert, "Airports and Congestion," op. cit. p. 38.
[9] Ibid.

tional airport capacity, and on the appropriateness of the landing allocations.

The rights approach has desirable flexibility: a carrier wanting to enter or expand service can "buy in," and face the same costs as any other firm. Rights would thus be allocated to their highest value uses. Of course, rights—just as airport capacity—should be subject to revision as demand for travel significantly changes.

Under either incentive approach, whether user charges or sale of rights, fares would come to vary over time, particularly with more flexible CAB pricing regulation. Fares would reflect the scarcity value of airport resources, and some passengers would be encouraged to shift travel plans to less congested times. Even if fares did not vary substantially, rational landing fees would discourage excessive scheduling competition at peak hours and encourage carriers to spread flights over the day. On the other hand, merely requiring or allowing air carriers to vary fares with airport congestion would not be an efficient solution, for it would provide no incentive for general avaiation flyers to shift away from the peak hours or overused facilities.

Administrative problems include setting and collecting fees for various periods. In addition, lease agreements between airlines and airports often set formulas for landing charges. Rational fees could raise total payments. Airport revenues might rise significantly. Revenues could be used to expand capacity, to build satellite airports, to improve air traffic control, or to compensate those damaged by airport construction or operation.

General aviation flyers will certainly be affected by higher fees. For some time, these users have enjoyed substantial subsidy at the expense of air carriers, their passengers and the general taxpayer. During the early 1970's the total subsidy to general aviation was estimated at well over $600 million annually, including more than $35 million annual congestion costs imposed on others. According to a leading authority ". . . it will commonly be the case that the *public at large contributes more toward the total cost of safely operating a light aircraft than the owner does himself.*"[10]

One partial solution would be to continue to arbitrarily allow some general aviation use at low fees or to assign some slots to general aviation as is now done under FAA quotas at a few congested airports.

In summary, in order for user charges to avert undue social costs, correctly guide resource allocation and serve equity, they must be designed to impose costs in relationship to all of the consequences of that use. Fees based on average construction or operating costs may have little or no relation to real social costs. And, as in the case of airports, they may provide perverse incentives, particularly when combined with subsidies. . . .

[10] Jeremy J. Warford, "Subsidies to General Aviation, in the Economics of Federal Subsidy Programs," op. cit. (sic), p. 853. The total estimated subsidy consisted of $445 million in Federal airways system costs. $30 million in Federal subsidies for airport development, $130 million in state and local subsidies to general aviation airports and $35 million in congestion costs, for a total of $640 million annually. (Ibid.). The congestion cost figure assumes no change in annual cost from an estimate for 1968. Though commercial flyers benefit from lessened congestion due to subsidies to special general aviation airports, it is clear that the balance of subsidy lies with general aviation. Emphasis in original.

Part Five

In one form or another, monopoly has long been a normal feature of economic life. The federal government operates several monopolies; they include the postal service, the production of fissionable materials for nuclear energy, the production of electric energy in several regions of the country, and of course the possession of ultimate physical coercion. Then in this country there are the regulated private monopolies in transportation and in the other public utilities. Under the copyright and patent laws, the federal government confers temporary monoplies on authors and inventors. The contemporary "problem" of monopoly has to do with unregulated private business monopolies. The monopoly powers that might reside in some labor unions and farmers' cooperatives are somehow widely regarded as less important.

Monopolies have long been present and considered evil. Legislation and other public measures against private monopolies can be traced far back. Many sticks have been wielded in ceaseless attacks on monopoly. Thus, monopoly is said to permit undue and irresponsible private power, to result in the denial of access and opportunity, to cause sluggishness in adopting new methods of production, and to bring about a misallocation of resources. This last criticism is the special contribution

Monopoly and Market Power

of economic theory to the attack on monopoly.

The chorus of economic criticism does not, however, contain full harmony. A few voices praise monopoly when it takes the form of the progressive big business that gathers together the best talent for production and research. Schumpeter's views on the creative powers of big business are well known. Some economists think that if basic research by business enterprises is to continue, the existence of large firms with monopoly positions in several markets must be accepted. It follows that a stronger antitrust policy might weaken the foundations of much of industry's research and development.

The word "monopoly" could be reserved for the situation where a firm is the sole seller in a market and has zero cross-elasticity of demand between its product and any other product in the economy. Few firms meet such definition. However, many firms face downward sloping demand curves for their products and so have a degree of market power. Firms with market power share some of the characteristics of strict monopolies. The question is how much market or monopoly power do firms have and what are its effects.

28 Parking is basically a competitive business until local government restricts entry.

THE PARABLE OF THE PARKING LOTS

HENRY G. MANNE
University of Rochester

In a city not far away there was a large football stadium. It was used from time to time for various events, but the principal use was for football games played Saturday afternoons by the local college team. The games were tremendously popular and people drove hundreds of miles to watch them. Parking was done in the usual way. People who arrived early were able to park free on the streets, and latecomers had to pay to park in regular and improvised lots.

There were, at distances ranging from 5 to 12 blocks from the stadium approximately 25 commercial parking lots all of which received some business for Saturday afternoon football games. The lots closer to the stadium naturally received more football business than those further away, and some of the very close lots actually raised their price on Saturday afternoons. But they did not raise the price much, and most did not change prices at all. The reason was not hard to find.

For something else happened on football afternoons. A lot of people who during the week were students, lawyers, school teachers, plumbers, factory workers, and even stock brokers went into the parking lot business. It was not a difficult thing to do. Typically a young boy would put up a crude, homemade sign saying "Parking $3." He would direct a couple of cars into his parents' driveway, tell the driver to take the key, and collect the three dollars. If the driveway was larger or there was yard space to park in, an older brother, an uncle, or the head of the household would direct the operation, sometimes asking drivers to leave their keys so that shifts could be made if necessary.

Some part-time parking operators who lived very close to the stadium charged as much as $5.00 to park in their driveways. But as the residences-turned-parking-lots were located further from the stadium (and incidentally closer to the commercial parking lots), the price charged at game time declined. In fact houses at some distance from the stadium charged less than the adjacent commercial lots. The whole system seemed to work fairly smoothly, and though traffic just after a big game was terrible, there were no significant delays parking cars or retrieving parked cars.

Reprinted with permission of the author from *The Public Interest,* No. 23 (Spring 1971), pp. 10–15.

But one day the owner of a chain of parking lots called a meeting of all the commercial parking lot owners in the general vicinity of the stadium. They formed an organization known as the Association of Professional Parking Lot Employers, or APPLE. And they were very concerned about the Saturday parking business. One man who owned four parking lots pointed out that honest parking lot owners had heavy capital investments in their businesses, that they paid taxes, and that they employed individuals who supported families. There was no reason, he alleged, why these lots should not handle all the cars coming into the area for special events like football games. "It is unethical," he said, "to engage in cutthroat competition with irresponsible fender benders. After all, parking cars is a profession, not a business." This last remark drew loud applause.

Thus emboldened he continued, stating that commercial parking lot owners recognize their responsibility to serve the public's needs. Ethical car parkers he said understand their obligations not to dent fenders, to employ only trustworthy car parkers, to pay decent wages, and generally to care for their customers' automobiles as they would the corpus of a trust. His statement was hailed by others attending the meeting as being very statesmanlike.

Others at the meeting related various tales of horror about non-professional car parkers. One homeowner, it was said, actually allowed his fifteen-year-old son to move other peoples' cars around. Another said that he had seen an $8,000 Cadillac parked on a dirt lawn where it would have become mired in mud had it rained that day. Still another pointed out that a great deal of the problem came on the side of the stadium with the lower-priced houses, where there were more driveways per block than on the wealthier side of the stadium. He pointed out that these poor people would rarely be able to afford to pay for damage to other peoples' automobiles or to pay insurance premiums to cover such losses. He felt that a professional group such as APPLE had a duty to protect the public from their folly in using those parking spaces.

Finally another speaker reminded the audience that these "marginal, fly-by-night" parking lot operators generally parked a string of cars in their driveways so that a driver had to wait until all cars behind his had been removed before he could get his out. This, he pointed out, was quite unlike the situation in commercial lots where, during a normal business day, people had to be assured of ready access to their automobiles at any time. The commercial parking lots either had to hire more attendants to shift cars around, or they had to park them so that any car was always accessible, even though this meant that fewer cars could park than the total space would actually hold. "Clearly," he said, "driveway parking constitutes unfair competition."

Emotions ran high at this meeting, and every member of APPLE pledged $1 per parking space for something mysteriously called a "slush fund." It was never made clear exactly whose slush would be bought with these funds, but several months later a resolution was adopted by the city council requiring licensing for anyone in the parking lot business.

The preamble to the new ordinance read like the speeches at the earlier meeting. It said that this measure was designed to protect the public against unscrupulous, unprofessional and under-capitalized parking lot operators. It required, *inter alia,* that anyone parking cars for a fee must have minimum capital devoted to the parking lot business of $25,000, liability insurance in an amount not less than $500,000, bonding for each car parker, and a special driving test for these parkers (which incidentally would be designed and administered by APPLE). The ordinance also required, again in the public's interest, that every lot charge a single posted price for parking and that any change in the posted price be approved in advance by the city council. Incidentally, most members were able to raise their fees by about 20 per cent before the first posting.

Then a funny thing happened to drivers on their way to the stadium for the next big game. They discovered city police in unusually large numbers informing them that it was illegal to pay a non-licensed parking lot operator for the right to park a car. These policemen also reminded parents that if their children were found in violation of this ordinance it could result in a misdemeanor charge being brought against the parents and possible juvenile court proceedings for the children. There were no driveway parking lots that day.

Back at the commercial parking lots, another funny thing occurred. Proceeding from the entrance of each of these parking lots within twelve blocks of the stadium were long lines of cars waiting to park. The line got larger as the lot was closer to the stadium. Many drivers had to wait so long or walk so far that they missed the entire first quarter of the big game.

At the end of the game it was even worse. The confusion was massive. The lot attendants could not cope with the jam up, and some cars were actually not retrieved until the next day. It was even rumored about town that some automobiles had been lost forever and that considerable liabilities might result for some operators. Industry spokesmen denied this, however.

Naturally there was a lot of grumbling, but there was no agreement on what had caused the difficulty. At first everyone said there were merely some "bugs" in the new system that would have to be ironed out. But the only "bug" ironed out was a Volkswagen which was flattened by a careless attendant in a Cadillac Eldorado.

The situation did not improve at subsequent games. The members of APPLE did not hire additional employees to park cars, and operators near the stadium were not careful to follow their previous practice of parking cars in such a way as to have them immediately accessible. Employees seemed to become more surly, and the number of dented-fender claims mounted rapidly.

Little by little, too, cars began appearing in residential driveways again. For instance, one enterprising youth regularly went into the car wash business on football afternoons, promising that his wash job would take at least two hours. He charged five dollars, and got it—even on rainy days—in fact, especially on rainy days. Another homeowner offered to take cars on consignment for three hours to sell them at prices fixed by the owner. He charged $4.00 for this "service" but his subterfuge was quickly squelched by the authorities. The parking situation remained "critical."

Political pressures on the city council began to mount to "do something" about the inordinate delays in parking and retrieving cars on football afternoons. The city council sent a stern note of warning to APPLE, and APPLE appointed a special study group recruited from the local university's computer science department to look into the matter. This group reported that the managerial and administrative machinery in the parking lot business was archaic. What was needed, the study group said, was less goose quills and stand-up desks and more computers and conveyor belts. It was also suggested that all members of APPLE be hooked into one computer so that cars could really be shifted to the most accessible spaces.

Spokesmen for the industry took up the cry of administrative modernization. Subtle warnings appeared in the local papers suggesting that if the industry did not get its own house in order, heavy-handed regulation could be anticipated. The city council asked for reports on failures to deliver cars and decreed that this would include any failure to put a driver in his car within five minutes of demand without a new dent.

Some of the professional operators actually installed computer equipment to handle their ticketing and parking logistics problems. And some added second stories to their parking lots. Others bought up additional space, thereby raising the value of vacant lots in the area. But many simply added a few additional car parkers and hoped that the problem would go away without a substantial investment of capital.

The commercial operators also began arguing that they needed higher parking fees because of their higher operating costs. Everyone agreed that costs for operating a parking lot were certainly higher than before the licensing ordinance. So the city council granted a request for an across-the-board ten per cent hike in fees. The local newspaper editorially hoped that this would ease the problem without still higher fees being necessary. In a way, it did. A lot of people stopped driving. They began using city buses, or they chartered private buses for the game. Some stayed home and watched the game on TV. A new study group on fees was appointed.

Just about then several other blows fell on the parking lot business. Bus transportation to the area near the stadium was improved with a federal subsidy to the municipal bus company. And several new suburban shopping centers caused a loss of automobile traffic in the older areas of town. But most dramatic of all, the local university, under severe pressure from its students and faculty, dropped intercollegiate football altogether and converted the stadium into a park for underprivileged children.

The impact of these events on the commercial parking lots was swift. Income declined drastically. The companies that had borrowed money to finance the expansion everyone wanted earlier were hardest hit. Two declared bankruptcy, and many had to be absorbed by financially stronger companies. Layoffs among car parkers were enormous, and APPLE actually petitioned the city council to guarantee the premiums on their liability insurance policies so that people would not be afraid to park commercially. This idea was suggested to APPLE by recent Congressional legislation creating an insurance program for stock brokers.

A spokesman for APPLE made the following public statement: "New organizations or arrangements may be necessary to straighten out this problem. There has been a failure in both the structure of the industry and the regulatory scheme. New and better regulation is clearly demanded. A sound parking lot business is necessary for a healthy urban economy." The statement was hailed by the industry as being very statesmanlike, though everyone speculated about what he really meant.

Others in the industry demanded that the city bus service be curtailed during the emergency. The city council granted every rate increase the lots requested. There were no requests for rate decreases, but the weaker lots began offering prizes and other subtle or covert rebates to private bus companies who would park with them. In fact, this problem became so serious and uncontrollable that one owner of a large chain proclaimed that old-fashioned price competition for this business would be desirable. This again was hailed as statesmanlike, but everyone assumed that he really meant something else. No one proposed repeal of the licensing ordinance.

One other thing happened. Under pressure from APPLE, the city council decreed that henceforth no parking would be allowed on any streets in the downtown area of town. The local merchants were extremely unhappy with this, however, and the council rescinded the ordinance at the next meeting, citing a computer error as the basis for the earlier restriction.

The ultimate resolution of the "new" parking problem is not in sight. The parking lot industry in this town not very far from here is now said to be a depressed business, even a sick one. Everyone looks to the city council for a solution, but things will probably limp along as they are for quite a while, picking up with an occasional professional football game and dropping low with bad weather.

MORAL: If you risk your lot under an apple tree, you may get hit in the head.

29 Theory says that monopoly prices are higher than competitive prices. But just how much higher? Theory has the answer to this, too, because the ratio of the equilibrium monopoly price to the equilibrium competitive price is $E/(E - 1)$, where E is the coefficient of price elasticity. This follows from the equality of marginal cost and marginal revenue in equilibrium, and from the relations among price, marginal revenue, and elasticity. However, not enough is quantitatively known about elasticities of demand facing firms to make it possible to compare monopolistic and competitive prices in this way.

In this selection, Kwoka explores the relationship between the price-cost margin or percentage markup and the concentration of sales among a few firms in the industry. After controlling for other factors that affect margins, Kwoka finds that higher market shares for the first and second largest firms are associated with higher margins. A larger third ranked firm, given the share of the first two however, is associated with lower margins for all the firms in the industry. If the largest firm has 26 or more percent of the market and the second firm has 15 or more percent while the other firms are all small, then the margins are 8 or 9 percent higher than if all the firms have small market shares.

THE EFFECT OF MARKET SHARE DISTRIBUTION ON INDUSTRY PERFORMANCE

JOHN E. KWOKA, JR.
Federal Trade Commission

I.

A central proposition of industrial organization is that the size distribution of sellers is an important determinant of an industry's profitability. Numerous studies have explored—and generally confirmed—such a relationship, but virtually all have been subject to a serious and binding constraint. The lack of individual market share data has forced use of the simple sum of the four (or eight) largest shares, i.e., the concentration ratio, as the variable representing firm size distribution. Nothing in theory, however, predicts that exactly four firms are crucial to industry performance, and nothing implies that they are equally important, as is implicit in their simple summation. . . .

Excerpted from John E. Kwoka, Jr., "The Effect of Market Share Distribution on Industry Performance," *Review of Economics and Statistics*, 61 (February 1979), pp. 101–109.

The views expressed in this paper are solely the author's and are not intended to reflect FTC opinions. Helpful comments from D. Gaskins, M. Lynch, J. Siegfried, and anonymous referees of the *Review of Economics and Statistics* are gratefully acknowledged.

II.

In this section we review the basic economic model and perform some preliminary regressions as the background for the more detailed analysis to follow. The methodology employed here draws on the rather substantial recent literature on price-cost margins (e.g., Collins and Preston, 1968, 1969; Rhoades and Cleaver, 1973; Weiss, 1974). As a measure of competitive performance, the price-cost margin has both sound theoretical roots and the considerable practical advantages of availability and reliability. Industry margins (*PCM*) are readily calculated from the 1972 *Census of Manufactures* (U.S. Bureau of the Census, 1975) as value-added minus payroll, divided by value of shipments. *PCM* is, therefore, a percentage margin of revenue over direct cost, and is regressed on a number of corrective and causal variables. Foremost among the latter, of course, are alternative features of the size distribution of firms in the industry (e.g., concentration, shares). A brief description of the other variables and their theoretical rationale follows.

(1) Since the margin calculation subtracts only direct costs, inter-industry differences in capital intensity, and hence in implicit capital costs, must be allowed for. A capital-output ratio (*KO*) is therefore included as an independent variable.[1]

(2) Similarly, a correction must be made to reflect the discrepancy between the national data compiled in the Census and the geographical extent of true economic markets. Considerable success has been achieved by using Collins and Preston's geographical dispersion index (*DISP*), defined in such a manner that its expected sign is negative.[2]

(3) Theory predicts that higher margins result from recent unanticipated growth in the industry. *GROW* is defined as the percentage change in industry shipments between 1967 and 1972.

(4) Price-cost margins fail to subtract advertising expenditures as costs due to Census definitions. The best currently available correction is a dummy variable *CDUM* equal to one for consumer goods industries and zero for producer goods industries.[3]

(5) Finally, the magnitude of scale economies in an industry creates barriers to entry which may permit existing large sellers to achieve above-competitive margins. In order to distinguish this from the behavioral effects of large market shares (i.e., collusion or cooperation), we explore alternative scale proxies. . . . *MID* is calculated as the share of an industry's mid-point plant size, a

[1] *KO* is calculated as the gross book value of fixed assets divided by value of shipments. All data are from the 1972 *Census of Manufacturers* (U.S. Bureau of the Census, 1975).

[2] *DISP* is the sum of absolute values of the differences between the percentages of all manufacturing value-added and a particular industry's value-added for all four Census regions of the country. Data are from the 1972 *Census of Manufactures*. See Collins and Preston (1969).

[3] Data are an update by the author of *Industry Classification and Concentration* (FTC, 1967), which was partly based on industry advertising/sales ratios. More detailed advertising data will appear in the 1972 input-output matrix.

variable generally correlated with minimum efficient scale.[4] *MCDR* is the interaction of *MID* with a "cost disadvantage ratio," the latter measuring the additional cost of entry at suboptimal scale. The interaction reflects the fact that, with modest cost disadvantages, suboptimal entry may be rational and entry barriers (and margins) lower than those implied by the minimum size variable alone.[5] . . .

III.

The market share data permit us to lift the veil of the concentration ratio and to establish the exact number, relative importance, and necessary size of the largest firms in determining industry performance. The procedure employed is to add successively each of the ten largest market shares, denoted $S1, \ldots, S10$, to the price-cost margin regression to see if significant additional explanatory power is achieved. In addition, a variety of non-linear terms and specifications are explored in an effort to determine whether one share's impact is dependent on the magnitude of others. Collinearity among such variables is often high and in some cases will temper our conclusions.

[The regression results of this process are reported in Table 1, which has been abridged for this anthology. The coefficients of the control variables have the expected signs: price-cost margins are higher in industries with higher capital-output ratios where there has been more recent growth, in consumer industries, and where there are larger scale economies. Margins are lower in industries that are more geographically dispersed.

The main concern here, however, is with the role of the market share of the largest firms. The regression reported indicates that the shares of the largest two firms are very strongly associated with larger margins. These results confirm the

[4] *MID* is based on the size of plant producing the fiftieth percentile of output in each industry, as estimated from the employment size classes in the *Census of Manufactures*. This computational procedure produces a high correlation with market shares and concentration and requires cautious interpretation of some later results. See Weiss (1963) and Weiss (1974, p. 224–227); for other evidence, see Scherer, et al. (1975, ch. 3).

[5] The "cost disadvantage ratio" is calculated as the value-added per worker in the smallest establishments producing 50% of industry output, divided by the value-added per worker in the largest plants accounting for the remaining 50%. For this variable *CDR* to measure the underlying cost difference, the top and bottom halves of the plant size array must not differ in product mix, technology, capital-labor ratios, labor quality, wage rates, advertising intensity, and R&D activities. (See Caves et al., 1975, p. 133). That these assumptions do not hold is confirmed by a number of cases in which $CDR > 1.00$.

Given such deficiencies of these data, Caves et al. convert the cost disadvantage variable into a zero-one dummy at various values of *CDR* less than unity. This reduces the importance of instances in which other factors clearly outweigh true cost disadvantages and focuses on "significant" differences in costs in developing the scale-barriers variable. They found a cutoff value of *CDR* of 0.80 to yield the best fit; the present data suggest 0.75, though in both cases close alternatives make little difference. Thus our *MCDR* is defined as *MID* when $CDR < 0.75$; $MCDR = 0$ when $CDR \geq 0.75$.

Table 1 Regressions of Industry Price-Cost Margins on Continuous Market Shares*

S^1	S^2	S^3	Capital-Output Ratio	Geographical Dispersion Index
0.0427	0.4572	−0.3243	0.0858	−0.0368
(0.80)	(3.56)	(1.74)	(4.72)	(2.75)

t-statistics in parentheses
*This table has been abridged from the original in Mr. Kwoka's article.

theoretical conclusion that industry concentration increases market power and so price-cost margins.

The market share of the third largest firm, however, is associated with *lower* price-cost margins. When the third largest firm holds a larger market share, the price-cost margins in the industry are lower. The existence of the large third firm seems to counteract the market power of the first two.

The market shares of the fourth through the tenth largest firms had no association with industry price-cost margins. The important issue of concentration seem to be size of the three largest.]

. . . The results in table 1 strongly suggest that the ability of an industry to secure above-competitive margins hinges on the sizes of the top two firms. Larger shares for subsequent firms do not generally contribute to the industry's efforts, and indeed may hinder them. These results imply that the coordination difficulties associated with more numerous firms set in at a very early stage. . . .

IV.

[The results in Table 1 use the market shares of the largest firms as continuous variables: the effect of a 1 percent increase in market share is assumed to have the same effect for the largest firm whether it already has only 10 percent or already has 75 percent of the market. Some previous studies have suggested a "critical value" of market share at which collusion or cooperation becomes effective. A statistical method searches for critical values for each of the three largest firms. The estimated critical value for the largest firm is where it has 26 or more percent of the market. The critical value for the second largest firm is 15 or more percent. The critical value for the third largest firm is 16 or more precent.]

. . . The economic implications of the results . . . are considerable. If the largest firm is at least 0.26 of the industry, price-cost margins are greater by about four percentage points. If the second share is at least 0.15, margins are greater by an additional five percentage points or so, *ceteris paribus*. . . . In addition, note that if $S2 \geq 0.15$, $S1$ must be at least as large and, hence, they

Table 1 Cont.

Industry Growth 1967–72	*Consumer Industry (binary)*	*Scale Variable*	*Constant*	$\bar{R}^2$
0.0422	0.0368	0.1783 *MCDR*		
(2.26)	(3.55)	(3.36)	.2072	.200

jointly control a minimum of 0.30 of industry output. If both exceed their critical values, as occurs in 37 industries in the sample, they total at least 0.41 of the industry. In such cases, their greater output control and tighter discipline raise margins by eight to nine percentage points, double either of their separate effects.

In this dichotomous formulation, the third share emerges as a large, negative, and clearly significant force on industry price-cost margins. It should be emphasized that the result is based on only five industries for which $S3 \geq 0.16$,[6] but its effect there is quite systematic and strong. A sufficiently large third firm causes industry margins to *fall* by 13 or 14 percentage points, wiping out the above-competitive margins secured by the large leading firms. . . . industry margins when all three firms are large are much the same as when all are small. Equality of size among three large firms appears to breed a rivalry capable of simulating competitive performance levels. . . .

VI.

Almost all literature relating firm size distribution to industry performance has focused on the four-firm concentration ratio. For reasons already outlined, such an arbitrary summary statistic is incapable of establishing exactly what features of industries are important, how important they are *in toto*, and what their relative importance is. The analysis in this paper demonstrates that the four-firm concentration ratio contains one irrelevant firm share ($S4$) and another with the wrong sign ($S3$). Large market shares for the two leading firms seem most decisive for industry price-cost margins, with a depressing effect from a sufficiently large third share. Moreover, these effects appear to be discontinuous,

[6] The five industries are SIC 2296, Tire Cord and Fabric: 2823, Cellulosic Man-Made Fibers; 3333, Primary Smelting and Refining of Zinc; 3482, Small Arms Ammunition; and 3672, Cathode Ray Television Picture Tubes. A referee has suggested that these industries sell to a few strong buyers who may use the large third seller as leverage against the top two. Additional data, currently unavailable, might permit testing this possibility.

For the three model specifications, the test statistics are $F(1,310) = 1.35$, and $F(1,305) = 2.70$, and $F(1,305) = 1.11$. Asymptotic $F(1,N) = 3.84$ at the 95% confidence level.

with breaks at $S1 = .26$, $S2 = .15$, and $S3 = .16$. The figures imply that industry margins are unaffected until output control by one or two firms reaches 25% to 35%, that past some point further domination by them has no effect on performance, and that three-firm coordination problems are so severe as to make a large third firm more likely a rival.

In addition to examining the effects of market share distribution, we have isolated the roles of several other independent variables, most notably scale economies.[7] Along with minimum efficient plant size, the cost disadvantage of small-scale entry has been shown relevant, thus replicating previous empirical work. The interaction of these factors produces a higher $\bar{R}^2$ and helps separate scale from market power effects of large shares. . . .

References

Bain, Joe S., "Relation of Profit Rates to Industry Concentration," *Quarterly Journal of Economics* 55 (Aug. 1951), 293–324.

Caves, Richard E., J. Khalilzadeh-Shirazi, and Michael E. Porter, "Scale Economies in Statistical Analyses of Market Power," this REVIEW 57 (Nov. 1975), 133–140.

Chamberlin, Edward H., *The Theory of Monopolistic Competition* (Cambridge: Harvard University Press, 1933).

Collins, Norman, and Lee Preston, *Concentration and Price-Cost Margins* (Berkeley: University of California Press, 1968).

———, "Price-Cost Margins and Industry Structure," this REVIEW 51 (Aug. 1969), 271–286.

Federal Trade Commission (FTC), *Industry Classification and Concentration* (Washington, D.C., Mar. 1967).

Fouraker, Lawrence, and Sidney Siegel, *Bargaining Behavior* (New York: McGraw-Hill, 1963).

Henning, John A., "Marginal Concentration Ratios: Some Statistical Implicatiions—Comment, *Southern Economic Journal* 36 (Oct. 1969), 196–198.

Kilpatrick, Robert W., "The Choice among Alternative Measures of Industrial Concentration," this REVIEW 49 (May 1967), 258–260.

Kwoka, John E., Jr., "Large Firm Dominance and Price-Cost Margins in Manufacturing Industries," *Southern Economic Journal* 44 (July 1977), 783–789.

Mann, H. Michael, "Asymmetry, Barriers to Entry, and Rates of Return in 26 Concentrated Industries, 1948–57," *Western Economic Journal* 8 (Mar. 1970), 86–89.

Miller, Richard, "Marginal Concentration Ratios and Industry Profit Rates," *Southern Economic Journal* 34 (Oct. 1967), 259–268.

[7] We have also failed to capture some variables like demand elasticity, and inadequately represented others such as advertising intensity.

———, "Marginal Concentration Ratios: Some Statistical Implications—Reply," *Southern Economic Journal* 36 (Oct. 1969), 199–201.

———, "Marginal Concentration Ratios as Market Structure Variables," this REVIEW 53 (Aug. 1971), 289–293.

Qualls, P. David, "Market Structure and Price-Cost Margin Flexibility in American Manufacturing, 1958–70," Federal Trade Commission, Bureau of Economics Working Paper No. 1, Mar. 1977.

Rhoades, Stephen, and Joe Cleaver, "The Nature of the Concentration—Price/Cost Margin Relationship for 352 Manufacturing Industries: 1967," *Southern Economic Journal* 39 (Apr. 1973), 90–102.

Scherer, Frederick M., *Industrial Market Structure and Economic Performance* (Chicago: Rand McNally, 1970).

Scherer, Frederick M., Alan Beckenstein, Erich Kaufer, and R. Dennis Murphy, *The Economics of Multi-Plant Operation* (Cambridge: Harvard University Press, 1975).

Stigler, George, "A Theory of Oligopoly," *Journal of Political Economy* 72 (Feb. 1964), 44–61.

Theil, Henri, *Principles of Econometrics* (New York: John Wiley, 1971).

U.S. Bureau of the Census, *1972 Census of Manufactures* (Washington, D.C., 1975).

Weiss, Leonard, "Factors in Changing Concentration," this REVIEW 45 (Feb. 1963), 70–77.

———, "Quantitative Studies of Industrial Organization," in Michael D. Intriligator (ed.), *Frontiers of Quantitative Economics* (Amsterdam: North-Holland, 1971).

———, "The Concentration-Profits Relationship and Anti-trust," in Harvey Goldschmid, H. Michael Mann, and J. Fred Weston (eds.), *Industrial Concentration: The New Learning* (Boston: Little, Brown and Co., 1974).

White, Lawrence, "Searching for the Critical Industrial Concentration Ratio: An Application of the 'Switching of Regimes' Technique," in Stephen Goldfeld and Richard Quandt (eds.), *Studies in Nonlinear Estimation* (Boston: Ballinger, 1976).

Technical Appendix

Market Share Data

Market share data are obtained from Economic Information Systems, Inc., of New York, which compiles a variety of information on the 120,000 manufacturing plants in the country with twenty or more employees. In 1972, such plants accounted for 35.2% of all manufacturing establishments, but more importantly 94.4% of value-added (1972 *Census of Manufactures*, v. 1, p. 5).

The EIS procedure for developing market shares begins with *County Business Patterns* statistics on employment by SIC for each county. Employment is allocated to individual plants in the county identified originally through a private mailing to 300,000 establishments. Those with fewer than twenty employees are excluded for reasons of cost and reliability of data. EIS then multiplies the employment estimate for each plant by a *Census of Manufactures* productivity factor (value of shipments per employee) for the appropriate employment size categories of plant in the four-digit SIC industry. The resulting estimate of shipments for each plant reflects some scale effects and technology differences among plant size classes, but, of course, it cannot capture individual plant variation.

This basic data set has been modified by the Bureau of Economics of the Federal Trade Commission to show the market shares of firms (with at least one establishment of twenty or more employees) by four-digit SIC industry. It is this version that is used in the present study.

Consistency with Census Data

This data set is linked to the 1972 *Census of Manufactures* by four-digit industry. Of the 451 "industries" comprising the Census, 70 denoted as "miscellaneous" or "not elsewhere classified" were deleted as not representing economically meaningful categories. Other problems resulted from the fact that the EIS data used "old" SIC definitions, while 1972 Census data were organized on the basis of a major revision of SIC industries. Of the 381 remaining Census industries, 77 differed significantly in definition between the classification systems. Twenty-four could be recovered by combining Census data into 11 "old" industries, but the remaining 43 defied any such treatment. The final data base thus consists of 314 industries.

Despite some inevitable inaccuracies of the EIS estimation process, the resulting data appear quite consistent with comparable Census numbers. For example, the 1972 Census four-firm concentration ratio (*CR*4) has a mean of 0.409, and its counterpart obtained by summing EIS market shares averages 0.398. Their simple correlation coefficient of 0.922 indicates that although they are not completely identical, they do capture much the same property of firm size distribution.

30

The loss of economic welfare caused by monopoly can be defined as the excess of the loss of consumers' surplus over the gain to the monopolist. The gain to the monopolist is his net profit which, in the constant-cost linear-demand model, is the difference between his price and the competitive price multiplied by the quantity he produces and sells.

By taking a model of monopoly with simple and convenient properties and by using statistics on profits, Professor Harberger makes an estimate of the dollar value of the welfare loss from monopoly. He finds the loss to be very small.

THE WELFARE LOSS FROM MONOPOLY

ARNOLD C. HARBERGER
University of Chicago

One of the first things we learn when we begin to study price theory is that the main effects of monopoly are to misallocate resources, to reduce aggregate welfare, and to redistribute income in favor of monopolists. In the light of this fact, it is a little curious that our empirical efforts at studying monopoly have so largely concentrated on other things. We have studied particular industries and have come up with a formidable list of monopolistic practices: identical pricing, price leadership, market sharing, patent suppression, basing points, and so on. And we have also studied the whole economy, using the concentration of production in the hands of a small number of firms as the measure of monopoly. On this basis, we have obtained the impression that some 20 or 30 or 40 per cent of our economy is effectively monopolized.

In this paper I propose to look at the American economy, and in particular at American manufacturing industry, and try to get some quantitative notion of the allocative and welfare effects of monopoly. It should be clear from the outset that this is not the kind of job one can do with great precision. The best we can hope for is to get a feeling for the general orders of magnitude that are involved.

I take it as an operating hypothesis that, in the long run, resources can be allocated among our manufacturing industries in such a way as to yield

---

Taken and adapted from Arnold C. Harberger, "Monopoly and Resource Allocation," *American Economic Review*, Vol. XLIV, No. 2, May 1954, pp. 77–79, 81–87. Reprinted by permission of the American Economic Association and of the author.

roughly constant returns. That is, long-run average costs are close to constant in the relevant range, for both the firm and the industry. This hypothesis gives us the wedge we need to get something from the data. For as is well known, the malallocative effects of monopoly stem from the difference between marginal cost and price, and marginal costs are at first glance terribly difficult to pin down empirically for a wide range of firms and industries. But once we are ready to proceed on the basis of constant average costs, we can utilize the fact that under such circumstances marginal and average costs are the same, and we can easily get some idea of average costs.

But that does not solve all the problems, for cost and profit to the economist are not the same things as cost and profit to the accountant, and the accountants make our data. To move into this question, I should like to conjure up an idealized picture of an economy in equilibrium. In this picture all firms are operating on their long-run cost curves, the cost curves are so defined as to yield each firm an equal return on its invested capital, and markets are cleared. I think it is fair to say that this is a picture of optimal resource allocation. Now, we never see this idyllic picture in the real world, but if long-run costs are in fact close to constant and markets are cleared, we can pick out the places where resources are misallocated by looking at the rates of return on capital. Those industries which are returning higher than average rates have too few resources; and those yielding lower than average rates have too many resources. To get an idea of how big a shift of resources it would take to equalize profit rates in all industries, we have to know something about the elasticities of demand for the goods in question. In Figure 1, I illustrate a hypothetical case. The industry in question is earning 20 per cent on a capital of 10 million dollars, while the average return to capital is only 10 per cent. We therefore build a 10 per cent return into the

FIGURE 1

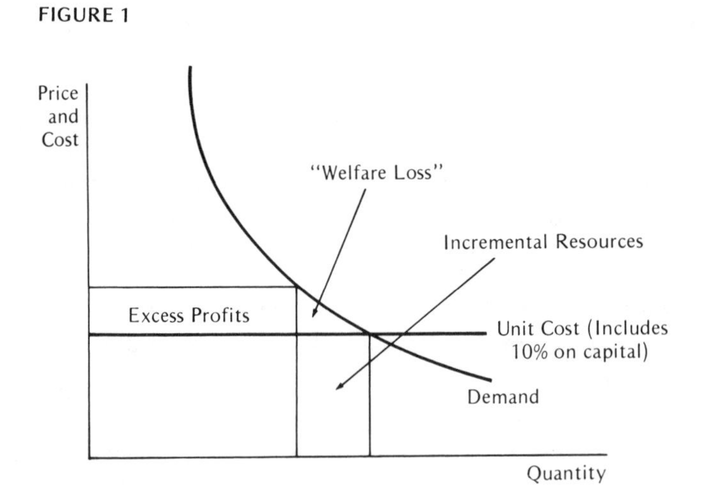

cost curve, which leaves the industry with 1 million in excess profits. If the elasticity of demand for the industry's product is unity, it will take a shift of 1 million in resources in order to expand supply enough to wipe out the excess profits.

The above argument gives a general picture of what I have done empirically. The first empirical job was to find a period which met two conditions. First, it had to be reasonably close to a long-run equilibrium period; that is, no violent shifts in demand or economic structure were to be in process. And second, it had to be a period for which accounting values of capital could be supposed to be pretty close to actual values. In particular, because of the disastrous effect of inflation and deflation on book values of capital, it had to be a period of fairly stable prices, which in turn had been preceded by a period of stable prices. It seemed to me that the late twenties came as close as one could hope to meeting both these requirements.

The late twenties had an additional advantage for me—because my choice of this period enabled me to use Professor Ralph C. Epstein's excellent study, *Industrial Profits in the United States* (National Bureau of Economic Research, 1934), as a source of data. Professor Epstein there gives, for the years 1924–28, the rates of total profit to total capital for seventy-three manufacturing industries, with total capital defined as book capital plus bonded indebtedness and total profit defined as book profit plus interest on the indebtedness. To get rid of factors producing short-period variations in these rates of return, I average the rates, for each industry, for the five-year period.

Now suppose we ask how much reallocation of resources it would take to eliminate the observed divergences in profit rates. This depends, as you can see in Figure 1, on the demand elasticities confronting the industries in question. How high are these elasticities? The elasticities in question are probably quite low. I think an elasticity of unity is about as high as one can reasonably allow for, though a somewhat higher elasticity would not seriously affect the general tenor of my results.

Returning again to Figure 1, we can see that once the assumption of unit elasticity is made the amount of excess profit measures the amount of resources that must be called into an industry in order to bring its profit rate into line. When I say resources here I mean the services of labor and capital plus the materials bought by the industry from other industries.

Using Epstein's data classified by industry, we find that in order to equalize the profit rate in all industries, we would have to transfer about 550 million dollars in resources from low-profit to high-profit industries. But this is not the end. Those of you who are familiar with Epstein's study are aware that it is based on a sample of 2,046 corporations, which account for some 45 per cent of the sales and capital in manufacturing industry. Pending a discussion of possible biases in the sample a little later, we can proceed to blow up our 550 million figure to cover total manufacturing. The result is

1.2 billion. Hence we tentatively conclude that the misallocations of resources which existed in United States manufacturing in the period 1924–28 could have been eliminated by a net transfer of roughly 4 per cent of the resources in manufacturing industry, or 1½ per cent of the total resources of the economy.

Now let us suppose that somehow we effected these desired resource transfers. By how much would people be better off? Again using Epstein's data, but this time estimating the counterpart of the triangle labeled "welfare loss" in Figure 1 for each industry, we find that the total improvement in consumer welfare which might come from our sample of firms turns out to be about 26.5 million dollars. Blowing up this figure to cover the whole economy, we get what we really want: an estimate of by how much consumer welfare would have improved if resources had been optimally allocated throughout American manufacturing in the late twenties. The answer is 59 million dollars—less than one-tenth of 1 per cent of the national income. Translated into today's national income and today's prices, this comes out to 225 million dollars, or less than $1.50 for every man, woman, and child in the United States.

Before drawing any lessons from this, I should like to spend a little time evaluating the estimate. First let us look at the basic assumption that long-run costs are constant. My belief is that this is a good assumption, but that if it is wrong, costs in all probability tend to be increasing rather than decreasing in American industry. And the presence of increasing costs would result in a lowering of both our estimates. Less resources would have to be transferred in order to equalize profit rates, and the increase in consumer welfare resulting from the transfer would be correspondingly less.

On the other hand, flaws in the data probably operate to make our estimate of the welfare loss too low. Take for example the question of patents and good will. To the extent that these items are assigned a value on the books of a corporation, monopoly profits are capitalized, and the profit rate which we have used is an understatement of the actual profit rate on real capital. Fortunately for us, Professor Epstein has gone into this question in his study. He finds that excluding intangibles from the capital figures makes a significant difference in the earnings rates of only eight of the seventy-three industries. I have accordingly recomputed my figures for these eight industries. As a result, the estimated amount of resource transfer goes up from about 1½ per cent to about 1¾ per cent of the national total. And the welfare loss due to resource misallocations gets raised to about 81 million dollars, just over a tenth of 1 per cent of the national income.

Finally, there is a problem associated with the aggregation of manufacturing into seventy-three industries. My analysis assumes high substitutability among the products produced by different firms within any industry and relatively low substitutability among the products of different industries. Yet Epstein's industrial classification undoubtedly lumps together in particular industries products which are only remote substitutes and which are produced by quite distinct groups of firms. In short, Epstein's industries are in some instances aggregates of subindustries, and for our purposes it would have been appropriate to deal with the subindustries directly. It can be shown that the use of aggregates in such cases biases our estimate of the welfare loss downward, but experiments with hypothetical examples reveal that the probable extent of the bias is small.

Thus we come to our final conclusion. Elimination of resource misallocations in American manufacturing in the late twenties would bring with it an improvement in consumer welfare of just a little more than a tenth of a per cent. In present values, the welfare gain would amount to about $2.00 per capita.

Now we can stop to ask what resource misallocations we have measured. We actually have included in the measurement not only monopoly misallocations but also misallocations coming out of the dynamics of economic growth and development and all the other elements which would cause divergent profit rates to persist for some time even in an effectively competitive economy. I know of no way to get at the precise share of the total welfare loss that is due to monopoly, but I do think I have a reasonable way of pinning our estimate down just a little more tightly. My argument here is based on two props. First of all, I think it only reasonable to roughly identify monopoly power with high rates of profit. And secondly, I think it quite implausible that more than a third of our manufacturing profits should be monopoly profits; that is, profits which are above and beyond the normal return to capital and are obtained by exercise of monopoly power. I doubt that this second premise needs any special defense. After all, we know that capital is a highly productive resource. On the first premise, identifying monopoly power with high profits, I think we need only run down the list of high-profit industries to verify its plausibility. Cosmetics are at the top, with a 30 per cent return on capital. They are followed by scientific instruments, drugs, soaps, newspapers, automobiles, cereals, road machinery, bakery products, tobacco, and so on. But even apart from the fact that it makes sense in terms of other evidence to consider these industries monopolistic, there is a still stronger reason for making this assumption. For given the elasticity of demand for an industry's product, the welfare loss associated with that product increases as the square of its greater-than-normal profits. Thus, granted that we are prepared to say that no more than a third of manufacturing profits were monopoly profits, we get the biggest welfare effect by distributing this monopoly profit first to the highest profit industries, then to the next highest, and so on. When this is done, we come to the conclusion that monopoly misallocations entail a welfare loss of no more than a thirteenth of a per cent of the national income. Or, in present values, no more than about $1.40 per capita.

I should like now to review what has been done. In reaching our estimate of the welfare loss due to monopoly misallocations of resources, we have assumed constant rather than increasing costs in manufacturing industry and have assumed elasticities of demand which are too high, I believe. On both counts we therefore tend to overstate the loss. Furthermore, we have treated intermediate products in such a way as to overstate the loss. Finally, we have attributed to monopoly an implausibly large share—33⅓ per cent—of manufacturing profits, and have distributed this among industries in such a way as to get the biggest possible welfare loss consistent with the idea that monopolies tend to make high profits. In short, we have labored at each stage to get a big estimate of the welfare loss, and we have come out in the end with less than a tenth of a per cent of the national income.

I must confess that I was amazed at this result. I never really tried to quantify my notions of what monopoly misallocations amounted to, and I doubt that many other people have. Still, it seems to me that our literature of the last twenty or so years reflects a general belief that monopoly distortions to our resources structure are much greater than they seem in fact to be.

Let me therefore state the beliefs to which the foregoing analysis has led me. First of all, I do not want to minimize the effects of monopoly. A tenth of a per cent of the national income is still over 300 million dollars, so we dare not pooh-pooh the efforts of those—economists and others—who have dedicated themselves to reducing the losses due to monopoly. But it seems to me that the monopoly problem does take on a rather different perspective in the light of present study. Our economy emphatically does not seem to be monopoly capitalism in big red letters. We can neglect monopoly elements and still gain a very good understanding of how our economic process works and how our resources are allocated. When we are interested in the big picture of our manufacturing economy, we need not apologize for treating it as competitive, for in fact it is awfully close to being so. On the other hand, when we are interested in the doings of particular industries, it may often be wise to take monopoly elements into account.

Finally I should like to point out that I have discussed only the welfare effects of resource misallocations due to monopoly. I have not analyzed the redistributions of income that arise when monopoly is present. I originally planned to discuss this redistribution aspect as well, but finally decided against it. All I want to say here is that monopoly does not seem to affect aggregate welfare very seriously through its effect on resource allocation. What it does through its effect on income distribution I leave to my more metaphysically inclined colleagues to decide. I am impelled to add a final note in order to forestall misunderstanding arising out of matters of definition. Resource misallocations may clearly arise from causes other than those considered here: tariffs, excise taxes, subsidies, trade-union practices, and the devices of agricultural policy are some obvious examples.

31 Professor Harberger's estimate (Selection 31) of the size of the welfare loss due to monopoly was the first to be made. He was subject to fairly strong criticism, some of it mentioned in this selection. Professor Schwartzman, however, gets similar estimates even though he employs a wholly different set of statistical data and a slightly different theoretical model.

THE BURDEN OF MONOPOLY

DAVID SCHWARTZMAN
New School for Social Research

A measurement of the effect of monopoly on price such as I have reported earlier in this *Journal*[1] is interesting for its implications for income distribution and resource allocation. The total of income transfers attributable to monopoly is the sum of monopoly profits, and I have shown that this sum is small.[2] The allocation effects of monopoly are the subject of this note.

So far, only A. C. Harberger has estimated the extent of misallocation due to monopoly and the resulting welfare loss. Applying Hotelling's model, Harberger has estimated the extent of monopolistic resource misallocation in 1953 at $4.6 billion and the welfare loss at $225 million.[3] These numbers are not large. George J. Stigler has criticized Harberger's method of estimating monopoly profits and also the assumption concerning the elasticity of demand in monopolistic industries which he used in calculating the reductions in output that result from monopoly.[4] Accordingly, I shall apply the same welfare model, but I shall substitute my own estimate of profits for Harberger's, and I shall assume a range of reasonable values for the elasticity of demand.

[1] "The Effect of Monopoly on Price" (August 1959), pp. 352–62.
[2] *Ibid.*, p. 362.
[3] "Monopoly and Resource Allocation," *American Economic Review* (May 1954), Proceedings, pp. 77–87; see also Harold Hotelling, "The General Welfare in Relation to Problems of Taxation and of Railway and Utility Rates," *Econometrica* (July 1938), pp. 242–69, esp. pp. 252 ff.
[4] "The Statistics of Monopoly and Merger," *Journal of Political Economy* (February 1956), pp. 33–40, esp. p. 35.

Reprinted from "The Burden of Monopoly," by David Schwartzman, *Journal of Political Economy*, Vol. LXVIII, No. 6, December 1960, pp. 627–630, by permission of The University of Chicago Press. In a later article, "The Effect of Monopoly: A Correction," *JPE*, Vol. LXIX, No. 5, October 1961, Professor Schwartzman corrected some of his estimates. The corrected figures have been inserted in this selection.

The Welfare Model

Figure 1 represents the usual model of monopolistic price determination except for the special assumption that the marginal-cost curve is constant. The output is *OF* and the price is *OA* under monopoly, compared with the competitive output, *OG*, and price, *OC*.

FIGURE 1

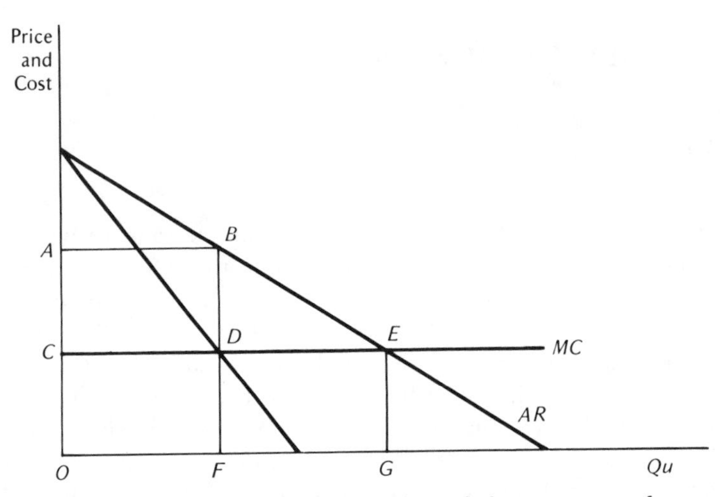

The extent of misallocation is the value of the resources that must be brought into the industry for the price to fall to the competitive level. This value is the competitive price times the difference between competitive and monopolistic outputs, *OC* times *FG*, or the rectangle *DEFG*.

The value of misallocated resources, *DEFG*, is related to monopoly profits, *ABCD*, as follows. The percentage change in price between *B* and *E* is *ABCD*/*CDOF*, measuring change from *E*; *DEFG*/*CDOF* is the percentage change in quantity between these points, measuring from *B*. Hence *DEFG*/*ABCD* is an estimate of the arc elasticity of demand between *B* and *E*. Let *DEFG*/*ABCD* equal *k*. But *k* tends to overstate the arc elasticity compared with what we would obtain by measuring changes in both price and quantity from *B*, the monopoly position, and to understate the arc elasticity measured from *E*, the competitive position. Thus the extent of misallocation is *k* times excess profits, where *k* is an estimate of the arc elasticity of demand between the monopoly and competitive positions on the demand curve.

The welfare loss is the sum of producers' and consumers' surplus or the area, *bde*, which approximately equals

$$\frac{\text{Increase in price} \times \text{reduction in quantity}}{2}$$

as Stigler has expressed it.[5] If we define the unit of output so that the competitive price, *OC*, is $1.00, the reduction in quantity, *FG*, equals *DEFG*, and the welfare loss equals

$$\frac{\text{Increase in price K } k(\text{monopoly profits})}{2}.$$

The assumption of constant marginal cost produces an upward bias in the estimates; a rising marginal-cost curve would mean smaller differences in price and in output between the monopolistic and competitive positions.

Harberger's Procedure

Harberger assumes that the demand curve facing each monopolistic industry has unitary elasticity throughout its length, which implies that *k* equals 1. The estimates of excess profits in monopolistic industries are based on Epstein's estimates of average profit rates by industry between 1924 and 1928.[6] These averages are assumed to be the long-run profit rates, and any excess of the individual averages over the average for all manufacturing is assumed to represent monopoly profits.[7]

Stigler argues that the elasticity of demand facing any monopolist at the point at which he is operating will be greater than unity.[8] However, the assumption refers to the industry demand curve rather than to that of the individual firm; the demand elasticity of General Motors is greater than unity, but that of the entire automobile industry may not be. Harberger's estimates of resource misallocation are for whole industries. Moreover, if we are interested in the value of resource misallocation by monopolistic industries as a group, the relevant demand elasticity is less than the average of the individual industry demand elasticities.

Stigler's objections to the estimates of monopoly profits may be stated as follows: (1) monopoly profits are capitalized, so earnings statements tend to report only competitive profit rates; (2) the average profit rate in manufacturing is above the competitive level, since monopoly is concentrated in manufacturing; (3) monopoly profits paid out to factors other than capital are not included. The estimates described are unobjectionable on these grounds.

The New Estimates

My estimate of the monopoly effect on price is 11.2 per cent of average variable cost. The estimate is based on data for 1954, and for that year total variable cost (direct cost) summed over all monopolistic industries engaged

[5] Stigler, *op. cit.*
[6] Ralph C. Epstein, *Industrial Profits in the United States* (New York: National Bureau of Economic Research, 1934), Tables 43D through 53D.
[7] Harberger, *op. cit.*, p. 79.
[8] Stigler, *op. cit.*

in manufacturing is \$43.6 billion. Excess profits are 11.2 per cent of this total, or \$4.9 billion. Following Harberger in assuming constant marginal cost and unitary elasticity of demand over the relevant range of the aggregate demand curve for monopolistic commodities, the extent of resource misallocation may be estimated at \$4.9 billion. Assuming that k equals ɒ2, the extent of resource misallocation is not greater than \$9.8 billion. I doubt whether any higher value for k need be considered.

To measure the welfare loss, we need a value for the monopolistic increase in price per unit of output, the unit being defined as the quantity which may be produced at a cost of \$1.00 under competition. This value equals

$$\frac{TR}{TR - E} - 1,$$

where TR is the total revenue and E is the excess profits of monopolistic industries. Substituting the aggregate value of shipments in monopolistic industries in 1954 for TR gives us a value of \$59.0 billion. As we have seen, E is \$4.9 billion, so that the increase in price per unit of output is \$0.083. The welfare loss is

$$\frac{\$4.9\ k \text{ billion K } 0.083}{2},$$

or \$202.5 k million. Since k is unlikely to have a numerical value greater than 2, the welfare loss probably is less than \$405 million, or less than 0.1 per cent of the national income in 1954.

Conclusion

Since the estimates are similar to Harberger's, they provide confirmation of Harberger's general conclusion that the welfare loss from monopoly has been small. We have already observed that the income transfers resulting from monopoly are also small in the aggregate.

Readers may object to the partial-equilibrium analysis which has been applied in this paper. As prices decline in monopolistic industries, the demand and cost curves may shift. However, the small size of the monopoly sector combined with the small size of the monopoly effect implies that the amount of resources that needs to be moved to achieve competitive prices throughout manufacturing is not large. Hence, the changes in the currently competitive sector would be small, and the partial analysis is adequate.

32 The welfare loss from monopoly is a loss of efficiency in the allocation of resources. In this selection Professor Leibenstein compares allocative efficiency with another kind, which he calls "X-efficiency." He contends that improvements in X-efficiency would give much greater results than improvements in allocative efficiency. Omitted here are extensive empirical materials on the existence of X-*in*efficiencies.

ALLOCATIVE EFFICIENCY VS. "X-EFFICIENCY"

HARVEY LEIBENSTEIN
Center for Population Studies,
Harvard University

At the core of economics is the concept of efficiency. Microeconomic theory is concerned with allocative efficiency. Empirical evidence has been accumulating that suggests that the problem of allocative efficiency is trivial. Yet it is hard to escape the notion that efficiency in some broad sense is significant. In this paper I want to review the empirical evidence briefly and to consider some of the possible implications of the findings, especially as they relate to the theory of the firm and to the explanation of economic growth. The essence of the argument is that microeconomic theory focuses on allocative efficiency to the exclusion of other types of efficiencies that, in fact, are much more significant in many instances. Furthermore, improvement in "nonallocative efficiency" is an important aspect of the process of growth.

In Section I the empirical evidence on allocative efficiency is presented. In this section we also consider the reasons why allocation inefficiency is frequently of small magnitude. Most of the evidence on allocative inefficiency deals with either monopoly or international trade. However, monopoly and trade are not the focus of this paper. Our primary concern is with the broader issue of allocative efficiency versus an initially undefined type of efficiency that we shall refer to as "X-efficiency" The magnitude and nature of this type of efficiency is examined in Sections II and III. Although a major element of "X-efficiency" is motivation, it is not the only element,

---

Taken and adapted from Harvey Leibenstein, "Allocative Efficiency vs. 'X-Efficiency,'" *American Economic Review*, Vol. LVI, No. 3, June 1966, pp. 392–394, 397, 398, 404–408, 409, 410. Reproduced by permission.

and hence the terms "motivation efficiency" or "incentive efficiency" have not been employed.

I. Allocative Inefficiency: Empirical Evidence

The studies assessing the importance of allocative efficiency are of two types. On the one side we have the studies of Harberger [Selection 30] and Schwartzman [Selection 31] on the "social welfare cost" of monopoly. On the other side we have a number of studies on the benefits of reducing or eliminating restrictions to trade. In both cases the computed benefits attributed to the reallocation of resources turn out to be exceedingly small.

Let us look at some of the findings. In the original Harberger study the benefits for eliminating monopoly in the United States would raise income no more than 1/13 of 1 per cent. Schwartzman's study which recomputes the benefits of eliminating monopoly by comparing Canadian monopolized industries as against counterpart competitive U.S. industries, and vice versa in order to determine the excess price attributable to monopoly, ends up with a similar result. Similarly, the benefits attributed to superior resource allocation as a consequence of the Common Market or a European Free Trade Area are also minute—usually much less than 1 per cent.

Why are the welfare effects of reallocation so small? Allocational inefficiency involves only the net marginal effects. The basic assumption is that every firm *purchases and utilizes* all of its inputs "efficiently." Thus, what is left is simply the consequences of price and quantity distortions. While some specific price distortions might be large it seems unlikely that all relative price distortions are exceptionally large. This implies that most quantity distortions must also be relatively small since for a given aggregate output a significant distortion in one commodity will be counterbalanced by a large number of small distortions in the opposite direction in quantities elsewhere. While it is possible to *assume* relative price distortions and quantity distortions that would be exceedingly high, it would be difficult to believe that, without intent, the sum of such distortions should be high. However, it is not *necessarily* so on purely *a priori* grounds.

There is one important type of distortion that cannot easily be handled by existing microeconomic theory. This has to do with the allocation of managers. It is conceivable that in practice a situation would arise in which managers are exceedingly poor, that is, others are available who do not obtain management posts, and who would be very much superior. Managers determine not only their own productivity but the productivity of all cooperating units in the organization. It is therefore possible that the actual loss due to such a misallocation might be large. But the theory does not allow us to examine this matter because firms are presumed to exist as entities that make optimal input decisions, apart from the decisions of its managers. This is obviously a contradiction and therefore cannot be handled.

II. X-Efficiency: The Empirical Evidence

We have seen that the welfare loss due to allocational inefficiency is frequently no more than 1/10 of 1 per cent. Is it conceivable that the value of X-inefficiency would be larger than that? One way of looking at it is to return to the problem of the welfare loss due to monopoly. Suppose that one-third of the industries are in the monopolized sector. Is it possible that the lack of competitive pressure of operating in monopolized industries would lead to costs 3/10 of a per cent higher than would be the case under competition? This magnitude seems to be very small, and hence it certainly seems to be a possibility. The question essentially, is whether we can visualize managers bestirring themselves sufficiently, if the environment forced them to do so, in order to reduce costs by more than 3/10 of 1 per cent. Some of the empirical evidence available suggests that not only is this a possibility, but that the magnitudes involved are very much larger. The spotty evidence on this subject does not prove the case but it does seem to be sufficiently persuasive to suggest the possibility that X-efficiency exists, and that it frequently is much more significant than allocational efficiency.

What conclusions can we draw from all of this? First, the data suggest that there is a great deal of possible variation in output for similar amounts of capital and labor and for similar techniques, in the broad sense, to the extent that technique is determined by similar types of equipment. However, in most of the studies the nature of the influences involved are mixed, and in some cases not all of them are clear to the analyst. In many instances there appears to have been an attempt to impart knowledge, at least of a managerial variety, which accounts for *some* of the increase in output. But should this knowledge be looked upon as an increase in inputs of production in all instances? Although the first reaction might be that such attempts involve inputs similar to inputs of capital or labor, I will want to argue that in many instances this is not the case.

It is obvious that not every change in technique implies a change in knowledge. The knowledge may have been there already, and a change in circumstances induced the change in technique. In addition, knowledge may not be used to capacity just as capital or labor may be underutilized. More important, a good deal of our knowledge is vague. A man may have nothing more than a sense of its existence, and yet this may be the critical element. Given a sufficient inducement, he can then search out its nature in detail and get it to a stage where he can use it. People normally operate within the bounds of a great deal of intellectual slack. Unlike underutilized capital, this is an element that is very difficult to observe. As a result, occasions of genuine additions to knowledge become rather difficult to distinguish from those circumstances in which no new knowledge has been added, but in which existing knowledge is being utilized to greater capacity.

Experience in U.S. industry suggests that adversity frequently stimulates cost-reducing attempts, some of which are successful, within the bounds of existing knowledge. In any event, some of the studies suggest that motivational aspects are involved entirely apart from additional knowledge. The difficulty of assessment arises because these elements are frequently so intertwined that it is difficult to separate them.

III. The Residual and X-Efficiency: An Interpretation

The main burden of these findings is that X-inefficiency exists, and that improvement in X-efficiency is a significant source of increased output. In general, we may specify three elements as significant in determining what we have called X-efficiency: (1) intra-plant motivational efficiency, (2) external motivational efficiency, and (3) nonmarket input efficiency.

The simple fact is that neither individuals nor firms work as hard, nor do they search for information as effectively, as they could. The importance of motivation and its association with degree of effort and search arises because the relation between inputs and outputs is *not* a determinate one. There are four reasons why given inputs cannot be transformed into predetermined outputs: (a) contracts for labor are incomplete, (b) not all factors of production are marketed, (c) the production function is not completely specified or known, and (d) interdependence and uncertainty lead competing firms to cooperate tacitly with each other in some respects, and to imitate each other with respect to technique, to some degree.

The conventional theoretical assumption, although it is rarely stated, is that inputs have a fixed specification and yield a fixed performance. This ignores other likely possibilities. Inputs may have a fixed specification that yields a variable performance, or they may be of a variable specification and yield a variable performance. Some types of complex machinery may have fixed specifications, but their performance may be variable depending on the exact nature of their employment. The most common case is that of labor services of various kinds that have variable specifications and variable performance—although markets sometimes operate as if much of the labor of a given class has a fixed specification. Moreover, it is exceedingly rare for all elements of performance in a labor contract to be spelled out. A good deal is left to custom, authority, and whatever motivational techniques are available to management as well as to individual discretion and judgment.

Similarly, the production function is neither completely specified nor known. There is always an experimental element involved so that something may be known about the current state; say the existing relation between inputs and outputs, but not what will happen given changes in the input ratios. In addition, important inputs are frequently not marketed or, if they are traded, they are not equally accessible (or accessible on equal terms) to all potential buyers. This is especially true of management knowledge. In many areas of the world managers may not be available in well-organized markets. But even when they are available, their capacities may not be known. One of the important capacities of management may be the degree to which managers can obtain factors of production that in fact are not marketed in well-organized markets or on a universalistic basis. In underdeveloped countries the capacity to obtain finance may depend on family connections. Trustworthiness may be similarly determined. Some types of market information may be available to some individuals but not purchasable in the market. For these and other reasons it seems clear that it is one thing to purchase or hire inputs in a given combination; it is something else to get a predetermined output out of them.

Another possible interpretation of the data presented is in connection with the "residual" in economic growth analysis. The residual manifests itself in three basic ways: (1) through cost reduction in the production of existing commodities without inventions or innovations; (2) the introduction of innovations in processes of production; and (3) the introduction of new commodities or, what is the same thing, quality improvements in consumer goods or inputs. We have ignored the introduction of new commodities, but the other two elements are pertinent here. The data suggest that cost reduction that is essentially a result of improvement in X-efficiency is likely to be an important component of the observed residual in economic growth. In addition, there is no doubt that, in some of the cases of reduced cost, new knowledge was conveyed to the firms involved, and this too is part of the residual. It is of special interest that such new knowledge involves knowledge dissemination rather than invention. The detailed studies suggest that the magnitudes are large, and hence a significant part of the residual does not depend on the types of considerations that have been prominent in the literature in recent years, such as those that are *embodied* in capital accumulation or in invention. We have considered the problem in terms of decreasing real costs per unit of output. It is clear that for a given set of resources, if real costs per unit of output are decreased, then total output will grow, and output per unit of input will also rise. Such efforts to reduce cost are part of the contribution of the residual to economic growth.

Both competition and adversity create some pressure for change. Even if knowledge is vague, if the incentive is strong enough there will be an attempt to augment information so that it becomes less vague and possibly useful. Where consulting advice is available it is significant that relatively few firms buy it. Clearly, motivations play a role in determining the degree that consulting advice is sought. The other side of the coin is that, where the motivation is weak, firm managements will permit a considerable degree of slack in their operations and will not seek cost-improving methods. We have instances where competitive pressures from other firms or adversity lead to efforts toward cost reduction, and the absence of such pressures tends to cause costs to rise.

IV. Conclusions

We have suggested three reasons for X-inefficiency connected with the possibility of variable performance for given units of the inputs. These are: (a) contracts for labor are incomplete, (b) the production function is not completely specified or known, and (c) not all inputs are marketed or, if marketed, are not available on equal terms to all buyers. These facts lead us to suggest an approach to the theory of the firm that does not depend on the assumption of cost-minimization by all firms. The level of unit cost depends in some measure on the degree of X-efficiency, which in turn depends on the degree of competitive pressure, as well as on other motivational factors. The responses to such pressures, whether in the nature of effort, search, or the utilization of new information, is a significant part of the residual in economic growth.

One idea that emerges from this study is that firms and economies do not operate on an outer-bound production possibility surface consistent with their resources. Rather they actually work on a production surface that is well within that outer bound. This means that for a variety of reasons people and organizations normally work neither as hard nor as effectively as they could. In situations where competitive pressure is light, many people will trade the disutility of greater effort, of search, and the control of other peoples' activities for the utility of feeling less pressure and of better interpersonal relations. But in situations where competitive pressures are high, and hence the costs of such trades are also high, they will exchange less of the disutility of effort for the utility of freedom from pressure, etc. Two general types of movements are possible. One is along a production surface towards greater allocative efficiency and the other is from a lower surface to a higher one that involves greater degrees of X-efficiency. The data suggest that in a great many instances the amount to be gained by increasing allocative efficiency is trivial while the amount to be gained by increasing X-efficiency is frequently significant.

33 Here is an objection to the finding that the welfare loss, or cost, of monopoly is very small. Professor Tullock thinks that the social costs of maintaining monopoly positions are themselves not small and are not taken into account in the usual methods of measurement. His analysis of the costs of tariffs is omitted here.

THE WELFARE COSTS OF MONOPOLIES AND THEFT

GORDON TULLOCK
Virginia Polytechnic Institute

In recent years a considerable number of studies have been published that purport to measure the welfare costs of monopolies and tariffs. The results have uniformly shown very small costs for practices that economists normally deplore. Judging from conversations with graduate students, a number of young economists are drawing the conclusion that tariffs and monopolies are not of much importance. This view is now beginning to appear in the literature. On the basis of these measurements Professor Harvey Leibenstein has argued "Microeconomic theory focuses on allocative efficiency to the exclusion of other types of efficiences that, in fact, are much more significant in many instances." [1]

It is my purpose to demonstrate that the tools on which these studies are founded produce an underestimation of the welfare costs of tariffs and monopolies. The classical economists were not concerning themselves with trifles when they argued against tariffs, and the Department of Justice is not dealing with a miniscule problem in its attacks on monopoly.

The Cost of Transfers

Generally governments do not impose protective tariffs on their own. They have to be lobbied or pressured into doing so by the expenditure of resources in political activity. One would anticipate that the domestic producers would invest resources in lobbying for the tariff until the marginal return on the last dollar so spent was equal to its likely return producing the transfer. There might also be other interests trying to prevent the transfer

[1] Harvey Leibenstein, "Allocative Efficiency vs. 'X-Efficiency'," *Am. Econ. Rev.*, June 1966, 56, 392–415.

Taken and adapted from Gordon Tullock, "The Welfare Costs of Tariffs, Monopolies, and Theft," *Western Economic Journal*, Vol. V, No. 3, June 1967, pp. 224–232. Reproduced by permission of the author and of the Western Economic Association.

and putting resources into influencing the government in the other direction. These expenditures, which may simply offset each other to some extent, are purely wasteful from the standpoint of society as a whole; they are spent not in increasing wealth, but in attempts to transfer or resist transfer of wealth. I can suggest no way of measuring these expenditures, but the potential returns are large, and it would be quite surprising if the investment was not also sizable.

Monopolies involve costs of a somewhat similar nature, and it follows that I will not be able to produce a method to measure their social costs. I will, however, be able to demonstrate that the welfare triangle method greatly underestimates these costs. The argument is customarily explained with the aid of a figure like Figure 1. The monopolist charges the monopoly

FIGURE 1

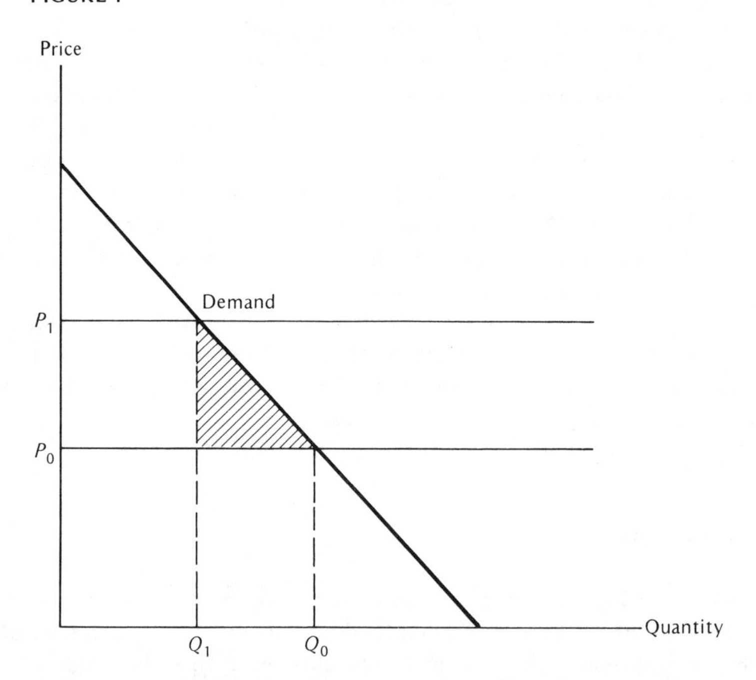

price P_1 instead of the cost P_0 for the commodity, and consumption is reduced from Q_0 to Q_1. The welfare triangle is a clear loss to the community but the rectangle to its left is merely a transfer from the consumers to the owners of the monopoly. We may object to the monopolist getting rich at the expense of the rest of us, but this is not a reduction in the national product.

In order to demonstrate that this line of reasoning ignores important costs, I should like to take a detour through the economics of theft.[2] Theft,

[2] The economics of illegal activities is an underdeveloped area, but Harold Demsetz discusses the subject briefly in "The Exchange and Enforcement of Property Rights," *Jour. of Law and*

of course, is a pure transfer, and therefore might be assumed to have no welfare effects at all. Like a lump sum tax, it produces no welfare triangle at all, and hence would show a zero social cost if measured by the Harberger method. This would, of course, be incorrect. In spite of the fact that it involves only transfers, the existence of theft has very substantial welfare costs. Our laws against theft do not deal with a trivial and/or unimportant problem any more than our laws against monopoly.

Figure 2 shows the situation confronting the potential thief. On the horizontal axis is shown the quantity of effort and capital (burglars' tools, etc.) he might invest in a career of crime. On the vertical axis are shown potential returns. The "opportunity cost" line shows the returns he could get for the same investment of work and material in other occupations. It is assumed

FIGURE 2

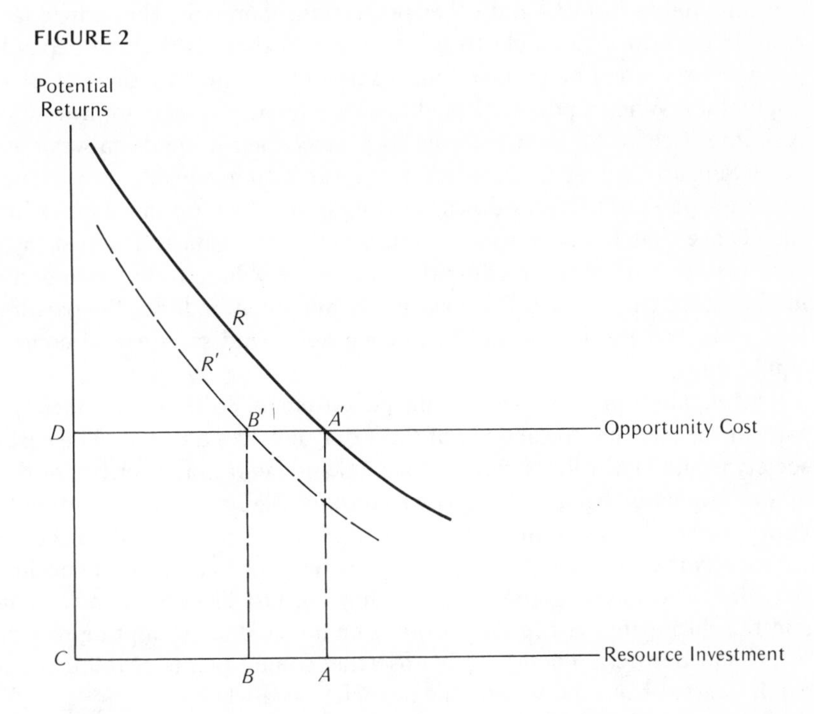

to be constant. Let us begin by assuming that taking another's property is not illegal. Under these circumstances the returns on various amounts of investment in the activity are shown by line *R*. The potential thieves would invest the quantity of resources shown at *A* in theft, the cost to him would

Econ., October 1964, 7, 11–26. J. Randolph Norsworthy's Doctoral Dissertation, *A Theory of Tax Evasion and Collection*, Virginia, 1966, is a more comprehensive examination of one type of illegal activity. Two unpublished items have been circulated among a few scholars. Gary Becker's "A Theory of Government Punishments and Rewards," and my own *Law and Morals*, the unfinished manuscript of a book which I began four years ago and which has languished in draft form for almost all of those four years.

be the rectangle AA′DC, and his net return on the investment would be the triangular area above A′D.

The situation of a person who wished to guard his own assets, who might, of course, be the thief hoping to hold onto his loot, may also be shown on Figure 2. On the horizontal axis are shown the resources invested in loss minimizing activities. The cost of each unit of resources put to this use is shown by the horizontal opportunity line, and the savings are on the vertical axis. The line *R* now shows the returns in the form of savings for each unit of "theft prevention." The total amount of resources invested would again be *A*.

The two situations are interrelated by more than the fact that they can be shown on the same diagram. The height of the *R* curve for the thief would depend upon the amount of resources invested by other members of the community in locks and other protections. Similarly, the individual in considering how many locks to buy would find that his *R* curve depended upon the resources being invested in attempts at theft by the rest of the population. When a potential thief invests money, say, in an improved lock pick, the *R* curve for people trying to protect their property moves downward. Similarly, hiring an armed guard to watch your valuables moves the *R* curve for potential thieves down. Putting a new lock on my door reduces the chance that I will be robbed, but whether the gain will be worth the cost will depend upon the effort the thieves are willing to put into getting in. Over time the interaction between the investment in locks, the payoff on lock picks and the investment in nitroglycerine and safes would come to equilibrium.

This equilibrium, however, would be extremely costly to the society in spite of the fact that the activity of theft only involves transfers. The cost to society would be the investments of capital and labor in the activity of theft and in protection against theft. If we consider Figure 2 as representing the entire society instead of individuals, then the social costs would be the area covered by the rectangle AA′DC. Transfers themselves cost society nothing, but for the people engaging in them they are just like any other activity, and this means that large resources may be invested in attempting to make or prevent transfers. These largely offsetting commitments of resources are totally wasted from the standpoint of society as a whole.

This lesson has been learned by almost all societies that have adopted a collective method of reducing this sort of income transfer. This collective procedure, laws against theft and police and courts to enforce them, can also be shown on Figure 2. On the horizontal axis we now have resources invested by police and courts, with their opportunity cost shown as a horizontal line. The "protection" given by each unit of resources invested in these activities is shown by the *R* line. The society would purchase *A* amount of protective services, and the total cost would be the usual rectangle. The effect of this would be to reduce the expected returns on theft and the savings to be made by private investment in locks, etc. The new returns are shown by the lower R' on Figure 2, and there is a corresponding reduction in the resources invested in each of these fields to B'. Whether the establishment of a police force is wise or not, depends upon an essentially technological question. If police activities are, for a range, more efficient than private provision of protection, then the R line will have the shape shown, and the police and court rectangle will have an area smaller than the sum of the two "savings" rectangles, for theft and locks.[3] This is, of course, what we normally find in the real world.

Note, however, that we do not carry investment in police protection to the extent that it totally replaces private protective expenditures. Clearly it is more efficient to have some protective expenditures by the owners of property. Automobiles are equipped with locks and keys, presumably because the expansion of the police force which could be paid for from the cost of leaving them off would be less effective in preventing theft than they are.[4] The total social cost of theft is the sum of the efforts invested in the activity of theft, private protection against theft, and the public investment in police protection. The theft itself is a pure transfer, and has no welfare cost, but the existence of theft as a potential activity results in very substantial diversion of resources to fields where they essentially offset each other, and produce no positive product. The problem with income transfers is not that they directly inflict welfare losses, but that they lead people to employ resources in attempting to obtain or prevent such transfers. A successful bank robbery will inspire potential thieves to greater efforts, lead to the installation of improved protective equipment in other banks, and perhaps result in the hiring of additional policemen. These are its social costs, and they can be very sizable.

But this has been a detour through the criminal law, our major subject is monopoly. To return to Figure 1, the rectangle to the left of the welfare triangle is the income transfer that a successful monopolist can extort from the customers. Surely we should expect that with a prize of this size dangling before our eyes, potential monopolists will be willing to invest large resources in the activity of monopolizing. In fact the investment that could be profitably made in forming a monopoly would be larger than this rectangle, since it represents merely the income transfer. The capital value, properly discounted for risk, would be worth much more. Entrepreneurs should be willing to invest resources in attempts to form a monopoly until the mar-

[3] It may be suggested that society should not be interested in the saving of the resources of thieves, and hence that the value of the protection afforded by the police should be measured by the lock rectangle only. This, however, would be correct only to the extent that the resources would not be reallocated to socially acceptable production.

[4] James Buchanan and Gordon Tullock, "Public and Private Interaction Under Reciprocal Externality," in *The Public Economy of Urban Communities*, Julius Margolis, Ed., Washington, D.C. 1964, pp. 52–73.

ginal cost equals the properly discounted return.[5] The potential customers would also be interested in preventing the transfer and should be willing to make large investments to that end. Once the monopoly is formed, continual efforts to either break the monopoly or muscle into it would be predictable. Here again considerable resources might be invested. The holders of the monopoly, on the other hand, would be willing to put quite sizable sums into the defense of their power to receive these transfers.

As a successful theft will stimulate other thieves to greater industry and require greater investment in protective measures, so each successful establishment of a monopoly or creation of a tariff will stimulate greater diversion of resources to attempts to organize further transfers of income. In Gladstone's England few resources were put into attempts to get favorable tariff treatment. In present day United States large and well financed lobbies exist for this purpose. The welfare cost in the first case was very low, in the second it must be quite sizable. An efficient police force reduces the resources put into the activity of theft, and free trade or an active antitrust policy will reduce the resources invested in lobbying or attempting to organize monopolies.

The problem of identifying and measuring these resources is a difficult one, partly because the activity of monopolizing is illegal. The budget of the antitrust division and the large legal staffs maintained by companies in danger of prosecution would be clear examples of the social cost of monopoly, but presumably they are only a small part of the total. That very scarce resource, skilled management, may be invested to a considerable extent in attempting to build, break, or muscle into a monopoly. Lengthy negotiations may be in real terms very expensive, but we have no measure of their cost. Similarly, a physical plant may be designed not for maximum efficiency in direct production, but for its threat potential. Again, no measure is possible. As a further problem, probably much of the cost of monopoly is spread through companies that do not have a monopoly, but have gambled resources on the hopes of one. The cost of a football pool is not measured by the cost of the winner's ticket, but by the cost of all tickets. Similarly the total costs of monopoly should be measured in terms of the efforts to get a monopoly by the unsuccessful as well as the successful. Surely most American businessmen know that the odds are against their establishing a paying monopoly, and they therefore discount the potential gain when investing resources in attempting to get one. The successful monopolist finds that his gamble has paid off, and the unsuccessful "bettor" in this particular lottery will lose, but the resources put into the "pool" would be hard to find by economic techniques. But regardless of the measurement problem, it is clear that the resources put into monopolization and defense against monopolization would be a function of the size of the prospective

[5] The margin here is a rather unusual one. Additional units of resources invested in attempting to get a monopoly do not increase the value of the potential monopoly, but the likelihood of getting it. Thus they change the discount rate, rather than the payoff.

transfer. Since this would be normally large, we can expect that this particular socially wasteful type of "investment" would also be large. The welfare triangle method of measurement ignores this important cost, and hence greatly understates the welfare loss of monopoly.

34 It is widely believed that many a monopoly position has been achieved through predatory price cutting that eliminates competitors. Professor McGee examines this belief and the most famous of all of the legends of discriminatory price cutting—the legend of the old (before 1911) Standard Oil Company. He finds that the belief has no foundation of economic logic and that, in fact, Standard Oil did not use predatory price discrimination to drive out its competitors. Professor McGee's 25-page analysis of the facts in the legal record is omitted here.

PREDATORY PRICE CUTTING

JOHN S. McGEE
University of Washington

The purpose of this paper is to determine whether the pre-dissolution Standard Oil Company actually used predatory price cutting to achieve or maintain its monopoly. This issue is of much more than antiquarian or theoretic interest. Settling it is of direct importance to present antitrust policy. At the very least, finding the facts should aid in defining certain hazy notions that now figure in discussions of monopoly and its control.

The Standard Oil Case of 1911

The *Standard Oil* case of 1911 [1] is a landmark in the development of antitrust law. But it is more than a famous law case: it created a legend. The firm whose history it relates became the archetype of predatory monopoly.

It is sometimes said that *Standard Oil* was influential because it revealed deadly and reprehensible techniques by which Monopoly on a heroic scale could be achieved and, probably more important, perpetuated. Historians tell us that the facts revealed in *Standard Oil* were in good part responsible for the emphasis that the antitrust laws came to place upon unfair and monopolizing business practices.

Perhaps the most famous of all of the monopolizing techniques that Standard is supposed to have used is local price cutting. Given the bad repute in which monopoly has long been officially held in this country, and

[1] Standard Oil Co. of New Jersey v. United States, 221 U.S. 1 (1911).

Taken and adapted from "Predatory Price Cutting: The Standard Oil (N.J.) Case." Reprinted with permission from *The Journal of Law and Economics,* Volume 1, October 1958, pp. 137–143, 168, 169.

the prominence of predatory pricing in *Standard Oil,* it is not surprising that the practice received special attention in the law. Monopoly was not new in 1911, but a predatory giant may have seemed novel. The vision of a giant firm that used a brutally scientific, and completely effective, technique for acquiring and maintaining monopoly must have aroused uncommon concern. Standard was invincible. Anything economists could say about the transience of monopoly must have seemed hopelessly unrealistic in view of the vigor and success with which Standard was said to have prevented entry.

In any case, by 1914, in the Clayton Act, predatory price discrimination was included among a select group of business practices the character or effect of which called for explicit statutory prohibition. The Robinson-Patman amendment of 1936 lengthened the list, but certainly did not weaken the hostility toward local price cutting. Indeed, its legislative history and subsequent interpretation reveal a continuing dread of the device.

Predatory discrimination thus occupies a special and almost unquestioned place in law and economics. This has led to a certain amount of difficulty, especially in connection with the Robinson-Patman Act. Some critics claim that this statute unnecessarily restricts rivalry, thereby softening competition. Yet even the critics apparently fear that if we permit the helpful kind of discrimination, we will encourage the lethal kind. Most are obliged to rely on the tenuous standard of intent to distinguish one kind from the other.

Predatory Price Cutting: Some Hypotheses

According to most accounts, the Standard Oil Co. of New Jersey established an oil refining monopoly in the United States, in large part through the systematic use of predatory price discrimination. Standard struck down its competitors, in one market at a time, until it enjoyed a monopoly position everywhere. Similarly, it preserved its monopoly by cutting prices selectively wherever competitors dared enter. Price discrimination, so the story goes, was both the technique by which it obtained its dominance and the device with which it maintained it.

The main trouble with this "history" is that it is logically deficient, and I can find little or no evidence to support it.[2]

In the beginning, oil refining in the United States apparently was com-

[2] I am profoundly indebted to Aaron Director, of the University of Chicago Law School, who in 1953 suggested that this study be undertaken. Professor Director, without investigating the facts, developed a logical framework by which he predicted that Standard Oil had not gotten or maintained its monopoly position by using predatory price cutting. In truth, he predicted, on purely logical grounds, that they never systematically used the technique at all. I was astounded by these hypotheses, and doubtful of their validity, but was also impressed by the logic which produced them. As a consequence, I resolved to investigate the matter, admittedly against my better judgment; for, like everyone else, I knew full well what Standard had really done.

petitive. Necessary capital was relatively slight, because of the modest quality demands imposed by consumer preferences and the primitive technological character of the refining process itself. The number of refiners was evidently large, since the Standard interests bought out more than a hundred of them. Standard Oil was not born with monopoly power: as late as 1870 it had only 10 per cent of the refining business.

The usual argument that local price cutting is a monopolizing technique *begins* by assuming that the predator has important monopoly power, which is his "war chest" for supporting the unprofitable raids and forays. Evidently the technique could not be used until the Standard interests achieved the necessary monopoly power.

A simpler technique did exist, and Standard used it. Unless there are legal restraints, anyone can monopolize an industry through mergers and acquisitions, paying for the acquisitions by permitting participation of the former owners in the expected monopoly gains. Since profits are thus expanded, all of the participants can be better off even after paying an innovator's share to the enterpriser who got the idea in the first place.

Under either competition or monopoly, the value of a firm is the present worth of its future income stream. Competitive firms can be purchased for competitive asset values or, at worst, for only a little more. Even in the case of important recalcitrants, anything up to the present value of the future monopoly profits from the property will be a worthwhile exchange to the buyer, and a bountiful windfall to the seller.

It is conceivable that Standard did not merge to the full size it wanted, but did achieve whatever size was necessary to use predatory techniques to grow the rest of the way. How would it go about using them? Assume that Standard had an absolute monopoly in some important markets, and was earning substantial profits there. Assume that in another market there are several competitors, all of whom Standard wants to get out of the way. Standard cuts the price below cost. Everyone suffers losses. Standard would, of course, suffer losses even though it has other profitable markets: it could have been earning at least competitive returns and is not. The war could go on until average variable costs are not covered and are not expected to be covered; and the competitors drop out. In the meanwhile, the predator would have been pouring money in to crush them. If, instead of fighting, the would-be monopolist bought out his competitors directly, he could afford to pay them up to the discounted value of the expected monopoly profits to be gotten as a result of their extinction. Anything above the competitive value of their firms should be enough to buy them. In the purchase case, monopoly profits could begin at once; in the predatory case, large losses would first have to be incurred. Losses would have to be set off against the prospective monopoly profits, discounted appropriately. Even supposing that the competitors would not sell for competitive value, it is difficult to see why the predator would be unwilling to take the amount that he would otherwise spend in price wars and pay it as a bonus.

Since the revenues to be gotten during the predatory price war will always be less than those that could be gotten immediately through purchase, and will not be higher after the war is concluded, present worth will be higher in the purchase case. For a predatory campaign to make sense the direct costs of the price war must be less than for purchase. It is necessary to determine whether that is possible.

Assume that the monopolizer's costs are equal to those of his competitors. The market has enough independent sellers to be competitive. Otherwise the problem of monopolizing it ceases to concern us. This implies that the monopolist does not now sell enough in the market to control it. If he seeks to depress the price below the competitive level he must be prepared to sell increasing quantities, since the mechanism of forcing a lower price compels him to lure customers away from his rivals, making them meet his price or go without customers. To lure customers away from somebody, he must be prepared to serve them himself. The monopolizer thus finds himself in the position of selling more—and therefore losing more—than his competitors. Standard's market share was often 75 per cent or more. In the 75-per cent case, the monopolizer would sell three times as much as all competitors taken together, and, on the assumption of equal unit costs, would lose roughly three times as much as all of them taken together.

Losses incurred in this way are losses judged even by the standard of competitive returns. Since the alternative of outright purchase of rivals would have produced immediate monopoly returns, the loss in view of the alternatives can be very great indeed. Furthermore, at some stage of the game the competitors may simply shut down operations temporarily, letting the monopolists take all the business (and all the losses), then simply resume operations when he raises prices again. At prices above average variable costs but below total unit costs, the "war" might go on for years.

Purchase has an additional marked advantage over the predatory technique. It is rare for an industrial plant to wear out all at once. If price does not cover average variable costs, the operation is suspended. This will often leave the plant wholly intact. In the longer run, it may simply be the failure of some key unit, the replacement of which is uneconomic at the present price level, that precipitates shut-down. In either case, physical capacity remains, and will be brought back into play by some opportunist once the monopolizer raises prices to enjoy the fruits of the battle he has spent so much in winning.

All in all, then, purchase would not be more expensive than war without quarter, and should be both cheaper and more permanent. It may at first be thought that predatory pricing more than makes up for its expense by depressing the purchase price of the properties to be absorbed. In effect, this requires that large losses reduce asset values less than smaller losses. This is not at all likely. Furthermore, assuming that the properties in question are economic, it is unlikely that their long-run market value will be much reduced by an artificially low price that clearly will not be permanent. The owners can shut down temporarily, allowing the monopolist to carry all of the very unprofitable business, or simply wait for him to see the error of his ways and purchase. Even if there is widespread bankruptcy, wise men will see the value to the monopolist of bringing the facilities under his control, and find it profitable to purchase them at some price below what the monopolist can be expected to pay if he must. Since the monopolist is presumably interested in profits, and has a notion of the effect of discount factors upon future income, he cannot afford to wait forever. Properties that a would-be monopolist needs to control can be an attractive investment.

Predation would thus be profitable only when the process produces purchase prices that are so far below competitive asset figures that they more than offset the large losses necessary to produce them. One empirical test, for those who suspect the logic, would be to examine prices paid for properties in cases where predatory pricing is alleged to have been practiced.

Some of the most strategic factors to be monopolized may be the skilled managerial and technical personnel of competitors. Reproducing them can be a much more formidable and longer job than the construction of physical facilities. But short of murder, the cost of which can also be expected to be high if undertaken in any quantity, the only feasible way of preventing their embarrassing and costly reappearance is to hire, retire, or share with them. None of these things can be accomplished well or permanently if these people are too much badgered in the process.

There are two other crucial issues that must be examined, the first dealing with the extent to which monopolization is profitable; the second, with the necessary conditions for its success. Monopolization as such will be carried only so far as is necessary to maximize profits, since it inevitably involves certain expenses of planning, purchase, and rationalization. In the case of a vertically integrated industry, the would-be monopolist will choose to monopolize the level that will produce the greatest net profit. This requires choosing that one which is both cheapest to control and over which control is likely to endure. If a monopoly can be achieved at the refining level, for example, there is little sense trying to achieve one at the crude oil producing level, or marketing. Standard Oil of New Jersey achieved a refinery monopoly; anything more would have been redundant.

This should not be taken to mean that the monopolist will not care what happens to the other levels, for he has every interest in seeing to it that the other levels are not monopolized by someone else. In marketing, for example, he would prefer that the product be distributed as cheaply as possible, since he can then extract full monopoly revenues from the level in his control. This point is important in interpreting the facts of the *Standard Oil* case.

Obstacles to entry are necessary conditions for success. Entry is the nemesis of monopoly. It is foolish to monopolize an area or market into which entry is quick and easy. Moreover, monopolization that produces a firm of greater than optimum size is in for trouble if entry can occur even over a longer period. In general, monopolization will not pay if there is no special qualification for entry, or no relatively long gestation period for the facilities that must be committed for successful entry.

Finally, it is necessary to examine certain data that are often taken to be symptomatic of predatory price cutting, when, in fact, they may be nothing of the sort. Assume that a monopolist sells in two markets, separated effectively by transport costs or other impediments to free interchange, and that he has a complete monopoly in both. Elasticity of demand is assumed to be the same in both markets, and monopoly prices are identical. Assume that, for some unknown reason, entry occurs in one market but not in the other. Supplies are increased in the first and price falls; price in the second remains unchanged. There are now two different prices in the two markets, reflecting the existence of alternative supplies in the first. The theory of the dominant firm, maximizing by taking into account the outputs of his lesser rivals at various prices, appears to fit the case. An objective fact-finder discovers that the monopolist is discriminating in price between the two markets. A bad theorist then concludes that he is preying on somebody. In truth, the principle established is only that greater supplies bring lower prices.

Compare this example with another. Assume that we have two separate markets and that each is in short-run competitive equilibrium with firms earning super-normal returns. Assume that, for some reason, entry takes place in one market but not in the other. Supply increases and price falls in one but not in the other. From this evidence of price changes in both the monopoly and competition examples, the inference is simply that greater supplies lower prices. We should not infer from the price data that either case has anything to do with predatory price-cutting.

To sum up: (1) Predatory price-cutting does not explain how a seller acquires the monopoly power that he must have before he could practice it. (2) Whereas it is *conceivable* that someone might embark on a predatory program, I cannot see that it would pay him to do so, since outright purchase is both cheaper and more reliable. (3) Because monopolization by any technique always involves some expense, a firm *qua* monopolizer will carry it to the one securest level in an integrated industry, not to all. (4) Actual variations in prices among markets may be accounted for in terms of variations in demand elasticities, but do not imply or establish that anybody is preying on anybody else.

Conclusions

Judging from the record, Standard Oil did not use predatory price discrimination to drive out competing refiners, nor did its pricing practice have that effect. Whereas there may be a very few cases in which retail kerosene peddlers or dealers went out of business after or during price cutting, there is no real proof that Standard's pricing policies were responsible. I am convinced that Standard did not systematically, if ever, use local price cutting in retailing, or anywhere else, to reduce competition. To do so would have been foolish; and, whatever else has been said about them, the old Standard organization was seldom criticized for making less money when it could readily have made more.

In some respects it is too bad that Standard did not employ predatory price cutting to achieve its monopoly position. In doing so it would surely have gotten no greater monopoly power than it achieved in other ways, and during the process consumers could have bought petroleum products for a great deal less money. Standard would thereby not only have given some of its own capital away, but would also have compelled competitors to donate a smaller amount.

It is correct that Standard discriminated in price, but it did so to maximize profits given the elasticities of demand of markets in which it sold. It did not use price discrimination to change those elasticities. Anyone who has relied upon price discrimination to explain Standard's dominance would do well to start looking for something else. The place to start is merger.

It should be quite clear that this is not a verdict of acquittal for the Standard Oil Company; the issue of monopoly remains. What this study says is that Standard did not achieve or maintain a monopoly position through price discrimination. The issue of whether the monopoly should have been dissolved is quite separate.

I think one further observation can tentatively be made. If the popular interpretation of the *Standard Oil* case is at all responsible for the emphasis that antitrust policy places on "unfair" and "monopolizing" business practices, that emphasis is misplaced.[3] This limited study suggests that what businessmen do *to* one another is much less significant to monopoly than what they find it useful to do together to serve their common interest.

[3] The Standard Legend may also be responsible for the strained analogy often drawn between business and war. Analogies to chess strike me as being equally weak. Chess is a competitive game which one player wins, while the other loses. Successful quasi-monopoly seeks to avoid the competitive game, since all players lose as soon as they begin playing it.

Part Six

The selections in this part deal with imperfect competition. The central issues are: What is the relevant market? How significant are barriers to entry? What is the effect of differentiated products? What is the effect of imperfect competition on prices and profits? There is also frequently an issue as to the appropriate scope for regulation

Imperfect Competition

by government, and the consequences of regulation. Regulation is also taken up in Part Eight.

Firms with market power follow strategies of erecting barriers to entry, of differentiating their products, of seeking government protection of price and markets. To what extent does this behavior enhance the well-being of consumers?

35 For the most part, price theory operates with quite simple concepts of the structures of markets. The sellers are either many or they are few; the products of the sellers are either homogeneous or they are differentiated. But when it is looked into, the market structure of an actual industry always takes on a complicated appearance and poses many an analytical problem. This selection on banking markets is just one example. Bank mergers and the activities of bank holding companies have aroused much interest in the strength of competition in banking markets.

THE STRUCTURE OF THE MARKET FOR BANKING SERVICES

ALFRED BROADDUS
Federal Reserve Bank of Richmond

The word "structure" refers to the number and size distribution of buyers and sellers making up a particular economic market. But one cannot determine the structure of a market until the market under consideration is carefully defined and delineated. . . . Speaking broadly, the market for any good or service consists of the individuals, business firms, and government agencies buying or selling the item in question. In practice, however, it may be quite difficult to designate precisely which buyers and sellers constitute a particular market. In defining a market, two especially vexing problems arise: (1) specification of the product or products exchanged in the market and (2) delineation of the geographic area covered by the market.

The *product specification problem* for banking markets is complicated by both product substitutability and product complementarity. With respect to complementarity, the essential question concerns the degree to which the wide variety of services banks provide are related. Banks make loans, accept deposits, process checks, and provide trust services. In addition to these traditional services, banks have expanded their activities in recent years to include the provision of such diverse services as investment consultation and the leasing of computer facilities. Do all of these services so complement one another that it is reasonable to speak of a market for "banking services"? Or, at the other extreme, does each of the individual services provided by banks constitute a distinct product for purposes of market definition?

Whether one views banking services as a composite product or as a group

---

Adapted from Alfred Broaddus, "The Banking Structure: What It Means and Why It Matters," *Federal Reserve Bank of Richmond Monthly Review*, November 1971. Reproduced by permission.

of distinct products, it is clear that nonbank financial institutions provide a variety of services similar to and, in varying degrees, substitutable for the services offered by commercial banks. Hence, in defining markets for banking services, one must determine which nonbank institutions should be included as sellers in these markets. This is the problem posed by product substitutability for the definition of banking markets.

Determination of the *geographic pattern of banking markets* is directly related to product specification. If a distinct market exists for each bank service, it seems reasonable to speculate that the geographic extent of these markets varies considerably from one service to another. For example, while markets for loans to small business firms appear to be local in character, the market for large loans to prime corporate borrowers is probably national in scope. Yet even where the decision is made to differentiate the markets for particular bank services extensively, the geographic area covered by the market for a specific service is often unclear. For example, do markets for loans to small business firms in urban areas include the entire metropolitan region or only some portion of the region? At the other extreme, if the aggregate group of bank services is considered a composite product for purposes of market definition, it becomes quite difficult to specify criteria for geographic market delineation.

One additional issue regarding the geographic specification of banking markets should be noted. In the United States, legal restrictions on bank branching differ from one state to another. Other factors aside, the market area for a given bank service may depend to some degree on the stringency of branching restrictions. Branching regulations are especially relevant to the designation of market areas in metropolitan regions. In cities where branching is permitted, each bank can, with the approval of the proper bank regulatory agencies, enter any neighborhood in the city through the establishment of a branch office. Where branching is prohibited (that is, where "unit" banking prevails), each bank must confine its facilities to a single office in a particular neighborhood or financial district. On these grounds, it has been argued that markets for such bank services as checking deposits cover the entire metropolitan area where branching is permitted, but that these markets are segmented in cities where branching is prohibited.

The Measurement of Banking Market Structure

As stated earlier, the structure of a specific market refers to the number and size distribution of buyers and sellers transacting business in that market. Often, the term is more restrictively employed to designate the number and size distribution of *sellers* in a given market. Throughout the remainder of this study, the phrase "banking structure" will be used in this more limited sense; that is, the term will refer to the number and size distribution of *banks* in particular banking markets.

Certain statistics are commonly employed to specify the structure of banking markets. These statistics include: (1) the number of banks in the market, (2) the number of bank offices in the market, (3) the ratio of banks or bank offices to the population of the market area, (4) "concentration ratios," which indicate the percentage of total deposits held by the largest banks in the market, and (5) the absolute size of individual banks in the market as measured by total deposits or total assets.

In evaluating such data, the essential point is that each statistic, if it is to provide useful structural information, must be appropriately applied to a particular market defined with respect both to product and geographic area. To take an extreme example, the number of banks in the United States or the percentage of total domestic deposits held by the three largest banks in the nation tells one little about the structure of local markets for small business loans or checking accounts. In practice, the difficulty encountered in developing useful data on the structure of banking markets arises at a considerably finer level of detail. In states where branching is permitted, for example, should the geographic market area for a particular bank service be defined to include the entire state, local regions, or portions of local regions? What groups of bank services constitute integrated banking service markets in given areas, and which nonbank financial institutions compete with banks in these markets? In short, the problem encountered in developing and evaluating information concerning the structure of banking markets amounts largely to the problem of defining banking markets. . . . Economists have devoted considerable effort to the analysis of banking markets, and some fundamental results have been achieved. Most economists agree that banking services form a group of related but distinguishable products rather than a composite product. Further, it is generally recognized that geographic market areas vary in extent from one service product to another. Finally, most students of financial markets agree that both bank and nonbank institutions compete in integrated markets for certain types of financial services.

A particularly important organizational phenomenon during the past decade has been the extensive growth of bank holding companies. The structural significance of bank holding companies is twofold. First, the holding company device can be used to bring two or more banks under common corporate control. Second, the device can be employed to bring one or more banks and one or more nonbank institutions under common corporate control. Therefore, bank holding company expansion can directly affect the number of independent banks operating in a market and the concentration of financial resources in the market. In addition, the linking of bank and nonbank activities by bank holding companies may broaden the market (with respect both to service product and geographic area) within which a given subsidiary bank operates.

What Determines the Banking Structure?

Since the banking structure refers to the number and size distribution of banks operating in particular banking markets, it follows that the factors which determine the structure of a specific market are the factors which affect the number and size distribution of banks operating in the market. . . .

Economic Factors

. . . Other things equal, the strength of demand in a market determines how many firms can operate profitably in the market. On the supply side, two especially important determinants of market structure are the technical characteristics of production and the relative ease with which new suppliers can enter the market. Regarding these latter two factors, it is well known that firms in certain industries enjoy economies of large-scale production: that is, decreasing average costs up to a certain level of output. If, in a given market, the output volume at which unit costs begin to rise is high in relation to total market demand, small firms will be driven from the market and new entry will be discouraged. Under these conditions, the market is likely to be characterized by a small number of large firms and a high degree of resource concentration.

Which of these economic determinants of market structure play active roles in shaping the structure of banking markets? The demand for banking services clearly influences the number of banks operating in particular areas. Moreover, demand conditions directly affect bank size. With respect to supply conditions, much attention has been given to the possibility that scale economies exist in the production of banking services. While statistical evidence suggests the presence of such economies, there is little agreement regarding their quantitative significance or their precise impact on the structure of banking markets.

Legal and Institutional Factors

Economic factors, such as those just outlined, only partially determine market structure. Of great importance is the regulatory environment within which a market functions. In the United States, market structure has been directly and extensively affected by the application of antitrust statutes to particular industries. Moreover, entry into several strategic industries is restricted by law or by regulatory authority.

It is quite clear that a principal determinant of the structure and organization of American banking markets is the complex dual system of federal and state banking regulations. Two categories of banking regulations directly affect the banking structure: (1) restrictions on the formation of new banks and (2) regulations which affect structure through their impact on bank organization.

Restrictions on bank formation are embodied in the chartering authority of federal and state regulatory agencies. Federal law and most state laws contain criteria to guide these authorities in approving or disapproving specific applications to establish new banks. These criteria include capital adequacy, the general character of proposed management, and probable effects on the convenience and needs of the community to be served. Because these guidelines are quite broad, regulatory agencies exercise, in effect, discretionary control over bank formation. Through the exercise of this authority, agency decisions directly influence the number of banks and the distribution of bank resources in specific markets.

What is the Significance of the Banking Structure

Some Theoretical Considerations

Perhaps the most significant hypothesis generated by general market theory concerns the relationship between the structure of a market and the efficiency with which the market allocates economic resources. Specifically, the theory asserts that the structure of a market determines the degree of competition in the market and that the degree of competition, in turn, affects the performance of producers with respect to the quantity of goods or services produced, efficiency in production, and prices charged in the market. Speaking generally, the theory draws the following conclusions. First, greater competition exists in markets characterized by large numbers of producers where no producer controls a significant share of the market. Second, given market demand, more competitive markets lead to greater output at lower prices. Hence, according to the theory, the aggregate welfare of the consuming public is improved by markets having numerous competitive producers.

With respect to banking, these theoretical propositions imply that the significance of the banking structure lies in its impact upon the performance of the banking industry in providing bank services to the public. Further, the theory seems to imply that markets with numerous competitive banks are preferable to markets exhibiting other structural characteristics.

The validity of market theory, however, depends critically on several highly restrictive preliminary assumptions regarding the nature of particular industries or markets to which the theory is applied. Where these preliminary assumptions do not correspond to reality, one cannot conclude that a competitive market structure is optimal.

Two of these assumptions are especially relevant to banking. First, the theory assumes that the rapid exit of relatively inefficient firms from competitive markets will not, in and of itself, detrimentally affect the functioning of the market. By eroding public confidence, however, bank failures may disrupt the operation of banking markets. It is true that deposit insurance mitigates some of the harmful effects of bank failures. Nonetheless, the fact that bank failures produce effects external to the failing banks themselves raises serious doubts regarding the desirability of unrestrained competition between banks.

Second, the theory assumes that the technically efficient level of an individual firm's total output is small in relation to aggregate market demand for the product in question. This condition is not met by firms engaged in productive activities characterized by significant economies of scale. Where scale economies exist, highly competitive market structures may be undesirable, since the numerous firms producing in such markets may be forced to operate at suboptimal output levels. As indicated above, several empirical studies have suggested the existence of scale economies in banking. The results of these studies are controversial and by no means conclusive. Nonetheless, they raise additional doubts regarding the desirability of competitive bank markets.

The Banking Competition Controversy

These considerations lie at the heart of what has become known as the "banking competition controversy." Essentially, this debate focuses on a single question: what is the optimal structure of the banking industry? The controversy has a long history and is reflected in the development of bank regulation during the past several decades.

During the 1920's and early 1930's, the highly unsettling effect of widespread bank failures stimulated an equally widespread distrust of unrestricted bank competition. As a result, the Banking Acts of 1933 and 1935 included provisions designed to reduce competition among banks. In particular, the 1935 Act established standards for chartering national banks which tightened restrictions on bank formation. At the same time, state governments imposed a variety of additional restrictions.

In conjunction with the introduction of deposit insurance, these regulations have reduced the rate of bank failure significantly. Within this regulatory environment, however, structural changes of a different sort have appeared during the past two decades. Specifically, the number of independent banks has declined during these years as a result of numerous mergers and bank holding company acquisitions. Consequently, many observers of bank activity have become convinced that too little rather than too much competition exists in banking markets, causing harmful effects on the consumers of bank services. This attitude received its principal practical manifestation when, in 1963, the United States Supreme Court held that a proposed merger of the Philadelphia National Bank with The Girard Trust Company Exchange Bank violated Section 7 of the Clayton Antitrust Act.

Statistical Evidence

In its present form, the banking competition controversy is essentially a debate concerning the effects of the apparent decline in banking competition on bank performance. To enlighten the debate, a number of studies have attempted to measure statistically the relationship between the banking structure on the one hand and bank performance with respect to the quality and pricing of bank services on the other. As indicated earlier, market theory suggests that producers in more competitively structured markets supply greater output at lower prices.

In order to test the validity of this hypothesis for banking markets, studies have employed two sets of variables designed to measure (1) the structure of banking markets and (2) the market performance of banks. Structural variables include the number of banks serving a market, the concentration of banking resources in the market (usually measured by the proportion of total market deposits held by the largest banks serving the market), and bank size. Performance variables include (1) price variables such as interest charged for various types of bank loans and interest paid on time and savings deposits and (2) quantity (i.e., "output") variables such as the ratio of loan volume to total deposits. Market theory suggests that, where other market characteristics are identical, banks will charge lower interest rates on loans, pay higher interest rates on time and savings deposits, and maintain higher loan-deposit ratios in markets having larger numbers of independent banks, larger numbers of competing nonbank financial institutions, and less concentration of banking resources.

The statistical studies have attempted to test these hypotheses. They have also analyzed other relationships between structure and performance and have attempted to determine whether or not economies of scale exist in the production of bank services. . . .

Several studies . . . attempted to determine whether or not the number of banks and nonbank financial institutions competing in particular markets affected bank performance in these markets. While some of the results tend to confirm the above hypotheses, other results either contradict these hypotheses or suggest that no systematic relationship exists.

Conclusions regarding the effects of banking resource concentration were also mixed. A number of studies . . . however, found that less concentrated markets generally exhibited lower interest rates on loans and higher interest rates on time and savings deposits, results which support the theoretical hypotheses.

The results of several studies . . . appear to suggest that, on balance, the performance of large banks is superior to the performance of small banks with respect to both interest rates and the proportion of total bank resources devoted to lending. This finding must be approached very cautiously, however, since large and small banks serve characteristically different types of customers.

Test results were generally inconclusive regarding the performance effects of the organization of banks into branch and bank holding company systems. Four studies . . . however, found that banks belonging to branch and holding company systems maintained higher loan-deposit ratios than banks not associated with such systems.

Economies of scale appear to exist in the production of many banking services. While some studies . . . found these economies to be quantitatively significant, two recent tests . . . concluded that they are relatively small.

While the findings of particular studies were often contradictory or inconclusive, this summary has indicated that, in some cases, several studies (usually employing quite different data) reached similar conclusions. One must be extremely careful, however, in generalizing on the basis of these results. Statistical tests of the sort employed in these studies are subject to inherent limitations. Moreover, the conclusions reached in several of the studies reflect the manner in which market areas comprising study samples were delineated. The earlier discussion of the problems encountered in defining banking markets, therefore, raises additional doubts regarding the validity of test results. In short, the findings summarized here can only be considered suggestive.

36 In models of price formation by industries, whether the competition is pure or monopolistic or oligopolistic, the mechanism of equilibrium includes the procession of firms into or out of an industry. Profits or losses entice or repel firms to enter or to leave. Since about 1950, economists have begun to give more and more attention to the activities of multiproduct firms, which can enter markets new to them simply by adding products to their existing product lines. In this selection, Dr. Hines examines entry by established firms, addressing himself particularly to the effectiveness of such entry in contributing to good competitive performance.

ENTRY BY ALREADY ESTABLISHED FIRMS

HOWARD H. HINES
National Science Foundation

"Entry" is the subject of much recent discussion, especially the growing recognition that the "entering" firm may be, not a newborn one, but an established firm (often a large one) moving into markets or industries where it has not previously participated. An increasing number of writers are pointing this out. But in revising our traditional conception of the mode of entry, should we also change our views about the probable *effectiveness* of entry in our society? Although many of the recent statements plainly imply that entry is much freer, and presumably more effective, than we had believed while thinking in terms of new-firm entry only, there does not seem to be any explicit analysis of this question as yet. The principal purpose of this paper is to try to approach this problem analytically by outlining what appear to be the major issues concerning the effectiveness of established-firm entry in the American setting, and by presenting some of the principal arguments bearing on them.

Requirements for Entry

Before we attempt to discover how *effective* the different forms of entry are likely to be, we shall consider briefly which kind of entry is easier and hence more likely to occur. "Entry" relates to the ease or difficulty with which a

---

Howard H. Hines, "Effectiveness of 'Entry' by Already Established Firms," *Quarterly Journal of Economics,* Vol. LXXI, No. 1, February 1957, pp. 132–150, Cambridge, Mass.: Harvard University Press.

firm can become a member of a group of competing firms by producing a close substitute for the products they are offering. Precise definition of this concept involves the difficulty that the idea of a "group" strictly implies a homogeneous product. There are fundamental logical objections to using the concept when one recognizes that each seller offers a different product. Under these conditions, an "entering" product may substitute closely for some "products" and hardly at all for others. Another entrant might affect a different constellation of sellers. This paper will nevertheless use the "common-sense" meanings of "entry" and "group," which assume that one can deal with an arbitrarily bounded range of substitutes, but the limitations of this procedure must be recognized.

Entry in this sense depends upon a number of specific factors, which it is convenient to classify as: (1) information about opportunities for profitable entry, (2) access to productive resources, (3) access to markets, and (4) ability to overcome immobilities and other frictions that slow the rate of adjustment. The following summary suggests some of the methods by which an established firm may be able to overcome handicaps that might effectively bar new-firm entrants:

1. *Obtaining information:* An established firm probably has unusually good knowledge of profit opportunities in markets contiguous to its own, particularly in those related vertically as suppliers or distributors. Accordingly, it might require a smaller uncertainty allowance than would a newcomer. For example, the diversified firm may adapt retail methods that succeed with one product to the distribution of other kinds of goods.

2. *Access to productive resources:* Capital, and after that managerial and other key personnel, are often strategic factors for entry, since actual markets for both are notoriously imperfect. However, large established firms (and small ones, too, if unusually profitable) may use some of their retained earnings or depreciation charges to open new lines of business. Moreover, as is well known, they obtain outside capital more cheaply than newcomers.

Sometimes, a firm may shift already-installed equipment and processes from one product to another more readily than a new firm could initiate production. Top management might also be already available within the firm; a number of observers have already commented on the generalized nature of managerial skills.

3. *Access to markets:* In addition to organizing economical production, the newcomer must find suitable marketing channels or perhaps build them himself. Once again the already-established firm may have an advantage in being able to adapt existing facilities, especially dealer organizations, to the marketing of new products. Brand preferences sometimes constitute barriers that might cost a fortune for a new firm to overcome by advertising. Yet they may in certain cases be offset cheaply by using a new product. And so sellers attach the brands "Hotpoint" to refrigerators and "Frigidaire" to stoves!

4. *Frictions and immobilities:* Probably the established-firm entrant

would have fewer advantages in overcoming frictions and immobilities than in the cases above. Indeed, if it is large or its management is "old," an established firm may suffer from bureaucratic inertia. On the other hand, a going organization with a fund of know-how may be able to move with far greater speed than a newcomer.

Oligopolistic Uncertainties and Large-Firm Entry

One fact must be kept at the center of attention when analyzing entry into oligopolistic markets. The probability of a new competitor entering such a market does not depend solely on technical or objective factors, such as his ability to match production costs, obtain market channels, and offer an attractive product. He must also be willing to hazard the uncertainties of oligopolistic rivalry. And even though a large, established firm could—if it were actually to make the attempt—enter a given market, survive possible retaliatory measures, and possibly gain a favorable position in a new oligopolistic rationale, it might prefer to avoid uncertainties by not making the attempt. This is all the more likely if established firms are more inclined than new enterprises to prefer a "quiet life." Consequently, our optimistic previous conclusions about ease of entry by established firms have to be modified when we take account of oligopolistic interdependence.

Effects on Market Performance of Entry by Outside Firms

What will be the effects of entry—and potential entry—by established firms on competitive behavior in oligopolistic markets? How will the results compare with what we should expect when the only form of entry would be by new firms? No easy answer is possible; after all, it is not easy to predict the outcome of oligopolistic behavior in general, even apart from entry. However, we shall attempt the more modest task of trying to discuss the directions in which the competitive process will move in the two cases, even if we cannot be certain about the destination. Which is more effective (1) when we take account only of actual entry, and (2) when we consider potential entry also?

Actual Entry

The first point is that there will be some cases in which new firms cannot enter at all, whereas established outside firms can. This method, then, will be the only way in which additional resources can move into the given area of the economy. And the arrival of new resources is probably beneficial, notwithstanding the familiar proposition that, where products are differentiated, the arrival of new sellers may cause each firm to produce at a smaller output and therefore at a higher unit cost, and higher price. For such a result can occur only if the group, as it enlarges in number, always renews its "understanding" of mutual dependence. The arrival of additional entrepreneurs is likely to be wholly beneficial, since the more decision-makers there are, the more difficult it would be to work out and maintain a nonaggressive mode of competition within the group.

Furthermore, there may be situations where entry by an existing firm would be more effective even though new, small firms could actually enter. Let us consider a typical market structure in order to illustrate the point. One frequently observes a small number of large firms, controlling a substantial share of the market, selling differentiated products at similar (if not necessarily identical) prices, while spending large sums on advertising and other nonprice competition. Around them cluster a number of small sellers whose share of the market is relatively small. If a new (small) firm can come into this sort of market at all, it is most likely to enter at either the upper or lower end. That is, it may try to offer specialty products at premium prices or to compete for low-income customers by designing products to allow a lower price. Gradually such entrants might cut into the share of the market held by the major firms. But unless their nibbling processes are unusually persistent, they are likely to remain at best merely part of a "competitive fringe," exerting a minimum disturbance on the price structure of the large sellers. By contrast, established-firm entrants (because of their large size or the strength of their brand or product appeal) might more probably move at once on a large scale into the central core of the market, where they will immediately influence pricing policies.

Potential Entry

Now we must also consider the effects of potential entry, since in oligopoly individual sellers can adjust their behavior for the purpose of forestalling entry. Would they adopt different strategies in the case of potential entry by new and by established outside firms?

The best defense against entry is low prices. While low prices may entail low profits, the latter alone—if caused by production inefficiency, excessive selling costs, and the like—may not deter entry. In the first place, the prospective entrant is likely to have much more information about present prices than about present profits. Also, he will be concerned with his *own* prospective profits, for which those of present operators are not necessarily a good index where there are differentiated products (and dynamic changes in them). Low prices, however, definitely discourage entry, since everyone must take them into account.

Firms already in the market may well overestimate the likelihood of entry by established outside firms. At least, they are more likely to do so than in the case of wholly new firms. Surely the ability of already-established firms to acquire resources and to gain access to markets will be more evident to them than the possible reluctance of those same firms to face oligopolistic uncertainties, the more so in cases where the insiders know that the market has ample room for another seller.

Consequently, considering the greater possible penalty they might have to pay for guessing wrong, sellers are much more likely to modify their competitive behavior to take account of possible entry by already established outside firms than by new ones. What is more, those already in the market may overcompensate for that possibility. The uncertainties of oligopolistic interrelationships will affect *insiders* as well as potential entrants. And the results are likely to benefit the public. Advertising and brand promotion are probably less effective against established outside firms than against new firms. Continuing technological progress would be a more certain protection, but it is difficult to attribute this to any one kind of incentive, still less to that of a particular type of entry. However, we would generally expect the upper limit for an exploitative price to be pressed downward. Indeed, one must interpret the useful notion of a "limit price"—usually specified as determined for those within a market by the average costs of the most efficient potential entrant—not as an objective but as a conjectural value, or as some kind of probability distribution of values. Moreover, potential entry might cause a nervous rival or two to depress the price toward the lower end of the now-narrowed discretionary range. If so, despite the fact that the uncertainties of oligopolistic relationships may diminish the likelihood of actual entry, they may intensify the significance of potential entry.

Social Effects: Career Opportunities

Up to this point, we have considered only the probable market performance effects. We recognize that the actual results of entry by established firms will vary with the facts of each individual case. It will not always succeed, as the recent experiences of Kaiser in automobiles and General Mills and International Harvester in home appliances exemplify. Even at a general and abstract level, we do not assert that actual and potential entry by existing outside firms will tend to bring "ideal" results in oligopolistic markets. The only point is, we do predict a *better* market performance than one would expect from models which assume that entry could occur only in the form of new firms, with the inference that (1) it would not be likely to take place at all, or (2) it would not affect the central oligopolistic core of the market even if it did take place. But this certainly does not imply that there is no need for antitrust or other public policies. And performance effects are not the only criteria for public policy. We must now consider broader social and political issues.

One of these broader standards of judgment concerns career opportunities. Our society holds wide freedom of choice among occupations, particularly for youth, to be an important value. The possibility of starting one's own business provides a desirable opening for a career. Where entry is impeded by barriers of one form or another, including economies of large-scale production and marketing, fields may be closed to young men. That established outside firms may be able to overcome these difficulties hardly means that young men are free to open entrepreneurial careers.

On the other hand, it seems unduly restrictive to identify personal occupational opportunities with owner-management of new firms. There are thousands of openings in government, in labor unions, and elsewhere outside of business. Even with respect to business careers, there are many possibilities within large firms, including the performance of entrepreneurial functions. Granting that entry by established firms does not afford the same kinds of openings for owner-management as new-firm entry is supposed to give, it does offer careers in other forms.

Business Size and "Concentration of Power"

Entry by established firms into markets where they have not previously operated affects not only those markets but also the entering firms themselves. They grow larger, and through diversification they undoubtedly gain in survival power. Consequently, we must evaluate not only "monopoly" in the sense of market control (as we have done above), but also the broader but less definite concepts of the "concentration of power" and "big business."

Despite oversimplification, exaggeration, and the very evident want of exact definition—not to mention quantification—it would be unwarranted to conclude that the concept of concentration of power is wholly unreal, and its problems, imaginary. And to whatever extent these problems are important, it is doubtful whether the predominantly favorable conclusions of the earlier sections of this paper on market performance apply to the later sections on social and political power. To the degree that we desire an individualistic society, a community where massive centers of power are absent, we can derive no comfort from the new views on entry.

Indeed, since firms grow larger as they enter new markets, big business and concentration of power may expand, and consequently social and political evils may result, despite improvement in conditions within specific markets. In the present state of knowledge, one can only speculate about these possibilities. But let one point be clear: The fact that we have given the larger part of our space to the subject of market control rather than to the concentration of power in the broader sense does not mean that the latter issues are less urgent for our society.

Summary and Conclusions

Entry may typically occur in the form of already-established firms, rather than new-born firms, as a number of recent writers have noted. Does entry of this kind perform all the traditional functions of entry, and perform them more effectively, in typical market settings?

Established firms are in almost all respects superior to new firms in their ability to overcome barriers to resources and markets, and to attain economical scales of operation in the face of oligopolistic rivalry. However, entry involves attitudes towards uncertainties as well as objective, technical considerations. Consequently, the uncertainties of oligopolistic interdependence might often deter existing firms from entering. Still, we have argued, firms *within* the markets may well overestimate the probabilities of potential entry by this kind of firm, and behave more competitively as a result. In particular markets, established-firm entry or potential entry should hamper the operation of an oligopolistic rationale, by narrowing the range of discretion in pricing and by tending to push prices toward the lower end of such a range. The probable effects on nonprice competition and particularly on technological innovation are less certain, but the outlook is mostly favorable. No claim is made that established-firm entry will insure "optimum" performance, but only that better results are to be expected than when entry and potential entry are disregarded altogether, or are conceived as new-firm entry only. This general conclusion is subject to modification in the light of the more detailed facts of specific industry or market situations.

While existing-firm entry draws rather good marks on the tests of market performance, it does not rate so well with respect to broader social and political criteria. To the degree that it tends to enlarge big business, established-firm entry may bring a number of results that many citizens would hold to be plainly undesirable. Unfortunately, however, the whole question of the social and political results of "big business" has been more characterized by rhetoric than by research.

37 How far do the prices and outputs of the oligopolistic industries in the American economy depart from the competitive ideal of efficiency? Satisfaction of consumers at minimum cost is the real meaning of efficiency. But consumers must be able to choose; within the constraints of the scarcities of resources, consumers must be able, in fact, to dictate to producers. Whether consumers in the modern economy are sovereign is a much debated issue. Professor Adams reviews the condition of competition in oligopolistic industries. He finds that vigorous competition and continuous innovation in these industries are essential to the maintenance of consumer sovereignty. This selection omits Professor Adams's three case studies because of their length. He shows how the automobile industry had to meet the challenge of foreign cars in the late 1950's, how the scheduled airlines were forced to adopt low-fare coach service in the late 1940's to fend off the cut-rate irregular air carriers, and how Tennessee Valley Authority's policy of low rates in the 1930's was imitated by private electric power companies. Thus there can be competition, or its effects, even in regulated oligopoly and regulated monopoly.

COMPETITION AND CONSUMER SOVEREIGNTY

WALTER ADAMS
Michigan State University

In economic theory, the specifications for "the good society" can be expressed in a few well-chosen propositions. With mathematical precision and logical elegance, it can be shown that an economy functioning according to classical competitive precepts is governed by the sovereign consumer—that free market choices determine the kinds of goods to be produced and the quantities of each. As the voter in a free society retains ultimate control over the political process, so the consumer in a free economy dominates the industrial machinery. In one case, the politician does the voter's bidding in the hope of gaining or holding public office. In the other, the entrepreneur does what the consumer demands in the hope of profit. Given the competitive assumptions, therefore, one may expect resources to be allocated so as to maximize consumer welfare in terms of overt market choices.

The relevant question, of course, is whether this theoretical model conforms to economic reality. To what extent, for example, is the American

---

Reprinted from "Consumer Needs and Consumer Sovereignty in the American Economy," by Walter Adams, *Journal of Business*, Vol. XXXV, No. 3, July 1962, pp. 264–270, 276, 277, by permission of The University of Chicago Press.

economy a democracy oriented to the dollar votes registered by free consumers in a free market, and to what extent is it an industrial autocracy controlled by entrepreneurs with varying degrees of monopoly powers? If it is responsive to consumer desires, does it reflect the wants of all consumers or only the will of a minority commanding a disproportionate share of spending power? If it does satisfy consumer wants in the short run, is it capable of generating an adequate growth rate to assure greater abundance in the long run? These are intriguing questions, and their brooding omnipresence is sure to create employment in the economics fraternity for some time to come. Our interest here, however, is more limited. We shall confine ourselves to a single (perhaps insoluble) empirical problem—the extent to which the American economy gives the consumer what he wants and needs.

I

One approach to this problem is negative—to measure the degree of monopolistic distortion in the allocation process. If monopolistic imperfections are pervasive, consumer sovereignty is *pro tanto* diminished.[1] If, on the other hand, monopoly elements have no more than a *de minimis* effect, and resource allocation approaches the competitive ideal, consumer welfare tends—all other things being equal—to be maximized.

Aggregate Measures of Misallocation

Two recent studies of the American economy shed some light on this subject. In one [Selection 31], Arnold Harberger has attempted to measure the influence of monopoly on resource allocation. He concluded that to correct misallocation and to achieve an optimal allocation of manufacturing resources would have resulted in an improvement of consumer welfare amounting to a little more than one-tenth of 1 per cent. In present values, this welfare gain would have amounted to approximately $2.00 per capita—hardly a heroic achievement.

Following Harberger's findings, David Schwartzman made a similar study [Selection 32] of differential profit rates in competitive and monopolistic manufacturing industries. Schwartzman concluded that, in the aggregate, the American economy is subject to only moderate monopolistic exploitation. He added, somewhat gratuitously, that on the basis of these findings an intensification of the government's antitrust program was not urgently needed.

[1] The reason should be obvious. With a given pattern of consumer preferences, the monopolist not only produces goods in the "wrong" quantities, but frequently the "wrong" goods. His price-output decisions—based on "ignorance" as well as "avarice"—interfere with consumer sovereignty over the use of resources and, at times, with his own profit maximization as well.

Industrial Concentration and Interindustry Competition

Other efforts to measure the significance of monopoly in America have focused on the concentration of power in particular industries. The findings have not been startling: in many industries concentration is high, and oligopoly is a pervasive phenomenon in the non-agricultural sector of the economy. In interpreting these findings, however, some students have cautioned against the use of industry concentration ratios as an index of monopoly power. The relevant index, they suggest, is not the concentration within industries but within markets. The tin-can industry, they point out, may be an oligopoly, but its product must compete in the same market as glass bottles, paper containers, and all sorts of plastic contraptions. Wool, cotton, and silk, as well as rayon, nylon, dacron, cellulose acetate, and many other synthetics, may be defined as separate industries, and some of them may be considered monopolies or oligopolies, but all must eventually compete in a common fibers market. Moreover, a product market which is monopolized in the short run tends to be undermined by dynamic innovations in the long run; it tends, according to this view, to be eroded by what Schumpeter has called the process of "creative destruction." Not only product monopolies but geographical monopolies are subject to the erosive forces of outside competition.

In the consumer goods market, according to a study by Clair Wilcox, oligopoly is not as ubiquitous as some more traditional scholars had supposed. Utilizing the theory of interindustry competition, Wilcox[2] analyzed consumer expenditures in order to measure the range of choice in such major categories as food, clothing, housing, etc. Wilcox concluded—with some justification—that most of the consumer dollar in America is spent under competitive conditions. While he conceded the crucial and pervasive importance of oligopoly in many producer goods markets, Wilcox emphasized that expenditures for food, clothing, housing and furniture are made in markets with an ample and competitive range of choice.[3]

[2] Clair Wilcox, "On the Alleged Ubiquity of Oligopoly," *American Economic Review, Proceedings*, May, 1950, pp. 70–72.

[3] In this connection, it is interesting to note the phenomenal growth of "discretionary" income in the United States. This is the portion of the consumer's income which remains after the basic necessities of life have been paid for. In 1940, discretionary income was estimated at $26.9 billion out of a total disposable income after taxes of $76.1 billion (or 35.3 per cent); by the middle of 1959, the comparable figures were $199 billion out of 335.3 billion (or 59.3 per cent) (see *Advertising Age*, April 18, 1960, p. 58). The significance of discretionary income, of course, is that it may be spent on such divergent items as travel, education, phonograph records, alcohol, etc., and that producers intent on capturing an increasing share of this income must compete for it aggressively—regardless of the degree of protection which their concentrated industries may seem to afford them.

Be that as it may, however, the importance of interindustry competition should not be exaggerated. Such competition can be subverted by merger, entry, or top-level financial control. Thus, when paper containers posed a threat to the tin-can duopoly, Continental entered the paper container industry; when magnesium challenged the aluminum monopoly, Alcoa joined the magnesium cartel; when aluminum threatened copper, Anaconda embarked on its venture

II

The foregoing studies are interesting, but far from conclusive, testimonials to the competitiveness of the American economy. Their chief virtue is negative. They help to guard us against the extremist critics, armed with slogans about "monopoly capitalism" and "Wall Street domination"—critics who confuse pejoratives with documentation. These studies are useful in defining the quantitative limits of the monopoly problem—suggesting that, in the aggregate, monopoly controls are less pervasive than generally supposed and that even in the concentrated industries the aspirations of monopoly are frequently subject to such checks and balances as interindustry competition and dynamic product innovation.

Nevertheless, these studies do *not* prove that the American economy gives the consumer what he really wants. To do this, I submit, we must develop some means of gauging the competitiveness, ingenuity, and progressiveness of entrepreneurs. We must approach the measurement of consumer satisfaction by examining producer rather than consumer behavior. After all, if the consumer at prevailing prices buys what he is offered; if there is equilibrium in the sense that no transfer of expenditure from one good to another will increase welfare; if producers earn no more than normal profits, can it be said that the economy serves the consumer as well as it might—that consumer satisfaction is indeed maximized? Obviously not, because this equilibrium is achieved only within a limited range of choice; because this equilibrium is "local" rather than "global"—because we can never know how much better off the consumer would be if his range of choice were expanded by the introduction of new products or by offering the old products at different prices. The real test of consumer welfare is not whether consumers buy what they are offered (i.e., whether the market clears), but whether entrepreneurs are constantly experimenting—testing the market for "dormant" layers of demand for old goods and "latent" tastes for new ones.

Noteworthy in this connection is Oscar Lange's observation that "*the real danger of socialism is that of a bureaucratization of economic life*, and not the impossibility of coping with the problem of allocation of resources." [4] This Weberian curse (from which capitalist societies are by no means immune) involves the danger that entrepreneurs will be essentially conservative—that they will not probe for better ways unless forced to do so by powers beyond their control. The bureaucratic mentality, whether it infests a socialist planner or private monopolist, transcends national boundaries and defies ideology. It is hostile to novelty. It is rigid. It is anti-experi-

---

in the aluminum industry. Today railroads control bus lines, newspapers control radio and TV stations, and radio licensees operate TV outlets. Moreover, in an extreme sense, interindustry competition is perfectly compatible with a fully monopolized economy.

[4] Oscar Lange and Fred M. Taylor, *On the Economic Theory of Socialism* (Minneapolis: University of Minnesota Press, 1938), p. 109. (Italics in original.)

mental. It is addicted to the status quo. It is activated not so much by a desire for monopoly profit as the search for the quiet life. It seeks to insulate itself from the winds of change. Imagination and initiative are outside its lexicon of virtues. Its slogan is to let well enough alone.

Here is the nub of the problem. If Lange is right, if bureaucracy is indeed the great danger, then the way to serve the consumer better is by curtailing bureaucracy rather than sanctifying it with official anointment. The solution lies in decentralization, dispersion of the centers of decision-making, autonomy for the seedlings of initiative. The solution lies in giving the market freer play, because the greatest threat to incrusted bureaucracy is the challenge of competition, the existence of a yardstick by which to measure performance, the presence of alternatives to decisions by the few for the many. Competition is what the bureaucrat fears most, because it compels him to do the customer's bidding, to submit to consumer choice. Where competition is effective, the entrepreneur can survive only by meeting the standards set by forces beyond his control. He can prosper only by turning in a performance superior to that of his rivals. In either case he cannot impose his will on the public; he is its servant, not its master.

Competition, then, is the obverse of bureaucracy. And the animus of competition consists of a willingness to experiment—to find out whether market expansion can be achieved through price reduction, and to do so against the prevailing judgment of the "experts." It is the willingness to be a nonconformist, a readiness to test new ideas which the traditional wisdom considers unworkable, an inclination to revolt against the conservatism of vested interests. This is the competitive animus which is the consumer's ultimate protection and most viable servant.

In the United States, this entrepreneurial spirit is not always or necessarily confined to the competitive segments of the economy. It *may* (and frequently does) operate in some highly concentrated industries, serving to produce market results surprisingly close to the competitive ideal.

Summary

Competitive entrepreneurship in the American economy is not *necessarily* confined to competitive industries, but may at times operate in unregulated oligopolies, regulated oligopolies, and regulated monopolies. The checks and balances which tend to break down the bureaucratic preference for letting well enough alone, and to compel entrepreneurs to submit to consumer sovereignty, are more widespread than is generally supposed. Be it the dictates of the competitive market, the pressure from imports or substitutes, the alternatives provided by the unregulated industry, or the yardstick imposed by government competition, there are forces at work which tend to erode, subvert, or render obsolete the conservative bias inherent in any organization devoid of competition. In the long run, it is these pressures—sometimes admittedly anemic, sometimes altogether too latent—which protect the consumer against outright exploitation or deprivation. It is these pressures which tend to assure the consumer that his "physical" desires are never too far removed from his effective demand. It is these pressures which the policy-maker must attempt to reinforce where they exist and to *build into* the market system where they are missing or moribund. The policy objective, throughout, must be to promote market *structures* which will *compel* market conduct and market performance in accordance with consumer sovereignty.

To the extent that a free enterprise system is built around this disciplining force of competition, it is—despite its faults—superior to a regime of socialist planning. For, even if we assume (with Oscar Lange) that the socialist is activated by the most noble of motives; even if we assume that he is basically consumer-oriented in his planning—he may still lack the willingness and inclination to pioneer untried trials, to explore paths which may lead to dead ends, to take risks which may not pay off, to try to make tomorrow better than the best.

In a word, consumer sovereignty without competition is sterile; and if competition did not exist, it would have to be invented.

38

This excerpt describes the consequences of regulation of Airline fares by the Civil Aeronautics Board (CAB). The regulation of fares led the airlines to compete in service quality. The validity of this analysis seems to be confirmed by the experience of the airlines following the deregulation of fares: fares dropped, service quality was reduced, and airline load factors increased.

DOMESTIC TRUNK AIRLINE REGULATION

THEODORE E. KEELER

In recent years, the domestic trunk airline industry has been the subject of numerous economic studies, nearly all of which have questioned the appropriateness of regulation of this industry, as practiced by the Civil Aeronautics Board (CAB). Largely as a result of these studies, there have been increasing pressures for regulatory reform in airlines and legislation to achieve such reform has been proposed by members of both the executive and legislative branches of the U.S. Government, and even by a special task force of the CAB itself.

In addition, since 1975, it has pursued a policy of deregulation based on the existing laws starting in the middle of 1977.

It is the aim of this chapter to provide an economic assessment of the desirability of airline regulation as it is currently practiced by the CAB, and to evaluate the alternatives for regulatory reform. . . .

Regulation of Fares

"The remarkable thing about the regulation of fare levels by the Board is how little of it there has been." So Richard Caves sums up the matter succinctly.[1] Caves backs this statement up with a persuasive argument that, in fact, during its first twenty years of existence, the Board consistently attempted to dodge the issue whenever it was asked to come up with an overall, consistent policy regarding the level and structure of fares. It was not until 1961, with the General Passenger Fare Investigation, that the CAB proclaimed general principles of cost accounting (i.e., cost of capital and depreciation guidelines) on which fares should be based. And it still skirted general issues such as the load factor (per cent of seats filled) on which fares should be based, and the first-class-coach

[1] Richard E. Caves, *Air Transport and Its Regulators* (Cambridge, Mass.: Harvard University Press, 1962), p. 140.

Excerpted from Senate Committee on Governmental Affairs, "Study on Federal Regulation," Appendix to Volume VI, *Framework for Regulation,* December, 1978, pp. 77–99.

differential. It was not until the Domestic Passenger Fare Investigation, in the 1970's (discussed below) that the CAB met these issues head-on, and attempted to develop such general principles.

But the mere fact that the CAB was for so long unwilling to openly articulate general policies regarding fares does not mean that it had none. It can be argued that the CAB preferred the flexibility provided by not having to apply general principles everywhere. Circumstances change, and the CAB had every reason to want to change with them.

Still, from the CAB's behavior over the years, certain dominant concerns can be traced. Consider first the pre-World War II period during the first years of Board regulation. It has been said that the Board and the carriers had no concern about fares at that time.[2] It might be more accurate to say that there was agreement between the Board and carriers as to what fares should be, and hence no conflicts arose. Both agreed on a discriminatory, "value of service," pricing scheme, based on the following premise. To promote the development of civil aviation, as required by law, it was necessary to have a nation-wide system, despite the fact that some routes were more profitable than others. To assure this, it was necessary that prices be set to make the service attractive on all routes. Thus, during those days, airline fares were based almost exclusively on first-class rail fares (indeed, they were roughly the same in most major markets).[3] The prices of the nearest substitute determined fares, and government subsidies made up the rest. It is not difficult to see why the CAB and the carriers should arrive at a tacit agreement as to the appropriateness of this scheme.

During the first 10 years of CAB regulation, fare changes occurred only when it was thought that the carriers' returns were excessive or inadequate. Thus, fare cuts were required during World War II in the face of high load factors and large profits. Fare increases were allowed after the war as profits declined.

But in the late 1940's, this situation changed: pressures arose for fare cuts, generated by the rise of the aforementioned nonskeds. The CAB's response to these pressures had a certain consistency to it: it was pervaded by a fear that airline revenues and profit would decline. Whenever the requested price cut was to a limited class of customers and allowed clearcut discrimination, without loss of revenues (as in the case of family fares), the CAB allowed the cuts.[4] On the other hand, when the proposed reductions threatened to lower the entire fare structure, the Board was at best reluctant to go along (the CAB's slowness to accept coach fares at the beginning and its reluctance to allow their spread is a case in point).[5] This behavior can be criticized as anti-consumer. But it must be remembered that during the late 1940's, the trunk industry was still subsidized directly, and only the benefit of hindsight allows us to see that direct subsidies would soon no longer be necessary. Under those circumstances, the

[2] Ibid., p. 141.
[3] Ibid., p. 357.
[4] A discussion of price-discriminatory policies of the CAB may be found in Caves, pp. 155–167.
[5] Caves, pp. 167–168.

CAB's fears of increased subsidy needs because of the onset of price competition were not irrational.

During the 1950's, however, the economic situation of the trunk carriers changed. They went off direct subsidies, and more or less all of their unprofitable routes were taken over by the local service carriers. Yet still the CAB tended to prevent fare cuts, and to prevent entry by lines who proposed such cuts. This was especially the case when carrier returns were below the official returns "allowed" by the CAB (discussed later in this section), or when a weak carrier was threatened.

Rate of Return Regulation

What are the motivations for this? One most certainly relates to a sincere desire that the airlines should be able to earn a "fair" rate of return. More specifically, as a result of the General Passenger Fare Investigation of 1961, the CAB established that a "reasonable" rate of return for the trunk carriers was 10.5 percent overall, including both debt and equity capital (i.e., the return to both stockholders' equity and bondholders' debt). As a result of the Domestic Passenger Fare Investigation of 1971, this overall return for the trunk carriers was raised to 12 percent.

There is little wonder that there should be competitive pressures to reduce fares set to yield these rates of return, because they are considerably higher than the rate which could be earned by an equivalent investment in a typical U.S. corporation (this "typical" return is called a "normal" return, or "the opportunity cost of capital," because it gives an indication as to what other typical investment opportunities will yield). More specifically, over the 40-year period between 1938 and 1968, the typical U.S. corporation earned an average return on investment of about 7.5 percent after taxes.[6] Thus, the CAB, in the returns which it has allowed over the past 15 years, may be building an incentive for price-cutting or overscheduling by setting them at "too high" a level.

Despite the CAB's persistent aim of a rate of return of 10.5 to 12 percent on investment for trunk airlines, the carriers have seldom been that profitable, and on the average, they, like the corporate sector, have earned an average of about 7.5 percent on their investment during peacetime years between 1938 and 1966.[7] Thus, CAB policies have been unsuccessful at achieving the above-normal profits embodied in its regulatory goals, despite the persistent vigilance on the part of the CAB to prevent price competition. We shall consider the reasons for this failure shortly. First, however, we investigate another reason why the CAB has desired to prevent price competition, and the degree of success it has had on this second count.

[6] For returns up to 1968, see Caves, p. 392. For returns past 1962, see Theodore E. Keeler, Resource Allocation in Intercity Passenger Transportation (Doctoral dissertation, Massachusetts Institute of Technology, 1971), pp. 20, 22.

[7] See Keeler, Resource Allocation, pp. 20, 22, and Caves, p. 392.

Cross-Subsidization

This second reason is the CAB's desire to minimize the need for Federal subsidies to unprofitable routes. The CAB has felt the political obligation to support service on these unprofitable routes for reasons described in the previous section. The idea here is that if some routes are profitable, the profits from these routes can be used to support losses on unprofitable routes (this is generally called "cross-subsidization" by economists). If, however, price competition is allowed on profitable routes, the profits will be dissipated, and subsidy requirements for unprofitable routes will increase (of course, competition in flight frequency may cause the same thing; this is discussed below).

A clear statement of the CAB's views on cross-subsidization came in the late 1940's, when "nonsked" carriers (previously mentioned) attempted to enter long-haul, high-density routes with scheduled service at fares considerably below those charged by the trunk carriers. The CAB rejected the nonskeds' proposals, for the explicit reason that such low fares would eliminate trunk profits from these routes, necessitating an increase in subsidies for unprofitable routes.[8]

The CAB applied its cross-subsidization doctrine again in the early 1950's when the local service carriers were new, and were expanding their routes. During these years, the CAB on several occasions withdrew the route authority of the trunk carriers from a given route, and gave it to a local service carrier, stating explicitly that if local service carriers had some profitable routes, it would greatly reduce government subsidy requirements. For example, in the *Southwest Renewal* case of 1952, the CAB suspended United's route authority (over United's strong protest) to four California cities and awarded them to a local service carrier. The Board noted that the local service carriers involved (directly and through connections) would gain an estimated $207,000 "which would ultimately revert to the Government in the form of reduced subsidy mail-pay requirements."[9] Numerous other cases of this can also be found during the period in the early 1950's when the local service carriers were developing their route structures.[10]

In the middle and late 1950's, with strong Congressional support for higher subsidies, the CAB lost interest in route-strengthening, and it worried less about it.[11] However, by the early 1960's, the situation changed again. President Kennedy's 1962 transportation message to Congress expressed a desire for the CAB "to develop . . . a step-by-step program, with specific annual targets, to assure sharp reduction of operating subsidies."[12] The Board again embarked on a route-strengthening drive, wherein it granted the local service carriers routes competitive with trunk carriers. Thus, whereas in 1955 only 19 percent of local service passenger-miles came from routes with the rivalry of more than one

[8] Caves, p. 173.
[9] Caves, pp. 224–225.
[10] Ibid., pp. 224–229.
[11] Ibid., p. 229.
[12] George Eads, *The Local Service Airline Experiment* (Washington, The Brookings Institution, 1971), p. 107.

carrier, by 1965 fully one-third of all local service passenger-miles came from such routes. Further route-strengthening was attempted between 1966 and 1972, and by 1970 fully 45 percent of all local service passenger-miles were generated on competitive routes.[13]

The success and the desirability of such attempted route-strengthening will be discussed below. The point here is that in awarding routes so as to reduce the subsidy needs of the local service carriers, the CAB was clearly admitting that some routes were more profitable than others, and acknowledging that its policy was indeed to use profits from some routes to support losses from others.

While the strongest evidence of desire to cross subsidize comes from the CAB's behavior toward the local service carriers, it has often behaved in a similar manner toward the trunks: a trunk carrier is often awarded a profitable new route if its existing route structure makes it unprofitable (after all, if a trunk carrier with unprofitable routes went out of business, the CAB might have to come up with subsidies to cover operations of its routes by subsidized carriers). An important example of this occurred in 1956, when the Board granted Northeast Airlines entry into the New York-Miami market, with the explicit goal of "strengthening" its route structure.

How successful have CAB policies on cross-subsidization been? Direct evidence on this count is difficult to get. However, there are several pieces of evidence from which to infer that little cross-subsidization goes on, at least at the trunk level.

First, it is worth noting that as soon as the trunk carriers went off direct subsidies, they were generally more than willing to abandon their unprofitable routes, allowing them to be taken over by local service carriers. Why should their stockholders be eager to subsidize service to small towns from their own pockets?[14] Then, as the local service carriers have been granted more and more profitable routes, they have been eager to go off subsidies, and to hand off their unprofitable routes to unregulated third-level or commuter carriers.[15] Thus, Allegheny has acquired enough profitable routes to go off subsidy completely, and has contracted out most of its unprofitable routes to third-level carriers using much smaller aircraft.[16] The point is that just as rapidly as the CAB seems to grant profitable routes to cross-subsidize unprofitable ones, the carriers involved attempt to abandon the unprofitable ones. And in the past 6 years or so, the CAB has been willing to grant such abandonments freely. . . .

Second, Caves provides direct evidence that even in the late 1950's, cross subsidies had ceased to exist on trunk level routes. Table 1 shows Caves' calculations as to the relationship between price and cost by route density and length of haul as of 1958. His results indicate rather clearly that there was

[13] Eads, p. 118.

[14] A complete discussion of the development of the local service carriers, and of the abandonment of various routes by the trunks, may be found in Eads, Chapter 6.

[15] Ibid., pp. 166–169.

[16] In 1974–1977, Allegheny received no subsidies. See Civil Aeronautics Board, *Air Carrier Financial Statistics* (December 1975), p. 23, (June 1977) p. 22.

Table 1 Caves' Estimates of the Ratio of Average Costs to Average Revenue per Passenger-Mile, by Distance of Trip and Volume of Traffic

Volume of Traffic (Passengers per Year)	*Distance (Miles)*				
	200 and Under	201–400	401–800	801–1,200	*Over* 1,200
Under 1,000	1.49	1.10	1.04	0.89	0.91
1,001 to 5,000	1.37	1.01	.86	.83	.89
5,001 to 25,000	1.09	.78	.74	.68	.77
25,001 to 100,000	1.06	.66	.60	.57	.60
Over 100,000	1.05	.64	.60	.57	.61

Source: Caves (1962), p. 409.

relatively little cross subsidy on routes above 200 miles in length and above 5,000 passengers per year in density. As Caves points out, practically all trunk routes by 1958 were 200 miles or longer and were above 5,000 passengers per year in length. It can be argued, however, that with the advent of the jet plane, the cost of long-haul travel relative to short-haul travel declined, and CAB fares by long-hauls.[17] However, this was corrected more or less completely by fare changes in the early 1970's.[18] Finally, the CAB itself gave evidence of rejecting the cross-subsidy doctrine in 1974. It stated that where fares exceed costs "rather than providing subsidization of short-haul services, . . . [they] merely subsidize wasteful competitive practices . . . Only if the domestic air transportation system consisted of a single monopoly carrier" could cross subsidy be expected to succeed.[19] (The "wasteful competitive practices" mentioned by the CAB will be discussed in the next section.) . . .

If cross subsidies are non-existent, and if the airlines have earned normal profits, one is tempted to believe that CAB regulation has had no effect on fares. And yet evidence from markets outside the reach of the CAB, the intrastate markets in Texas and California, would imply that this is not the case. Thus, intrastate fares in California, brought about by competition from non-CAB regulated carriers (most importantly Pacific South-west Airlines (USA)), have consistently been 30 to 50 percent below fares on equivalent interstate routes. Similarly, since the entry of an intrastate carrier in Texas, Southwest Airlines fares in that State have been lower by similar amount.[20] Moreover, potential entrants to interstate routes have proposed fares similarly lower than CAB regulated fares on long-haul routes. Most notably, World Airways, a charter carrier, has proposed New York–California service at fares 40 percent below

[17] "Airline Regulation and Market Performance," p. 419.
[18] The increase in fare markup over costs with distance observed for 1968 seemed to have disappeared by 1972. See Keeler (ibid.), p. 420.
[19] CAB order 74-382, pp. 71–72, as cited in Kennedy Report, p. 64.
[20] This is documented in detail in the following section.

prevailing CAB regulated fares. Finally, the CAB has itself authorized fares to Hawaii and Puerto Rico far lower than long-haul mainland fares for similar distances, and the eagerness of carriers to provide this service without subsidy is evidence that this service is profitable.[21] More detailed evidence on these fares will be considered shortly. The main point here is that there is ample evidence that CAB policies have indeed rigged trunk air fares in continental United States at levels well above what an unregulated market would provide for.

Service Quality Competition

If, indeed, fares are rigged at such high levels, where do the money (and, more importantly, the accompanying resources) go? We have already noted that they do not go into excess profit, and there is little evidence to support the notion that it goes into cross subsidizing low-density routes.

This seeming paradox is not likely to be a quandary to anyone who flies, and the answer has been noted in numerous studies. As the present writer put it in 1972, "with fares set at high cartel levels, the airlines have competed away profits through excess capacity. Since more frequent flights mean more business, there is an incentive to compete through flight frequency instead of prices, and the resulting excess capacity appears to keep profits down to a normal level."[22] Of course, service quality competition can occur in dimensions other than flight frequency. Holding frequency constant, larger aircraft with more seats make it easier to get reservations during peak periods: roomier seats, lounges, movies, sumptuous meals, and fast baggage service are other ways to compete in service quality, as well.[23] Different students of the industry may disagree as to just how close the industry has come to earning normal profits, and to just what types of service quality competition have been used to compete profits away. But all economists studying the problem (and the Senate Subcommittee on Administrative Practices and Procedure) seem to agree that the airlines do compete away more or less all excess profits in service quality competition, thereby negating CAB efforts to raise trunk profits above a normal level, and to cross-subsidize service on lower-density lines. . . .

The Domestic Passenger Fare Investigation—Scope and Intention

The CAB has for some time been aware of the service quality competition of the sort noted above, and has attempted to do something about it. More specifically, the Domestic Passenger Fare Investigation of 1971–74 (DPFI) was

[21] Kennedy Report, pp. 49–51.
[22] "Airline Regulation and Market Performance," p. 421.
[23] Lower load factors make it easier to get reservations during crowded periods. This notion will be discussed in more detail in the following section.

intended to develop (for the first time) an all-around fare policy, and to deal with the service quality competition problem, and some others, as well.[24] Let us therefore briefly consider the DPFI, the policy changes resulting from it, and the actual changes in fares and service qualities which in turn resulted from these policy changes.

The first change in CAB goals resulting from the DPFI was to up the target rate of return to be built into fares from 10.5 to 12 percent rates of return (in both cases this is the after-tax return on all assets, debt and equity combined). The appropriateness of this change is highly questionable, especially given that the industry has managed to get all too much capital at a much lower (but normal) return of 7.5 percent after taxes.

In addition to a rate of return standard, the DPFI resulted in a load-factor standard of 55 percent overall, i.e., fares were to be set such that a carrier could earn exactly a 12 percent after-tax return on all assets if 55 percent of the seats were filled. This change, unlike the target rate of return, was based on a new principle. The CAB has previously set target rates of return, but it had not set a target load factor. Previously, if the return was "inadequate," the Board could authorize fare increases; but if additional service competition drove the return back down to an "inadequate level," another fare increase would be needed, and so on. This "rachet effect" could theoretically drive fares ever higher, with no increases in cost at a given load factor.[25]

In principle, the notion of a 55 percent load factor standard on which to base fares was an improvement, relative to past practice, which was vulnerable to the aforementioned rachet effect. However, there are at least two reasons why the policies resulting from the DPFI may fall well short of what is feasible by way of economic efficiency (note we say "may" here, because a complete discussion of economic efficiency in the airline industry is deferred until the next sction).[26]

First, the assumption of a 55 percent load factor is arbitrary, and there is little, if any, evidence that it represents an optimal trade off between fare and service quality (i.e., the ease of flying when one wants to fly) on a significant number of routes. In fact, evidence presented in the following section indicates that on most routes a higher load factor would be appropriate. Furthermore, it is likely that the optimal load factor will vary from route to route, making a single universal number inappropriate.

Second, we have already presented evidence that a 12 percent rate of return is probably higher than the opportunity cost of capital, and higher than the airline industry has historically generated. On the basis of past evidence, one would expect rates set to generate a 12 percent rate of return at a 55 percent load factor to, in fact, generate a lower post-tax return (say, 7.5 percent), as

[24] A more detailed discussion of the DPFI may be found in Douglas and Miller, pp. 150–169.

[25] The term "rachet effect," applied to this phenomenon, was first used by Douglas and Miller. See pp. 54–57.

[26] For a more detailed critique of the DPFI, see the Kennedy Report, pp. 121–122, and Coleman, pp. 6–13.

service quality competition drives the load factor overall below 55 percent.[27] That is, load factors would be driven down until airline profits equaled the opportunity cost of capital.

So far, we have been primarily concerned with describing the goals and policies of the Civil Aeronautics Board in its execution of the Civil Aeronautics Act of 1938, with only a hint here and there as to the economic appropriateness of its policies. It is now time to turn to a more systematic economic evaluation of these policies.

The Impact of CAB Regulation: An Economic Analysis

At the end of the previous section, I described a hypothesis about airline regulation on which most students of the area agree—that, although the CAB has set trunk airline fares at high, "cartel" levels, the potential profits from these fares are competed away through frequency and service quality competition on the part of the airlines. As a result, the airlines do not gain profits from the regulation, and the consumer is left paying a fare much higher than he would prefer, with lower load factors and presumably higher service quality than he would prefer.[28]

This section is concerned with examining the evidence regarding this hypothesis, and with providing an estimate as to the likely welfare loss or gain from CAB regulation. Consideration must be given to costs and benefits to several groups: consumers in high-density markets, consumers in low-density markets (which perhaps currently are cross subsidized), carriers, and suppliers of inputs to carriers. . . .

Evidence of the Impact of CAB Regulation on Fares and Service Qualities—The Intrastate Routes

In order to test the hypothesis that CAB regulation has held fares at an unnaturally high level, and load factors at an unnaturally low level, the first place one would be inclined to look would be domestic markets outside the reach of the CAB's powers. Such markets currently exist on intrastate routes in California and Texas.

Markets in both States have enjoyed considerably less regulation, both of fares and of firm entry, than have the intrastate trunk routes controlled by the CAB. Both are regulated to some degree, however, in California by the California Public Utilities Commission, and in Texas by the Texas Aeronautics Commission.

[27] At no time in the past 20 years have the airlines earned a return as high as 12 percent overall. If the cost of capital of 12 percent assumed by the CAB were correct, most firms would have gone out of the industry years ago. See Kennedy Report, pp. 121–122.

[28] The idea here is that higher service quality comes from higher fares, and there is a limit to what the typical traveler is willing to pay for high service quality. This is discussed at length below.

In California, both fares and firm entry were almost totally unregulated until 1965, except that a new firm had to meet safety standards set by the Federal Aviation Administration, and the PUC could set maximum rates, but not minimum ones. In 1965, the Public Utilities Commission was given the right to control both fares and entry of firms, with the aim of achieving an " . . . orderly, efficient, economical, and healthy intrastate air network . . ." along with stability, low fares, and frequent service.[29]

The Texas Aeronautics Commission (TAC) has complete control over entry of firms, as does the California PUC, but very limited control over fares. Technically, it has control over an intrastate carrier's fares; but it claims no control over the fares of intrastate operations of interstate carriers, so it has effectively allowed pricing freedom for both carrier types.[30] The law requires the TAC to "further the public interest and aeronautical progress by providing for the protection, promotion, and development of aeronautics."[31]

In both States, the relevant regulatory agencies have been considerably more liberal than the CAB in allowing new firms to enter, and in allowing downward price competition. Thus, after 1965, 16 new carriers entered the California market, and after 1965 two new carriers have been allowed to enter in California. Of these 18 carriers, however, only two important ones, Pacific Southwest Airlines (PSA) and Air California have survived.[32] In Texas, one carrier, Southwest Airlines, has entered the market, and then only after lengthy court litigations although the Texas Aeronautics Commission favored entry of Southwest Airlines from the beginning, Texas law allows court appeal of TAC decisions by interested parties, including carriers already serving the routes proposed for service by Southwest.[33]

The numbers of intrastate carriers succeeding in each market (one in Texas and two in California) may seem small. But even these small numbers would seem to be enough to instigate vigorous price competition. They cut fares sharply and forced the CAB-regulated carriers to match the cuts for intrastate traffic.[34] As a result, fares on every intrastate route are significantly below fares on routes of equivalent length and traffic density as CAB routes.

Fare Differences To give an idea of these differences, Table 2 presents some current California intrastate fares (and yields per mile) alongside equivalent

[29] Simat, Helliesen, and Eichner, vol. I, p. 11.

[30] Testimony of Charles A. Murphy, Executive Director, Texas Aeronautics Commission, before U.S. Senate, Committee on the Judiciary, Subcommittee on Administrative Practices and Procedure. Hearings on Oversight of Civil Aeronautics Board Practices and Procedures, Feb. 14, 1975, 94th Congress, First Session, vol. II (Washington, U.S. Government Printing Office, 1975), p. 528.

[31] Simat, Helliesen, and Eichner, vol, I. p. 11.

[32] It is worth noting, however, that the carriers which went out of business in California tended to be very small and short-lived (under a year, usually). Thus, this experience does not indicate that a well-established carrier would be likely to go out of business with deregulation. See Jordan, pp. 14–33.

[33] Simat, Helliesen, and Eichner, pp. 17–18.

[34] A full discussion of this pricing behavior may be found in Jordan, Chapter 5 for California, and in Simat, Helliesen, and Eichner, vol. II, chapters II and III for California and Texas, respectively.

Table 2 Fares on Intrastate and Comparable Interstate Routes

	Fare (Includes Tax)	*Nonstop Distance (Miles)*	*Fare per Mile*
Los Angeles to San Diego	$12.25	109	$0.112
Fresno to San Francisco	16.00	165	.097
Fresno to Los Angeles	20.00	213	.094
Los Angeles to San Francisco	25.50	337	.076
Los Angeles to Sacramento	26.50	373	.071
Cleveland to Pittsburgh	27.00	105	.257
New York to Hartford	27.00	106	.255
Baltimore to Norfolk	31.00	159	.194
Detroit to Dayton	32.00	166	.192
New York to Syracuse	36.00	209	.172
New York to Washington	37.00	215	.172
Chicago to Minneapolis	49.00	334	.147
Pittsburgh to New York	48.00	340	.141
Boston to Baltimore	51.00	370	.138
Los Angeles to Phoenix	45.00	370	.121

[1] La Guardia to Washington National. See Simat, Helliesen, and Eicher, vol. 1, exhibit 7.
Source: Official Airline Guide, Feb. 1, 1977.

figures for routes of similar length on CAB-regulated intrastate routes.[35] The results are revealing. They indicate that fares on interstate routes are consistently greater than fares on equivalent California routes by 70 to 120 percent. Thus, the fare for the Pittsburgh-Cleveland route (105 miles) is $27, or over 120 percent greater than the Los Angeles-San Diego fare of $12.25 (for a trip of 109 miles). Similarly, the fare from New York (La Guardia) to Washington (National), a distance of 215 miles, is $37, or 80 percent greater than the fare for Los Angeles-Fresno of $20 (for a trip of 213 miles). As the reader can verify, the results are more or less the same for comparison of any of the other comparable city-pairs.

Similar fare savings are available in Texas. Between Dallas and Houston, a distance of 222 miles, the current fare is $25 on weekdays before 7 p.m., and $15 for evenings and weekends (both figures include taxes).[36] This compares with a fare of $37 (including taxes) for the New York-Washington route, a distance of 215 miles (Table 2).

The low fares provided by the intrastate carriers in California and Texas are

[35] It was pointed out at the beginning of this chapter that by 1977 the CAB had already embarked on a program of very modest deregulation; this means a 1977 comparison might not show the full effect of deregulation of CAB routes, relative, say, to 1974. However, these comparisons are for regular fares, whereas in early 1977, it was mainly in discount fares that the trunk carriers made reductions.

[36] Dallas-Houston fares come from the Official Airline Guide, Feb. 1, 1977, p. 451.

not achieved at the cost of safety or modernity of aircraft. The intrastate carriers use aircraft identical to those of interstate carriers on equivalent routes, and their safety records are excellent in comparison with CAB-certificated carriers.[37] Furthermore, it is not clear that the service quality provided by the intrastate carriers is overall inferior to that provided in coach service on equivalent routes by interstate carriers. Both generally use coach seats 18 inches wide pitched 34 inches apart. Although the intrastate carriers do not serve meals, the trunk carriers do not generally serve meals or free snacks on the hops of 65 to 350 miles served by the intrastate carriers. As regards flight frequency, the evidence from a number of routes where new low-fare competition has been instituted by an intrastate carrier would suggest that the low fares charged by intrastate carriers will induce sufficient new demand to support more flights than the higher fares previously charged by CAB-certificated carriers. Finally, the intrastate carriers have made considerable use of "satellite" airports, providing service to and from more points in a metropolitan area than generally occurs on interstate routes, and making for a higher level of passenger convenience. It is thus not obvious that intrastate passengers have inferior service compared to interstate coach passengers.

Causes of Lower Intrastate Fares How do the intrastate carriers achieve these lower fares? It is certainly not by accepting lower profits than the CAB-certificated carriers. Once start-up costs were covered, intrastate carriers have consistently enjoyed profits as great or greater than those of CAB-certificated carriers. Thus, in 1972 through 1974, Air California earned a return on over 24 percent after taxes on its equity investment.[38] Over the same period, PSA earned 4 to 6 percent after taxes which, although it may seem low, it is not out of line with earnings of CAB-certificated carriers in the same years.[39] And Southwest Airlines, now that heavy startup costs have been covered, is also profitable, having earned a return on investment of 12.6 percent in 1974.[40]

How, then do the intrastate carriers achieve profits in combination with fares substantially lower than those charged by the CAB-certificated carriers? The answer lies in a number of considerations, but most importantly in two: the seating capacity of the aircraft, and the load factor. Thus, in the case of the Boeing 727-200 (one of the most widely-used aircraft ever built) PSA puts 158 seats in each aircraft, compared with 120–133 seats in trunk aircraft.[41] Does this mean that the passenger enjoys less space on intrastate aircraft? In the case of coach passengers, any space improvements provided by interstate carriers on short-haul routes are minimal, for the six-abreast seating with 34-inch[42] pitch

[37] Testimony of J. Barnum, Hearings on *Oversight of Civil Aeronautics Board Practices and Procedures*, vol. I, p. 10.
[38] Coleman, p. 75.
[39] Ibid., p. 75.
[40] Simat, Helliesen, and Eichner, vol. I, p. 8.
[41] Simat, Helliesen, and Eichner, vol. II, p. IV-4.
[42] Pitch is the distance from a given spot on one seat to the same spot on the seat in front or behind it.

used by PSA is common among the trunk and local-service carriers on short hauls. The difference in seating capacity would seem to be accounted for by two things: first class service on trunk carriers (but not PSA), and galley space (but, as we have already noted, meal service to coach passengers on trunk routes is rather rare for the short hauls of relevance here). Air California and Southwest Airlines (in Texas) get similarly larger numbers of seats into their Boeing 737's.[43]

As regards load factors, all three intrastate carriers have consistently achieved higher load factors than have the interstate carriers. Thus, over the early 1970's, Air California achieved an average load factor of 70 percent; PSA achieved a load factor of 60 percent or more on all its high-density routes, which in turn account for over two-thirds of its traffic. And, after its initial start-up period, Southwest Airlines achieved a load factor of 58 percent in 1974, and 62 percent in the first three quarters of 1975. The trunk carriers, on the other hand, have consistently achieved lower load factors of 52.1 percent in 1972, 51.9 percent in 1973, 55.7 percent in 1974, and 54.8 percent in 1975.[44]

It might be argued that the lower load factor provided by CAB-regulated carriers does produce a superior quality by making it easier to get a reservation at the preferred time.[45] If such benefits occurred, however, they accrued exclusively to the privileged ten per cent of interstate passengers who flew first class. In 1974 and 1975 alike, the coach load factor was nearly 59 percent, roughly the same as that achieved by PSA and Southwest.[46]

Evidence from the intrastate markets, then, strongly supports the contention that interstate trunk fares are being set "artificially" high by the Civil Aeronautics Board, and that the potential excess profits from these high fares are being competed away through service quality and flight frequency competition. . . .

[43] Air California puts seats into a 737-200 (Hearings of Subcommittee on Administrative Practices and Procedures, vol. I, p. 450), and Southwest puts 110 seats in the same aircraft (ibid., vol. II, p. 1243). On the other hand, United and Western's 737's seat only 95. See Simat, Helliesen, and Eichner, p. II-75.

[44] Intrastate load factors come from Simat, et al., pp. 4, 8; Interstate load factors come from U.S. Civil Aeronautics Board, *Air Carrier Operating Statistics*, December 1973 and December 1975.

[45] This matter is discussed at length later in this section, under the discussion of Douglas and Miller's schedule delay model.

[46] See U.S. Civil Aeronautics Board, *Air Carrier Operating Statistics* (December 1975) for interstate load factors; PSA and Southwest load factors are mentioned above. A full discussion of the impact of CAB regulation on coach service quality is presented below in this section.

39 When does product differentiation become brand proliferation? This report from *Business Week* concerns an analysis of the ready-to-eat breakfast cereal industry by the Federal Trade Commission. The issue is whether product differentiation can be pursued so aggressively as to limit the entry of new firms.

TOO MANY CEREALS FOR THE FTC

BUSINESS WEEK

Whatever its fault, U.S. business has won high marks for its capacity to please consumers, who enjoy a seemingly limitless variety of products that crowd supermarket shelves and department store racks. The Federal Trade Commission, however, is arguing that, in the case of ready-to-eat breakfast cereals, the presence on the market of more than 80 different branded varieties actually hurts consumers by raising prices while protecting the monopoly power of major producers. FTC lawyers are asking an administrative law judge to call for the breakup of the three leading cereal makers—Kellogg, General Mills, and General Foods, which together account for nearly 86% of industry sales and nearly all of the brands. Such a move would allow new blood into the market.

The FTC's main economic ammunition in this case is a study by economist Richard L. Schmalensee of the Massachusetts Institute of Technology which was first presented at the annual meeting of the American Economic Assn. last December. He argues that the ready-to-eat cereal industry has followed a "brand proliferation" strategy, crowding supermarket shelves with different cereal brands so that "the pieces of the market left are so small that outside companies do not find entry attractive." The result, says Schmalensee: high profits for the major cereal companies, which, in turn, cost consumers roughly $200 million a year in higher prices.

The FTC's reliance on Schmalensee's study signals that the regulatory agency will be widening its scope and moving far beyond its traditional focus on "predatory pricing" as an industry's way of protecting its market from outsiders. If the new approach proves successful, it will "doubtless provide a viable way of analyzing other industries as well," says an FTC staffer, and could generate an avalanche of new cases. Most economists, indeed, agree that the brand-proliferation argument could be applied to nearly all nondurable consumer products, from cosmetics to detergents. Adds FTC economist William Burnett: "Schmalensee has led me to question what competition really means."

Chocolate-Flavored

Schmalensee bases his argument on an economic theory of localized competition that was first advanced by Harold Hotelling in 1929. The theory holds that in industries where products are clearly differentiated—such as in cereals, where brands differ in crunchiness, sweetness, and flavor—products compete more with one or two others that share similar characteristics, rather than with every other product on the market. For example, if the price of Kellogg Co.'s Cocoa Crispies falls, it would likely affect the demand for and the price of other chocolate-flavored cereals, such as General Mills Inc.'s Cocoa Puffs, but not the price of Kellogg's Corn Flakes or Post Raisin Bran, argues Schmalensee.

This intense competition among a few highly similar products gives the market its "localized" structure, while inviting anticompetitive behavior, says the MIT economist. Although there is no overt collusion, companies are anxious to avoid destructive price competition, so they compete instead by introducing more and more new brands. Each company thus positions its brands so that new products launched by other companies already in the industry will not erode its profits, Schmalensee says. "The result is brand proliferation, which yields excess profits to existing companies but leaves little hope that new companies will get much of a foothold in the overall industry because they have to start competing for tiny slices of the market," he adds.

In most industries, of course, established companies have an advantage over prospective entrants, since it costs less to expand an existing product line than to start up a new one from scratch. Nevertheless, if high profits exist in the industry, new companies will be attracted in droves. But, argues Schmalensee, the cereal market has become so fragmented that the high profits for a new company are dwarfed by the capital costs of the estimated $150 million investment required for those not already in the market to produce and sell a new brand. He says that new companies cannot expect to secure the 3% to 5% share of the market that, in his estimation, permits them to become efficient enough to break even. And this explains, he adds, "why even giant companies that have an interest in food processing, such as Procter & Gamble and Colgate-Palmolive, have never entered the cereal market seriously."

Rigid Prices

The major cereal companies indeed appear to be enjoying high profits, at least according to the FTC. The commission finds that aftertax rates of return on investment for the five largest cereal makers averaged more than 15% from 1958 to 1970, nearly twice the U.S. manufacturing average. Rates of return for General Mills, the industry profit leader, averaged more than 20% after taxes. Similarly, the commission found that ready-to-eat cereal prices have been unusually rigid over the past 20 years, and that makers rarely give trade deals to retailers or offer lower-price private-label brands. Despite high profits, says the FTC, there has been little significant entry into the industry for more than 30 years.

Based on these findings and Schmalensee's analysis, the FTC is charging the three major cereal makers with operating a "shared monopoly." In addition to breaking up the companies, the commission is proposing a system of trademark licensing that would enable new or smaller companies to readily imitate leading brands. For a nominal fee, a new company, for example, could buy the right to sell Puffed Wheat which, says the FTC, would foster competition and bring down prices.

But the FTC's position and Schmalensee's analysis are coming under sharp attack by the industry and by laissez-faire economists. For one thing, the critics argue that Schmalensee cannot prove that cereal companies are not simply trying to satisfy consumers, who happen to enjoy picking among a variety of brands. They say that companies try to satisfy consumer preferences, however fickle or diverse. "Brand proliferation is the direct outgrowth of reasoned consumer decisions," says Phillip Nelson, of the State University of New York at Binghamton. "If this means that it is difficult for new companies to introduce new brands into the market, it is not Kellogg's fault."

Brand Name Defense

Nelson argues that a small number of companies dominate the cereal industry because consumers prefer their products to others on the market. For this reason, he accuses the FTC of trying to "break up companies that consumers have deemed winners." Adds Robert Rifkind, a lawyer for Cravath, Swaine & Moore, which represents Kellogg: "The FTC should worry when companies are not introducing new products, instead of when they are."

Furthermore, the commission's proposed trademark licensing plan will "demand a homogeneity of products when people don't want it," says Nelson. And Stanley I. Ornstein, an economist at the University of California at Los Angeles, warns that trademark licensing "gives companies a strong incentive to lower quality," since consumers won't be able to associate high-quality cereals with specific brand names.

Nevertheless, the Schmalensee study has its defenders. "I find his argument persuasive," says Harvard University economist Michael E. Porter. "It does not mean that companies can't introduce new brands to please consumers, but that new and smaller companies should be doing the introducing." Says Steven Salop, an economist at the Civil Aeronautics Board: "The study is important to economic science because it offers a new way of analyzing anticompetitive behavior."

The FTC is just now wrapping up its case against the three cereal companies. Charges against Quaker Oats Co., also named in the original 1972 complaint, but which accounts for only 9% of industry sales, were dropped last month. Later this month the cereal companies will present their side. While the case could well stretch into 1979 before a decision, the betting in Washington is that the FTC will not wait before pushing ahead with new investigations into what it sees as the anticompetitive effects of brand proliferation.

40 Prices and profits in an oligopolistic industry with a differentiated product are affected by the ease or the difficulty of entry to the industry. The elasticity of demand and the information available to consumers also influence prices. Professor Blackwell gives results from his empirical study of the funeral industry; some of his statistical materials are, however, omitted here. His study includes an analysis of the conditions of entry.

PRICE LEVELS IN THE FUNERAL INDUSTRY

ROGER D. BLACKWELL
Ohio State University

Until recently, one of the major industries in the United States was discussed only in a hushed, hurried voice. The topic of death was as taboo as the subject of sex had been 50 years earlier. In terms of dollars expended, however, the purchase of a funeral is one of the more important decisions in which the consumer will become involved. With the advent of two popular books on the subject[1] acting as a catalyst and with numerous voices of concern being heard about rising funeral prices,[2] the need became apparent for a serious inquiry into the economic structure of the funeral industry and its pricing practices.

In view of the paucity of previous economic research in the funeral industry, a priority was established for questions that should be answered. The following questions are among those investigated in a doctoral dissertation on price levels in the funeral industry.[3]

(1) What is the economic structure of the funeral industry?

(2) What pricing practices are found in the funeral industry?

(3) What is the effect of entry regulation on price levels in the funeral industry?

[1] Jessica Mitford, *The American Way of Death* (New York: Simon and Schuster, 1963), and Ruth Mulvey Harmer, *The High Cost of Dying* (New York: Crowell-Collier, 1963).
[2] US Senate, Committee on the Judiciary, *Antitrust Aspects of the Funeral Industry*, Hearings before the Subcommittee on Antitrust and Monopoly on S. Res. 262, 88th Cong., 2nd Sess., 1964.
[3] Roger D. Blackwell, "Price Levels of Funerals: An Analysis of the Effects of Entry Regulation in a Differentiated Oligopoly" (unpublished Ph.D. dissertation, Northwestern University, 1966).

Taken and adapted from Roger D. Blackwell, "Price Levels in the Funeral Industry," © 1967, *Quarterly Review of Economics and Business*, Vol. 7, No. 4, Winter 1967, pp. 75–84.

The Investigative Model

The funeral industry does not have a national market. The industry is a composite of local markets which possess the characteristics of oligopoly involving a differentiated product. The studies of Paolo Sylos-Labini[4] and Joe S. Bain[5] and the synthesis of these works by Franco Modigliani[6] appeared to provide a framework within which to investigate the funeral industry and the effects of entry barriers upon pricing. The synthesis of their research, termed the S-B-M model, has served to generate hypotheses about the variables and relationships which influence pricing decisions by oligopolists such as those found in the funeral industry.

A theorem developed from the S-B-M analysis is that firms within a local market evaluate the difficulty of entry by potential competitors either explicitly or implicitly. They then use this calculation in supporting an industry price which will maximize short-run profits, yet not be high enough to induce additional entry into the industry sufficient to force serious adjustments in the output or price of existing firms.

The entry-preventing, or critical, price is defined as

$$P_o \simeq P_c\left(1 + \frac{1}{eS}\right)$$

where

P_o = entry-preventing, or critical, price,

P_c = purely competitive equilibrium price,

e = elasticity of demand in the neighborhood of P_c, and

S = market size ratio, where S is defined to be equal to the total output of the market if it were purely competitive divided by the scale of output for a firm operating at the optimal position on its cost curve.

The S-B-M model is particularly useful in analyzing the funeral industry because it indicates that the entry-preventing price will rise most above the competitive price when the market is so structured that the optimal scale of output for an individual firm is relatively high in proportion to market demand. This may occur where there are significant economies of scale and where demand tends toward inelasticity. The data in this study support the conclusion that both of these conditions are typical in the funeral industry.

From the S-B-M model it may be hypothesized that conditions which increase the perceived difficulty of entry encourage a higher entry-preventing price than if entry were not impeded. The S-B-M model does not deal ex-

[4] Paolo Sylos-Labini, *Oligopolio e progresso tecnico* (Milan: Giuffre, 1957).
[5] Joe S. Bain, *Barriers to New Competition* (Cambridge: Harvard University Press, 1956).
[6] Franco Modigliani, "New Developments on the Oligopoly Front," *Journal of Political Economy*, Vol. 66, No. 3 (June 1958), pp. 215–32.

plicitly with legal restrictions as a barrier to entry, although their existence is recognized by both Bain and Sylos-Labini. Specifically it relates price levels to the probability of calculation of entry difficulty made both by existing firms and by potential competitors. It therefore suggests that legal restrictions which increase difficulty of entry into an industry contribute to higher price levels than those which would be found in their absence.

Structure of the Funeral Industry

Many Small Firms

The funeral industry is composed of many small firms and only a few large ones.[7] In 1963 the modal group of establishments in the United States received annual revenue of $30,000 to $50,000 with an annual case load (number of deaths handled) of 65. The mean size, however, is somewhat larger. The mean revenue per establishment was $63,259 and the mean annual case load was 88. Funeral firms averaged less than three paid employees per establishment, with a total of 58,849 employees in 1963.

Large firms appear to be more effective competitors than small ones, when measured by the proportion of total business and their growth in recent years. About 10 per cent of the industry's establishments received nearly 40 per cent of the total revenue. Growth rates of establishments having annual volumes of over $100,000 are much faster than those among small establishments.

The data also show that the funeral industry has a very low exit rate as well as a very low entry rate. What appears to be occurring is that small firms continue to operate except for the normal attrition due to death and similar reasons but that expanding demand resulting from increased population is allocated among the large firms. The industry has not experienced aggressive price competition of the type that might squeeze out some of the small firms in the industry. This suggests that the industry may be operating at price levels which are based upon the cost curves of the many small firms rather than upon the cost curves of large firms which can spread overhead costs over large volume.

Incentive for Expansion

The proportion of fixed costs to total costs seems to be high in the funeral industry. The wholesale cost of caskets constitutes the principal variable cost. Labor costs produce the same effect in the short run as they would if they were fixed for two reasons: the specialized nature of the skills involved and a market structure which makes it difficult to employ personnel on

[7] All of the statistical data in this section are computed from US Department of Commerce, *Census of Business: Selected Services*, and other government statistical services. To evaluate reliability, they were compared with several industry sources and the results of field interviews.

other than a salaried, fairly permanent basis. Because of the nature of demand for funerals, this ordinarily results in considerable excess capacity. In other industries, the incentive to absorb excess capacity would normally stimulate the use of highly competitive marketing tactics in order to enlarge the market share held by an individual firm. The funeral industry, however, has not experienced the development of aggressively competitive marketing strategies, in spite of the incentive to do so.

Pricing Practices and Trends

There is much confusion about pricing practices in the funeral industry because of misunderstanding about what constitutes the product sold by funeral service firms. Consumers typically think of the funeral as a service to the deceased, but this is a misleading viewpoint.

One purpose of the funeral is disposal of the remains of the deceased. This could be accomplished in a variety of ways, at relatively little expense. The second purpose of the funeral is to give assistance to the survivors in their efforts to adjust to the new relationships caused by death. It is this latter function that causes most of the cost of funerals. Funerals are a service to the living, not the dead, and consumption decisions must be evaluated with this in mind.

Low Level of Price Competition

There is a striking absence of price competition in the funeral industry. This may be partly attributable to the general lack of discussion of funeral subjects. Consumers are reluctant to speak of death and funerals, even though they secretly would like more information about the subject. People regard death as an improbable event for themselves and frequently manifest this attitude in joking about it in order to avoid serious consideration.

The absence of such discussion about funerals and funeral prices among consumers may explain some of the rationale for laws which have developed to restrain marketing strategy in the funeral industry. Because consumers have very little information with which to judge competitive claims and service, funeral directors frequently assert that price advertising, soliciting, and other forms of competitive marketing tactics would serve to mislead uninformed consumers. They therefore support laws which prohibit price advertising, burial contracts, personal salesmen, and other forms of aggressive marketing strategy.

Unit Pricing

An absence of specific prepurchase planning typifies consumer behavior concerning funerals. This phenomenon helps to explain why unit pricing is characteristic of the industry. The unit price is determined by the quality of the casket and includes all other elements of service and merchandise provided by the funeral director. Except for a few items such as clothing and vaults, consumers usually are not asked which of the services provided by the funeral firm they wish. The funeral is purchased as a unit and paid for as a unit in most cases. Funeral directors frequently assert that unit pricing is necessary because consumers are not sufficiently informed to decide upon individual items that they might want included in a funeral.

The concept of the complete funeral had its origin in the manner in which the industry developed. Early funeral directors in the United States were primarily builders and marketers of caskets. By the end of the 19th century, competition had forced most casket-builders to offer embalming and other funeral services as well. Since the price charged was historically for the casket, however, this system was retained, even though the product sold had evolved to one primarily of personal service rather than of merchandise.

The procedures for establishing funeral prices to the consumer today vary in specifics among funeral firms. Usually, however, they are related directly to the cost of the casket. The calculations may be either a multiple of wholesale casket cost or may be average overhead plus retail price of casket, but the final price has until very recently been quoted to the consumer entirely on the basis of the casket selected.

Inelastic Demand

The number of funerals demanded in a time period is inelastic, although selection of the casket quality may be sensitive to price differences. The number of funerals in a market area may be reliably estimated with demographic data, and within normal price ranges it is unaffected by price changes. The quality of the casket that is selected, however, is affected by price and by such variables as social class, income level, age, ethnic membership, and religion.

Price Trends

The mean price of funeral services in 1963, the most recent year for which government data are available, was $716. This figure compares with $616 in 1958, $502 in 1954, and $396 in 1948. Funeral prices have risen a little more rapidly than the consumer price index and the price index for services. The funeral price rise has been slightly less rapid than that of medical services. There have been, however, substantial quality changes in funerals during the period; some of the price rise reflects increased service standards and improved facilities.

The measure of price used throughout this analysis refers only to the amount which accrues to funeral service firms. Excluded are the charges for cemetery lots, cremation and other items which represent cash advances to agents of the funeral director. Thus the price concept used here is used only to evaluate the charges of funeral service firms; it is not a measure of the total magnitude of allied funeral expenses.

Nature of Legal Restrictions

Very serious restriction upon entry is found in the funeral industry in the United States in the form of regulatory codes and laws. Every state and the District of Columbia provide regulation of some type of the funeral industry; Massachusetts provides the most extensive regulation and Alabama provides the least.

Control over marketing practices is achieved in some states by fines and sentences, but restraint upon marketing action is also frequently exercised through the power to suspend or revoke licenses of firms violating regulations on business practices. The intensiveness and ubiquity of regulation is an intriguing finding and one which serves to emphasize the extent to which business decisions are made under restraints imposed by the legal environment. Such legal restrictions are of three broad types.

(1) *Individual entry restrictions.* Most states regulate individual entry into the funeral industry. They impose the prerequisite of technical skills such as embalming upon an individual even if he may be interested only in the management of funeral-directing. The effect of this type of regulation is to prevent an individual seeking to utilize his marketing, financial, or management skills from doing so unless he is willing to perform the technical activities of the industry.

(2) *Capital barriers.* The regulations of many states serve to increase the fixed costs and the optimum output level for entering firms. Such laws require specific facilities to be maintained which might not be required by the entering firm, prohibit the sharing of facilities among small firms, and contain other provisions which serve to increase the capital requirements for entry. The effects of such laws are especially severe in a market in which total demand is fixed. In some states the corporate form of organization is prohibited; such laws make the raising of capital difficult. This serves both to restrict entry and to limit large-scale expansion by existing firms.

(3) *Limitations on marketing strategy.* Many states have regulations which limit the forms of marketing strategy or the instruments of competition that may be used. Funerals are purchased infrequently, and there appears to be considerable loyalty to existing firms. Therefore an entering firm might logically want to use extensive advertising, personal selling to institutions (and perhaps even to final consumers), and other tactics to obtain volume at an early stage. These strategies are often prohibited or discouraged by the state regulations. In many cases, specific types of advertising

that normally might be used in the marketing mix of a firm are outlawed in the funeral industry.

From an analysis of state laws, it can be concluded that there are numerous and substantial legal restrictions on entry into the funeral industry and that in some instances they do serve to discourage potential and existing competitors from using the business strategies that they might otherwise adopt. Such laws are barriers to entry and also serve in the funeral industry to restrict intensive interfirm rivalry of the type normally desired in a competitive system.

Effect of Entry Restrictions on Price Levels

The effect of legal restrictions on entry upon funeral prices was investigated by using the technique of multiple regression analysis and correlation. From the S-B-M model, it was predicted that states with more severe legal barriers to entry would have higher price levels than states with less restrictive entry conditions. This hypothesis was supported by the analysis of the regression of price levels on entry restrictions.

Approximately .12 of the variation in price levels between states could be explained (r^2) by variation in the difficulty of entry index, a measure of entry restrictions. This was a partial correlation coefficient between price level and entry regulations, holding constant the association with economic conditions affecting the market. This supports the hypothesis generated from the S-B-M model that a higher critical or entry-preventing price will tend to be supported in markets where entry is perceived to be difficult by existing and potential competitors.

Policy Implications

The desirability of entry restrictions in the funeral industry is clouded because of the justification advanced for such laws. The rationale for obtaining such regulation is usually that the restrictions have a salutary effect upon public health by preventing the spread of disease which might result if the bodies of deceased persons were not properly handled. Additionally, it is recognized that death is a phenomenon with important psychological effects upon the survivors and that this must be considered when evaluating the desirability of permitting aggressive marketing strategy.

Any such evaluation therefore must be tempered by relevant sanitary and psychological health questions. These suggested policy implications are based only upon the economic goal of lowering price levels for the consumer and are developed in the light of the economic analysis presented earlier. Where there is competent evidence to show that these suggestions are in conflict with medical or other relevant social goals, modification would be expected.

Separation of Technical and Business Functions

Regulatory laws in the funeral industry should be designed so that individuals could enter the industry and perform business functions without meeting the technical qualifications. To accomplish this, the licensing of the technical services such as embalming and funeral counseling would need to be separated from the business management operations such as financial management, administration and personnel management, and marketing.

If aggressive competition is the goal, entrepreneurs should be allowed to enter the funeral industry, so long as they can provide service which meets sanitary and legal standards necessary to protect the public health and welfare. Whether the entrepreneur provides this through his own skills and knowledge or whether he employs technically trained and licensed personnel should not affect his right to enter the market. Deletion of laws which require all owners to be licensed funeral directors might result in strict regulation of firms (as opposed to the present practice in many states of regulating only individuals) to ensure that they meet sanitary codes.

Encouragement of Competition

Findings from sociology and psychology show that consumers typically have little information and do little planning for funeral purchase decisions. Because consumers are uninformed, purchase infrequently, and avoid prepurchase planning, regulatory codes should be rewritten to encourage rather than to discourage the type of marketing strategy which stimulates more attention to the funeral purchase decision and which disseminates information about comparative facilities, services, and prices.

There is ample evidence to indicate economies of scale and a great deal of unused capacity in the funeral industry. Increased competition would enable firms to obtain additional market share through the promotion of better facilities or lower prices. Permitting the use of aggressive marketing tactics, so long as they meet ordinary prohibitions against deception and fraud, should result in the realization of the economies associated with large-scale operation. This in turn should result in lower prices for the consumer where intense rivalry between firms (including the threat of potential new entry) exists.

Encouragement of Large-scale Firms

Regulations which prohibit the corporate form of organization, multiunit operations, and other conditions usually associated with large-scale operations should be removed where the goal is lower prices. State regulatory boards should recognize the characteristics of oligopoly and attempt to promote aggressive rivalry within such a framework. It appears more desirable to permit firms large enough to realize economies of scale than to restrict competition to small firms, even though the result would be fewer firms in the market. The goal of regulatory agencies should be to maintain rivalry between large firms in hopes that their cost curves, rather than the cost curves of the small firms, would be the basis of industry price and service levels.

Competitive rivalry is not restricted to price, of course. Other variables more valued by the consumer than price may be emphasized; but in a competitive market, the consumer should be the final judge as to which marketing mix best satisfies him.

A policy encouraging the growth of large firms carries with it the danger of conspiratorial prices. This danger is inherent in the nature of oligopoly. No attempt has been made in this study to ascertain to what degree conspiratorial price determination exists in funeral markets as they are now regulated, but it is frequently asserted to be common.

Nonindustry Members of Regulatory Boards

The state boards of funeral regulation are composed primarily of funeral directors. There are a few states which require the state director of public health to be an ex officio or regular member and at least two states in which a clergyman may be appointed to the state board. For the most part, however, policy decisions and enforcement of legal restrictions upon entry are controlled wholly by existing firms within the industry.

The state boards, if they are to continue to maintain control over entry, should include some individuals with no vested interest in the industry. Appointments might be made from among persons trained as economists, psychologists, sociologists, lawyers, physicians, clergymen, or other knowledgeable and responsible citizens. The effect would be partly to transfer entry control from existing firms in the industry to individuals who should have no vested interest in maintaining difficulty of entry.

Implications for Other Service Industries

Although there are many characteristics of the funeral industry which make it unique, the findings of this study may have relevance to other service industries. The determination of price levels in the professional and service industries is relatively unstudied compared with other subjects in the pricing literature. As service industries increase in importance, much more attention to the pricing practices and problems of the service firm would seem to be warranted.

The S-B-M analysis and its application to the funeral industry suggests that there is a systematic body of theory which is appropriate for studying service industries. Such a model proves extremely helpful by providing concepts, isolating relevant variables, and suggesting testable hypotheses in the funeral industry and undoubtedly in many industries other than manufacturing, for which it was originally developed.

Part Seven

Here are analyses of business pricing practices and policies and of profit renegotiation by the government. The basic issue is whether and to what degree firms actually price products so as to maximize profits. Most of the selections suggest that marginal calculations are at work, but that application of marginal principles are filtered through the experience of managers rather than being a formal exercise. Costs and especially demand change too rapidly for a formal analysis to be relevant for very long. On the other hand, marginal calculation of an informal kind appears to be

Business Pricing

part of the nature of business decision making. Within the limits of imperfect knowledge, a firm seeking maximum profits can only grope and feels its way.

The essay by Qualls deals with managerial versus profit motives. When ownership is diffused among thousands of persons, no one of which has a large share, managers may have more flexibility and so may not aggressively seek profits. If so, then their prices might follow sales maximization or other pricing goals. Qualls examines these alternative views of business behavior.

41 Hardly recognized in the literature on price theory, the expression "administered prices" continues to flourish in public debates on big business, monopoly, and inflation. Back in the 1930's some observers blamed the length and severity of the depression on administered prices. In the late 1950's and again in the early 1970's administered prices were said to be a main fuel of inflation. Professor Adelman's comments still have a fresh ring.

A COMMENTARY ON "ADMINISTERED PRICES"

M. A. ADELMAN
Massachusetts Institute of Technology

"Administered prices" is a catchy phrase which promises everything, explains nothing, and thereby gets in the way of our learning something.

Anyone trying to understand a market and its prices is confronted by an array of disorderly facts about prices, products, customer channels, etc., which must somehow be sorted out. In general, if each individual firm regards only its own particular interest, it will always produce and sell more of any product if the price of that incremental output will exceed its cost. But there is usually a greater industry profit to be had by not letting that much be produced, and by not letting prices be driven down that far; restricting capacity or output to where the price remains higher than the incremental cost is nearly always more profitable. In that case the price is governed by the prices of the nearest substitute products. The price of telephone service, for example, would absent regulations be set by the competition of postal service, telegraph, and airline fares—and it is competition all right. But competition is a matter of degree. In general, any time an industry spokesman tries to justify or explain a price as being set by the competition of outside substitutes, he is justifying a monopoly price—unless, of course, he is only parroting a public-relations line.

The monopoly of a single firm is a built-in safeguard against the temptation to produce and sell a bit more if incremental cost is less than the price. The monopolist always thinks of what's good for the industry as a whole, because he is the industry as a whole: Like Louis XIV he can say, "the industry—that's me!" With more than one company in the business, this is no longer true and there are always a few in every crowd who may not listen to what's good for the industry as a whole; like the character in King John they

---

Reprinted from M. A. Adelman, "A Commentary on 'Administered Prices,'" in *Administered Prices: A Compendium on Public Policy.* Subcommittee on Antitrust and Monopoly of the Committee on the Judiciary, United States Senate (Washington, D.C.: GPO, 1963), pp. 22–24.

say: "Bell, book, and candle will not drive me forth, when gold and silver beckon me come on." And those who see the name by which this character is called will conclude that Shakespeare, as usual, is wonderfully up to date.

How is this ever-present temptation to be resisted? Perhaps by everyone agreeing to accept as true (and probably believing) that unless it is resisted, everybody must infallibly end up selling below cost and being ruined. This is a legend in every industry except the few natural monopolies, but if believed it can have some effect. Or firms may get together and collude on what is a fair price and a fair and reasonable return—the details, to the extent we have them, of the notorious Philadelphia electrical case, sound just like the arguments for farm price supports, and of course the economic rationale is no different. And where collusion is illegal or impractical, industry "statesmanship" may be not without effect. Usually it cannot do nearly as much as outright collusion, but it may be able to do something. The variety of situations is almost infinite. But the essential point of them all is mutual reassurance—that if any firm X conforms, all others will conform and vice versa. If a firm knows that nobody else will chisel, then they will probably—not necessarily—also refrain from chiseling, and thereby do what is best for the industry as a whole, and ultimately, themselves.

With a large number involved, say of the order of 20 equal-sized companies or more, it is impossible to keep everyone in line without outright collusion. With fewer firms or greater inequality among the group—which is to say, the equivalent of fewer firms—it becomes possible though by no means assured. These are the markets hardest to understand. The problem has nothing to do with "the giant corporation." Absolute size, as someone has well said, is absolutely irrelevant. What counts is the size of the market and the number and size distribution of the firms within it.

Even the number and size distribution of firms in a market cannot be settled until and unless one has found out where the presence of substitutes sets the boundaries, and on what terms—recall our telephone example. But any effective control may yet be impossible because the nature of the product makes it impossible to exchange assurances and check up on compliance. Or costs may be so different that one company's best price is too far from another's for any agreement short of very detailed collusion. Or the market may be growing rapidly, and the rewards of successful innovation may be too much to be resisted. Or there may be large and price-conscious buyers prowling around to confront every firm with the offers of every other firm, and if need be use "threats" and "coercion" and "pressure" to get prices down in the direction of incremental costs. Large buyers need not be monopsonists and they almost never are in fact. I do not refer to "countervailing power," another catchy and meaningless phrase. A large buyer able to bring or hold down prices is merely translating potential competition into actual.

In many industries, therefore, for one reason or another, firms cannot possibly resist the competitive pressure; Government may step in. Farm price supports are probably the most effective monopoly price existing today. Less effective but still important are such exemptions and loopholes in the antitrust laws as the Robinson-Patman Act and the fair-trade laws; tariffs; judicious stockpiling at the right moment, etc.

Without the obstacle—governmental or private—the price would come down from the noncompetitive level, and there would be a profit squeeze. Less efficient facilities, and even some whole firms, would be pushed out of business. Their labor and capital would be put to more productive use. The products would be more cheaply available. On both counts, national income and productivity would be greater, and so would our potential for the means of defense, for trade rivalry in an increasingly competitive world, and for other useful kinds of public and private expenditure. But if we want surplus farm capacity or surplus steel capacity, then we must avoid the profit squeeze and try to set a "fair" price which will allow a "fair" income for not only low-cost producers running at full capacity but for high-cost producers running at half capacity.

What does administered prices supply in understanding either price formation or public policy? Less than nothing, because it is a waste of time, which is a valuable resource, and lulls us into a false satisfaction which becomes one more barrier to cross. By mouthing phrases we head off thinking ideas. The fact is that the overwhelming bulk of wholesale prices, and just about all retail prices, are administered. They are announced in a deliberate manner rather than being thrown out, as on the stock or commodity exchanges, as the sparks from a constant stream of individual transactions. But this is form, not substance. To explain why a price and a pattern of output is what it is and not something else takes analysis of supply, demand, and market control; setting up models of competition, monopoly, collusion, imperfect collusion, etc., and seeing which best fits. All this labor is saved, and in addition one has the nice feeling of being profound and up to date by saying: "Administered prices."

42 Here are excerpts from a careful study of the policies of a group of business firms recognized as being well managed. In general, Professor Earley finds that most of the firms do indeed tend to behave marginally; they do tend to make their decisions in such ways as to aim at maximum profits. Part of the background of Professor Earley's investigation is the controversy over full-cost pricing.

Observe that in the well-managed companies examined by Professor Earley, the accounting data are handled so as to furnish the basis for marginalist decisions.

MARGINAL POLICIES OF "EXCELLENTLY MANAGED" COMPANIES

JAMES S. EARLEY
University of Wisconsin

In a recent article[1] I presented evidence from management literature that leading cost accountants and management consultants are currently advocating principles of accounting analysis and decision-making that are essentially "marginalist" in character and implications. The present article reports on a questionnaire survey designed to test empirically the acceptance and influence of these new principles among leading American manufacturing firms. It seeks to ascertain what relationships there are between organizational and accounting practices and the policies of the firms employing them. It seeks above all to test the validity of certain "nonmarginalist" propositions concerning business behavior found in recent economics literature, and the "marginalist" hypotheses derived from the management literature.

The survey does not purport to cover a cross section of American business by size and type. It is deliberately restricted to leading firms, which are presumably in the vanguard in the use of the newer management techniques. Through diffusion, direct imitation, and the competitive pressures they create, they are likely to set the dominant patterns of *future* business practice. Inquiry is also directed especially towards multiproduct and mul-

[1] "Recent Developments in Cost Accounting and the 'Marginal Analysis,' " *Journal of Political Economy*, June 1955, XLIII, 227–42.

Taken and adapted from James S. Earley, "Marginal Policies of 'Excellently Managed' Companies," *American Economic Review*, Vol. XLVI, No. 1, March 1956, pp. 44–48, 56–58, 66, 67. Reproduced by permission of the author and of the American Economic Association.

timarket companies, both because marginal accounting has most applicability in these cases and because such firms appear to be becoming increasingly representative of American business. It is confined to fairly large companies for similar reasons.

The basic list of companies to which the questionnaire was sent is that of the entire group of 217 manufacturing companies rated as "excellently managed" by the American Institute of Management;[2] 110 usable replies were received.

More than most empirical studies of business policies, this one relies upon inference from indirect evidence. Only a few direct questions concerning policies were asked. Most of the evidence refers to organizational structure, accounting practice, and certain oblique judgments of management, from which inferences as to behavior are drawn. This strategy was deliberately chosen in the belief that it would yield more reliable evidence of wider theoretical value than more direct questioning. The inferential approach is fortified by two special features of the analysis—the search for *patterns* of responses, and *tests of consistency* of the patterns.

It is suggested by many recent theoretical and empirical studies in economics that the modern business firm behaves nonmarginally in at least two essential respects: in having predominantly a long-run and defensive viewpoint in its pricing, production, and investment policies (rather than an alert attitude towards its near-at-hand profit opportunities); and in using, in the main, a full-cost rather than incremental-cost calculus in its pricing, production, and investment decisions. These are the major nonmarginalist hypotheses tested in this survey.

The major hypotheses from the management literature, which run counter to those above, and in this respect and others are considered to be "marginalist" in their implications, are the following:

1. Among well-managed multiproduct companies there will be found a substantial amount of what I call marginal accounting. The essential characteristic of such accounting is systematic (1) segmentation and (2) differentiation of costs (and, where appropriate, also revenues). By segmentation is meant the separate calculation of the costs and revenues of each of the firm's operations and prospective actions (so-called "segments")—*e.g.*, each process, product or product group, market area, "function," division, plant or contemplated action. Cost differentiation, which is as far as possible carried out for each segment, takes two forms: (1) the breaking apart of

[2] Each year the Institute "continues its comparative study of over 4,000 American and Canadian companies in all branches of business," and selects an "excellently managed" list, which is published in its *Manual of Excellent Managements* (New York: American Institute of Management, 125 East 38 Street). The 1954 *Manual* lists 348 "excellently managed" companies, of which 217 were considered to be primarily in manufacturing. Questionnaires were sent to all of these. In the third mailing 11 companies being considered for listing by the Institute were added. Twenty-five responded that they did not consider the questionnaire applicable to their line of business because they were mining companies, worked on a government cost-plus basis, or for other reasons. Of the remaining 203 companies, 110 or 54 per cent responded in sufficient detail to afford usable responses.

fixed and variable costs to obtain a variable cost function; and (2) differentiation between those fixed costs that can be specifically assigned to a segment and those that must be considered common to the enterprise as a whole.

Such accounting is "marginal" in two essential respects: first, it provides discrete data for considering each segment as an alternative field of management action; and second, in place of average cost information it provides data for estimating the *differences* in costs (and in revenues) that any action would entail.

2. In multiproduct, multiprocess enterprise, marginal accounting (and the basing of policies upon it) will be associated with, and facilitated by, an organizational structure differentiated, administratively and technically, along lines of major segments, such as product-lines, functions, and market areas. This facilitates the above-mentioned segmentation and differentiation of costs and revenues and helps management focus upon each major sector of the enterprise as a profit-making entity.

3. Marginal accounting data will be found useful in a wide range of managerial problems, including (1) evaluation and control of operating efficiency; (2) minimizing costs (as by proper selection of processes and methods); (3) determination of the relative stress that should be placed among products and markets in selling; (4) pricing decisions, both short-range and long-range; (5) selecting, adding, or dropping products or market segments; and (6) product- and market-related investment (including disinvestment).

4. Marginal accounting analysis will lead firms to employ marginal techniques of planning and decision-making (called by the National Association of Cost Accountants "cost-volume-profit analysis" and "marginal income analysis"), and to adopt marginalist viewpoints and policies. The basic principle of such marginalism being to concentrate upon the differences in costs, revenues, and profit that decisions involve and to neglect "inescapable" costs not affected by them, special attention will be given to ratios between price and variable costs ("marginal income ratios" in NACA terminology), and to differences between revenues and variable-plus-separable costs (so-called contribution margins). Overhead allocations and full-cost computations will tend to fall into disuse for decision-making purposes.

Specific policies likely to flow from marginal accounting analysis are: much reference to variable costs in short-range pricing decisions and in "selective selling"; attention to both variable and separable fixed costs in choices among markets and products and in product-related investment decisions; and differential pricing and other forms of "market segmentation" according to estimates of differing variable/fixed cost compositions, competitive pressures, and demand elasticities.

5. Such analyses and policies, especially if accompanied by budgeting and "profit planning," will be associated with a short-dated time horizon (at least as far as pricing and other product-related decisions are concerned), and a fairly keen and short-dated search for increased profit.

6. Pricing, product, and investment decisions will be made with a lively sense of impending innovation and obsolescence; hence the possible long-run reactions of rivals to the profits currently being made will not greatly influence these decisions. This is in contrast to full-cost theories in particular, which implicitly assume that firms make their decisions within the horizon of a given function.

Pricing Policies

One question concerned the company's general pricing objective. A full-cost pricing philosophy could be expected to lead management to try at least to maintain more or less equal margins between prices and full costs on its various product and market segments. Yet almost three-quarters of the companies responded that this was not their policy. Most of these companies apparently either consciously pursue the advantages of price-cost differentiation or make so many exceptions to uniform full-cost-plus pricing that it has ceased to be recognized as an objective.

There followed questions on three factors that if frequently made the basis of modifications of price-cost ratios among multiple products, would indicate either marginal policy or marginalist behavior regardless of policy: differing V/F cost compositions of products, differing buyer sensitivity to price, and differences in expected competitive pressures.

Of these, the highest proportion (84 per cent) of the companies declared they modify their relative price-cost relationships to "reflect differences in the degree of competitive pressure" expected from other companies. While the full-cost theory recognizes, and even emphasizes, that business will pay close heed to threats of market invasion in its pricing, this response strongly suggests: (a) that in most cases invasion expectations differ considerably among the products and market areas of the same company; and (b) that full-costs are not generally considered a reliable measure of what prices it is safe to charge in different cases.

Another question sought to ascertain whether estimates of differences in elasticity of demand among buyers are given any systematic recognition in modifying price-cost relationships of multiple products. The percentage of companies indicating that this is done is somewhat lower than that of those who pay attention to differing competitive pressures, but is still very high. The proportion of consistent "marginal" patterned responses is also very impressive in comparison with that of consistent full-cost responses, being 79 per cent as compared with only 33 per cent.

The proportion of companies that "take into consideration the extent to which costs of different products are made up of variable as against fixed costs" (61 per cent) is appreciably lower than those modifying price-cost ratios for the other two factors investigated. And only 60 per cent of the companies whose responses indicate a differential pricing objective explicitly recognize differing V/F ratios as a basis for such differentiation. These lower percentages indicate that the implications of differing V/F cost ratios, in situations in which competitive pressures and market elasticities differ among products, are less well understood in connection with general pricing policy than in connection with short-run price adjustments, product selection, and possibly pricing new products.

Certain questions bear inferentially on the companies' pricing policies, and reinforce the evidence that marginal pricing is the norm for the type of company being studied. Thus the fact that 73 per cent of the respondents stated that in pricing their new products they give primary attention to expected demand elasticities over the "first few years" of introduction rather than over longer periods, tends to gainsay the basic rationale of the full- or average-cost pricing theory that companies give primary consideration to the danger that if they price above present normal costs, including "reasonable overhead allocations" they will open themselves to competitive market invasion. In the same direction points the fact that 58 per cent of the companies state their new products can "usually command a higher price in relation to their costs than [their] well-established products." Presumably these companies, at least, recognize the "life cycle" of many products from distinctiveness to comparative obsolescence that results from gradual market saturation and the appearance of new products and methods, and differentiate price-cost ratios between their new and older products accordingly.

Impressive evidence of "marginalism" and of distrust of "full-cost" pricing is also provided by the very high proportion (89 per cent) of the companies stating in response to the final question that they consider the speed with which they improve their products and production and selling processes more important to their profitability and growth over the years than "close pricing of products in relation to costs."

Conclusions

A reasonable inference would seem to be that the use of marginal accounting techniques and a short-time perspective and innovation sensitivity are each *independent* influences tending towards marginalist pricing. The kind of costing which is appropriate to something akin to conventional theory's short run is itself sufficient to incline companies towards pricing on essentially marginalist lines. The addition of other conditions that may lead management to take especially short views of their needs and opportunities simply increases this tendency.

When combined with other results of the survey, this conclusion has, it seems to the author, interesting theoretical and practical implications. The significant pattern of results can be summarized as follows: (1) short views, innovative sensitivity, marginal costing, and marginal pricing are all preponderant among the responding companies; (2) where considerable segmented variable cost data are brought to management's attention, the companies' short-range policies (inferred from the substantial attention given to variable cost functions in the various problems covered in question 6) are consistent with their longer-range costing, pricing, and other product-related policies; (3) with such companies marginalism is apparently not dependent upon—though it is increased by—a short time perspective.

It appears reasonable to conclude from this pattern that the bulk of these "excellently managed" companies do not conceive of short-run *vs.* long-run profitability as alternative and inconsistent goals, and that they seek to "maximize" their long-run welfare by alertly trying to maintain and increase their current profits within their practicable horizons. With regard to such companies, there arises a serious question whether it is valid to build our analytical models on theoretical time periods, short or long, as presently conceived. What seems to be typical of these companies is not "marginalism sitting," short or long run, but "marginalism-on-the-wing."

In any case, the major messages seem to be fairly clear: (1) Marginal accounting and costing principles have a strong hold among these companies, and the bulk of them also follow pricing, marketing, new product, and product-investment policies that are in essential respects marginalist. (2) Whether interested in short-run profits or long-run health, very few of these companies give any evidence of ignoring the opportunities and/or necessities of practicing marginalism in the above range of problems.

Whether the same will be found true of most American firms only further study—and perhaps the passage of time—can tell. "In the long run," it is safe to say, the influence of firms such as these is bound to be substantial. At least as long as a reasonable amount of company autonomy and rapid innovation prevail, their influence is likely to be strongly in the direction of growing "marginalism" in American enterprise.

43 Many economists believe that most retailers woodenly set their prices by adding fixed percentage margins to their wholesale costs. In this selection, however, the authors find that margins vary and that changes in them, at least for the retailers studied, are consistent with the formal principles of profit maximization. To be maximizers, retailers do not have to know the mathematics of marginal revenue, price, and elasticity. All they need is an eye for a dollar and a trained instinct that tells them how their customers respond to prices.

PROFIT MAXIMIZATION AND MARGINS IN THE RETAILING OF PERISHABLES

W. A. LEE
Pennsylvania State University

L. E. FOURAKER
Graduate School of Business Administration, Harvard University

In the numerous studies of retail margins for perishables, many patterns of variation have been observed.[1] Certain patterns of variation have been observed sufficiently often to suggest basic forces at work. It has been observed that during periods of low wholesale prices, the dollar-and-cent retail margin on many perishable items is less than in periods when wholesale prices are high. On the other hand, the percentage retail margin is higher when wholesale prices are low than when wholesale prices are high. In other words, retailers in the aggregate apparently use pricing practices that result in margins somewhere between a constant dollar markup and a constant percentage markup. This is a description of the result of pricing practices, but not an explanation.

An example of such variation in margins was observed during the 1953 calendar year in the marketing of potatoes. During the spring of 1953, toward the end of the storage season for the 1952 crop, the most usual price

[1] As used in this article, retail marketing margins represent the difference between the wholesale price paid for a good by retailers and the retail price paid for the same good by consumers. Margins can be measured in absolute terms in dollars and cents or as percentages of either the retail or wholesale price. When expressed in percentage terms in this article, they are measured as percentages of the retail price.

Reprinted from *Journal of Marketing*, published by the American Marketing Association, "Profit Maximization and Margins in the Retailing of Perishables," by W. A. Lee and L. E. Fouraker, Vol. XX, No. 2, October 1955, pp. 171–173.

for Pennsylvania potatoes in Pennsylvania retail stores was 99 cents per peck. At the same time, the price received by growers through the Pennsylvania Cooperative Potato Growers Association was 75 cents per peck delivered to stores. Thus, the absolute retail margin was 24 cents per peck, while the percentage margin was approximately 24 per cent during this period of high wholesale prices. In the fall of 1953, after the harvesting of the 1953 crop, the most usual price for Pennsylvania potatoes in the same stores was 49 cents per peck, and farmers were receiving 35 cents per peck. At this low level of wholesale prices, the absolute margin was 14 cents per peck, while the percentage margin was approximately 28 per cent.

One reasonable explanation of such variation is that businessmen alter their margins in an attempt to increase profits. This would imply that the characteristics of the cost and revenue functions were important determinants of margins. It seemed appropriate to suppose that the wholesale price was the most important variable cost and that any one retailer could buy all of the product he wished to handle at the same wholesale price.[2] If raising the absolute margin—when the wholesale price increases—improves the profit position of the firm, then physical sales volume must vary less for a given price change in the high range of retail prices than in the low range of retail prices. Similarly, if reducing the relative margin—when the wholesale price increases—improves the profit position of the firm, then the relative response (that is, percentage change in quantity divided by percentage change in price) for a given price change must be greater in the high retail price range than in the low.[3] These are characteristics of consumer reaction on which retailers have opinions.

Thus it was felt that retailers' opinions of the reaction of their customers to price changes could be predicted on the basis of their margin practice and vice versa provided the retailer tried to maximize profits. This does not mean that retailers will maximize profits even though they try. Retailers as

[2] This view was confirmed in interviews with retail produce merchandisers. Monopsonistic elements might exist occasionally for chain stores in the factor market, but evidence of this was not sufficient to justify the assumption of a positively sloping marginal cost curve for the factors.

[3] These relationships were derived from the assumptions that wholesale price equals marginal cost, marginal cost equals marginal revenue (profit maximization), and marginal revenue equals price multiplied by one minus the reciprocal of the absolute measure of elasticity of demand. Thus, the retail price minus the wholesale price (the margin) is equal to an algebraic complex that reduces to the retail price divided by the elasticity measure. It follows that if the firm maximizes profits by having a high absolute margin when retail prices are high and a low absolute margin when retail prices are low, the elasticity at the high price must be less than the product of the low price's elasticity and the ratio of the high price over the low one. This reduces to the proposition concerning the reaction of sales volume to price presented above.

The proposition regarding the relative margins was derived by a similar process. If the absolute margins are equal to the retail price divided by the elasticity, the relative margins will equal the reciprocal of the absolute measure of elasticity. Therefore, if maximization of profits is served by lowering the relative margin as the wholesale price rises, it implies that the elasticity of demand at high retail prices is greater than at low retail prices.

Throughout this analysis it is assumed that the change in the wholesale price came about as a result of a shift in supply rather than a shift in demand.

well as economists have difficulties in measuring consumer reaction to price changes. We are not concerned here with the accuracy of retailers' opinions of consumer reaction but with the logical consistency between these opinions and resultant margins.

Interviews were conducted with retail produce merchandisers. These businessmen were asked to explain the variation of their margins on potatoes from the spring to the fall of 1953.

The first businessman interviewed was the produce manager of a branch of a large, national, chain-store organization. When asked about the nature of variation in margins on potatoes from the spring to the fall of 1953, he confirmed that the margins for his branch were similar to those described above. That is, the absolute retail margin was larger during the period of high wholesale prices in the spring of 1953 than during the period of low wholesale prices in the fall of 1953. The percentage margins were the reverse.

When asked why he took a smaller absolute margin during periods of low wholesale prices, he explained that when prices are low consumers can be impressed by price features and will respond greatly to further reductions in price. The use of psychological pricing—particularly the practice of pricing on nines in the produce industry—accentuates this situation. For example, if a price of 29 cents per unit would provide a reasonable retail margin, it would have to be lowered to 25 cents or even 19 cents to make a good price feature.

On the other hand—this businessman argued—when prices are high, it is difficult to create the impression of a good price feature. Since competitors would not feature the commodity under such circumstances, there would be little pressure to cut prices, and a higher dollar-and-cent margin would be taken. However, he also pointed out certain limitations resulting from the need to give consideration to long-run public relations. High food prices are likely to antagonize consumers. A retailer would be in a vulnerable position if it were to become known that his percentage margin was higher than usual during periods of high prices. Consequently, while he may be in a position to take a higher dollar-and-cent margin during periods of high prices, he would not risk carrying this to the point where it resulted in a percentage margin as high or higher than during periods of low prices.

With one exception, the businessmen interviewed experienced a pattern of margin variation similar to that described above. The reasons given, for all the businessmen except one, were also similar to those described above. Without exception, all retailers concluded that the most important considerations in setting prices were (1) the level of the wholesale price and (2) the way they believed their customers would react to changes in the retail price.

The one exception to the margin pattern described above was the owner of a small independent grocery located in a suburban village three miles distant from a larger retail center. This retailer indicated that, in general, his absolute retail margin was larger at low wholesale prices than at high wholesale prices. This being the case, his percentage margin at low wholesale prices was also larger than his percentage margin at high wholesale prices. For this margin practice to be consistent with profit maximization, consumers would need to be more responsive to price changes when prices are high than when prices are low.

The explanations offered by this retailer for his margin practice indicated that he believed this to be the case. He felt that when prices are high, his customers are concerned about the high price of food and would respond to lower prices if they exist in other stores, particularly in the chain stores located in the shopping center three miles distant. Thus, he felt that consumers would respond unfavorably to further price increases when wholesale prices are high, and—since his wholesale cost is higher than the cost to chain stores—he felt it was necessary to squeeze his margins during periods of high prices.

On the other hand, when prices are low, he felt that customers would not be sensitive to price differences between his store and the chain stores in town and would still patronize his store because of the convenience element. During this period, he could obtain the margins necessary to cover costs. Furthermore, since his potential market is small, he did not feel that he could gain much by lowering prices still further when prices were low.

In summary, this investigation appears to indicate that profit maximization is an important factor in the pricing decisions of retailers of some perishable products. For the small sample involved, it was possible to approximate the businessman's description of his customers' reactions to price changes on the basis of his margin practice and the assumption of profit maximization. In this case, the revenue and cost concepts of economic analysis proved to be useful tools in the study of margins.

44 The federal government buys billions of dollars of commodities every year, many of them having no other purchaser. This vast market has only recently been put under the scrutiny of economic analysis. One activity about which almost nothing has appeared in economic literature is the renegotiation of the profits from sales to the government. This activity is explained and analyzed by Dean Burns, who has been a consultant to the Renegotiation Board of the federal government. His article was written especially for this volume.

THE GOVERNMENT RENEGOTIATES PROFITS

ARTHUR E. BURNS
The George Washington University

Profit limitation imposed by government takes many forms. State regulatory commissions set rates for electricity, gas, and local telephone calls to limit utility profits to a fair return on investment. Federal agencies set rates on interstate telephone communications and natural gas transmission to hold profits to a fair return on investment. In war-time, excess profits taxes are common as a means of profit limitation. Business firms that negotiate contracts to sell products and services to the military, the space agency, and a number of other agencies, have their contract fees (profits) limited by law. Other forms of profit limitation could be cited.

Perhaps the least known of these, to all but those directly affected, is renegotiation. Renegotiation is the process in which business firms with contracts to supply goods and services to government agencies[1] are examined annually by the Renegotiation Board,[2] a federal agency, to ascertain whether these firms made excess profits on this business. If excess profits are found, the Board solicits an agreement from the contractor firms to return this excess as a refund to the government. Failing agreement, the Board issues an order to refund. The amounts repaid are adjusted for the corporate income taxes previously paid by the companies on this portion of their profit.

When business firms (contractors) negotiate contracts with government agencies, the contract stipulates a fee to be paid to the contractor for the work to be performed. There are many kinds of fee arrangements: cost-plus-

[1] The Department of Defense, Departments of the Army, Navy, and Air Force, the Maritime Administration, the Federal Maritime Board, the General Services Administration, the National Aeronautics and Space Administration, the Federal Aviation Agency, and the Atomic Energy Commission.
[2] Created by the Renegotiation Act of 1951, Public Law 9, 83rd Congress, as amended.

fixed-fee, various kinds of incentive fee arrangements, and fixed price contracts. The fees paid on this business show up in the profit column of the firm's income statement—unless through miscalculation or bad luck the firm's costs wipe out the fees, and a loss results. These profits are subject to renegotiation—not the individual contract fees, but the aggregate fees which make up the fiscal year profits of the contractor.[3]

The sales to government reviewed by the Board are termed "renegotiable sales," and the profits made on such sales are "renegotiable profits." The sales and profits of such firms in the commercial markets, or sales to government not covered by the Renegotiation Act, are termed "non-renegotiable." Contractors report both categories of sales and profits to the Board annually. In 1967, renegotiable sales totalled some 33 billion dollars.

Renegotiation as a policy made its appearance in 1942 to recapture excessive wartime profits. More than 11 billion dollars were judged to be excessive and recaptured in the war years and immediately after. The present Renegotiation Board has recaptured over 950 million dollars since 1951, ranging from $153 million in 1956 to nearly $8 million in 1962. Moreover, many large contractors have reported voluntary refunds and price reductions to the Board, amounting to 1.3 billion dollars.[4]

Firms subject to the Renegotiation Act must report sales, profits, losses, and other financial data annually to the Board. The number so reporting has ranged from nearly 4,000 to over 8,000 a year. Many report losses on renegotiable business; most of the others are "cleared" by the Board upon cursory examination of sales and profits. Some 15 to 20 per cent of the firms report profits deemed by the Board to need close scrutiny. While the Board eventually clears most of these, it does find excessive profits in some cases—as noted above, amounting to some 950 million dollars since 1951, in nearly 4,000 findings of excessive profits. Ninety per cent of these firms repaid the excessive profits by agreement with the Board; the other 10 per cent would not agree and were issued refund orders. About 150 firms in this latter group petitioned the Tax Court of the United States for a redetermination. More often than not, the Court has upheld the Board's findings of excessive profits.[5]

The renegotiation process and the cases taken to the Tax Court raise the fundamental question: What is a fair and reasonable profit? And what is excessive? This is a contentious issue; unavoidably, the answer is a normative judgment. From this stems much of the strong business opposition to the renegotiation process.

[3] Not all government business is subject to renegotiation. There are many exemptions, and many government agencies fall outside the scope of the Renegotiation Act.

[4] Hearings before the Committee on Ways and Means, House of Representatives, March 11 and 12, 1968, page 16. These voluntary actions were probably taken to forestall a Board finding of excessive profits.

[5] See annual reports, The Renegotiation Board, Washington, D.C.

The Meaning of Excessive Profit

The Renegotiation Act defines profit generally as the excess of receipts or accruals under government contracts and subcontracts over the costs paid or incurred that are allocable to them. Under the Act [SEC 103(e)] the term excessive profits means "the portion of the profits . . . which is determined (by the Board) to be excessive." This, of course, is no definition of excessive profits.

As guidelines for the Board's determination of excessive profits, the Act states that [SEC 103(e)]

> In determining excessive profits favorable recognition must be given to the efficiency of the contractor or subcontractor . . . and in addition, there shall be taken into consideration the following factors:
>
> (1) Reasonableness of costs and profits, with particular regard to volume of production, normal earnings, and comparison of war and peacetime products;
> (2) The net worth, with particular regard to the amount and source of public and private capital employed;
> (3) The extent of risk assumed, including the risk incident to reasonable pricing policies;
> (4) Nature and extent of contribution to the defense effort, including inventive and developmental contribution . . . ;
> (5) Character of business, including source and nature of materials, complexity of manufacturing technique, character and extent of subcontracting, and rate of turnover;
> (6) Such other factors the consideration of which the public interest and fair and equitable dealing may require. . . .

The most that can be said for these statutory guidelines is that directly, indirectly, and vaguely, nothing relevant to the question goes unnoticed. But the Act needs clarification and precise meaning on these matters to minimize the interminable disputes that arise in the renegotiation process. As written, the language simply places an unnecessarily heavy burden on judgment. It complicates the answer to the question: What is a fair and reasonable profit? And what is excessive?

The Measurement of Profit

This question is further complicated by a number of analytical issues that arise in the renegotiation process. As the Act defines renegotiable profit, no notice is given to the fact that some portion (and perhaps all, in some cases) is properly an imputed interest or other income, and not profit at all.[6] This

[6] The excess of receipts or accruals over cost is roughly what is meant by "business profits." It is not "pure" profit in the economist's sense, which excludes imputed interest, rent, and in some cases, a management income. For a useful review of corporate profits, see Stevenson, H. W., and Nelson, J. R. (eds.), *Profits in the Modern Economy*, Univ. of Minnesota Press, 1967.

distinction, however, needs attention. Contractors doing business with government show great diversity in their capital commitment to this business. In some cases it is entirely equity capital; in others there are varying degrees of reliance on long-term capital. Some contractors carry out work in government-owned plants and with government-owned equipment, with varying amounts of their own capital committed to contract work. For these and other reasons, the equity capital-output ratios among contractors show considerable variation, as does the imputed interest component of the reported profits. These issues are largely neglected by both parties to the renegotiation process.

A related analytical issue is this: Against what base are renegotiable profits related? Profit must be expressed as a ratio of some base, for business purposes to determine profitability and to make decisions, and for renegotiation purposes to warrant a judgment on the reasonableness of profits. For both purposes, the ratio or ratios of profit for any given firm must be compared with a norm, usually a relevant statistical average.

There are a number of conventional and useful financial ratios that relate profit to some base. Profit may be measured as a per cent yield on invested capital;[7] it may be measured as a per cent (margin) of renegotiable sales. There are other standard ratios, but these two have figured prominently and controversially in the renegotiation process. (Many elements, of course, other than these ratios are involved, but they usually relate back to profit ratios.) What is the appropriate measure of profit? On this basically crucial question there is often little or no agreement in renegotiation cases.

This lack of agreement on the relevant measurement is seen in the major renegotiation cases brought to the Tax Court by many of the air frame firms.[8] Their profits from Korean War contracts were found excessive by the Renegotiation Board. The subsequent litigation brought the profit measurement issue to the fore. Profits as a per cent of invested capital (net worth) for these firms ranged from nearly 100 to over 300 per cent. By contrast, the earnings of some 50 major manufacturing firms for the same years averaged between 20 and 24 per cent on capital employed. On the other hand, the profit margin—per cent profit to sales—was approximately 8 per cent (for Boeing and North American Aviation), about equal to the average profit margin for manufacturing companies as a whole. Which is the relevant profit ratio? The air frame companies argued for the profit margin; since their margins equalled the average, they were therefore not excessive. The Tax Court ruled otherwise; profit in relation to capital invested was held to be excessive.

This issue goes to the core of the renegotiation process. What is the ap-

[7] The capital base may be stockholders equity or equity plus long-term debt, or assets. For present purposes these complexities need not be explored. Suffice it to say that profit must be *related* to *some* invested capital base in all capital-using enterprises.

[8] Boeing Company, 37 TC 613 (1962); North American Aviation, 39 TC 207 (1962).

propriate ratio for the measurement of profit? In an entirely different field of profit limitation, public utilities, the answer has long since been given: the allowable profit is measured as a rate of return on what is essentially the capital base. The diversity of firms and industries subject to renegotiation, however, does not permit sole reliance on such a measurement. The Board, in fact, looks at both the return on capital and the profit margin. So does the Tax Court. The companies subject to renegotiation do likewise. When the issue is joined, however, each side to the dispute tends to rest its case on one ratio and denies the validity of the other. Perhaps this is unavoidable in adversary proceedings, but it obscures the analytical issues.

Clarification of the measurement issue may be advanced by (1) a classification of business firms, ranging from highly capital-intensive to highly labor-intensive in their renegotiable work, and (2) a classification of the functions performed for which profit is compensation. For example, a manufacturing firm using its own plant and equipment to produce Army trucks differs functionally from a firm managing a government facility under contract, or one undertaking a research project. The first is capital-intensive; the latter two, labor-intensive. Should both be tested as to reasonableness of profit the same way? Perhaps not. The truck producer uses much capital in his operation; an adequate yield on that is of utmost importance. The management contract and the research contract call upon the contractors to *do* something quite different from what the truck maker does. It is not that the products in all cases are different, but the functions involved differ. And the contractors are paid fees to perform the requisite functions.

The functions performed for which profits (negotiated fees) are a compensation include (a) capital supply, (b) assumption of capital risk, (c) mobilization of the requisite resources, (d) management of these resources, and (e) innovation in products or processes.[9] The extent to which these functions are performed varies considerably from one contractor to another. Some employ considerable amounts of capital and assume the attendant risks of capital; others supply negligible capital of their own. The functions of mobilizing the requisite resources and managing them efficiently are in some cases routine. In other cases the mobilizing and managing of highly specialized resources for sophisticated work, e.g., a new space or weapons system, entail much skill, particularly when many specialized subcontractors must be mobilized and directed. Some types of contracts require high-level innovative work, others of a routine character do not. There are instances of contractors who do little more than sign the contract, collect the fee, and subcontract the work to others.

Despite this great variety in functional performance, the fees for most of them range narrowly between 5 and 7 per cent of the contract cost. What are the fees, and the profits that derive from them, paid for? The suggested

[9] Uncertainty is absent from this list. The government procurement market reduces the uncertainties of the conventional market by contract provisions and by the supply of government-owned facilities in the major procurement areas.

functional analysis of profit is one approach to this answer. This, then, would suggest the answer to that difficult question: What is a reasonable profit? It is that profit which compensates the functions performed. Anything more than that is excessive.

Conceptually, this is clear. The difficulty lies in the *valuation of the functions* that are performed. Here the two ratios—rate of yield and the per cent of sales—may usefully be combined.

The capital supply and assumption of risk functions may be compensated by an imputed interest which varies with the degree of risk. The capital markets supply a structure of rates which could guide the valuation of these functions; or the yields allowed to the utility industry might be useful here. The component of renegotiable profit attributable to capital supply and risk would loom large in the case of a contractor using only his own plant and equipment; it would be negligible for those who rely heavily on government plants and equipment. The remaining functions in such a case could be valued by allowing additional percentage points to the yield, e.g., 1–2 per cent to compensate for mobilizing the requisite resources, 0–5 per cent for degrees of efficiency in management, and 0–10 per cent for whatever innovative elements might be involved. These figures, of course, are suggestive; both the suggested functions and compensations need much examination.

The profit margin, alternatively, might be used to value the other functions, with a range to account for differences in functional importance. Certainly, the margin might be the relevant basis for valuing functions that exclude anything but a negligible capital supply, e.g., a research organization.

The functional approach to renegotiable profit is complex. It is not absent in the renegotiation process, but its analytical framework is inchoate. One of the central elements is presently missing: the proper allocation of a firm's capital to its renegotiable business. The Board tentatively allocates this capital on a cost-of-sales basis. That is, if a company's business is one-half renegotiable and one-half non-renegotiable, the firm's capital is allocated accordingly, and the return on renegotiable capital is thus computed. But suppose a company also uses government-owned plant and equipment, which never appears on its balance sheet. In the above case, the allocation would still be fifty-fifty, which, of course, is untenable. This method produces a nonsense result when output changes greatly with changes in the employment of government-owned capital.

Complexities in profit measurement extend well beyond those briefly described in this paper. The problem needs more analytical attention than given to it in the past. A functional analysis is a promising, though difficult, approach. It seeks to answer the question: What are renegotiable profits paid for? This is largely unanswered at present. An answer to this question, and the valuation of the functions as suggested above, points directly to the further question: What are reasonable, what are excessive, profits? An analytically tenable functional theory yields an answer.

Why Renegotiation?

This question comes up constantly. Opponents of renegotiation deny its need, asserting that "competition" can be depended upon to assure fair prices and reasonable profits. The rivalry among contractors for contracts is given as evidence of competition. The fact that profits on total renegotiable business in recent years have averaged about 3 per cent of sales is taken as further evidence of competition. In short, the government procurement market is considered only a sector of the competitive market mechanism, with competitive forces limiting profits.

In their detailed study of major weapons systems procurement, Peck and Sherer have much to say on this point.[10] They characterize the arguments for the competitive way, or the free enterprise approach, as "vague talk" and generalities. They conclude:

> It is not only that a market system does not exist in the weapons acquisition process. We can state the proposition more strongly. A market system in its entirety can never exist for the acquisition of weapons.[11]

In a similar vein, Congressman Wilbur D. Mills, Chairman of the Committee on Ways and Means, set forth the economic bases underlying policy:[12]

> The central truth . . . is there simply is no traditional market place to guide pricing for a large part of the defense and space procurement. The Navy cannot go out in the ordinary market place and buy a Polaris Missile. NASA cannot buy commercially a Surveyor or an Apollo. . . . With the elements of cost uncertainty (and) product complexity, the government procurement market is fundamentally different in many respects and in many instances from the private competitive market. This unique set of characteristics provides the economic basis for renegotiation.

In elaboration, Mr. Mills pointed to the facts that (a) prices are negotiated, (b) price competition over much of the procurement market is weak or non-existent (single-source suppliers), (c) cost estimates are often too uncertain to assure reasonable pricing, (d) many major contractors work with government plant and equipment and may be financed by progress payments, and (e) individual contract fees give no clue as to the profit outcome from all renegotiable business of the contractors.

The fact is, the government procurement market is highly diverse. At one end of the spectrum the transactions are scarcely distinguishable from ordinary commercial transactions. Over the rest of the spectrum there are differences ranging on up to transactions bearing no resemblance to those in

[10] Peck, M. J. and Sherer, F. M., *The Weapons Acquisition Process: An Economic Analysis*, Harvard University Press, 1962, especially pages 55–64.
[11] *Ibid.*, p. 57.
[12] *Hearings*, Loc. cit., p. 17.

the private market mechanism. Rivalry, but no price competition, exists. In the absence of price competition renegotiation is the policy instrument to limit profits to reasonable amounts. This is in general the analytical case for renegotiation.

Conceivably, the British approach could be followed as an alternative to renegotiation. British authorities negotiate contract fees so as to produce a 7–10 per cent yield on capital. Contractors must supply detailed financial data on capital invested, source of capital, capital turnover, the allocation of capital between defense and non-defense business, cost data and cost allocation, and other delicate financial data. U.S. business is not likely to submit to such a financial inquisition; faced with the choice, it would probably embrace renegotiation as the lesser of two evils.

To limit profit at the contract negotiation stage, or to recapture any excess profit later in the renegotiation process, has the same economic origin: the imperfections or absence of competition over much of the government procurement market. This answers, Why renegotiation? but not What is a reasonable, and What is an excessive profit? A functional analysis of negotiated profits may yield that answer: a reasonable profit is that which just compensates the combination of functions performed by contractors.

45 This selection reports a study of the effect on price–cost margins of differences in control of firms by owners or by managers. The hypothesis is that managerially controlled firms will seek profits less agressively than owner controlled firms. Qualls states the hypotheses clearly, tests them ingeniously, and comes up with intriguing findings.

MARKET STRUCTURE AND MANAGERIAL BEHAVIOR

P. DAVID QUALLS
University of Tennessee

I. Introduction

Forty-four years have passed since Adolf Berle and Gardiner Means (1932) first propounded the thesis that a "managerial revolution" was taking place in American industry. In their view, the growing dispersion of stock ownership under the corporate form of business enterprise was conferring basic decision making control of the firm upon "hired" managers, whose behavioral motivations might not coalesce with the profit interests of stock owners. "Classical" economic theory was being rendered invalid owing to its crucial reliance on the role of the rapacious, decision making, risk taking, profit receiving entrepreneur, who no longer existed.

This view is still being debated today. If it is essentially correct, much of the work in the modern field of industrial organization adopting the structure-conduct-performance paradigm outlined by Professor Bain and relying implicitly on a profit maximization assumption for business enterprises, may rest on a somewhat shaky foundation. This chapter critiques recent empirical tests of the managerial behavior hypothesis, distinguishes among alternative behavioral hypotheses, and presents some new empirical evidence. . . .

III. Economic Profit Margin Implications of Nonmaximizing Behavior

There are at least three different types of profit nonmaximizing behavior that could have implications for long run price–economic cost margins. One has to do with constrained sales revenue maximization. A second is related to orga-

---

Excerpted from Chapter Five of Robert T. Masson and P. David Qualls, eds., *Essays on Industrial Organization in Honor of Joe S. Bain* (Cambridge, Mass.: Ballinger, 1976), pp. 89–104, 266, and 267. Reprinted with permission from *Essays on Industrial Organization,* Copyright 1976, Ballinger Publishing Company.

nizational slack and X-inefficiency, and a third (which to my knowledge has not been discussed in this context previously in the literature) concerns risk-averse behavior in a stochastic limit pricing framework.

Sales Revenue Maximization

For firms which enjoy some monopoly power there should be a tendency for management-controlled firms to have lower economic profit margins than owner-controlled firms, if the sales maximization hypothesis for management firms is correct. In a heterogeneous product industry, management firms should tend to charge lower prices relative to given costs than would owner-controlled firms in that industry. In either homogeneous or heterogeneous product industries dominated by management-controlled firms, industry price levels should be lower relative to given costs than those for other industries (of similar market structure) dominated by owner controlled firms.

Overall, across a large sample of industrial firms enjoying some market power, there should be a tendency for management-controlled firms to have lower economic profit margins than would owner-controlled firms. And the profit margin differences should be greater as market power, indicated by higher industry concentration and/or entry barriers, is greater. With higher achievable price—economic cost margins, the difference between achievable economic profit margins and the economic profit margins that result from sales maximization behavior should be greater, otherwise constrained sales maximization is not really behaviorally different from profit maximization.

The assumption here is that higher concentration and higher barriers to entry have positive and interactive effects with regard to firms' monopoly power and potential monopoly profits. A second assumption is that the minimum profit constraint is not systematically and significantly higher as concentration and barriers to entry are higher. If the profit constraint were higher for higher concentration and higher barriers, the profit maximization and constrained sales maximization assumptions would yield the same general predictions for price–economic cost margin performance in market structure analysis. The sales maximization assumption does not predict positive relationships of price–economic cost margins to seller concentration and barriers to entry unless it is assumed that the minimum profit constraint is higher for firms in more highly concentrated, higher barriers industries.

Organizational Slack

Another suggested result of management control is that of higher costs. With isolation from owner control, management may become less diligent with resultant X-inefficiency. Or managers may elect to allocate resources to "non-productive" expenditures which yield some managerial utility.

With higher costs, management-controlled firms would tend to exhibit lower price-cost margins than would owner-controlled firms in the same industry or in other industries with similar market structures. Again, however, this would follow only for firms in industries whose market structures confer some monopoly power. In workably competitive industries, competition should prevent this for surviving firms. The higher the degree of seller concentration and/or entry barriers, the greater would be the cost increasing possibilities and opportunities for this organizational slack and the greater would be the expected difference in price—economic cost margins between management-controlled and owner-controlled firms.

Stochastic Limit Pricing

Limit pricing behavior is usually discussed in a context of certain knowledge regarding the new firm entry that will result from current pricing policy. However, firms may be able to assess only the ***probability*** of entry. In this stochastic framework a reasonable assumption is that established firms regard the probability of a given amount and "type" of entry (a minor amount of small firm entry or a major amount of large firm entry, for example) as being higher as current price is higher relative to cost. Risk-neutral firms would elect current pricing policies designed to maximize the expected present discounted value of present and future profits. In this context, a risk-averse firm would deliberately establish a current price lower than that which would maximize expected present value. This would be tantamount to sacrificing some expected present value for a reduced probability that the target expectation would be nonrealized as a result of entry.

A managerialist behavioral hypothesis might well argue that, in this sense, management-controlled firms would tend to behave in a more risk-averse fashion than would owner-controlled firms. To some extent, stockholders have the opportunity of balancing profit risks in their portfolio holdings. To the hired manager group, however, entry presents the prospects of declining market share, a smaller bureaucracy than otherwise and perhaps declining employment tenure probabilities. And managers do not have the same opportunity to balance this sort of bureaucratic employment risk as do stockholders concerned with the profit risks involved in stochastic limit pricing.

In short, a managerialist hypothesis would be that management-controlled firms will tend to establish lower prices relative to cost than will owner-controlled firms, given the same stochastic entry function. An important point here is that if this behavior occurs, one would expect it to be most clearly observed in industries characterized by moderate to high seller concentration coupled with only low to medium barriers to entry rather than high barriers. Limit pricing considerations presumably are relevant only where interdependent pricing policies are feasible—moderate to high concentration.

Moreover, an assessment of the barrier to entry as being "very high" quite likely also implies less uncertain knowledge concerning the entry function and less entry risk to be hedged. As a result of this sort of behavior, clearly observable differences in price–economic cost margins would be most likely expected, or larger differences would be expected, in moderately to highly concentrated industries in which barriers to entry are regarded as low to medium, rather than very high.

In order to attempt to shed some empirical light on these phenomena, the remainder of this chapter is concerned with the results of a statistical study of the hypothesized interactive relationships between long run price–economic cost margins and market structure and type of control in the enterprise.

IV. The Data Sample

The data sample utilized here covers 205 large American industrial firms.[1] This is the intersection of the 231-firm sample studied by Shepherd (1972) and the 450-firm sample studied by Palmer (1973). For each of these firms, Shepherd calculated a concentration index as the weighted average of the adjusted four-firm concentration ratios in each of the industries in which the firm had significant operations.[2] For each firm, Palmer developed a barrier to entry estimate—"high," "medium," or "low"—as a weighted average assessment of the magnitude of entry barriers in each industry in which the firm operated.[3] Palmer designated each firm as "strong owner" controlled, "weak owner" controlled, or "management" controlled, depending on whether the largest block of voting stock held by any one "party" was equal to or greater than 30 percent, as great as 10 percent but less than 30 percent, or less than 10 percent of the firm's total voting stock, respectively.

In addition, I calculated excess profits as a percentage of sales (the price–economic cost margin) for each firm for 1960–1968. For each year, 6 percent times beginning of the year stockholder equity was subtracted from net after-tax accounting profit, and the difference—economic profit—was expressed as a percentage of net sales revenue. Averaging arithmetically over the nine-year period yielded the dependent variable observation for each firm.[4] Baa corporate bond yields averaged 5.4 percent over 1960–1968. Six percent seems to be a reasonable estimate of the opportunity cost of equity capital for these firms. . . .

VI. Empirical Findings

As indicated in Tables 1 and 2, the concentration and barriers to entry cell means conform to the traditional Bain hypotheses. Average price–economic cost margins are higher for "high" than for "medium" concentration, which are, in turn, higher than those for "low" concentration. Class means are higher

[1] Each of these firms was on the *Fortune* 500 list for 1965 and 1967.

[2] Shepherd adjusted some of the SIC four-digit industry concentration ratios for local or regional product market characteristics, and for industry product definitions that were too broad or too narrow.

[3] With regard to the barrier to entry assessments for the *industries*, Palmer placed heavy reliance on previous estimates by Bain (1956), Mann (1966), and Shepherd (1970). I made one change. In keeping with a previous argument (Qualls, 1972), I designated the barrier to entry in the liquor industry as "medium" rather than "high." This affected one firm (Seagram's) in the sample.

[4] As indicated above, this calculation approximates the Lerner measure of monopoly. For a full discussion of the mechanics and justification of this approach, see Qualls (1972). The raw data were taken from *Moody's Industrial Manuals* and Standard and Poor's Compustat tapes. The independent variable observations centered on 1963 and 1965, hence the selection of the time period 1960–1968.

Table 1 Average Economic Profit Margin Percentages, 1960–1968: 205 Firms Classified by Concentration Level and Type of Control

	Type of Control				
Concentration Class	*Management*	*Weak Owner*	*Strong Owner*	*Owner (Strong & Weak)*	*All Control Types*
High, CR4A > 80, N = 50	5.1	6.2	6.1	6.2	5.6
Medium, 60 < CR4A < 80, N = 81	3.2	4.1	3.4	3.8	3.4
Low, CR4A < 60, N = 74	1.8	1.8	1.8	1.8	1.8
All concentration classes	3.1	4.0	3.5	3.7	3.3

for "high" barriers than for "medium" barriers, which are, in turn, higher than those for "low" barriers.

In the "medium" and "high" concentration classes and the "medium" and "high" barriers classes, the "owner" control class means are slightly higher, for the most part, than the "management" control class means (in the "high" barriers class the "strong owner" control average is less than the "management" average). This seems mildly supportive of the managerial hypothesis. On the other hand, the "strong owner" averages are slightly lower than the "weak owner" averages. This seems contradictory to the managerial hypothesis. . . .

Table 2 Average Economic Profit Margin Percentages, 1960–1968: 205 Firms Classified by Barriers to Entry and Type of Control

	Type of Control				
Barriers to Entry	*Management*	*Weak Owner*	*Strong Owner*	*Owner (Strong & Weak)*	*All Control Types*
High, N = 47	5.0	5.9	4.8	5.4	5.2
Medium, N = 101	2.9	4.4	3.5	3.9	3.2
Low, N = 57	1.9	1.9	2.6	2.2	2.0
All barriers classes	3.1	4.0	3.5	3.7	3.3

In Table 3, the firms are classified three ways—by concentration, barriers to entry, and type of control—and class means are presented. Unfortunately, there are some empty cells. Nevertheless, a couple of factors do stand out. First, there is no clear tendency for "owner" control averages to be higher than "management" control averages where concentration and barriers to entry are "high." Whereas the "weak owner" average is slightly above, the "strong owner" average is slightly below the "management" average. For the fourteen "owner" ("weak" plus "strong") firms the average is 6.2 percent as opposed to 6.0 percent for the eighteen "management" firms.

Table 3 Average Economic Profit Margin Percentages, 1960–1968: 205 Firms Classified by Concentration, Barriers to Entry, and Type of Control

Concentration	*Barrier to Entry*	*Type of Control*	*No. of Firms*	*Economic Profit Margins (percent)*	
High	High	Strong owner	6	5.5	6.1
		Weak owner	8	6.8	
		Management	18	6.0	
	Medium	Strong owner	2	5.6	4.2
		Weak owner	2	6.1	
		Management	12	3.6	
	Low	Strong owner	1	10.1	6.3
		Weak owner	1	2.5	
		Management	—	—	
Medium	High	Strong owner	—	—	3.5
		Weak owner	2	2.4	
		Management	9	3.8	
	Medium	Strong owner	10	3.7	3.3
		Weak owner	10	4.0	
		Management	41	3.0	
	Low	Strong owner	1	1.0	3.8
		Weak owner	1	7.7	
		Management	7	3.6	
Low	High	Strong owner	1	.5	2.2
		Weak owner	—	—	
		Management	3	2.7	
	Medium	Strong owner	4	2.2	2.3
		Weak owner	2	4.6	
		Management	18	2.1	
	Low	Strong owner	8	1.8	1.5
		Weak owner	10	1.2	
		Management	28	1.4	

This contradicts the managerialist view that for firms with significant market power, management control will lead to distinctly lower prices with given costs, or higher costs with given prices, and strongly suggests that whatever slight overall tendency there is in the sample for price–economic cost margins to be higher for owner controlled firms cannot be explained by simple reference to sales maximization or X-inefficiency. Mostly, differences between "owner" and "management" class means seem to cluster in the "medium" to "high" concentration and "low" to "medium" barriers categories. This suggests that the slight overall tendency toward higher economic profit margins for owner controlled firms in the sample, if not the simple result of random variation, is more likely explained as management firms in concentrated, lower barriers to entry industries behaving in a risk-averse fashion and pricing lower relative to cost in order to increase the probability of entry preclusion.

All this was tested further by estimating the following three regression equations:

$$
\begin{aligned}
PM = \; & \underset{(-1.424)}{-1.267} + \underset{(4.813)}{.073(CR \cdot HB \cdot S)} + \underset{(6.223)}{.089(CR \cdot HB \cdot W)} \qquad (9) \\
& + \underset{(6.445)}{.082(CR \cdot HB \cdot M)} + \underset{(4.466)}{.073(CR \cdot M \cdot S)} \\
& + \underset{(5.123)}{.083(CR \cdot MB \cdot W)} + \underset{(4.481)}{.063(CR \cdot MB \cdot M)} \\
& + \underset{(3.561)}{.079(CR \cdot LB \cdot S)} + \underset{(2.948)}{.070(CR \cdot LB \cdot W)} \\
& + \underset{(3.376)}{.066(CR \cdot LB \cdot M)} \\
& \qquad R^2 = .275 \qquad F = 8.199
\end{aligned}
$$

$$
\begin{aligned}
PM = \; & \underset{(-1.472)}{1.302} + \underset{(6.528)}{.083(CR \cdot HB \cdot O)} + \underset{(6.515)}{.083(CR \cdot HB \cdot M)} \qquad (10) \\
& + \underset{(5.344)}{.078(CR \cdot MB \cdot O)} + \underset{(4.544)}{.063(CR \cdot MB \cdot M)} \\
& + \underset{(3.732)}{.074(CR \cdot LB \cdot O)} + \underset{(3.430)}{.066(CR \cdot LB \cdot M)} \\
& \qquad R^2 = .268 \quad F = 12.071
\end{aligned}
$$

$$
\begin{aligned}
PM = \; & \underset{(-1.549)}{-1.365} + \underset{(7.089)}{.083(CR \cdot HB)} + \underset{(5.062)}{.069(CR \cdot MB)} \qquad (11) \\
& + \underset{(3.858)}{.071(CR \cdot LB)} \\
& \qquad R^2 = .254 \quad F = 22.852
\end{aligned}
$$

Here, *CR* is the Shepherd individual firm concentration index (a continuous variable), *M* is a 0–1 dummy variable for "management" control, and *LB* is a 0–1 dummy for "low" barriers. . . . [The other variables are also dummy variables: *HB* for high barriers to entry; *MB* for medium barriers; *PM* for the price–economic cost margin; *S* for strong owner; *W* for weak owner; *O* for owner (includes both strong and weak); *M* is management control.] Given the theorized interaction between concentration and barriers to entry and between market structure and type of control, this interactive specification is appropriate.

The concentration slope coefficients are all positive and highly significant, providing strong support for the Bain concentration hypothesis. Holding the type of control constant, the coefficients are larger where barriers to entry are "high" rather than "medium"—i.e., the concentration–profit margin relationship is "steeper" with "high" barriers, providing support for the barriers to entry hypothesis.[5] Where barriers to entry are "high" there is no clear tendency for the coefficients to be higher for "owner" control than for "management" control. Where barriers are "medium" and "low" there does seem to be a tendency for the coefficients to be higher for "owner" control.

This can be seen most clearly in equation (10), where "strong" and "weak" are combined into a single "owner" designation. There the high barriers–owner coefficient is exactly equal to the high barriers–management coefficient (when rounded off)—i.e., the concentration–profit margin relationship is no steeper for "owner" control than for "management" control. However, where barriers are "medium," the second pair of slope coefficients, the concentration–profit margin relationship is steeper for "owner" control. The difference between the two coefficients is statistically significant at the .01 level.

This again suggests that the slight overall tendency toward higher economic profit margins for "owner" control, if not the result of pure random variation, is the result of more risk-averse limit pricing behavior for "management" firms rather than simple sales maximization or X-inefficient behavior. If the latter were the case, the first slope coefficient in equation (10) should be significantly greater than the second. . . .

VII. Conclusions and Policy Implications

If the interpretation of empirical results stated above is reasonably accurate, the Berle and Means "managerial revolution" does not present much of a problem either for economic theory or public policy.

With regard to theory, the assumption of profit maximization appears to be virtually as meaningful (with perhaps one slight exception) for management-controlled firms as it is for owner-controlled firms. X-inefficiency seems to be no more of a problem for management-controlled firms than it is for owner-controlled firms. Market structure is important for market performance, but whether firms are controlled by managers or owners doesn't really matter very much.

[5] The concentration–profit margin slopes are not greater for "medium" barriers than for "low" barriers. This can be seen most clearly in equation (11), where the type of control dummies are dropped out. There the "low" barriers concentration coefficient is slightly and insignificantly higher than the "medium" barriers concentration coefficient. This is consistent with the Bain view (1956) that many firms in highly concentrated, low barriers to entry industries may engage in entry inducing pricing. The "high" barriers concentration coefficient is greater than the "medium" barriers coefficient and the difference is significant at approximately the .01 level. The statistic used to test for significant differences in regression coefficients was $[(\hat{\beta}_j - \hat{\beta}_k)/S(\hat{\beta}_j - \hat{\beta}_k)] \sim t_{n-k}$. For an explanation of this, see Kmenta (1971, p. 372).

The only noticeable behavioral difference may be that management-controlled firms faced with serious but uncertain threats of potential entry, hedge against the entry risk to a greater extent by setting lower prices relative to cost than would owner-controlled firms in similar market structural circumstances. In a normative sense this may be regarded as *good* rather than *bad*. Although it may make for less actual entry and "turnover" overall, it means that in some cases potential competition may lead to more nearly competitive price performance where established firms are management-controlled rather than owner-controlled.

Finally, two recent studies (Lewellen, 1971; Masson, 1971) have concluded that executive compensation schemes provide financial incentive for managers to pursue the goal of profit maximization. The evidence presented here suggests that, by and large, managers behave in accordance with that incentive.

References

Bain, J. *Barriers to New Competition*. Cambridge, Mass.: Harvard University Press, 1956.

———. "Relation of Profit Rate to Industry Concentration: American Manufacturing, 1936–1940." *Quarterly Journal of Economics* (August 1951): 293–324.

Berle, A. and G. Means. *The Modern Corporation and Private Property*. New York: Macmillan, 1932.

Kamerschen, D. "The Influence of Ownership and Control on Profit Rates." *The American Economic Review* (June 1968): 432–447.

Kmenta, J. *Elements of Econometrics*. New York: Macmillan, 1971.

Larner R. *Management Control and the Large Corporation*. New York: Dunellen, 1970.

Lerner, A. "The Concept of Monopoly and the Measurement of Monopoly Power." *Review of Economic Studies* (June 1934):157–175.

Lewellen, W. *The Ownership Income of Management*. New York: Columbia University Press, 1971.

Mann, H. "Seller Concentration, Barriers to Entry, and Rates of Return in Thirty Industries, 1950–1960." *Review of Economics and Statistics* (August 1966):296–307.

Masson, R. "Executive Motivations, Earnings, and Consequent Equity Performance." *Journal of Political Economy* (November–December 1971):1278–1292.

Monsen, R., J. Chiu and D. Cooley. "The Effect of Separation of Ownership and Control on the Performance of the Large Firm." *Quarterly Journal of Economics* (August 1968):435–451.

Palmer, J. "The Profit-Performance Effects of the Separation of Ownership

From Control in Large U.S. Industrial Corporations." *The Bell Journal of Economics and Management Science* (Spring 1973):293–303.

Qualls, D. "Concentration, Barriers to Entry and Long Run Economic Profit Margins." *The Journal of Industrial Economics* (April 1972):146–158.

———. "Stability and Persistence of Economic Profit Margins in Highly Concentrated Industries." *Southern Economic Journal* (April 1974):604–612.

Scherer, F. *Industrial Market Structure and Economic Performance*. Chicago: Rand McNally, 1970.

Shepherd, W. *Market Power and Economic Welfare*. New York: Random House, 1970.

———. "The Elements of Market Structure." *Review of Economics and Statistics* (February 1972):25–37.

Weiss, L. "Quantitative Studies of Industrial Organization." In *Frontiers of Quantitative Economics*. Michael D. Intrilagator (Ed.). Amsterdam: North-Holland, 1971.

———. "The Concentration-Profits Relationship and Antitrust." In *Industrial Concentration: The New Learning*. H. Goldschmid, H. Mann, and J. Weston (Eds.). Boston: Little, Brown, 1974.

Part Eight

A generation ago, the interest of economists in the public utility and transportation industries found its center in the public control of monopoly prices. Economists played a prominent role in the evolution of state and federal regulation of public utility rates. These rates were, and still are, established so that they cover average costs plus a "fair" return to investors. Thus successful regulation achieves a sort of compromise between investors and consumers. In a rough way, the compromise is consistent with the norm of long-run competitive equilibrium, in which prices equal full average (and marginal) costs plus normal profits (which however are not identical with "fair" profits).

Within the last generation, however, the concern of economists with the public utility industries has shifted. One reason is that interproduct and inter-

Public Utility Pricing

service competition has become strong: the railroads now have to compete with air carriers and motor carriers and water carriers; the electric power companies have to compete with the natural gas companies, and so on. Thus the problem of monopoly exploitation has become modest. At the same time the older pattern of regulation continues, though it no longer fits the realities of the new competition in and among the public utility industries. Accordingly, economists have been seeking fresh solutions to the questions of public utility regulation. Some of them advocate relaxation of much regulation to give greater sway to competition, while other economists propose a drastic change, namely, that public utility prices be made equal to marginal, not average, costs.

46 This selection is a statement, with one small omission, prepared in 1962 under the auspices of the Association of American Railroads. To prepare the statement, Mr. Burton N. Behling, economist of the Bureau of Railway Economics of the Association, engaged as consultants the other economists and transportation specialists whose names are given below. All of these men subscribe to the statement "in substance, and they specifically agree with the conclusions as set forth in the summary at the end of the statement."

COST CALCULATIONS FOR MINIMUM RAILROAD RATES

WILLIAM J. BAUMOL *Princeton University*
BURTON N. BEHLING *Association of American Railroads*
JAMES C. BONBRIGHT *Columbia University*
YALE BROZEN *University of Chicago*
JOEL DEAN *Columbia University, Joel Dean Associates*
FORD K. EDWARDS *Edwards and Peabody*
CALVIN B. HOOVER *Duke University*
DUDLEY F. PEGRUM *University of California (L.A.)*
MERRILL J. ROBERTS *University of Pittsburgh*
ERNEST W. WILLIAMS, JR. *Columbia University*

Increasing competitiveness in transportation has stimulated debate regarding the principles which should guide the determination of any floor below which particular railroad rates will not be permitted to fall. A central issue in this debate is whether particular rates should be cost- or market-oriented. This statement examines the issue—bringing to bear accepted principles of economics that apply throughout the economy. It sets forth the role of cost in pricing and in so doing shows that prices must be *both* cost- and market-oriented.

Examining first the basic cost concepts and then the nature of railroad costs, the analysis concludes that incremental costs provide the valid cost

Taken, adapted, reprinted from "The Role of Cost in the Minimum Pricing of Railroad Services," by William J. Baumol and Associates, *Journal of Business,* Vol. XXXV, No. 4, October 1962, pp. 358–366, by permission of The University of Chicago Press.

guide for minimum pricing and that "fully distributed" costs must be rejected as an economic test of any particular price or rate. These conclusions are reached by reference to the interest both of the pricing carrier and of society as a whole, and they have the same force and relevance for pricing within modes of transport as among modes.

Underlying Cost Principles

The increase in total costs resulting from an expansion in a firm's volume of business is commonly referred to as *incremental cost.* This cost is of vital economic significance. For the businessman, it provides an essential guide to his production and pricing policy. If he is considering a reduction in price, he needs to know whether the increase in total revenues from greater volume will more than cover the additional costs that will be incurred. For the whole economy it is incremental (not fully distributed) cost that is the relevant cost guide to how much of what shall be produced and how much should be invested in various lines of production. This cost, which is measured by the value of the additional resources that will be used up when more of anything is produced, represents the real cost to society.[1] Incremental costs indicate (by comparison with the incremental revenues they will bring) whether additional outputs of any commodity are worth producing and (by incremental cost comparisons) which of the alternative ways of satisfying wants or requirements is the most efficient.[2]

But not all costs can be identified causally with specific quantities of production. Much of the controversy over cost concepts stems from the false notion that all costs can be traced and attributed to specific blocks of output. Although many costs are *traceable,* there are also *non-traceable* costs which simply do not lend themselves to this method of identification:

a. *Fixed Costs.* Some costs, called *fixed costs,* do not change in magnitude when the quantity of output for a given plant varies. Hence, it is impossible to assign any specific portion of these costs to a particular unit of output (e.g., to a particular ton-mile of traffic). Rather, a fixed cost must be imputed to the entire supply of the type or types of service with which it is associated.

b. *Joint Costs.* Different services may sometimes share their costs, as, for example, when the same roadbed is employed to transport both food products and lumber.

Such common and joint conditions are frequently encountered in the

[1] Social costs which are escaped by the enterprise must also be included in the calculation.

[2] In addition to those costs which vary with rate of output for a given investment level, incremental costs include cost increments associated with new investment. For example, if special equipment is acquired in order to handle certain additional traffic, the costs are incremental to that traffic.

railroad industry as well as elsewhere. Wherever incremental costs are also either joint or common costs, the resulting difficulties of allocation cannot be side-stepped. Here the standard distinction between common costs and joint costs can have practical importance. *Common costs* are outlays devoted to either of two or more classes of services which may be variably proportioned at the discretion of management, with the result that it is, in principle at least, possible to trace them to individual services. *Joint costs*, in contrast, are costs for which the proportions of output are not variable, so that supplying one class of service in a given amount results automatically in making available another class of service in some unalterable amount. The practical consequence is that incremental joint costs are not traceable to individual railroad services and can be allocated only arbitrarily. In contrast, those common costs which are incremental are traceable in principle, although it may be impossible over a considerable range to do so in practice.

For any business or industry there is no rigid division between variable costs and fixed costs. Some cost elements which are fixed in the very short term or with small changes in output may over a somewhat longer period or a broad range of output become incremental if additional investments or other inputs are required. However, an indefinitely long-term view of incremental costs is not appropriate, for some fixed costs may be expected to remain fixed over any time period and range of output that is reasonable to consider in setting a price floor. Depending on the particular circumstances, incremental costs might contemplate a range of short terms. The only general rule for deciding which measure of incremental cost to use as a *cost* guide for minimum pricing is that the choice of incremental cost functions must be geared to the duration of the expected revenue change.[3]

Each particular situation requires its particular cost analysis by management. For example, a cost structure will be affected significantly by the extent of unused capacity in the production factors involved. Where unused capacity is substantial and persistent, the fixed cost elements per unit of output are correspondingly greater and more enduring, and the incremental costs proportionately smaller.

Arbitrary apportionments of non-traceable costs among particular kinds of outputs must be employed in the calculation of "fully distributed costs." This measure will be further considered later in particular reference to railroad rate-making. However, it is apparent from what has been said that fully distributed costs have no true economic content because their derivation falsely assumes that all costs can be traced to particular kinds or quantities of output and can rationally enter directly into pricing decisions. The

[3] More specifically, the decision is governed by such revenue dimensions as the nature and amount of the contemplated change in volume, the length of the commitment to carry the traffic, the duration and geographic scope of the changed rate, the alterations of the service that might require added investments, and the time period in which changes may legally or practically take place.

greater the degree of non-traceable costs, the more inappropriate is the use of fully distributed costs as a guide to minimum prices.

Nature of Railroad Costs

Fixed costs, which are independent of volume and are not attributable to specific amounts of traffic, are an important characteristic of railroad cost structures. Large portions of railroad investment costs represent expenditures for long-lived facilities that have been "sunk" in the enterprise at various times in the past. The facilities involved are of such specialized nature that they are not generally transferable to other pursuits without great loss. Fixed costs associated with sunk physical investments, as well as organizational or other cost factors which are underutilized, are irretrievably committed to an essential public service unless disinvestment, organizational shrinkage, or, as a last resort, abandonment occurs.

Because of the long but varied lives of their facilities and the inherent uncertainties of forecasting, adjustment of railroad capacity to changing requirements is difficult. Unutilized railroad capacity is a chronic problem which demands effective steps to retain existing traffic and to attract additional traffic. Moreover, railroad investments in recent years which were intended for modernization and greater efficiency have in many instances also increased capacity, although this has not usually been the purpose. Significant technological improvements include heavier rail and track structures, electronic yards, centralized traffic control, and better communications, as well as improved locomotive power and higher-capacity freight cars. Realization of the potential economies of these and other interrelated improvements depends on large and increasing traffic volumes.

The railroads own, and hence must fully pay for, the costly plant facilities they use. In contrast, highway, water, and air carriers use publicly owned rights of way and facilities. To the extent that they repay the economic costs of these facilities furnished to them, their payments are mainly through use charges which make their costs of this sort predominantly variable. For these and other reasons, these rival carriers can adjust their capacities to fluctuating demand more promptly and precisely than can the railroads.

The public interest requires maximum economic utilization of the vast capacity of the railroads' plant and operating organization. To this end, it is essential that the burden of fixed costs be spread over as large a volume of traffic as can be developed with attractive rates in excess of the relevant incremental costs. This mode of operation is desirable not only for the railroads in providing them with the opportunity for reasonable investment returns. It may also be advantageous to the shippers in lower shipping costs. Above all, it is in the public interest because it provides the maximum amount of transportation service for the resources which are employed for this purpose.

Relevant Incremental Costs

In determining incremental costs, it is necessary to distinguish between sunk and prospective investments. Sometimes the pertinent incremental costs involve making added investment (e.g., cars or locomotives). In that event, all the added costs to be incurred (including use-depreciation and cost of capital) should be recognized as incremental. Sometimes capacity is so excessive that the traffic at issue can be handled without added investment. The investment costs then are sunk and may become fixed for long periods. Once the commitment has been made, and if a plethora of capacity subsequently develops, the recovery of anything more than incremental cost is better than nothing.

Prudent railroad management should certainly be aware of the threat to long-term profitability, and even survival, from fixing rates on a substantial proportion of traffic near strictly short-term incremental costs. Nevertheless, in the complex and varied circumstances of the railroads, there will be some situations where pricing of particular services on the basis of short-term considerations will improve utilization and will yield accretions to net income not otherwise obtainable. In view of their primary responsibility to make effective use of their vast facilities through volume retention and development, railroad managements require considerable latitude in estimating relevant costs as well as in pricing decisions. There is no single cost formula which will always and automatically be appropriate.

In rapidly expanding industries operating with short-lived facilities and highly flexible organization, recognition of the transitory nature of fixed costs and their tendency to be transformed rather quickly into incremental costs is an essential costing precept for pricing purposes. But railroad costs cannot be cast in such a simple mold. The reality of their fixed costs cannot be made to disappear with a general assumption of variability with traffic volumes if the time period is stretched out long enough. With the persistent and serious underutilization of capacity which is characteristic of the railroads' basic plant and organization, large amounts of fixed costs remain fixed indefinitely. The least effective way to cope with unutilized railroad capacity would be to include its fixed costs in floors for pricing. For the high prices which would result could only discourage utilization of these facilities and aggravate the condition.

Neither extremely short-run nor extremely long-run incremental cost is an economic concept of general applicability to all minimum pricing problems encountered in the railroad industry. The determination of the relevant incremental costs appropriate for a particular pricing decision is not simple[4] but must reflect complex railroad cost conditions that arise from

[4] The relevant incremental costs are a function principally of the prospective volume in relation to present volume and unutilized capacity in existing plant and organization. The rate over time at which the prospective volume is likely to be achieved, the prospects for its continuance over the longer term, and its distribution over stated time periods (for example, sea-

persistent excess capacity, irrelevant fixed-cost elements, and such interrelated dynamic factors as changing volume, changing labor and material costs, technological innovations, and improved operating techniques. Where such dynamic forces are at work the incremental costs of additional traffic, which may be induced by a reduced rate, may be quite different from those indicated by past experience.

More penetrating analysis of specific cost elements is needed for a better understanding of their relationship to traffic volumes. Such analysis, which is beyond the scope of this statement on cost concepts, should be intensified by the railroads. Particularly urgent is the need for cost determinations which are "tailored" to specific situations instead of the commonly used general measures which are vitiated by excessive averaging.

Costs and Pricing

Forward-looking costs are essential because the pricing decisions they must guide necessarily look to the future. The estimation of such costs must reckon with changes in operating techniques which may result from expanded volume and associated or unassociated technological innovations. Because of these factors, historical experience provides no sure basis for determining those future incremental costs which alone are relevant in setting price floors.

As a general rule, any rate below incremental costs is both unprofitable and socially wasteful of resources because the additional (incremental) revenue obtained is less than the additional cost incurred.[5] However, this does not mean that the railroads should set rates *at* that cost level or that they should be required to do so. On the contrary, this cost reference is uniquely important as a guide in determining the specific rates which will provide the maximum contribution to the overhead burden and thus to net income. The margin above incremental costs which maximizes this contribution depends upon the price sensitivity of demand, determined primarily by the alternatives available to shippers. The judgment of management should be relied upon to make this determination, subject to limitations imposed by regulation of maximum rates and discrimination. Thus, while incremental

sonality and peaking characteristics) are all relevant to the determination of appropriate incremental costs. From consideration of the prospective volume and its characteristics, it may be feasible to estimate those elements of plant and organization which will require ultimate replacement, allowances for the use of which should figure currently in costs. If volume promises to build up substantially over time, the likelihood and cost of the required expansion in capacity must be recognized in the computation of the price floor.

[5] The application of this principle in particular situations may require special care in estimating the pertinent incremental costs and incremental revenue. Especially in the short run they may be different from what they superficially appear. Example: the hidden incremental costs of dismissing and later reassembling a key work-force; and the hidden, foregone incremental revenue that may result in losing a profitable customer by refusing to take an occasional order below incremental cost.

costs should not *determine* prices or rates, they set the lower boundary (and demand conditions and regulate the upper boundary) within which pricing decisions should be made.

Railroads produce a multiplicity of different services in many markets with dissimilar demand characteristics. For example, the demand for the transportation of coal for three hundred miles eastbound may be entirely different from the demand for the transportation of the same commodity three hundred miles westbound because of competitive or market influences. Basing rates on demand (as well as on incremental costs) to attain the maximum contribution means, therefore, that rates for all services will not be the same either absolutely, or in relation to cost, or in contributions to the net income of the carriers.

Since demands for rail services have become increasingly elastic as alternative means of transportation (both for-hire and private) have become ever more available, the greatest total contribution to net income will for many items and hauls result from a low unit margin above incremental cost and a large volume. Estimating the volume of traffic which might move at different levels of rates and the effect on net income is a key aspect of pricing. This vital function is a primary management responsibility which should be performed on the basis of managerial and not regulatory judgment. Rates so determined, however, can legitimately continue to be subject to regulation of maximum rates and to legal rules against unjust discrimination.[6]

Differential pricing is consistent with the public interest in the economical utilization of resources. It can yield significant benefits to the users of rail services by encouraging the retention of traffic and the development of greater traffic volumes and improved profits, thus fostering the adoption of improved technology and service, as well as lower rates.

Pricing designed to achieve such results should not be condemned as "destructive" or "unfair" competition. Rather it is necessary for constructive competition and maximal economy and efficiency in the utilization of resources. By the very nature of competition, some are hurt by it. It may well be that realistic assessments of incremental costs as a pricing guide would encourage rate reductions where carrier or regulatory policies have stressed preservation of historic rate structures or keeping rates high enough to maintain "fair" market sharing. Indeed, reductions designed directly to improve profits may do so mainly by shifting traffic away from firms operating by other modes, which are thereby hurt or even destroyed. But this does not constitute predatory competition. Predatory practices must be taken to refer to temporary price reductions designed to eliminate competition in order to clear the way for high and monopolistic rates in the future. Ease and low costs of re-entry of trucks and other modes make predatory competition by the railroads unprofitable and, hence, unlikely. Moreover, such un-

[6] The railroads also are subject to the limitation of a reasonable over-all "return," but this regulatory limitation has not for many years of low earnings been a matter of real concern. If excessive profits were ever achieved, it would be the lawful responsibility of the regulatory authorities to apply the appropriate restraints.

desirable practices constitute a legitimate concern of the regulatory authorities. Regulatory powers should not, however, be used to prevent price reductions which are designed to improve or maintain profits by increasing or retaining traffic volume. Such prevention is particularly undesirable socially, because of the low rates of utilization of the large property investments of the railroads.

"Fully Distributed" Cost an Invalid Basis for Minimum Pricing

The relevant incremental costs constitute all the cost information pertinent to the determination of floors in the pricing of particular railroad services. "Fully distributed" cost, measured by some kind of arbitrary statistical apportionment of the unallocable costs among the various units or classes of traffic, is an economically invalid criterion for setting minimum rates, from both a managerial and a regulatory standpoint. No particular category of traffic can be held economically responsible for any given share of the unallocable costs. Whether any particular rate is above or below some fully distributed cost is without real economic significance for minimum pricing.

Stated differently, the appropriate aim of the railroads is to determine that margin above incremental costs, traffic volume considered, at which a rate produces the maximum total contribution toward fixed costs and net income. Fully distributed costs cannot serve this vital economic purpose. They present an entirely false picture of traffic profitability. Their use would drive away great quantities of profitable, volume-moving traffic now handled at rates below fully distributed costs.

Another misconception is the view that if some railroad rates are below fully distributed costs, a burden is imposed on other traffic which must pay more to make up the "deficiency." But, when the true significance of unallocable costs is understood, it becomes apparent that a particular rate which maximizes the contribution to such costs over and above the relevant incremental costs cannot possibly burden other traffic even though rates on the latter may be higher. If such contributions from lower-paying traffic were lost because of unattractive rates, railroad earnings and expenditures for improvements would suffer, and the ability to provide good service would be impaired. Traffic which is not moved cannot possibly help to bear the unallocable costs. It is the fully distributed cost doctrine which, by pegging minimum rates on a false economic premise, would burden not only railroad shippers but the economy as a whole and would tend to bankrupt the railroad system by artificially restricting the economic use of railroad facilities and services.

Especially in competitive industries, no cost system can really assure that all costs will be covered and a "normal" profit earned, for sales volume will play a significant role. If guaranteed coverage of all costs and a normal profit are the objectives of fully distributed cost pricing, it cannot succeed.

For that matter, neither can pricing based on relevant incremental costs plus a maximum contribution to fixed costs and net income, as determined by conditions of market demand, provide such a guarantee. But if these contributions are maximized throughout the pricing structure, the best result has been achieved and no further improvement is possible under prevailing market conditions.

Thus, the fully distributed cost doctrine does not reflect valid principles of pricing, where fixed costs are significant. Application of this false criterion in the railroads' present competitive environment would bring about prices which (for much traffic) would shrink volume. If the same total constant costs were then distributed on the shrunken traffic volume, even greater fully distributed unit costs would result, and if this should cause the railroads to raise rates still higher relative to the prices of other modes of transportation, then rail traffic volume would probably be still further reduced. A costing procedure which can inaugurate such a destructive cost-price spiral is not qualified to serve as a basis for pricing in the railroad business or in any other with unallocable costs and unused capacity.

The social costs of such a pricing method could be enormous. The railroads could not function economically and quite possibly could not survive the use of this misguided basis of pricing. Under it, much traffic either would not move at all or would be moved only by modes of transportation with higher actual economic costs. The end result would be a greater total transportation cost borne by the whole economy in return for a reduced volume of transportation service.

"Full Cost of Low-Cost Carrier" Also a False Standard

An offshoot of the fully distributed cost fallacy is the contention that rail rates should not be permitted to go below the "full cost of the low-cost carrier" (such carrier being determined on the basis of comparative fully distributed cost), whether it be that of a railroad or a different mode of transport. This contention, also, has no validity as a measure of "inherent advantage" or relative economy in the utilization of economic resources of the nation. For the reasons pointed out above, the low-cost carrier is properly identified by incremental cost, not by so-called "full" cost.

Only a railroad's own incremental costs are of any significance as a guide in establishing its minimum rates; and this same principle applies as well to other modes of transport and other industries. Imposing a different and higher *cost* standard deprives railroads of traffic which they can transport more economically, artificially stimulates the growth of uneconomic transportation by other means including private transportation, deprives the shipping public of the benefits of low-cost service, and imposes higher commodity prices on the consuming public. However computed, the use of fully distributed costs would be wasteful of economic resources by misdirecting their use and by keeping them idle or underutilized.

In addition to its inherent defect, this specious "cost" proposal has another deficiency. To whatever extent carriers which operate on public facilities may not have to meet full economic costs in conducting their business, their "fully distributed costs" are not consistent with those computed for the railroads. For the railroads a fully distributed cost computation embraces the entire costs. The effect of the use of the "full cost of the low-cost carrier" doctrine is to obstruct the railroads in pricing their services in competition with other modes to the extent that they may be subsidized. Thus, this proposal constitutes umbrella rate-making to protect any subsidized modes of transportation from legitimate competition by the railroads.

Summary

1. In the determination of cost floors as a guide to the pricing of particular railroad services, or the services of any other transport mode, incremental costs of each particular service are the only relevant costs.

2. Rates for particular railroad services should be set at such amounts (subject to regulation of maximum rates and to legal rules against unjust discrimination) as will make the greatest total contribution to net income. Clearly, such maximizing rates would never fall below incremental costs.

3. Pricing which is not restricted by any minimum other than incremental cost can foster more efficient use of railroad resources and capacity and can therefore encourage lower costs and rates. This same principle applies to other modes of transportation.

4. The presence of large amounts of fixed costs and unused capacity in railroad facilities makes it especially important that railroad rates encourage a large volume of traffic.

5. Reduced rates which more than cover incremental costs and are designed by management to maximize contribution to net income do not constitute proof of predatory competition.

6. "Fully distributed" costs derived by apportioning unallocable costs have no economic significance in determining rate floors for particular railroad services. The application of such a criterion would arbitrarily force the railroads to maintain rates above the level which would yield maximum contribution to net income and would deprive them of much traffic for which they can compete economically. For similar reasons, restriction of railroad minimum rates according to the "full cost of the low-cost carrier" is economically unsound.

POSTSCRIPT

The July 1963 issue of the *Journal of Business* carried three articles criticizing the statement by the ten economists and transportation specialists. One critic said that the statement calls for more discriminatory pricing by the railroads, which could be contrary to the public interest. Another objected to "incremental pricing." The third critic raised questions about the model of pure competition and its applicability. In reply, the authors of the preceding statement issued a "Statement of Clarification." In this they reaffirmed their position on how costs should be viewed for price making. Incremental costs, they repeated, should not determine prices; rather, they are normally the relevant costs to be included in calculations of prices. Whether prices are unduly discriminatory is another matter.

47 The trucking industry has been regulated by the Interstate Commerce Commission (ICC). The ICC makes entry of new firms difficult, and limits price changes. Has this regulation raised or lowered rates of return to trucking firms? Has the regulation increased or decreased efficiency in trucking services?

A PARADOX OF REGULATED TRUCKING

MILTON KAFOGLIS
Emory University

Adam Smith wrote in *The Wealth of Nations* that "every individual necessarily labours to render the annual revenue of the society as great as he can . . . and he is in this, as in many cases, led by an invisible hand to promote an end which was no part of his intention." In other words, the public interest is best served through the pursuit of private interest. This apparent paradox is quickly resolved when we identify the "invisible hand" as the competitive market—an arrangement that permits the individual to pursue his own self-interest without penalizing other members of society. Indeed, many economists have devoted their lives to examining the intricacies of "Smith's paradox" in complex situations.

When a benign government seeks to serve the public interest by substituting its visible, frequently coercive, and often selective hand for Smith's invisible, volitional, and impersonal hand, new paradoxes appear. Unlike Smith's, some of these cannot be rationally resolved and are, therefore, absurdities. Our subject is one of these.

Consider the following. The trucking industry is said to be earning no more than a "competitive" return on its assets, but entrepreneurs are paying large sums for the right to operate as truckers in this "competitive" market. That is, they spend millions of dollars each year to purchase existing operating rights from other truckers and millions more to obtain new operating rights from the Interstate Commerce Commission (ICC). If returns to the transportation-related assets were in fact competitive, truckers would not pay such sums for operating rights, because this would force their rate of return below the competitive level—below what these assets could earn elsewhere.

Since the ICC controls the supply of operating rights (also called "operating authorities" or "operating certificates"), the question that arises is whether the

---

Reprinted from Milton Kafoglis, "A Paradox of Regulated Trucking," *Regulation,* September/October 1977, pp. 27–32.

The author of this article expresses his thanks to James C. Miller III, who suggested and encouraged this research effort.

commission creates an artificial scarcity of supply or in some other way permits the industry to earn excessive returns. If it does, we no longer have a paradox—just poor or unnecessary regulation.

The commission argues that because truckers are not permitted to include the value of their operating rights in the assets on which they are entitled to a return, the existence of these rights does not lead to higher truck rates. The commission also argues that it does not significantly limit the supply of operating rights, since it approves over 80 percent of the applications it receives. If rights are easy to acquire and if truck rates are set so that the industry earns a "competitive" return on its transportation-related assets, the paradox reappears, and one is left wondering about the business sense of those who pay huge sums for these rights.

Background

At this point we should note the historical origins of the apparent contradiction we have identified. The basic structure of trucking regulation was established by the Motor Carrier Act of 1935. At that time the economy was in the throes of the Great Depression, and there grew a demand that industry be protected from the evils of "destructive competition." Conditions seemed particularly bad in the trucking industry. The business was an easy one for enterprising individuals to enter and provided an alternative to industrial unemployment. With considerable new entry occurring, truck rates declined as hard-pressed truck operators struggled to compete for customers.

The gains to consumers from lower trucking rates did not persuade the policy-makers of that time. Instead, they accepted the argument that equipment was being inadequately maintained, that driving times had lengthened, and the "unethical" operators were creating unsafe conditions. The railroads and large trucking firms, whose established markets were being threatened, were joined by large shippers and the ICC, which was concerned about the viability of "common carriage," in demanding an extension of regulation to the trucking industry. The principal purposes of regulating the truckers were to "protect" the common-carrier system from competition by treating motor carriers like railroads and to stabilize prices and capacity in trucking.

The essential techniques of railroad regulation—a system designed to control monopoly—were applied to the diverse and atomistic trucking industry in an environment characterized not by monopoly but by intense rivalry. First, with some exceptions, the ICC was granted power to approve and suspend rates charged by for-hire motor carriers. In determining just and reasonable rates the commission did not, as is usually the case in public utility regulation, directly establish a fair rate of return on investment. It considered a number of factors, but relied most heavily on the operating ratio (the ratio of operating costs to revenues) as a criterion for evaluating rate increases. This type of regulation, along with the antitrust immunity subsequently granted to motor-carrier rate bureaus (organizations used by truckers to establish rates through joint "agreement"), has led to inflexible prices and the virtual elimination of price competition among truckers.

Second, the ICC was granted control over entry into the industry. Common carriers (those which provide services to the general public) must obtain from the ICC "certificates of public convenience and necessity" to transport particular classes of goods over particular routes.[1] The "need" for a new certificate is easily contested by carriers already operating in the particular transportation market. These certificates—or rights—contain various restrictions, including specification of routes, gateway restrictions (that is, restrictions on the routes a carrier can use when passing from the territory of one ratemaking bureau to that of another), limitations that increase empty backhauls, and restrictions on particular commodities hauled. As a result, route structures are often circuitous, and route and service offerings quite inflexible to changes in the demand for service. Some of these inefficiencies have been relieved by ICC action and by the carriers themselves as larger firms have bought certificates from smaller firms in order to make their routes more efficient. But the problem is far from resolved.

What Are Operating Rights Worth?

According to a 1974 report of the American Trucking Associations (ATA), "Recent acquisitions in the motor carrier industry indicate that amounts paid for operating authorities are approximately 15% to 20% of the annual revenue produced by those authorities." Indeed, the report describes operating rights as the industry's "most important asset."

Operating rights are issued only if the proposed service "is or will be required by the present or future public convenience and necessity" (49 U.S. Code, section 307). The commission seldom grants an application that threatens the financial health of existing carriers. Regulatory policy thus supports the survival of existing firms and significantly reduces entrepreneurial risk. The ICC thinks this is desirable because it leads to "stability" and lower borrowing rates for truckers. Bankers tend to view operating rights as assets that can be sold in the event of bankruptcy, as protection from harsh competition, and as representing a preferential claim on new business.

The commission grants over 4,000 operating rights a year, denying only a small portion of those that are requested. In view of this, why are existing operating rights purchased for huge sums? Why do not truckers simply apply directly to the commission and receive their rights for no more than the expense of hiring an attorney? The answer is that if they really intend to compete with existing firms, they will necessarily "injure" those firms. Doubtless, many

[1] Most of the operating rights in existence today arose under the so-called grandfather clause of the Motor Carrier Act. Congress made special provision to protect the interests of motor carriers in bona fide operations prior to the passage of the act by not requiring these carriers to prove public need in order to continue in operation.

truckers who want rights are advised by their attorneys not to apply because they cannot meet the "no injury" standard.[2] Beyond these basic regulatory obstacles, the application procedure is lengthy and costly, involving legal and other costs far in excess of those available to most would-be entrepreneurs.

The fact that the commission acts favorably on most applications does not mean that entry is easy. The new operating rights that are granted are generally specific and narrow with respect to the origins and destinations of traffic and the commodities to be carried. They are granted, for example, when a new plant opens (and may limit the carrier to serving just that plant) or when they are simple extensions of existing rights not contested by other truckers. Entry that creates direct, new competition is rare, notwithstanding the leniency claimed by the ICC. Thus entrepreneurs wishing to set up trucking businesses of any size or to extend their operations substantially usually must purchase expensive operating rights. (These purchases must be approved by the ICC, but this is a routine procedure and imposes no impediment to such transactions.)

Over the ten-year period, 1963 through 1972, total investment in operating rights shown on the balance sheets of Class I common carriers of general freight grew from about $65 million to about $300 million according to the ATA—or at an annual compounded rate of approximately 16 percent. The balance sheet increase resulted primarily from the sale of these rights at prices above book value, meaning that the truckers who bought the rights carry them on their books at higher values than the truckers who sold them. Since book values increase only when rights are sold, existing rights not recently traded are seriously undervalued on the books. Thus, the figure of about $300 million for year-end 1972 grossly understates their market value. For example, Associated Transport, Inc., carried operating rights on its balance sheet at $976,000 but sold them in 1976 at public auction for $20.6 million. The same year, Eastern Freightway, Inc., sold rights carried on its books at $450,000 for about $3.8 million.

The ICC recently released information on forty-three transactions in operating rights from 1967 through 1971 (see Table 1). These transactions involved no assets beyond the operating right. The forty-three rights were purchased originally for a total of $776,800 and were later sold for a total of $3,844,100. The average length of time they were held is 10.1 years, so that their aggregate value increased at a compounded annual rate of 17 percent. Adjusting the sales figure to constant (1972) dollars reduces the annual increase to 13 percent. The "average" trucking company (as represented by the forty-three transactions) thus earned a "capital gain" of 13 percent a year on its operating right (in real terms), plus an after-tax return on its investment in other assets of 9 to 17 percent (the 1970–1975 range).[3] The after-tax return on investment of 9 to 17 percent

[2] Competition typically involves the provision of a better service or lower prices than are provided by the existing firm and will thus lead to a weakening of the existing firm's financial condition. A potential entrant who would make consumers better off thus would have difficulty meeting ICC standards.

[3] After-tax returns on investment of Class I motor carriers ranged from a low of 9.0 percent in 1970 to a high of 17.5 percent in 1972, and averaged 13.27 percent in 1975 (ICC annual reports, 1971–1976). According to *Business Week* (November 15, 1976), the average rate of return on equity for the year ending September 30, 1976, was 13.7 percent for the all-industry composite and 20.9 percent for the truck companies included in the survey.

exceeds that earned by public utilities and compares quite favorably with results in unregulated markets. The higher return from the sale of operating rights, of course, raises the truckers' overall return. Given the degree of protection from competition that is inherent in a regulated industry and the low risk of failure, this return—putting it mildly—seems high.

It is interesting to note that the rate of return earned on the operating rights covered in the table (that is, the rate of increase in their value) declined with the length of time the rights were held. One possible reason is that as a route structure grows older it becomes less efficient because—owing to ICC restrictions—it cannot be adjusted to changes in transportation demand. Another is that competition develops along older routes and reduces profits—but, given the problems of entry, this seems unlikely.

Since the sample of forty-three transactions is small and includes only operating rights that were actually sold, we should not place a great deal of confidence in the precise results. Yet, the results do conform generally to the ATA figures cited earlier and are conservative compared with some recent unpublished estimates made by Thomas G. Moore.[4]

The ICC is aware that operating rights increase in value over time. A February 1972 statement issued to motor carriers by the ICC's Bureau of Accounts states that "in a preponderance of cases where carrier operating rights are acquired through a business combination we are of the opinion that the value of those rights tends to increase rather than diminish. However, we are undecided as to the underlying cause of the increase." This conclusion seems incredible and suggests that the commission has made little effort to evaluate this crucial asset. There must be some reason why the operating rights increase in value over time, and that reason may be related to failures in the regulatory system.

Why Do Operating Rights Increase in Value?

The value of an operating right is the present value of profits in excess of those needed to maintain investment in the industry. In a genuinely competitive industry, the rate of return earned on investment is equal to that required to maintain and attract capital. Economists refer to this rate of return as the "cost of capital." It happens that in the regulated trucking industry a "gap" has been created between the actual return and the cost of capital. Such a "gap" can be created by permitting excessive rates and may be widened if control of entry creates some monopoly power. If this "gap" is expected to persist, the excessive return will become capitalized, giving value to the operating right. A continuous rise in the value of an operating right suggests that the present value of the

[4] When rights are purchased, carriers are required to file a "giving effect" statement with the ICC. This statement includes an estimate of the profit that would have been earned had the rights been owned in the most recent period. Moore examined ten such statements and found that the expected return on the investment in rights was 35 percent. The "giving effect" statement probably gives undue influence to near-term factors so that Moore's figure may be related to the returns on the rights in our sample that have been held a short period of time. (Thomas G. Moore, "Beneficiaries of Trucking Regulation," preliminary discussion paper, June 21, 1976, p. 21.)

Table 1 Rates of Return Earned on 43 Transactions in Operating Rights, 1967–1971

Years Rights Held	Purchase Price (000)	Sale Price (000)	Compound Annual Rates of Return: Current Dollars	Compound Annual Rates of Return: 1972 Dollars
1	3.0	23.0	667%	620%
1	2.5	17.0	580	576
1	15.3	100.0	554	554
1	29.4	151.6	416	390
1	3.0	15.0	400	329
1	17.5	50.0	186	186
1	16.8	22.5	34	27
1	30.0	31.9	6	2
1	10.0	10.0	0	0
2	20.2	50.8	58	51
2	25.6	20.0	−12	−14
3	10.0	40.0	58	51
3	18.0	50.0	40	34
4	10.0	400.0	151	138
5	1.1	40.0	105	98
7	9.8	265.2	60	56
7	8.8	80.0	37	33
7	102.7	349.4	19	16
7	10.8	35.0	18	14
7	26.0	65.0	13	9
7	38.0	38.0	0	0
7	5.0	1.0	−20	−23
9	25.3	50.0	8	4
10	25.8	274.2	27	24
10	13.0	55.0	16	12
11	11.0	350.0	37	33
11	2.3	10.0	14	11
11	10.0	25.0	8	5
12	15.0	15.0	0	1
15	32.8	175.0	12	9
16	2.8	45.0	19	16
16	13.5	85.0	12	10
17	2.5	30.0	16	13
17	105.0	113.5	0	−2
18	5.5	340.0	63	25
18	4.1	23.0	10	7
20	22.0	90.0	7	4

Years Rights Held	Purchase Price (000)	Sale Price (000)	Compound Annual Rates of Return	
			Current Dollars	1972 Dollars
22	2.5	20.0	10	7
22	9.4	59.0	9	6
22	24.6	75.0	5	2
24	16.0	100.0	8	5
28	6.2	50.0	8	4
29	14.0	14.0	0	−4
Average life: 10.1 years				
Totals				
Current dollars:	776.8	3,844.1	17	
Constant (1972) dollars:	1,163.1	4,181.4		13
Mean percent return (unweighted), 1972 dollars:				78
1 year				298
0–5 years*				203
5–10 years				15
10–20 years				11
Over 20 years				3

* Includes one-year rights
Source: Data provided by Interstate Commerce Commission.

stream of excess profits becomes successively higher each year *and that this had not been predicted* (that is, not capitalized).

What has caused this constant reevaluation upward in the expected stream of excess profits? There is no obvious answer, but let us suggest two possible explanations: (1) rates of return may *continuously* exceed those required to maintain firms in the industry, and (2) inflexible route structures may become inefficient over time, leading to a market for the trading of operating rights among firms seeking to improve their route structures.

Effects of Excessive Rates of Return

Consider the first possibility. Suppose that an entrepreneur is willing to invest in the trucking business at an after-tax return on total investment of 10 percent, but that the ICC views 12 percent as the appropriate return and regulates the trucker accordingly.

Suppose now that the entrepreneur is granted an operating right, invests $80,000, and reinvests the profits. In the first year, the trucker will earn a profit of $9,600 (12 percent) on the original $80,000 investment, including $1,600 in excess of the 10 percent minimum he or she is willing to accept. This excess return will be capitalized, and the operating right will now be valued at $16,000 ($1,600 divided by .10). If the earnings of $9,600 are reinvested, the trucker will have physical assets of $89,600 and, the next year, will earn $10,752 on this amount, or $1,792 more than could have been earned at a 10 percent rate of return. The value of the operating right thus becomes $17,920 (that is, $1,792 divided by .10). The percentage growth in the value of the operating right is, under our assumptions, precisely equal to the percentage growth in assets invested. Thus, the value of operating authorities grows in direct proportion to the growth of the industry.

This scenario may help to explain the continuous compounded rate of growth in the value of the operating right. As indicated, the original value of the operating right is created by the capitalized value of an expected excess return, and the growth in value is created by the continuous earning of excess returns on new assets and by the inclusion of these excess earnings in the value of the right.[5] A difficulty here is that if it were known that assets would grow, the "excess" associated with new assets would also be capitalized, the compounding process would not occur, and the value of operating rights would stabilize. But of course, though growth can be predicted, it cannot be known with certainty.

The analysis suggests that the return to regulated trucking is excessive, so that we should expect individuals to attempt to enter the industry and "undercut" existing truckers. Since entry is limited, this should lead to illicit operations and imaginative schemes for entering the industry without ICC authority. This, in fact, seems to be the case. For example, agricultural cooperatives are exempt from trucking regulation provided that they haul agricultural products. A major problem for the ICC has been to prevent the creation of "sham" cooperatives that illegally transport commodities at rates lower than those established by regulation. There are numerous examples of such schemes to enter the industry without authority. To me, this means that regulated rates are excessive and fortifies the analysis set forth here.

[5] It could be argued that the payment for an operating right is a payment for "goodwill." There may be some truth in this view. To the extent that the concept of goodwill refers to monopoly advantages (location) and the return on a protected investment, it includes some of the elements noted above. But as an explanation of why operating rights have value and why this value grows, it is not a significant factor. In the view of analysts at the Chase Manhattan Bank: "[Operating rights] are an asset with unique and truly identifiable value which is unlike patents, goodwill or those values rising out of a merger or purchase, which may diminish in time." (Chase Manhattan Bank, *1976 Financial Analysis of the Motor Carrier Industry*, p. 10.)

Effects of Route Inflexibility

As we have noted, truckers must operate within the limits of their operating rights and cannot easily adjust their route structures as the pattern of demand for trucking changes. Over time, these "frozen" structures lose earning capacity. Inefficiencies appear in the form of increased circuitousness, interlining, and underutilization. Rates of return may decline and operating ratios may increase, leading to increases in costs and to justification for rate increases.

The trucker who wishes to expand or rationalize an outmoded route structure may be unable to do so if that would infringe on routes served by others. So, instead, he will purchase a right from another trucker and perhaps sell a portion of his own right to a third trucker who has similar problems. This trading in rights—if rational—will almost always increase trucking efficiency because the purchaser has a more profitable use for the right than the seller. The payments are thus, in part, payments to overcome the complex web of inefficiencies created by detailed ICC regulation of routes, commodities, and services. One trucker must pay another in order to serve the public interest.

There are thousands of operating rights, each of which fits into the jigsaw puzzle that truckers put together at considerable cost in the form of payments for the rights, as well as for legal fees and other items. After a while, transportation demands shift, the puzzle falls apart, and another must be constructed. This is a costly game, one that would not have to be played if there were more flexibility at the regulatory level. And, of course, it is the shipper, and ultimately the consumer, who pays the costs of the game.

It has been noted that the annual compounded rate at which an operating right grows in value diminishes with the length of time that the right has been held. This relationship suggests that the value of "old" rights reflects the decreased efficiency that occurs as frozen route structures become less suited to market demand. On a slightly different point, the behavior of the values of operating rights held for a short period of time suggests the possibility of sophisticated short-term speculation, a possibility that requires further examination.

Conclusion

The evidence we have examined suggests that the cost of shipping goods by regulated motor carriers is excessive, that truckers who are granted new operating rights receive large windfall profits, that those who purchase existing rights receive excess returns on them over time, and that large payments must be made to overcome route inflexibilities.

The value of an operating right is the capitalized value of the "excessive" returns it enables its owner to earn. In a sense, high truck rates (or, perhaps more accurately, regulation-induced monopoly power) lead to high values for operating rights, rather than operating rights creating the high rates or monopoly power. So long as the rate of return earned by regulated truckers consistently exceeds that which would exist in a competitive market, operating rights will retain value and may rise in value over time. Though rate-of-return considerations have been emphasized here, it is important to bear in mind that route inflexibility is a significant contributor to higher costs.

A recent task force report prepared by the staff of the ICC makes special note of the high price of operating rights. The thrust of its brief discussion is that the high prices paid for rights look bad and that, perhaps, it would be desirable to put a "cap" on these prices or restrict in some manner the transfer of rights. One could infer that the ICC staff is, indeed, confused by the paradox we are trying to unravel. Placing a cap on sale prices or restricting the transfer of operating rights would lock operators into even greater inflexibility and result in ever higher costs of motor-carrier transportation.

Curiously, the commission seems not to have recognized that the aggregate value of operating rights is an excellent measure of the efficiency of its regulation. If operating rights command high prices, this is an indication that the commission is artificially constraining service, raising costs to consumers, and creating excess profits for owners of the rights. There should be little doubt that the paradox of valuable operating rights in a "competitive" industry can be explained by the existence of regulation that permits little real competition.

48 For some time, economists have been discussing and arguing the merits of having public utility rates set so that they would be equal to marginal costs. In contrast, the principle in actual operation is for regulatory commissions to establish public utility rates at levels where they equal average costs plus "fair" profits. Economists who advocate marginal cost pricing do so on grounds of economic efficiency, i.e., of the optimum allocation of resources. Competitive equilibrium furnishes the standard of efficiency, where marginal cost equals price. If unit costs are rising in the relevant range, marginal cost exceeds average cost; to set price equal to marginal cost is to stop production of units of output whose extra cost exceeds their value to the consumers. If unit costs are falling, marginal cost is less than average cost; to set price equal to marginal cost here is to cause the whole enterprise to operate at a loss. And this causes complications.

MARGINAL COST PRICING FOR PUBLIC UTILITIES

WILLIAM VICKREY
Columbia University

The principle of marginal cost pricing is not in practice to be followed absolutely and at all events, but is a principle that is to be followed insofar as this is compatible with other desirable objectives, and from which deviations of greater or lesser magnitude are to be desired when conflicting objectives are considered. On the other hand, I propose to maintain that marginal cost must play a major and even a dominant role in the elaboration of any scheme of rates or prices that seriously pretends to have as a major motive the efficient utilization of available resources and facilities.

Some of the conflicting considerations may be mentioned briefly. There is always the cost involved in the determination, publication, and administration of a rate structure. The relative importance of this consideration obviously declines as the value of the unit of sales becomes larger, so that, for example, one could expect that more refinement would be justifiable in the case of overseas airline fares than for short-haul train trips. Ability of the consumer to respond intelligently is also a limiting factor of a somewhat similar force. Thus a service used frequently by the same individual, such as local transit, will bear relatively more complexity than a service used rarely, such as parcel checking. And services used primarily by business firms,

---

Taken and adapted from William Vickrey, "Some Implications of Marginal Cost Pricing for Public Utilities," *American Economic Review,* Vol. XLV, No. 2, May 1955, pp. 605–614, 617–620. Reproduced by permission of the author and of the American Economic Association.

whose choices among alternatives are in the hands of relatively expert specialists, will also bear more complexity. Thus freight tariffs can stand being fairly complex, though this is by no means a justification of the present jumble.

Another point at which prices based on marginal cost may require modification in practice is where such prices come into too violent conflict with popular notions of equity. For example, it is clear that on marginal cost principles, transit fares should be substantially higher during rush hours than during off-peak hours. Yet a proposal of this sort is likely to be considered inequitable by many if not most of the lay population on such grounds as that rush-hour riding is less comfortable, is more of a necessity, is more heavily concentrated among low-income groups or at least among working people; or is, according to some naïve method of cost allocation (as by first computing a cost per vehicle-mile and then dividing this by the average load at various times), less costly. Some of these notions of equity may be considered to be valid in their own right, as the above consideration for the relative income level of the rush-hour riders would be if the facts as to the income distribution of riders actually bore out the assumption. Other notions of equity may be so strongly held as to require, as a matter of practical politics, some consideration in the design of rate structures if the proposals are to succeed. But while the economist may have a role to play in the design of such compromise measures, these compromises should in most cases be regarded as inferior solutions to be superseded by better ones as soon as public opinion can be educated to a more rational view.

The Question of Subsidies

By far the most important of the considerations that conflict with the strict application of marginal cost pricing is the need for revenues. Many of the more extreme advocates of marginal cost pricing for decreasing-cost industries seem tacitly to assume that the government has some perfectly costless and neutral source of revenue that is capable of very substantial expansion without ill effects.

Obviously, it will not pay, on any concept of the public welfare, to carry a marginal cost pricing policy all the way to the limit, so that the last dollar of subsidy barely yields a dollar's worth of benefits to the using public, when the securing of this dollar for the subsidy imposes burdens of more than a dollar.

There is very little to be said for the shibboleth that the rates should be above marginal cost by an amount just sufficient to produce revenues just covering average cost, however this may be defined. To be sure, there are often political and administrative advantages to having operations of a public utility carried on by independent agencies, whether private or public, rather than as governmental departments on a par with other nonrevenue-producing agencies of government. It is often argued that this can only be done if the agencies are financially self-supporting. But to me this would be taking a far too defeatist attitude towards our ability to develop appropriate political institutions.

This is not to say, however, that there are no impediments to the pursuit of a thoroughgoing marginal cost pricing policy by independent agencies. In particular, attempts to adjust prices to variations in marginal cost produced by the installation of large units of capacity or by unforeseen scarcity or surplus may, in the case of a public agency, produce financial difficulties of a sort that may well give rise to demands for revision of the subsidy provisions that would be too strong to resist. Even so, if this breakdown of independence could be resisted and the substantial fluctuations in earnings weathered by appropriate financial measures such as borrowing or the accumulation of reserves, such fluctuations would yield better resource utilization than a policy of keeping earnings as even as possible from year to year.

In the case of a regulated private utility, the incentives that would result from such a short-run marginal cost pricing policy for delaying expansion so as to raise marginal costs and with them the rates that would be warranted and consequently profits, would produce additional difficulties. If to prevent this the regulatory agency is empowered to dictate the installation of capacity, little discretion indeed would be left to private management, even if regulation could be kept from breaking down under the added administrative burden. Thus, whether the agency be public or private, it does appear that it would be difficult to preserve political independence and still provide for the variations of rates in accordance with short-run excess or deficiency of capacity.

Marginal Cost Pricing and Competition

Another important consideration to be kept in mind is that marginal cost pricing will not be adopted everywhere simultaneously, and where closely competing services continue to be rendered at rates substantially above marginal cost, reduction of the rates under consideration to marginal cost might well produce a poorer allocation of resources than somewhat higher rates. Indeed, if the only consideration were the allocation of a given demand between two closely competitive forms of service, the proper price for the service under consideration would be one that makes the differential between the prices of the two services reflect the differential in marginal cost, at least where the application of this principle leads to a unique result. It should be noted that it is an equal absolute differential and not an equal percentage relationship that is sought.

There may also be several competing services, differing in the degree to which their rates exceed marginal cost. In which case, some sort of compromise will be necessary, with the influence of each competing service weighted according to the appropriate cross-elasticity of demand. For example, if rates for water transportation are to be set, it may not be possible to do this in such a way as to cause the rate differentials to agree with the marginal cost differentials for both rail and truck shipments, if the rates for these latter are not to be disturbed. Of course, where a single agency, such as the ICC, has control over the rates of all of the competing services, all of the rates can be adjusted together to a common margin above marginal costs and there is no difficulty in preserving the competitive relationships among the various services whatever the general level of rates decided upon, except possibly where it is necessary to distort the relationship in order to give the agency providing each service a fair return and no more on its investment.

Of course, in a general sense, every service competes with all other commodities and services for purchasing power and for the use of resources, and it is sometimes claimed that, since imperfect and monopolistic competition prevail fairly widely in the private sector of the economy, producing prices considerably above marginal cost on the average; therefore, public utility prices should likewise be above marginal cost by a like percentage. This argument must be used with caution, however. At most, the presence in the economy of a substantial sector that appears to be genuinely competitive in the relevant sense would bring the average discrepancy between marginal cost and price down to a more moderate figure than would be thought of if attention is focused primarily on the imperfectly competitive sectors.

But whatever arguments may be advanced for departing in various degrees from a strict marginal cost pricing policy, no sound pricing policy can be developed without using marginal cost as one of the principal determinants. Indeed, while marginal cost pricing has been discussed most frequently in a context of decreasing cost situations and subsidies, marginal cost has an important role to play even where economies of scale are absent and there is no problem of self-liquidating versus subsidized operation. Adequate consideration of marginal cost in the setting up of a price structure often leads to structures quite different from those in general use, wholly aside from the question of the proper general level of rates. Even where economies of scale are substantial, marginal cost considerations may be much more important in relation to the structure of rates than to the level.

Fluctuating Marginal Costs

If the only implication of marginal cost pricing were that in decreasing-cost industries the price structure should be reduced more or less uniformly by a percentage reflecting the amount by which the elasticity of the long-run production function falls short of unity, one might be justified, in many cases, in feeling only a very restrained enthusiasm. For example, studies I have made of the marginal costs for railroad freight service indicate a level in the neighborhood of 80 per cent of average costs, on a long-run basis. Subsidies of the order of 2 billion dollars a year, which would be indicated in order to enable rates to be cut to a marginal cost level, would produce a net gain in national product of some 250 billions, assuming an elasticity of demand of about unity. In view of what has been said above concerning the marginal costs of public revenues, this would seem to have relatively little to promise. Actually, in such a case, one could probably rest content with recommending that taxes bearing on freight transportation in one way or another be abated as far as administratively possible.

Capacity limits on output of nonstorable services often operate to produce rather drastic fluctuations in marginal costs that are regular and predictable enough to be used as the basis for rate-making. For subway service in New York, for example, it has been estimated that the marginal cost of a fairly long rush-hour trip would be on the order of 30 to 50 cents, while a comparable nonrush-hour trip would have a marginal cost of only 8 to 10 cents, and rush-hour trips in a direction opposed to the major flow of traffic would in most cases be a surplus by-product service with a marginal cost substantially zero. Costs per passenger mile will vary equally drastically for different portions of a single trip on a single train. An evening rush-hour trip from Coney Island to Bedford Park in the Bronx would have a zero marginal cost for the Brooklyn portion of the trip, a cost rising to about 5 cents per mile for the upper Manhattan portion of the trip and falling off to 1 or 2 cents per mile for the Bronx portion of the trip.

Capacity limits are, however, not always rigid. The usual way of expressing a somewhat elastic capacity limit is in terms of a more or less sharply rising marginal cost curve. In many cases, however, while the capacity limits on the volume of service offered are quite rigid, elasticity at the capacity limit is provided by impairment in the quality of the service offered. It may not be possible to run more trains or longer trains on a given route, at least in the short run, whether from lack of track capacity or of equipment; an increase in traffic will be accommodated by having a larger proportion of standees, or more intense crowding. Costs to the operating agency may be very little affected, and in this sense one might say that marginal cost is very low; the cost, however, is to be measured in terms of the deterioration in the value of the service to the former passengers. It is not often realized how great a marginal cost computed in this way can easily be. If the addition of 20 passengers to a car already containing 200 passengers creates increased crowding that the original passengers would on the average pay 3 cents each to avoid, this is a cost of $6.00 to be divided among the 20 passengers causing it, resulting in a marginal cost of 30 cents each. Or as demand approaches the theoretical capacity, the slack necessary to insure taking care of customers as they apply may vanish, with the result of longer and longer queues or delays in getting service. The queue or the delay may operate to cut down to some extent the demand for service, but in general this will be an inadequate deterrent without substantial increases in the rate as well, since the operative deterrent for the individual is the average delay, not the much greater increment in total delays that will be caused by the addition of one person to the demand: not only will the additional customer have to wait while he works his way to the head of the queue, but all customers after him will have their waits increased by the time required to service the added customer, until such time as either the queue is entirely worked off or some potential customer is discouraged by the increased length of the queue.

In an extreme case where the control of the queue may require diversion of resources from the providing of the service, as for example may occur in some situations in telephone service, overload may even reduce the amount of service that can actually be rendered below what it would have been had demand been more moderate. For example, repeated attempts of thwarted subscribers to place calls may absorb the time of operators or of certain types of common equipment in an automatic exchange such as registers, senders, markers, and the like. Considerable additional complexity of central office equipment is often necessary to prevent paralysis in such contingencies.

Fairly extreme results also tend to occur in poorly controlled situations such as curb parking. Very marked differences in the amount of time which a would-be parker will have to spend in finding a place to park, and also in the distance that he will have to walk to get to his ultimate destination, on the average, according to whether, out of say 1,000 parking spaces in a given area, 999 are, again on the average, occupied, or whether the average occupancy is only 995 or 990. Again, the deterrent to say the 990th parker is only the amount of time he will have to search, and he takes no account, ordinarily, of the added searching time that his occupancy of a space will impose on those who come after. Metering of curb parking space on marginal cost principles would thus require rather substantial fluctuations in the rate per hour as the degree of occupancy fluctuates in the neighborhood of 100 per cent.

Economic Efficiency

In summary, then, marginal cost pricing must be regarded not as a mere proposal to lower rates generally below the average cost level, but rather as an approach which implies a drastic rearrangement of the patterns and structures of rates. Indeed, it is this restructuring of rates that is likely to be the greatest contribution of marginal cost pricing to the improvement of the over-all efficiency of our economy, while the further gains that might be obtainable from the reduction of rates from a self-sustaining level to a marginal cost level, once the pattern of rates has been made to conform as closely as possible to marginal cost, are likely to be relatively small. The issue is not primarily one of subsidized versus nonsubsidized operation, though this is still an important issue. The dominant issue is one of whether the pattern of rates should be based on tradition, inertia, and happenstance, or whether it is to be developed by a careful weighing of the relevant factors with a view to guiding consumers to make an efficient use of the facilities that are available.

Perhaps some indication of the outstanding absurdities that occur in present utility rate structures may be worthwhile in conclusion. For example, in New York a new vehicular tunnel was opened a few years ago from the Battery to Brooklyn. Since it is a new facility and undoubtedly much more easy and pleasant to use than the old East River bridges, it must, forsooth, be made to pay for itself by the imposition of tolls starting at 35 cents, the practical consequence of which is to encourage continued heavy use of the Manhattan bridge for all trips for which that route is shorter than the tunnel, with the result that the streets near the Manhattan end of the bridge are the scene of some of the worst traffic congestion in the city. Marginal cost considerations would call for the collection of a substantial toll on the old East River bridges, at least during hours of heavy congestion, and a smaller toll or none at all for the tunnel, even though this might mean that the users of the bridges might be "paying for" the tunnel.

In suburban railroad service, the lowest fares offered are almost invariably the weekly and monthly commutation tickets used predominantly by commuters who travel almost exclusively in the rush hour when marginal costs are highest; next highest are multiple-ride tickets used by family members, often at the rush hours, but somewhat less frequently so. Users of one-way or round-trip tickets, on the other hand, are more likely to be off-peak or even counter-rush riders with very low marginal cost. Nor can this pattern be defended on the basis of elasticity. The daily commuter rides from almost absolute necessity, in most cases, whereas the occasional trips of other family members are often dispensable trips; further, the use of the family car for such trips is much more often a strong competitor, since the car is then not needed at home, the schedules are less frequent and convenient than in the rush hour, and many persons may be riding together. To be sure, in the long run there is elasticity to the daily commuter traffic in that the fares influence the decision to move to the suburbs, but even to the extent that this is a significant factor, it will be some weighted average of the commutation and multi-trip ticket that would be the relevant rate to be considered by the prospective suburbanite. Political pressures seem to be partly responsible for this state of affairs: regular commuters have both a sufficient stake and a sufficient appeal to the public sentiments to bring effective pressure to bear on regulatory bodies. Some roads have been of late making tentative progress towards putting in a reduced-rate type of ticket good only during the nonrush hours, but the attempt in most cases seems to have been rather half-hearted, as the rate offered is usually still higher than that available in the multi-trip family ticket. Marginal cost pricing here would go much further than this and just about reverse the entire pricing structure.

The same delusion often gets a foothold in the local transit field. Philadelphia, probably on the basis of political pleas, has recently adopted a plan for selling strips of ten tickets, good for one week only, which, of course are used predominantly by the high-cost rush-hour riders.

The rapid obsolescence of that great American institution, the open-section Pullman car, is in many ways the work of an inefficient pricing policy, itself in large measure the product of inefficient working arrangements between the Pullman Company and the railroads. No serious attempt seems ever to have been made to vary rates so as to balance the demand for upper and lower berths, so that what was and could still be a device for furnishing a satisfactory low-cost service is fast being relegated to the scrap heap.

And so it goes. One may, for various good and sufficient reasons, hesitate to embrace marginal cost pricing in all of its ramifications as an absolute standard. But no approach to utility pricing can be considered truly rational which does not give an important and even a major weight to marginal cost considerations. And when adequate weight is given to such consideration, important changes in present pricing practices will be indicated in many areas.

49 Commissions for trading stocks on the New York Stock Exchange were fixed by the Exchange until May 1, 1975. A change in federal regulation mandated competitive rates. The resulting deregulation of brokerage lowered prices and led to the unbundling of brokerage services.

REGULATION OF THE SECURITIES MARKETS

HANS R. STOLL
The Wharton School, University of Pennsylvania

Since passage of the Securities Act of 1933, regulation of securities markets has primarily been concerned with providing for full disclosure and eliminating fraud and manipulation in order that securities prices resulting from the free interplay of market forces may as nearly as possible reflect fundamental values. The new-issue prospectus and continuing reporting requirements of corporations and direct regulation against fraud and manipulations have been the primary means to assure this objective of market efficiency and fairness.

Under the principle of self-regulation, relatively less attention was for many years paid to the internal workings of stock exchanges and the efficiency with which brokers and dealers provided transactions services. The cost to the public of transactions services are twofold. First, the broker, who acts as an agent, is compensated by a commission for the services of communicating with other traders, executing, clearing and recording the transaction. Second, when another investor cannot be found for the other side of a transaction, the services of a dealer, who acts as a principal and is compensated by the bid-ask spread, may be required. This study is concerned only with the brokerage function.

Under long standing New York Stock Exchange practice, unchanged by Federal regulation until May 1, 1975, commissions for brokerage services were fixed above the competitive level and membership on the Exchange limited to a fixed number of "seats". The justification of fixed commission rates for brokerage services was based on market failure arguments and arguments based on equity considerations. It was alleged that without fixed commission rates,

---

U.S. Senate Committee on Governmental Affairs, "Study on Federal Regulation," December 1978, Appendix to Volume VI, *Framework for Regulation,* pp. 589–591.

The author of this article gratefully acknowledges the research assistance of Ronald Judy and the assistance of the staff of the Securities and Exchange Commission's Directorate of Economic and Policy Research in the conduct of some of the empirical work, and he thanks Donald Farrar for his helpful comments. He wishes to thank the University of Chicago, Graduate School of Business, where this study was first written during the second summer of his term of visit in 1975–1976, for the provision of excellent facilities. Since then the study has been completely revised to incorporate data through the third quarter of 1977. The basic conclusions withstood the test of time. It was unnecessary to alter any of them because of the more recent evidence.

markets would fail because continuing economies of scale for the brokerage firm and a fixed-to-variable cost ratio conducive to "destructive competition" would lead to monopolization of the industry or its domination by a few large firms. Small and regional firms, not necessarily the least efficient, would fail and industry capital and therefore its capacity to serve the public would be impaired. Markets would also fail because of the inability to internalize all costs and benefits. NYSE members, unwilling to bear the costs of running the exchange without receiving high fixed commissions, would leave the NYSE; and this would cause markets to become fragmented and would reduce liquidity. Research would decline because the cost of producing it would not be recaptured under competitive rates; the first recipient could resell the research at less than costs of production. Competitive rates were said to be undesirable on equity grounds because they would lead to discrimination against the small investor who would not have the bargaining power of institutional investors.

The arguments against fixed commission rates are the arguments against cartel pricing of any service: competition would lead to lower prices and a higher level of output. Competitive rates would eliminate roundabout and costly procedures for rebating commissions and the production of unrelated services that not all investors desire. Potential conflicts of interest that arise in the provisions of some services to institutional investors would be lessened. Market fragmentation would not result; instead, investors would have a greater incentive under lower competitive rates to channel transactions to the NYSE. Finally, competition would eliminate inefficiency and lead to greater innovation in the provision of brokerage services.

On the basis of extensive hearings and studies conducted between 1968 and 1975, the Securities and Exchange Commission and committees of the House and Senate reached the conclusion that the evidence did not support the argument for fixed commission rates. On May 1, 1975, fixed rates of commission were abolished.

Empirical investigations of the arguments for and against competitive rates and the experience since the introduction of competitive rates indicate, almost without exception, that competitive rates have been beneficial to consumers without resulting in the harmful and disruptive effects anticipated by the opponents of competitive rates.

Under competition, commission rates have declined an average of about 15 percent according to the Securities and Exchange Commission. They declined much more on transactions of institutional investors and hardly at all on transactions of individuals. However, both institutions and individuals have the opportunity to pay commissions lower than the average when fewer services are required, an opportunity not available under fixed rates. There is no evidence that discrimination against small investors has occurred.

Adjustment of NYSE member firms to competitive rates has been relatively easy because of a surge in stock market activity. However, even brokerage firms serving institutional investors, which suffered a commission revenue decline of over 30 percent according to the SEC, adjusted quickly by finding other business and reducing costs. Nevertheless, profits are lower than they would have been under fixed rates because monopoly profits have been eliminated, a fact which is reflected in much lower NYSE membership prices.

The fear that one firm would dominate the industry and that small and regional firms would, in particular, be driven out of business as a result of competitive rates has not been realized. Although there has been an increase in the share of commission revenue going to the very largest firms, this is a longer-term trend not affected by the introduction of competitive rates. In fact the trend is less after the introduction of competitive rates. The trend appears to reflect some economies for national full line brokerage firms and the use of mergers to bail out failing firms. The evidence on the firms leaving the NYSE in 1975 through 1977 indicates that both large and small firms failed; the growth in market share of the very largest cannot be said to be at the expense of the smallest firms. Furthermore, the cost structure of the industry does not exhibit the high level of fixed costs usually associated with destructive competition that might lead to domination by one firm. Except for occupancy and equipment costs, brokerage costs are quite variable, and this fact has helped the industry to adapt so well to competitive rates. There is also no indication that large firms cut commission rates more than small firms in an attempt to drive small firms out of business. In fact, it appears that the innovators in discount commissions for individual investors have been small brokerage firms.

Markets have not become fragmented as a result of competitive rates. Instead the trend is to more trading on the NYSE, not less. Use of commission dollars to buy research has apparently declined, although judging from the number of research analysts hired it is difficult to say that the amount of research produced has declined. It does seem clear that fixed commissions are not necessary effectively to compensate those who produce research. Finally, measures of the liquidity afforded large block transactions and more general measures of market quality do not indicate any deterioration since the introduction of competitive rates.

50 One of the problems of large urban communities is the struggle between the advocates of freeways and of rapid transit, a struggle that often seems to become an ideological war rather than a debate over the objective issues. One of the issues is the cost of private automobiles; another is their owners' continued preference for driving them downtown. Professor Sherman addresses himself to these issues in a contribution to the literature on the efficient allocation of resources to personal transportation.

A PRIVATE OWNERSHIP BIAS IN TRANSIT CHOICE

ROGER SHERMAN
University of Virginia

The continuing defection of public transit riders in big cities suggests that eventual dominance by private automobiles may be inevitable. A Chicago survey has indicated that only a very large subsidy would persuade a significant number of auto travelers to switch to public modes. There remains a question, however, whether the private auto is gaining ascendancy by genuine consumer choice or because private costs differ sufficiently from social costs to produce a misallocation of resources in favor of autos. There are tendencies toward overinvestment in highways through our political decision process, which builds highways to relieve congestion but also distributes them free so that congestion is inevitable, Such studies suggest that present institutional arrangements may not enable consumers to choose the allocation of transit resources they prefer.

On the reasonable assumption that costs decrease for each transit mode, we demonstrate in Section I a bias in consumer choice that favors private autos over public transit. The bias arises as a result of an auto traveler's commitment to auto ownership, which forces a choice between auto and other modes and also makes the average price he pays per mile vary with his usage while for public modes it does not. Also, constant prices for decreasing cost public transit modes can prevent optimal allocation among them, thereby making them a less effective substitute for auto travel. Section II describes one way of financing public transit that will avoid this particular allocation bias.

Condensed slightly from Roger Sherman, "A Private Ownership Bias in Transit Choice," *American Economic Review*, Vol. LVII, No. 5, December 1967, pp. 1211–1217. Reproduced by permission.

I. Private Choice: Automobile, or Public Transit?

Broadly, there are two alternative travel means, the private automobile and public means, including bus, railroad, taxi, airplane, or rental vehicles. We should expect a consumer to choose either automobile or public transit, not both, because auto ownership carries with it a substantial commitment to the automobile as a means of travel. If used-car markets were perfect this might not be so, for a consumer could then buy a car for one trip and sell it afterward. But transaction costs in automobile markets are high. Not only does the purchase of an automobile require time and effort, its sudden sale at an inopportune time will result in financial sacrifice. A tendency of persons to travel either by auto or public transit is evident in data from a Chicago study of commuters. Of those who owned cars (85 per cent owned cars), four out of five used the car in traveling to work, three out of four traveling all the way into the city by car. Of those who did not own cars, 85 per cent traveled to work via public transit.

Over a short period, the marginal cost of auto travel will be very low for an auto owner while for a nonowner, transaction costs make short-period marginal cost very high. Thus, the short-run choice between public and private transit will depend on whether the chooser already owns an automobile. Analysis of choice must extend over a time period long enough to permit an effective choice, enough time for a consumer to purchase or sell an automobile and satisfactorily amortize his transaction costs. The average period of automobile ownership in the United States is a little more than three years, and we shall assume that the auto-traveling consumer bases his choice on an estimate of his auto travel costs over that period. To avail himself of such long-run costs, however, he must commit himself to auto travel for the period. Failing such commitment, he will have to confine his travel primarily to the public mode.

Some costs of auto travel vary with time (e.g., insurance, licensing, garaging, some depreciation) and others vary with miles traveled, so traveling more miles over a given time period will lead to a lower average cost per mile. Notice that the cost per auto mile, or consumer price per mile, will therefore be different for different consumers, depending on how many miles they travel. The effect of miles traveled on price per mile will, in turn, affect the consumer's decision regarding the number of miles he travels. By thus affecting planned travel miles, marginal cost exerts an influence on the eventual average price per auto mile, making the average cost lower for consumers who travel more. Average cost per mile also decreases with more miles traveled via public transit. In the public transit case, however, there can exist one average cost per mile, when fixed costs are allocated over the total number of passenger miles traveled. As a consequence of such cost allocation a single, constant price per mile can be charged users of public transit and related to the cost per passenger mile. Since we wish to examine allocation in the absence of subsidies, and because we consider a combination of public modes some of which are not subsidized, we shall assume that cost and price per mile are equal. In the public transit case, then, one consumer's price is not affected by his usage. To see the difficulties this arrangement causes for resource allocation among transportation modes, consider the consumer's utility-maximizing problem.

Well-known conditions for the consumer to maximize his utility require that his marginal utility from each good divided by its marginal price be equal for all goods and services consumed, this ratio of marginal utility to marginal price being the consumer's marginal utility of income. In planning his possible auto travel over a three-year period, the consumer must first reduce income available for all goods by making fixed payments associated with auto ownership. Consumption of all goods (ignoring inferior goods) is reduced as a result. At the same time, a lower marginal price is used to evaluate auto miles traveled, and this invites the consumer to travel more than he would if he paid a constant average price per mile. In planning possible public transit travel, in contrast, the consumer bases his usage on a constant average price which equals average cost but is greater than marginal cost. The private auto arrangement has an advantage for utility maximizing that can be illustrated easily. Regard as private transit an automobile, privately purchased. Consider as a public transit alternative an automobile that can be rented, the rental rate per mile for one person being regulated at an average price equal to average cost. If a person is given a private or public choice in these terms, he will always prefer the private alternative, for he can reach the same consumption goods mix that is available to him under the public arrangement and because of a lower effective marginal price can reach a preferred position as well (assuming only that the marginal rate of substitution between travel and other goods diminishes).

When this example is extended to a genuine public transit service, there will be only one average price for all public transit consumers rather than a different one for each consumer. That single average price is affected not by one's own usage of the service, but by the usage of all other consumers combined. Those whose marginal utility from travel diminishes rapidly are then likely to prefer public transit because the price per public transit mile is lower than they can achieve privately. Those who travel much, however, will face a lower cost per mile via auto travel. It is this effect that is troublesome in decreasing cost industries, where long-run average cost can be lowered by higher rates of usage. The commitment that will enable an individual to achieve the benefits of his own higher usage is a commitment to automobile ownership, which will simultaneously reduce the usage of public transit services. It does so because the auto owner enjoys a low marginal price per mile by auto once he commits himself to ownership, and is therefore less likely to seek public transportation at a price equal to its average cost. Thus, if benefits of higher usage are available only through the private auto transportation mode, that mode will be made more attractive, while passenger miles lost to it from public modes will raise the average cost of service via those modes.

The allocation problem is further aggravated by the presence of many separate public transit modes. From the utility-maximizing model we know that in choosing among public transit modes, a consumer's marginal utility from each mode divided by its marginal price must be equal for every mode that is used. If marginal costs of public transit modes are not proportional to average costs, consumers who face prices equal to average cost are sure to reach an equilibrium that is nonoptimal. Exchanges among the consumers, at marginal costs, could improve their welfare. Thus, the coordination of different public modes through single, fixed prices is imperfect. And failure to achieve an optimal combination of the different modes reduces the effectiveness of public transit as a substitute for auto travel.

II. Avoiding Ownership Bias

One way to achieve an efficient combination of public transit services, and at the same time offset the advantage of marginal cost influence in private auto choice, is to subsidize all public transit modes so that they may price at marginal cost. Unfortunately, this will not solve the problem completely, for it makes inefficiencies necessary elsewhere in order to finance the subsidy. More important, it implicitly raises the question: should an automobile be given to every family as well, so that only short-run marginal costs will influence the choice between public and private transit? The costly duplication that would result from such a scheme reveals the importance of affording long-run as well as short-run choice; consumers must take into account all costs when expressing their preference, not just short-run marginal costs. But to cover all costs, the fees would have to be in two parts: one for short-run marginal costs, and another for fixed costs which depend on time rather than usage.

Since coordination of public transit modes is needed to make public transit effective as an alternative to the private automobile, a collective institution such as a public transit club would offer genuine advantages. Membership fees could correspond to fixed costs of the modes chosen by the member. Non-members could still have access to the public modes but at higher prices per mile than members, who would pay only marginal costs. The club could of course serve as a credit institution as well, for it would be a billing and collection agency. Fixed fees could be distributed among the modes by the club, dividing the fee among different firms within each mode in proportion to the direct services provided by the firms. To be sure, allocating investment risks and fixed costs of the modes among members in the form of fixed fees is not easy. The degree of commitment to an automobile is evident to any owner; he makes an investment in an auto and he assumes risks of ownership. Unlike the automobile case, public transit investment does not occur in separate parts that are identified with each user. Nevertheless, the fixed costs of a public transit mode, e.g., vehicles, roadbed, and structures, will depend on the number of passengers it must be capable of carrying, not just on passenger miles. Indeed, the number of rush-hour passengers has repeatedly been revealed to be a crucial determinant of costs for different public transit modes. And if members can influence their average price per public transit mile by making a fixed payment and then paying a marginal price equal to marginal cost, the bias in favor of automobiles will be eliminated.

It would be possible to accommodate many variations in a membership institution. When several agencies offer service by the same mode, differences in variable fees are possible and would enforce competition *within* those modes. Classes of service could also be distinguished, in fixed or variable fees or in both. Where different services share fixed costs jointly it might be desirable to grant access to both services, at appropriate prices per mile, for only one fixed fee. Peak load pricing can be accommodated, too. For example, limited memberships which deny rush hour access might be offered at lower fees. Our purpose is only to register feasibility, and so we shall not elaborate further on these possibilities. Fortunately, large, established public transportation institutions already exist. Thus, the major problems would be those that accompany transition to an institutional form which would unify pricing, not problems associated with the initiation of new transit agencies or modes.

Organizing such an institution is not a simple matter, to be sure. Especially difficult is the question of its geographic scope. It seems most appropriate for individual cities, yet one of its advantages is coordination of all transit modes into an effective consumer service including intercity railroads and airlines, which would suggest national scope. The most practical form might be a federation of metropolitan Riders' Clubs, each serving major urban centers in the country. Whether the Riders' Clubs be public or private enterprises is an interesting issue we cannot open here. Our objective is only to sketch an alternative institution which might enhance the effectiveness of consumer choice and of the competitive process among those who provide transportation services.

III. Summary

A resource allocation bias can favor private autos when an ownership commitment encourages an either/or choice between private and public modes, assuming that all transit is characterized by decreasing costs, and that public transit must cover its costs and uses single, constant prices to do so. Possible misallocation among the public transit modes was also demonstrated. To compensate for these allocative biases, we proposed a collective institution to implement fixed and variable fees. The proposed institution would enable each consumer to plan his transit usage, taking account of approximate marginal social costs, and on that basis make a forward commitment either to private or public transit means. In this way investment in transit resources, as well as short-run usage, can be coordinated. The rise in alternative transit modes makes this approach more appropriate than the traditional regulation of separate monopolies. The argument is relevant primarily for urban areas, where substitution possibilities are greatest, where necessary organizing is most feasible, and where transit resource allocation problems are most urgent.

Part Nine

Factor prices are fully as important as final-product markets because they are a central determinant of incomes. Although many factor-market issues have important macroeconomic dimensions, for example unemployment, the microeconomic dimensions are also significant. Wage determination is the focus of these readings because wages are the largest source of income.

Factor Pricing

The readings are concerned with the shape of demand and supply relationships in factor markets, the presence of market power and imperfections, and dynamic dimensions of factor markets. The minimum wage is an important policy issue for factor markets.

51 The shapes of supply curves in precapitalistic or underdeveloped countries have been much discussed and disputed. Negatively sloped supply curves can represent an obstacle to economic development if they are caused by the workers' desires for fixed or target incomes. Economic development is the result of human effort, among other things. Development lags if effort ceases once a traditional (and low) income is achieved.

Dr. Berg analyzes supply curves for labor in Africa and how and why they have been changing. Watch for the important distinctions between individual and aggregate supply curves, and between supply curves in international and in national markets.

SUPPLY CURVES FOR LABOR IN AFRICA

ELLIOT J. BERG
University of Michigan

Few discussions of labor supply in underdeveloped countries fail to bring up the backward-sloping labor supply function. Wage-earners in newly-developing countries are alleged to have relatively low want schedules or high preference for leisure as against income, so that they work less at higher wage rates and more at lower ones. In the underdeveloped world, and notably in Africa, this has been the almost universal opinion of foreign employers of native labor, an opinion shared by outside observers. It was no less common a view in eighteenth-century England, where a typical complaint was that "If a person can get sufficient in four days to support himself for seven days, he will keep holiday the other three; that is, he will live in riot and debauchery."

The widespread conviction that labor supply functions in countries in early stages of development tend to be backward-sloping is no mere intellectual curiosity. It is one of those ideas in history which has had genuine impact on the practical world of affairs. It has served as a rationale for wage and labor policies which influenced the course of economic and political development not only in Africa but elsewhere as well. It has also been brought into the arena of methodological debate to serve as part of the un-

---

Reprinted by permission of the publishers from Elliot J. Berg, "Backward-Sloping Labor Supply Functions in Dual Economies—The Africa Case," by Elliot J. Berg, *The Quarterly Journal of Economics,* Vol. LXXV, No. 3, August 1961, pp. 468–475, 478–488, 491, 492. Cambridge, Mass.: Harvard University Press.

derpinning of theories which claim that the analytic tools of "Western" economic theory are inapplicable to "dual" societies.

Given its popularity and its influence, it is surprising that this hoary concept of the backward-sloping labor supply curve has been exposed to so little systematic analysis, particularly since there runs through most discussions of the matter a considerable confusion over fundamentals. The sources of this confusion are twofold. First, many writers tend to mix the present with the past; they write of contemporary nonindustrial societies as ideal types of pre-industrial societies untouched by contact with the market economy. Most contemporary nonindustrial societies, however, even in Africa's isolated corners, are societies in varying degrees of transition. They have been in contact, however sporadic and tangential, with the goods and ideas of the outside world for two or three generations at least. They have consequently undergone changes which have made them responsive to the money economy outside the villages. Discussions of labor supply which heavily underscore the immobilities of labor in underdeveloped countries, the unwillingness of villagers to enter wage employment, the indifference to monetary incentives are concerned more often with the past than the present.

The second and more important source of confusion derives from a general fuzziness about *which* labor supply functions are at issue. Conclusions about aggregate labor supply have been drawn from individual labor market behavior. But this is correct only with the implicit assumption—the classical assumption—that the size of the labor force is some constant proportion of the total population. However useful this assumption is in analysis of the labor supply in industrial countries, it is obviously misleading in countries with large non-market sectors. Aggregate man-hours of labor available for paid employment is a function not only of average time spent in employment by individuals in the labor force; it depends also on the number of people at work (the labor force participation rate) in a given population, a variable which is subject to considerable short-run fluctuation, particularly in dual economies. No *a priori* statements about aggregate labor supply can, therefore, be derived from observations about the time each worker spends in employment.

In this paper, an attempt is made to avoid these common confusions by explicitly recognizing the fact of change over time, and by sorting out several of the various labor supply functions pertinent in the African context. We try to show the sense in which labor supply curves were in the past or are presently backward-sloping. The analysis centers on the factors determining the shape of three labor supply curves—that of the individual, that of the exchange economy as a whole, and that of the country or territory—the standard political unit. While the analysis refers specifically to sub-Saharan Africa, it has applicability to other areas of similar economic structure.

The Dual Economy and the Migrant Labor System

African economies are "dual" in both the structural and the sociological sense. A modern exchange or money sector and a traditional subsistence sector exist side-by-side. Though the extent of the money economy varies widely between the different parts of the continent, in Africa as a whole a relatively large proportion of land and labor resources are devoted to subsistence production. Out of a total African population of perhaps 160–170 million in Africa south of the Sahara only about 8 million work for wages during any part of the year.

Most of the unskilled workers employed in the exchange sector are temporary emigrants from the villages of the subsistence sector; the characteristic feature of the labor market in most of Africa has always been the massive circulation of Africans between their villages and paid employment outside. In some places, villagers engage in wage-earning seasonally. More commonly today they work for continuous though short-term periods of roughly one to three years, after which they return to the villages. Tendencies toward more or less permanent stabilization in wage-earning are increasingly emerging, especially in southern Africa, the ex-Belgian Congo, and some of the West African towns. But even today the majority of wage-earners in most African countries are not permanently fixed in towns or wage employment. It is with these migrant workers that we are concerned.

The Individual's Offer of Labor

What are the factors that determine whether and for how long an individual African villager will offer his labor for paid employment in the exchange sector? In general terms, they are the same factors that determine how much labor an individual in any market economy will offer for hire: the nature of the individual's preference between income and leisure, the level of his non-wage income, the rate of wages. The potential migrant laborer balances the benefits to be obtained from income-earning outside against the inconveniences of a given spell in wage employment. He decides to migrate when, given the rate of wages and his "leisure"-income preference function, the anticipated satisfactions from his net expected income exceed the costs to him of migrating, "costs" being defined as sacrificed "leisure." [1] Since the villager usually has non-wage sources of money income (i.e., marketed portions of village output), his decision to migrate and the length of time he

[1] There is some conceptual difficulty connected with the notion of "leisure" in transitional societies. In that part of the total society already wholly integrated into the modern market economy, it does not involve too great a distortion of reality to regard "leisure" as simply time not spent at "work." In the traditionally oriented sector, however, which is to say in most villages, "leisure" is the sum of village activities not immediately or directly concerned with production. Within village society, it is by no means easy to distinguish between "economic" and "noneconomic" activity, between "work" and "leisure." Because of these considerations, "leisure" is placed within quotation marks throughout the discussion in this paper.

will stay in employment depend also on the level of his village income and the effort-price of income in wage employment as compared with the effort-price of income in alternative income-earning pursuits. The major factors determining the individual's decisions therefore are: (1) the intensity of his preference for money income as against "leisure" in the village; (2) the level of his income from village production; (3) the effort-price of income earnable in the village; (4) the effort-price of income earnable outside the village.

For the reluctant villager with a fixed income goal, the key elements determining the decision to migrate and the amount of time to stay in employment are the level of his demand for money income (the size of his income goal), the level of his income from village sources, and the rate of wages in the exchange sector. The size of his income goal depends mainly on tax rates and the accumulated level of his wants; it can be taken in the short run as given. It is therefore the level of the individual's village income and the rate of wages which are the decisive short-run factors in determining the quantity of labor which he will offer in the exchange economy. Given his income goal, and supposing all other factors unchanged, the function relating the time he is prepared to spend in employment with the rate of wages in the exchange sector is a curve of unit negative elasticity—a rectangular hyperbola; if wage rates rise (fall), the migrant spends proportionally less (more) time in paid employment. Similarly, given his income goal and the rate of wages outside, his "time spent in employment" function varies inversely and proportionally with respect to changes in village income; if harvests are good and his village income rises, he spends correspondingly less time in paid employment. If village income is sufficient to allow him to attain his income goal, he will not go out to work regardless (within realistic limits) of the rate of wages.

Analysis in terms of a "leisure"-income preference function characterized by extreme reluctance to leave the village and by a rigid target income goal is useful for a number of reasons. It provides, first, a limiting case, permitting analysis of labor-supply reactions under the most restrictive possible assumptions about African willingness to work for economy. It would apply, for example, to the villager who had absolutely no demands for money income beside tax money. Second, it is in fact an approximation to the actual preferences of many Africans, particularly in the early decades of European contact. In the early years, most villagers had only sporadic contact with the exchange economy. Wants were few and land relatively abundant. Knowledge of the outside was sparse and transport difficult. The choice between emigrating and staying at home involved much more than simply exchanging some "leisure" for some income at the margin. It involved abandoning (temporarily) the security of a traditional way of life for the risks and discomforts involved in a venture into a radically different social environment. Most Africans in the past (and many today) could therefore be regarded as reluctant—indifferent to the appeals of money income attainable outside the village; the fact that higher incomes were available outside was not sufficient to induce them to emigrate. Like most men in pre-industrial societies or those in early stages of transition, African villagers had great attachment to their traditional social system and generally preferred, in the absence of strong "push" factors, to remain within it. It is no surprise that until about 1930 in most of the continent, the securing of a labor force in the exchange sector depended largely on the exercise of direct or indirect coercion. And since force or some special need for money drove them out of the village, they would work only long enough to meet this need; they could be regarded as target-workers.

Finally, this analysis provides a convenient framework for summarizing the effects of change over time on economic behavior. The process of economic and social change, as it affected the villager and his willingness to work for money, can be characterized as changing both the target goal of income and the elasticity of the individual's labor-supply curve. In the period of early contact, the target income of most villagers was low and inflexible; the amount of labor offered by the individual varied inversely with the rate of wages or village income. In later years, increasing contact with the outside and a consequent expansion of wants and needs for money income increases the target income and blurs it at the edges, so to speak. The income level at which the villager refrains from entering paid employment undergoes continuous increase, and the growing flexibility of wants erodes the rigidity of the relationship between the level of wage rates and time spent in employment, reducing its negative elasticity. In contemporary Africa, the average target income, to the extent that targets can be said to persist, is not only much higher than earlier; it is much more plastic, less well-defined.

The Supply of Labor to the Exchange Economy as a Whole

A great many factors influence the rate of emigration in any given area and hence determine the size of the aggregate labor supply available for employment in the exchange sector. The most significant of these are the level of village income, wage rates, the size of the African population in the area concerned, the extent and intensity of the need for money income (which in turn depends on the degree of penetration of new wants, tax levels, the size of the bride price, etc.), the degree of compulsory recruiting (which is of minor importance today outside of Portuguese Africa), the scarcity or abundance of jobs and the "agreeableness" of these jobs, the nearness of employment centers to population concentrations and transport costs and difficulties, the intensity of contact between the villages and the exchange sector, the habits and customs of the particular ethnic groups in the area, the degree of knowledge about conditions existing outside the village. We will look at two of these factors: the level of money income from village sources and the rate of remuneration in the exchange sector. Changes in these two variables are most important in explaining short-run changes in the aggregate labor supply available outside the villages.

The level of income derived from village sources, and changes in the level of this income are major influences on the supply of labor presenting itself for employment in the exchange sector. First, at any moment of time, differences in the average per capita village income between areas are closely associated with differences in the rate of emigration. Within a given country or region, those areas where village incomes are relatively high tend to have relatively low emigration rates. Evidence of this tendency is plentiful, and can be found in all parts of Africa. In addition, in any given area the rate of outmigration varies over time with fluctuations in the level of village income. These fluctuations arise, in the short run, from variations in the size of village harvests or changes in the prices of the crops grown.

When village harvests are bad, the number of migrants increase. In places where income-earning outside is required to provide foodstuffs for the subsistence sector (as in much of southern Africa), a bad harvest means more men must go out to fill the subsistence gap. In places where Africans live in the neighborhood of famine much of the time (Ruanda-Urundi, Northern Nigeria, parts of East Africa), increased emigration when harvests are abnormally low is a necessary alternative to hunger. More commonly, a bad harvest means difficulties in meeting the customary money needs of the villagers, for taxes and commodities regarded as essential. If these needs cannot be satisfied by selling local crops, then they can only be met by increasing the export of labor.

If the effect of a bad harvest (low village income) is to stimulate more villagers to migrate, the effect of a good one is to keep more men at home. Enough food or cash-crop production can be sold to meet subsistence needs, to buy necessities not produced in the village, and to pay taxes.

Although for many Africans in various parts of the continent migration is no longer simply a way to pick up "pocket money," but has become an absolute necessity, the effect of village harvests remains significant. The Annual Report of the Labour Department of Tanganyika for the year 1953 notes: "The most outstanding feature of labour supply during the year was the fact that owing to the failure of the rains in many areas and consequential restricted harvests of staple foodstuffs, most districts had no lack of manpower." And the *Economic Survey of the Colonial Territories* (1951) stated, with reference to Kenya: "Labour supply is held generally to be dependent on harvests of various crops. Years of large crops will be years of labour shortage, which will be seen in urban as well as rural areas."

Fluctuations in village incomes depend, of course, on prices obtainable for marketed crops as well as on the size of the harvests. Price fluctuations thus entered from the beginning as a factor determining the size of the labor force in the exchange sector. A decline in the price of cash crops tends to increase the rate of outmigration in two ways. First, it results in lower village incomes (other things equal) and brings the income of some villagers below their minimum income goal. Second, it raises the effort-price of income earned in the village. This is a particularly important consideration in the case of annual cash crops—cotton, peanuts, tobacco, maize, rice, etc., for the villager has each year the option between growing such a cash crop or emigrating. A fall in cash-crop prices leads some villagers to migrate, since the effort-price of income from growing cash crops (given expected yields, marketing facilities and transport costs), increases relative to the effort-price of income from paid employment outside (given the rate of remuneration, the cost of transport and subsistence while away).

During the early years, the second effect—balancing of effort-prices of income earnable in the village and outside—did not come into play to any great extent. Since departure from the village was generally repugnant to most men, it was only when cash crop prices fell to the point where income goals were unattainable in the village that the rate of outmigration was significantly affected.

With time, increasing knowledge of the outside world and the establishment of patterns of migration, the trip to work outside for wages became less forbidding, less risky, less distasteful. More Africans came to consider a spell in wage earning outside as a possible alternative to income earning in the village, even when income needs could be met by expanding or diversifying village production. At this stage, the relative effort-prices of income in cash-crop production and paid employment outside became an important factor determining the size of the migrant labor force. The supply of migrant labor became much more sensitive to small changes in the prices of cash crops. When there is a fall in peanut prices in Senegal or Nigeria, cotton prices in Uganda, French-speaking Equatorial Africa, or parts of the Congo, tobacco and maize prices in East and Central Africa, the supply of migrant labor available to employers outside the villages increases.

In considering the relationship between changes in wage rates and changes in labor supply to the exchange economy as a whole, let us simplify the analysis by assuming that: (1) the unskilled labor supply of the exchange economy consists only of migrants from the subsistence sector; (2) all these migrants are what we earlier called "modified" target workers; (3) the total labor supply in the exchange economy has only two dimensions: the number of men in paid work and the amount of time they work. The aggregate labor supply, that is, consists of the number of men at work for wages multiplied by the average amount of time each spends in wage employment.

Now suppose all other determinants of the supply of labor are constant. How do changes in the level of wages offered in the exchange sector affect the aggregate labor supply in that sector? Given the stated conditions, any change in wage levels will influence the supply of labor in each of its dimensions. It will change the number of men presenting themselves for hire, and it will change the amount of time the men in employment are prepared to remain in employment. The two dimensions of labor supply, however, react in opposite directions. An increase in wage rates will tend to draw more men out of the subsistence sector; but the increase of wage rates also means that those who are in wage employment will work shorter periods of time since they can attain their targets more quickly at the higher rates. Whether an increase in wages increases or diminishes the total supply of labor depends, therefore, on whether the fall in average time worked has greater or less impact than the increase in the number of men working.

The effect of any wage change on the aggregate supply of labor in the exchange sector is therefore ambiguous. Even under the most restrictive assumptions about the individual African's economic behavior once he is in wage employment—that he is a target worker—it is not possible to conclude anything *a priori* about the shape of the aggregate labor supply curve to the exchange economy.

We can, however, speculate about the likely magnitude of the diverse effects of wage changes. To do so meaningfully, it is essential to recognize that the behavior of the two dimensions of labor supply varies according to the historical period being considered.

Even during the early years of African development, a wage increase tended to increase the number of men seeking work outside the villages. The higher rate reduced the effort-price of income; given consumption goals could be reached with smaller expenditure of time and effort in paid employment. This lower effort-price was just enough to convince some men in each village that it was now worthwhile to emigrate temporarily; it also made migration a more attractive way of earning income than production in the village. Further, with given transport costs, every wage increase widened the geographical extent of the labor market; at the higher wage, it paid men from more distant villages to migrate.

In these early years, however, the positive elasticity of labor supply with respect to wage increases tended to be slight. Because of sociological factors and because the level of wants and hence the need for money income was restricted, the subsistence sector responded sluggishly to wage rises in the exchange sector. Most villagers were deaf to the appeal of wages. They went out of the village to earn money when necessary. Most of them were unconcerned with marginal differences in income-earning possibilities; they were simply out of the labor market. Furthermore, the geographical impact of wage changes tended to be limited because of lack of transport and communication facilities.

In the early years, therefore, changes in wage levels had limited effects in augmenting the number of migrants into paid employment. At the same time, a wage increase was likely to result in a decided shortening of the length of time most migrants stayed in employment. When opportunities to earn money income first appeared, those who left the villages voluntarily were mainly target workers with rigidly fixed goals. The goals were so clearly defined that the possibility of earning a little more for the same time spent in employment did not appeal to many migrants. So when the early wage earners were granted higher wage rates, they tended to return earlier to their villages or stay longer at home between trips. In the early period of contact, then, the net result of a wage increase was not likely to be a substantial increase in aggregate labor supply, and was quite possibly a reduction. The aggregate supply function of labor to the exchange economy as a whole was either highly inelastic or negatively elastic through most of its range. For while the "men in employment" function (relating numbers of migrants to rates of wages) was positively sloped, the "average time in employment" function (relating average time spent in paid employment to wage rates) was sharply backward-bending, and the effect of the latter probably outweighed the effect of the former.

In the later period and in contemporary Africa, more villagers have moved to the margin of possible inducement; they can be drawn into wage employment by relatively small changes in wages. Transport and communication facilities have been improved. Knowledge of the outside is widespread in the villages. The geographical extent of the labor market has widened. Men move many hundreds of miles from village to workplace. When wages rise, the number of men in paid employment thus increases much more substantially than formerly.

At the same time, African wants have become greater and less definitely structured. Many men no longer quit their jobs sooner when wages rise; they stay as long as they had planned to, and are happy to bring back to the villages a richer collection of goods. Though many others remain target workers in a vague sense, their target goals have become hazier. The sharply backward-bending "time in employment" function of the early years has become a more gently backward-turning curve.

In most parts of Africa today, then, the aggregate supply curve of labor to the exchange economy as a whole (the relation between the general level of wages and the total quantity of labor available in the exchange sector) is positively sloped throughout most of its length. The positive "men in employment" reaction to wage changes now swamps the negative "average time in employment" reaction. Except at relatively high and low wages, it tends to be inelastic; the target tendencies of the labor force brake the increase in aggregate labor supply when wages rise. Moreover, at each wage rate, much more labor is available now than formerly; the curve has shifted outward. This is due to population increase, faster, better and cheaper transport and communication, and the continuing expansion of wants and hence of income needs.

Our earlier analysis, then, which related to the supply of labor available to the exchange economy as a whole, has to be amended to take account of the international character of labor markets for African labor. The aggregate labor-supply function to any given country (say the Union of South Africa, or the Ivory Coast or Uganda) may have been backward-sloping in the early years of African development; but when these countries are placed in their regional context, this becomes unlikely. Where the connections with other countries were strong, as in the Ivory Coast and South Africa, there is in fact good reason to suppose that almost from the beginning the aggregate labor-supply function of labor within these countries was positively-sloped in its relevant portions. That it is so shaped in most African countries today is certain.

Summary and Conclusions

By distinguishing various types of labor supply functions, and by attempting to take account of changes over time, we have tried to see in what sense and during what historical period it is legitimate to speak of backward-sloping labor-supply curves in Africa.

First, the quantity of wage labor offered by the individual African tends to be inversely related to changes in village income and changes in wage rates in the exchange sector. This relationship was pronounced in the early years, when migrants tended to be reluctant target workers whose elasticity of demand for income, once their target income was achieved, approached zero for everything except "leisure." In contemporary Africa, the target income concept is losing its applicability as wants increase in size and flexibility. It does not apply at all to "committed" workers who no longer shuttle between village and outside employment.

Second, the *number* of individuals in wage employment varies with the level of village income and changes in the level of village income; the income-elasticity of labor supply is negative, "income" referring to village income. This was markedly true in the early period of contact and remains a strong tendency today.

The shape of the aggregate labor-supply function—the "ordinary" function relating aggregate quantity of labor to wage rates—cannot be predicted *a priori*, since it depends on the net outcome of two contrary changes that follow a wage change: changes in the number of villagers in wage employment and changes in the average time each man spends at work. In the early years, the aggregate supply of labor to the exchange economy as a whole probably tended to be backward-sloping in relevant ranges; a rise in wages induced few new men into employment while it encouraged many of those in paid employment to cut short their stay. In contemporary Africa, this is no longer true; a wage rise stimulates relatively many more men to emigrate into paid jobs and leads far fewer to reduce their time in paid employment. And when account is taken of the international character of African labor markets, it is most unlikely that for any given country (*a fortiori* for any given industry or firm) the aggregate supply of labor was ever negatively elastic with respect to wage rates.

52

This selection deals with the monopolistic practices of professional baseball leagues as well as with the market for baseball players. This selection builds on the demand ideas discussed in selection 9 by considering issues of market power and behavior in factor markets.

MAJOR POLICY PROBLEMS IN PROFESSIONAL BASEBALL

GERALD W. SCULLY
Southern Methodist University

[I. Overview]

Despite the rough sailing in Congress over the proposed NBA-ABA merger, the passage of an Anti-TV-Blackout Law and some erosion of league operating rules in the Courts as they apply to contracting player services, professional team sports continues to operate in a milieu of special privileges.[1] Leagues are free to monopolize sports markets and employ players under extraordinarily restrictive contractual terms. This extreme *laissez-faire* public policy was fashioned in an era in which professional sports appeared to be more of a sporting than a business activity. It was believed that the incorporation of the public interest, through the application of antitrust laws, would seriously undermine the character of professional sports. It was alleged, and is still argued by league representatives, today, that breaking up the sports monopolies or restricting their monopolistic business practices would encourage the formation of competing leagues, which would lower the absolute quality of play and inflict a great degree of financial instability on the teams.

Failure to support the reserve clause and player drafting procedures, which governed player contracts, was viewed as potentially leading to big city team domination in the leagues and to an escalation of player acquisition costs.

Whatever the original justification for the current public policy toward sports, recent analyses of professional sports have shown that this policy cannot rectify

[1] The changing legal milieu in which professional sports operates is described by Steven R. Rivkin in "Sports Leagues and the Federal Antitrust Laws," in Roger G. Noll (ed.), *Government and the Sports Business,* The Brookings Institution, Washington, D.C., 1974. An up-to-date statement is contained in *Professional Sports and the Law,* A Study by the Select Committee on Professional Sports, House of Representatives, Ninety-Fourth Congress, Second Session, August, 1976.

Excerpted from U.S. House of Representatives, Select Committee on Professional Sports Hearings, *Inquiry into Professional Sports,* September 14, 1976.

several major problems inherent in the industry.[2] First, a number of business practices of the leagues serve only to enlarge profits. These practices are not necessary to the production of sports contests of high quality, and are frequently in conflict with the public interest. Secondly, in general, the reserve and the option clause and the system of player drafting cannot bring about equalization of team playing strengths. Such restrictions on player movement cannot be justified on this basis. The reserve and option clause and the drafting procedures exist solely to reduce player acquisition costs. Other remedies are needed to achieve the goal of equalization of playing strengths. Inequality of team playing strengths and the territorial restrictions incorporated in league constitutions have brought with them the problem of franchise shifts.

The sporting public justifiably is concerned by the abuse of power visited upon them by owners who move franchises at whim, raise ticket prices at will, trade players like bushels of corn and select the games that can be viewed on television. Many issues in professional sports need to be resolved, but we will focus on only four major areas of concern. In these problem areas we seek to incorporate the public interest more fully by: (1) restricting some of the monopolistic business practices of the leagues that adversely affect the public interest, (2) reducing the number and frequency of franchise shifts, (3) incorporating methods that truly equalize team playing strengths, and (4) seeking alternatives to the reserve clause beyond those currently being discussed. The operating rules that govern the various sports leagues are in serious need of an overhaul to more equally balance the interests of the fans, the players and the general public. However, reforms must be made which will not alter the basic characters of the sports. The reforms suggested below incorporate this dual objective.

II. Monopolistic Practices of Sports Leagues

Maintaining the highest possible absolute quality of play and establishing a champion among the contenders are sufficient justifications for the continuance of sports leagues as monopolies. Whether the form of the monopoly is a single league or multiple leagues, which establish the champion through post-season interleague championship play, is relatively unimportant. Championships are more conclusively established when one league exists, since more games are played between the contenders and the outcomes are less subject to random factors. World Series or Superbowl methods of establishing the champion may

[2] See, for example, Roger Noll, *Ibid.*, and Gerald W. Scully, *The Economics of Professional Sports*, Schenkman, Cambridge, Mass., in press for analyses of the economics of professional sports, which form the basis for the conclusions in this paragraph. Space limitations prevent the development of the arguments in detail, but the interested reader can pursue the background arguments in these works.

be exciting and profitable, but frequently yield ambiguous results because of the relatively small number of games between the premier teams.

Recognition of the basic need of some form of monopoly status for professional sports leagues in no manner justifies the variety of monopolistic practices promulgated by the leagues. Many of these practices do not serve the public interest, but are important devices for earning monopoly profits. Restrictions on such practices, rather than removal of the monopoly status of the leagues, would serve the public interest without adversely affecting the character of the games. In this section, three major areas of concern are discussed: team territorial rights; league expansion procedures; and, franchise shifts.

Territorial Restrictions

Part of the terms of membership in a sports monopoly is the granting of an exclusive territorial right to the owner. This right permits the team to field the only league game in town. Such a monopoly right means little in a small city, where only one franchise can be supported, but conveys large monopoly rents to the owners of franchises in New York, Chicago, Los Angeles, Detroit, Philadelphia and other large metropolitan areas.[3] These exclusive territorial rights bring with them wide differences in attendance and team revenues, and, hence are a major barrier to equalizing team playing strengths within a league. An alternative policy would allow the number of franchises in a city to increase to the point where each franchise was just financially viable.

An example from a regulated industry with an analogous problem will illustrate the point. Airline routes are federally regulated. There are imperfections in the regulations but the main criterion in allocating routes is that each of the carriers earn a normal rate of return. Public policy permits monopolization of air routes, because it is in the public interest. A route from Parkersburg to Charleston, West Virginia, for example, may not generate sufficient air traffic to viably support more than one carrier. A monopoly on the route is encouraged, since it serves the public interest. In the absence of a monopoly on the route, no air service would exist. On the other hand, the air route between New York and Chicago could be monopolized, but larger monopoly profits and potentially inferior service would result. Carriers are added to the route until each airline earns a normal rate of return. This approach, broadly, is applicable to professional sports. Exclusive territorial rights are justified in the interest of league

[3] For example, in major league baseball it was found that during the 1968 and 1969 seasons, each one million additional population in an SMSA with a major league team brought nearly $500,000 in revenues, independent of other revenue determining factors, including the team's win-loss record. Thus, the monopoly rents associated with the exclusive location of a league franchise in New York or Los Angeles could be worth several million dollars annually in revenues. On this point see Gerald W. Scully, "Pay and Performance in Major League Baseball," *American Economic Review*, Vol. 64, No. 6, December, 1974, p. 920.

stability when it can be demonstrated that the entry of a new league team would seriously undermine the financial viability of the existing team. When cities are capable of supporting more than one franchise it is not in the public interest to allow the existing team to block entry solely to protect its monopoly profits.

League Expansion

Decisions concerning the expansion of the leagues are in the exclusive domain of team owners. Because we have, today, about one hundred teams scattered over 34 American cities, the problem of expansion does not seem very important. Businesses normally expand when excess demand for their products and services exist in a market. Monopolies do not expand for such reasons. Monopolies expand only because of a threat of entry of a competing monopoly due to the excess demand. Many cities finally got a major league baseball franchise, not out of an attempt by the National and American Leagues to satisfy demand, but because of the threat of the establishment of a competitive league—the Continental League led by Branch Rickey. The same fact holds true in other sports. From a public policy perspective, expansion of leagues should be encouraged if two conditions are met. First, the potential site must be economically viable. Second, the expansion of the league should be league balancing. That is, new teams should be located in areas that will potentially reduce the wide dispersion in team attendance found in most team sports. Allowing team owners to decide when and where additional teams will be located within a league permits them to exercise an exclusive concern for monopoly profits rather than a concern for satisfying the public interest.

Franchise Shifts

The trauma caused by the transfer of the Washington Senators to Dallas, Texas, brought the problem of franchise shifts into focus. Fans, particularly in relatively small cities, have come to realize that their home town team may be here today and gone tomorrow. Even the fans in larger metropolitan areas are not immune, as the Brooklyn Dodgers and New York Giants moves testify. The sporting public has no control over the movement of franchises. This decision is largely in the hands of the team owners. Theoretically, authority for a franchise shift rests with the league, but, as a matter of fact, owners rarely veto a franchise move. The Washington Senators move was not a particularly rare occurrence. From 1953–72, a total of 10 franchise moves occurred in major league baseball. Franchise shifts in football and hockey have been less extensive, but basketball franchise moves are very frequent. From 1947 to 1971, in the NBA, and from 1967 to 1971, in the ABA, there were 10 franchise shifts in each league.

There are solid economic reasons for these franchise shifts. In general, the franchises that moved were located in population centers, which, from the beginning, were too small to viably support the sport. In Table 1, the ten teams

Table 1 Franchise Moves in Baseball and Basketball[4] [amounts in thousands]

Franchise Move	*Population of City, Premove*	*Population of City, Postmove*
Major league baseball, 1953–72:		
Boston to Milwaukee	1,297	1,270
St. Louis to Baltimore	1,053	1,804
Philadelphia to Kansas City	2,172	1,093
Brooklyn to Los Angeles	3,565	6,039
New York to San Francisco	3,565	2,649
Washington to Minnesota	2,064	1,482
Milwaukee to Atlanta	1,404	1,390
Kansas City to Oakland	1,257	1,555
Seattle to Milwaukee	1,422	1,404
Washington to Texas	2,861	1,556
(Average)	(2,066)	(2,024)
National Basketball Association, 1947–71:		
Tri-Cities to Milwaukee	281	1,233
Milwaukee to St. Louis	1,233	2,105
Rochester to Cincinnati	733	1,268
Fort Wayne to Detroit	232	3,762
Minneapolis to Los Angeles	1,482	6,039
Chicago to Baltimore	6,221	1,727
Philadelphia to San Francisco	4,343	2,649
Syracuse to Philadelphia	564	4,343
St. Louis to Atlanta	2,327	1,390
San Diego to Houston	1,221	1,867
(Average)	(1,864)	(2,368)
American Basketball Association, 1967–71:		
Pittsburgh to Minnesota	2,401	1,667
New Jersey to New York	897	2,505
Minnesota to Florida	1,667	1,268
Anaheim to Los Angeles	1,420	7,032
Minnesota to Pittsburgh	1,667	2,401
Oakland to Washington	1,555	2,861
Houston to Carolina	1,867	443
Washington to Virginia	2,861	474
New Orleans to Memphis	1,064	770
Los Angeles to Utah	7,032	558
(Average)	(2,243)	(1,998)

[4] Sources: James Quirk, "An Economic Analysis of Team Movements in Professional Sports," in Journal of Law and Contemporary Problems, winter, 1974, and the testimony of Robert Nathan, in U.S. Congress (1972), House: "The Antitrust Laws and Organized Professional Team Sports Including Consideration of the Proposed Merger of the American and National Basketball Associations." Hearings before the Antitrust Subcommittee, 92d Cong., 2d sess.

that moved in baseball from 1953 to 1972 are shown to have been located in smaller cities, on average, than the average league size city of 2.7 million. Of the ten franchise shifts in baseball, four were to smaller size cities, four were to equivalent size cities and only two, Brooklyn to Los Angeles and Saint Louis to Baltimore, were to larger size cities. For the ten moves, the average pre-move size city was 2,066,000, while the average post-move size city was 2,024,000. Therefore, generally, one cannot justify these franchise shifts on the basis of their potential equalizing effect on the league. The moves were motivated by several factors all related to the short-run profitability of the franchises. The first general reason for these franchise moves was poor attendance. This in turn has been linked mainly to rather lackluster performances by the teams. Owners expect mainly two benefits from a franchise shift. First, they expect attendance to rise due to a "honeymoon" effect in the new location. As an example, consider the migration of the Milwaukee franchise. In 1948, while in Boston, with a first place finish, the team drew 1,455,000. In 1952, its last year in Boston, the team finished in seventh place and drew 281,000.

The first season in Milwaukee, with a second place finish, drew 1,827,000 and with good finishes through 1960, the team had attendance in the range of 1.5 to 2.2 million. The Milwaukee population was about the same size as the Boston population but, due to the "honeymoon" effect, the team was drawing about 500,000 more per season for an equivalent finish than it was in Boston. In 1960, with a second place finish the team drew 1,498,000 similar to its 1948 draw in Boston. The "honeymoon" period lasted about six years. In 1965, with a fifth place finish, Milwaukee closed its season with 55,000 fans. Its first year in Atlanta, with an equivalent size population as Milwaukee and with a similar finish, saw 1,540,000 fans pass through the turnstiles. Attendance remained in the 1.1 to 1.5 million range for three years despite an average fifth place finish. The record of the team deteriorated from 1970 to 1972 and attendance in 1972 was down to 753,000. The pattern in attendance is similar in each of these franchise moves. Attendance increases due, at least in part, to the novelty of the presence of the team and then the novelty wears off and either the team turns in a winning record or its attendance falls. In the long run, Milwaukee would have done as well in Boston, but whether it was in Boston, Milwaukee, or Atlanta, to maintain high attendance, the team had to finish well. Perhaps, much to the chagrin of these traveling franchises, the "honeymoon" effect seems over at least in baseball. The recent move of Washington to Texas is testimony to the elimination of short run gains in attendance through franchise shifts.

A second inducement for moving, peculiar to baseball, because broadcast rights to a large measure are locally negotiated, is the availability of better TV contracts. TV revenues played a substantial role in the moves of Washington to Minnesota, Milwaukee to Atlanta and Kansas City to Oakland, where gains in the TV contract were reported to be in the $400,000 to $800,000 range. The prospect of pay-TV, which did not materialize, was said to have been of considerable influence in the moves of the Dodgers and Giants. TV revenues seem to have been a factor in about half of the franchise shifts in baseball. Because NFL and NBA teams share TV revenue equally, broadcast rights play no role in franchise shifts.

The pattern of franchise movement in the NBA stands in sharp contrast to the franchise moves in baseball. In the NBA, seven of the ten franchise shifts have been to larger size cities. Only the moves from Chicago to Baltimore, Philadelphia to San Francisco and St. Louis to Atlanta led to further league imbalance. Therefore, overall, franchise shifts in the NBA have been league balancing. In the ABA, only four out of ten franchise moves served to balance the league. The moves of franchises from Houston to North Carolina, Washington to Virginia and Los Angeles to Utah were particularly imbalancing for the league.

There is considerable franchise shifting in baseball and basketball and very little in football. The reason for the different behavior among these sports is that revenues in baseball and basketball are determined almost exclusively at the home team rate. The gate split (85–15 overall in baseball and 100–0 in basketball) and the prevalence of local broadcast rights in baseball, ties a team's financial destiny to the home town folks. In football, a 60–40 gate split, an equal division of TV revenues and season sellouts, led to little revenue difference between the teams. No gains can be made by moving a franchise. The easiest way to end franchise shifts in baseball and basketball is through the adoption of a 50–50 gate split and equal division of revenues. Such an arrangement would completely remove the incentive for teams to relocate, since any short run gains in attendance would be equally shared with the other teams in the league. Furthermore, an equal division of revenues would cause team owners to be concerned about the geographical distribution of franchises, particularly expansion franchises, since, under such a revenue sharing rule, the location of each franchise in a smaller than league average size city would reduce the profits of every team in the league. In the NBA, the established franchises such as the Knicks and the Lakers, in their battle with the ABA, cared little about where the expansion franchises located, since under a 100–0 gate split, they earned no revenues from games on the road. Rather, NBA expansion strategy was to block entry of ABA teams into potentially viable locations for ABA teams. Similarly, baseball teams earn only a small percent of their revenues from road games and, hence, had little concern about the sizes of the cities of the expansion franchise.

Other remedies can be considered, such as encouraging necessary franchise shifting followed by a moratorium on franchise relocation for an extended period. Such a proposal could work if the franchise moves were league balancing, i.e., movement of franchise toward the league average size city. A complete prohibition on franchise shifts would not be in the public interest, since numerous franchises in baseball and basketball are in cities too small to support the teams and judicious relocation of these franchises would enhance the relative quality of play within the league. Equal revenue sharing among the teams, however, seems the best method of eliminating the excessive franchise shifting in baseball and basketball.

III. Equalization of Team Playing Strengths

I assert that in addition to the aesthetic satisfaction of watching teams and players of a certain absolute level of technical competence, fans are also concerned about the relative quality of team play, i.e., the dispersion of team finishes within a league. If the relative strengths of teams were so unequal that team A always was victorious over teams B, C, D, . . . in the league, and team B always beat teams C, D. . . . , etc., the outcome of the contests would be certain, and watching such games would be a colossal bore. If such win-loss records existed within a league, a condition of absolute inequality of play would prevail, and the relative quality of play would be at its lowest. Uncertainty of outcome is a necessary feature of competitive team sports, and this uncertainty is determined primarily by the relative playing strengths of the teams. The more equalized the playing strengths of the teams within a league, the more competitive are the contests and the more uncertain are the outcomes of the games. The relative quality of the play within a league is highest when the win-loss records are equal among the teams. However, it is important to distinguish between a distribution of playing strengths that lead to mathematical equality of play (all teams having 500 records) and a distribution of playing skills that results in statistical equality of play (all teams having records deviating to only some small degree around 500 due to random factors or to short-run gains from superior strategy on the playing field). In this discussion, we will use the concept of equalization of team playing strengths in the statistical sense, whereby team win-loss records deviate by small margins and the winners and losers change from year to year, but over the long haul all teams have statistically identical records.

League operating rules have a substantial impact on relative team playing strengths. It is widely held that the most important league rule affecting relative team quality is the reserve clause. Other league rules governing roster size limits, playing rules, gate sharing arrangements, the drafting procedures and the distribution of minor league team ownership among the major league teams, also have significant effects on the distribution of playing talent. We will first establish analytically the effects of the reserve clause and the drafting procedures on the distribution of playing strengths among the teams, and then briefly document the historical trend in relative team playing strengths in various sports leagues.

The Effect of the Reserve Clause on Relative Team Strengths

Like any business, the *raison d'etre* for production is profit. Teams jointly produce games of a certain level of quality to earn profits. It has been shown that team revenues are determined by the size of the metropolitan areas in which teams play and by their win-loss records.[5] If two teams with similar win-loss records are in different size metropolitan areas, we would expect the team which draws fans from the larger population to have a higher attendance. Since fans derive satisfaction from seeing the home team win, holding the effect of population size constant, we would expect the team with the higher win-loss record to draw more attendance.

Franchise owners established, with the reserve clause in baseball and hockey and option clause in football and basketball, an alleged means of equalizing team playing strengths, within an economic milieu where team revenues are largely determined by the size of the franchise city and the team's record on the field. They argue that, in the absence of restrictions on player movements, the wealthy teams located in the large metropolitan areas of the country would acquire all of the prime athletic talent and cause a significant loss of fan interest, because the wealthy teams would always dominate the league. Furthermore, they have introduced the drafting procedure based on the inverse order of finish of the teams as a means of allocating the rights to the best new players to the teams with the worst records. Their argument contains two implications: (1) that size of the metropolitan area is a major factor in the distribution of playing talent, because larger cities have higher gate receipts and hence can pay higher salaries for better players, and (2) the distribution of playing talent is more equal under the reserve clause and drafting proceudre than in its absence.

To establish the effect of the reserve clause on relative team playing strengths we will assume a league consisting of two teams, the owners of which are profit maximizers.[6] Team 1 is located in a relatively small city, and Team 2 in a relatively larger city. Because of its favored monopoly location, Team 2 earns higher revenues for each increment in its performance relative to Team 1. However, we would expect that for both teams increments in their win-loss records would produce declining increments in team revenues. That is, we assert that there are diminishing returns to team wins. In economic parlance this means that team marginal revenues (the change in total revenues) decline with respect to increments in team wins. Team costs are a function of team quality. We assert that in view of the relative scarcity of prime athletic talent team costs rise relatively with successive increments of team skill. Intuitively, this is sensible. It would cost relatively more to increment team skills to the level that would exist on a team composed of all Hank Aarons and Sandy Koufaxs than to increment team skills from the level of a Bush league team to

[5] The support for this view is contained in Scully, "Pay and Performance."

[6] Treating more than two teams complicates the discussion without altering the conclusion. The case of non-profit maximizers is treated later on in the discussion.

the level found on the weakest teams in the major leagues. For this reason we assert that marginal cost (the increment in total team costs) rises with increments in team skills.

In Figure 1, we relate team marginal revenues to team marginal costs, over various levels of playing skills, which are indexed arbitrarily from 0 to 1,000. The index of playing skills is an abstraction, which manifests measures of team playing quality (say, for example, pitching and hitting abilities in baseball). The scaling of the index is unimportant. What is important is that, for example, a team with a playing index of 600 has 50 percent more playing skills than a team with an index of 400.

In the absence of the reserve clause, players would be willing to sell their skills to the highest bidding team. If all teams in the league face the same player supply function, which is a reasonable assumption, team marginal costs would be represented by the line marked "marginal cost without the reserve clause" in Figure 1. The equilibrium level of playing skills selected by profit maximizing Teams 1 and 2 would be governed by their respective marginal revenues. Since Team 2 is located in a relatively larger city, its marginal revenue is higher, and it selects an index of playing skills equal to 600. Team 1's profit maximizing level of playing skills is 400. Why are these levels of playing skills uniquely determined? There are three reasons. First, the teams face an exogenously derived demand for team skills, determined by the local fans demand for home town victories. Secondly, they face an exogenous player supply function. Thus, their marginal revenues and marginal costs are governed in the markets for

FIGURE 1 Effect of the Reserve Clause on the Absolute and Relative Quality of Team Play

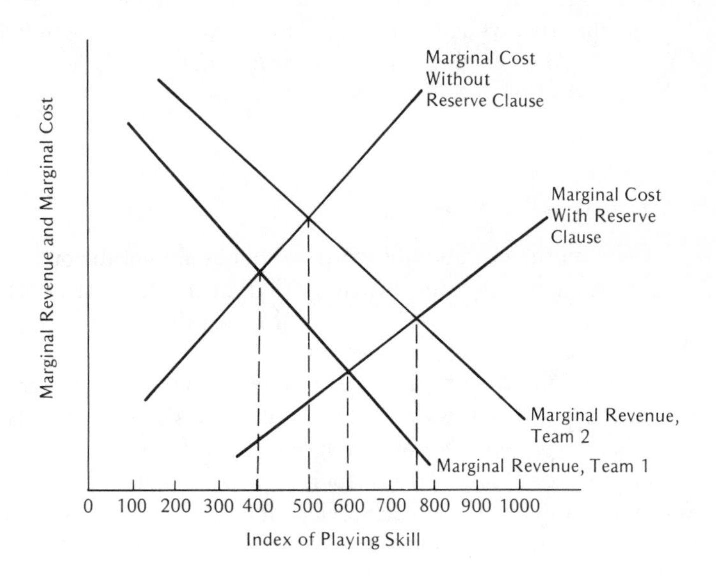

attendance and players. The only situation that the team can control itself is the level of playing skill. Profit maximization requires that the team select a level of skill such that marginal revenue equals marginal cost. This occurs for Team 2 at a level of playing skill of 600 and for Team 1 at 400. A level of skill above these corresponding equilibrium values would require that more be added to team costs than to team revenue. A level of skill below these values would mean more could be added to revenue than to costs by increasing the level of playing skill. Thus, any values other than 600 for Team 2 and 400 for Team 1 would produce less than maximum profits.

Now, introduce the reserve clause. The effect of the reserve clause is to reduce player acquisition costs (marginal costs). This is so because under the reserve clause players are no longer free to sell their services to the teams where their services are most highly valued. The reserve clause binds the player to the team that acquires rights over the player. This lowering of team costs through the reserve clause is shown conceptually in Figure 1 by the line marked "marginal cost with the reserve clause." What are the effects of the reserve clause? First, since marginal costs are lower with the reserve clause than without it, team profits rise. Thus, we can conclude that the reserve clause positively affects the profitability of sports franchises, and, hence, that its elimination would reduce that profitability. Secondly, the absolute level of skill fielded by the team rises, in the example in Figure 1, to 750 for Team 2 and to 500 for Team 1. The increase in skill fielded under the reserve clause is arbitrary in the figure. What is not arbitrary is that the increments in playing skill of Teams 1 and 2 are such that relative team playing strengths remain unaffected by the reserve clause. That is, Team 2 is still 50 percent better than Team 1. This is due to the fact that the reserve clause lowers player acquisition costs equally for all teams in the league, so that there is a downward shift in marginal cost. We can conclude therefore, that while the reserve clause increases the absolute quality of play in a league, by allowing teams to own more talent at a lower per unit cost, it does not affect relative team playing strengths.

Capital Gains in Sports Franchises

Current profits from the operation of sports franchises are not the only, nor the major, source of profits for team owners. Profits in the form of capital gains accrue to the owners of professional teams, if they sell the clubs' assets at prices greater than the original purchase prices.

Professional team sports have the rather unique economic features that there are little in the way of fixed assets of a team and that the important factor of production is labor (players). Normally, at least three factors of production or inputs are necessary for production: (1) labor, (2) capital, and (3) entrepreneurial ability. Businesses are owned by the suppliers of capital, but consider what are the necessary inputs in the production of professional team contests. The necessary inputs are (1) a league or a group of teams recognized as an entity, (2) a set of rules which minimize disputes on the field and govern the behavior of the teams within the league, (3) a stadium or field of play, (4) equipment, (5) decision makers, and (6) players. Not one of these inputs constitutes capital in the normal sense. A league is nothing more than a collection of teams agreeing to compete and abide by a set of rules which regulate their behavior. Decision makers, i.e., managers, coaches, related team personnel, business managers and front office staff are all contracted for salary. The only need for capital in professional sports if for a field of play and for equipment. Equipment costs are modest. Moreover, even under private ownership of teams, three-quarters of the stadiums are publicly owned and, therefore, rented.[7]

The point to recognize is that capital, in the classic economic sense, plays a very small role in the production of professional team contests. One can reply, however, that it would take $20 to $25 million in *capital* to buy, for example, a National Football League franchise today. Therefore, isn't that amount, the capital input, necessary to the production of games? The answer is in the negative. The $20 to $25 million required to purchase an NFL franchise consists of the transfer of a monopoly right (an exclusive territory), a monopsony right (reserved or option-contracted players), and the capitalized value of the tax shelter. Thus, almost all of the purchase price is in intangible assets, the value of which depends critically on the ability of leagues to maintain their monopoly in the product market, the reservation rights to the players and tax laws governing the depreciation of player contracts. Very little of the transfer price of a franchise is allocated to tangible assets. More importantly, these monopoly and monopsony rights, which exist exclusively as a result of public policy, are not necessary to the production of professional team contests.

Examination of the record of sales of franchises indicates how extensive are capital gains in the industry. In the recent history of team sales I have found only one sale in which a franchise apparently was sold as a loss, and only two qualified cases without substantial capital gains. Kansas City acquired its franchise for $3.5 million through the move of the Philadelphia Athletics in 1954. In its last year in Philadelphia the A's drew 305,000 fans. In their first year in Kansas City, attendance was 1,393,000. However, without any improvement from their perennial cellar position, Kansas City's attendance dropped. In 1964, with attendance at 642,000, Charles O. Finley purchased the team for $3.0 million. Thus, the sale of one of the weakest baseball franchises resulted in a capital loss of $500,000, or about $50,000 per year. When Milwaukee was sold in 1971 for $11.0 million, this represented only a $200,000 increase over the 1970 purchase price. The New York Yankees were purchased by CBS for $14 million in 1964 and sold for $16 million in 1970, a modest capital gain. However, in both of these cases previous sales had occurred, which probably had already capitalized any of the future gains.

[7] Benjamin A. Okner, "Subsidies of Stadiums and Arenas," in Roger G. Noll (ed.), *op. cit.*

In the case of Milwaukee, the team originally sold for $5.6 million in 1969. The gain in the transfer had been $5.2 million when it was sold in 1970. Therefore, litte capital gain could be expected in the sale of the franchise in the following year. In the case of the New York Yankees, the team had been purchased for $2.8 million in 1945 and when sold to CBS in 1964, showed a capital gain of $11.2 million. This represented a capital appreciation rate of 21 percent per year. Therefore, with a lackluster performance and competition at the gate from the New York Mets, capital appreciation was modest.

The usual case is that franchises appreciate in value at phenomenal rates. In baseball, the largest total capital gain occurred with the sale of the New York Mets. The team was purchased in 1962 for $3.75 million and sold in 1971 for $20.0 million, representing a capital gain of $16.25 million. Annual capital appreciation of the Mets franchise was $2.3 million or about 48 percent per year. On the average, for the cases studied, capital appreciation has totaled $5.6 million per team in baseball. *Forbes Magazine* estimated that the aggregate increase in the value of baseball franchises, since their purchases, is between $72 to $122 million in the American League and $46 to $160 million for the National League.[8] This indicates an increase in franchise value between $6–$10 million per club in the American League and $4–$13 million per team in the National League. In football, capital appreciation has been even more spectacular. . . .

V. Alternatives to the Reserve and Option Clause

Until recently the reserve and option clauses, which are a feature of the standard player contracts, were extraordinarily restrictive obligations. These clauses significantly suppressed player salaries from rising to their market levels. In *Flood vs. Kuhn* (1972), the Supreme Court upheld the original premise of *Federal Baseball Club vs. National League* (1922) and *Toolson vs. New York Yankees* (1953) that organized baseball was free of Anti-trust restrictions. However, continued player association legal attacks has led to three very significant rulings: *In re Arbitration of Messersmith* (1976), *Mackey vs. National Football League* (1975), and *Yazoo Smith vs. Pro-Football* (1976). These rulings, along with the growing strength of the player unions, seriously erode owner prerogatives in setting salary levels and allocating amateur players. In this period of restructuring the market for player services it will be useful to consider some alternatives to player reservation clauses and their consequences.

Apparently, a redeeming feature of the reserve (option) clause is that it imparts a degree of stability to the distribution of playing talent within a league. Part of our viewing pleasure at the ballpark is seeing not only the game, but certain players as well. Numerous fan clubs and the rubbernecking of the crowd to

[8] *Forbes Magazine,* April 1, 1971.

catch a glimpse of Hank Aaron or Joe Namath testifies to the fact that who is playing is an important feature of the fans' enjoyment of the game. The reserve clause allegedly prevents musical chairs from being played with the players. In the absence of such restrictions, it is held that excessive player movement would occur. Fans could not identify with a team of faceless players who were here today and gone tomorrow. However, the reserve and option clauses do not spare us from excessive player movement. There is a tremendous amount of owner-initiated player movement in the big leagues. Examination of the weekly regular season data on major league baseball player deals reported in *The Sporting News* reveals that in the 1973 season about 750 players were either traded, sold or released from major league and Triple A rosters. In professional football about 800 player transactions were reported during the regular 1972 season. About half of these transactions were internal movements on and off the "move list." Under the restrictions of the "move list," a club may place no more than 12 players at one time on the list during the regular season with the provision that the players remain off the active roster no less than two games or 10 days, and no more than seven games. Despite this substantial proportion of internal roster transactions, considerable player trading, sale and disposal exists. Given this magnitude of movement of players in the professional ranks, it seems rather unclear, that in the absence of the reserve or option clause, whether player-initiated moves would be any longer than owner-initiated moves.

There are a number of alternatives to the reserve and option clauses, which can improve player opportunities without compromising fan interests. One alternative is contained in the July 12, 1976 collective bargaining agreement between baseball owners and players' representatives. A result of the *Messersmith* decision and collective bargaining a player will be reserved for six years, but may opt to become a free agent after that time. As a free agent such a player will be free "to negotiate with a maximum of 12 teams starting with the inverse order of the previous season standings."[9] Additionally, there are restrictions on the clubs with respect to the numbers of free agents that can be signed. Clearly, this new agreement between the baseball owners and the players is a hallmark and a model for other sports. However, it does not substitute a competitive market as the mechanism for allocating players among the teams, and, hence, while an improvement, remains restrictive. In addition, there are some unfortunate side effects. Journeyman players, who are likely to be in the large pool of players with six years or less in the majors, are reserved as were all players prior to the *Messersmith* decision. As a result, one is very likely to observe a widening salary differential between those with six or fewer years of service (the reserved players) and those who have more than six years of service and opt for free agent status.

A most radical solution would be to place all players under a *one season* contract. Negotiations with other teams for the next season would have to be restricted to the off-season period to insure the integrity of the game. In season,

[9] "Professional Sports and the Law," *op. cit.*, pp. 18–19.

owner-initiated trades might be possible under such a plan, but, in the absence of the reserve clause, could only occur with the consent of the affected players. Such a system would make players completely free agents between seasons. In view of the analysis above, the reader should be aware that the distribution of playing talent would not be fundamentally different under such a plan, since the distribution of players is governed by their incremental contributions to team revenues in various locations are not the reserve clause. However, owners would lose the monopsony rents associated with the clause. Player salaries would increase to a level equal to their incremental contribution to team revenues, as inter-team competition transferred these rents. The main objections to such a plan are that it would lead to excess player turnover and would reduce team investments in player development in baseball and hockey. However, in light of the previous discussion, these may not be serious objections.

Rather than one year contracts between players and teams, a system of multiple year contracts could be adopted. If players signed renewable contracts for a 3–5 year period, the commitment of the players to the home town franchise would be evident. A stipulation of first refusal by the current contract holder would serve to reduce player movements at the end of the contract period, but retain the feature of competitive determination of player salaries. The issue of player-training investments only applies to baseball and hockey, since football and basketball players are trained by colleges. Long term player contracts allow recovery of team training investments. As long as the minor leagues are owned by the teams, the major leagues will need rights to an extended, but not indefinite period of player services or the flexibility to sell or trade players. If the minor leagues were owned or operated by the leagues as a whole, player development costs and returns would be equally shared and, hence, there would be no need to recover the development costs of any particular player. Even if the incentive for the teams to invest in player development was eliminated, it does not follow that the level of skills of new entrants into the game would fall. Under the current system, teams bear all of the direct costs of training and recover all of the returns. In the absence of teams providing such training, alternative sources of training would become available perhaps through an increased development of college baseball, or, through the creation of baseball training schools, which charge tuition. In the so-called individual sports like tennis and golf, the players bear the cost and recover the benefits of their training. In any case, the argument of a collapse of training opportunities for baseball and hockey players, with the removal of the reserve clause, is a gross overstatement of the consequences. We have suggested that league ownership of the minor leagues will allow training investment recovery and considerable player initiated mobility.

VI. Conclusions

League operating rules mainly serve the interest of owner profits at the expense of the public interest. Many of these rules actually are barriers to achieving the primary goal of competition among the teams on the playing field. A public policy which grants the leagues autonomy in their business practices, a status of special privilege, is inconsistent with the public interest. Continuation of this policy will inflict upon the sporting public continued inequality of playing strengths on the field of play, further player-management disputes, which may jeopardize the playing seasons, inter-league wars and their consequences, rising ticket prices, profit motivated rule changes, etc., all of which erode fan enjoyment in the games.

A new public policy toward professional team sports is required. Such a policy must be an enlightened one in that remedies are sought which incorporate the public interest without imposing the heavy hand of bureaucratic interference. There are several routes to the implementation of this objective. One personal would create a Federal Sports Commission. In 1972, Senator Marlow Cook introduced legislation, which would have created a Federal Sports Commission within the Department of Commerce to regulate franchise and player movements, drafting procedures and broadcast rights. Past experience suggests that such regulatory bodies are rather inefficient and ineffective regulators. For these reasons, the public interest is not likely to be well served through the creation of a Federal Sports Commission. A possible alternative to regulation of the operations of the industry is legislation directed at the problematic league operating rules. A number of alterations in the league operating rules have been suggested. For example, to bring about equalization of playing strengths, a ban could be imposed on all trades and sales of players that were not league balancing. To protect fans, all proposed expansions and franchise shifts could be required to demonstrate in advance their potential financial viability and their favorable impact on league balance. To protect players, resolution of salary disputes by automatic, binding arbitration could be required. Theoretically, a more equal weighing of conflicting interests in professional team sports could be achieved by judicious legislation of league operating rules. But, who would interpret and enforce such rules? In the absence of governmental interpretation and enforcement of such rules, conflicts would emerge. Moreover, there are real incentives and rewards in circumventing such rules. For these reasons, legislating league constitutions to incorporate the public interest appears to be an unpromising route to achieving the goal.

Actually, the publc interest can be well served by some rather simple changes in league operating rules that require no external interpretation or enforcement. The most important modifications in league operating rules would be to change the gate sharing arrangements from their current levels to an equal division of revenues among the teams within a league. Equal division of revenues has been shown to be the critical factor in equalizing team playing strengths and in minimizing player movements. Furthermore, under such a plan, the incentive for franchise shifts is removed and expansion is more carefully considered. This simple rule change will go a long way toward protecting the interests of the fans without altering the character of sports in any manner.

Second, player interests need to be more fully protected. The removal of the reserve clause and the option clause and the substitution of multiyear contracts, with a first refusal stipulation, is the best way of protecting player interests. With an equal division of revenues, there will be no incentive for players to move from one city to another in response to salary differentials, since such differentials will not exist. Equal division of revenues among the teams will mean that players will be worth the same, for example, in Oakland as in New York.

53 Here is an economic explanation of the postwar shortages of engineers and scientists. The explanation uses a special model of the adjustments of demand, supply, and price. The model fills a gap in conventional theory, which had given little or no attention to the reaction *speeds* of demand, supply, and price.

The model used is a competitive model, giving good results in spite of the heterogeneity of the services of engineers and scientists. Notice that demand and supply are given, for this analysis, sharp and special definitions. The quantities in both functions are those calculated by buyers and sellers when *they* are in equilibrium, i.e., when they have made complete and rational calculations.

THE DYNAMICS OF THE "SHORTAGE" OF ENGINEERS AND SCIENTISTS

KENNETH J. ARROW
Harvard University

WILLIAM M. CAPRON
Harvard University

The frequent and loud complaints of a shortage of engineers and scientists heard since about 1950 or so might be taken as indicating a failure of the price mechanism and indeed have frequently been joined with (rather vaguely stated) proposals for interference with market determination of numbers and allocation. It is our contention that these views stem from a misunderstanding of economic theory as well as from an exaggeration of the empirical evidence. On the contrary, a proper view of the workings of the market mechanism, recognizing, in particular, the dynamics of market adjustment to changed conditions, would show that the phenomenon of observed shortage in some degree is exactly what would be predicted by classical theory in the face of rapidly rising demands.

In this paper, we present a model which explains the dynamics of the market adjustment process and applies the conclusions drawn from this analysis to the scientist-engineer "shortage."

Reprinted by permission of the publishers from "Dynamic Shortages and Price Rises: The Engineer-Scientist Case," by Kenneth J. Arrow and William M. Capron, *Quarterly Journal of Economics,* Vol. LXXIII, No. 2, May 1959, pp. 292–308. Cambridge, Mass.: Harvard University Press. Reprinted by permission of John Wiley & Sons, Inc. The full paper is part of an economic analysis of the engineer-scientist market conducted for The RAND Corporation, by A. A. Alchian, K. J. Arrow, and W. M. Capron (RM-2190-RC, June 1958).

Equality of supply and demand is a central tenet of ordinary economic theory, but only as the end result of a process, not as a state holding at every instant of time. On the contrary, inequalities between supply and demand are usually regarded as an integral part of the process by which the price on a market reaches its equilibrium position. Price is assumed to rise when demand exceeds supply and to fall in the contrary case.[1] A shortage, in the sense of an excess of demand over supply, is then the normal concomitant of a price rise.

If we assume stability of the market mechanism, the shortage observed during the equilibrating process is transitory and tends to disappear as the price approaches equilibrium. If, however, the demand curve is steadily shifting upward at the same time, the shortage will persist, and the price will continue to rise. We argue that the interaction of rising demand with price movements which do not instantaneously equate supply and demand provides a plausible interpretation of the recent history of the engineer-scientist market in the United States from about 1950 to date. We also suggest a more detailed account of the price-adjustment mechanism than the bare statement that price varies according to the inequality between supply and demand.

Shortages and Price Rises

In what follows, we use the terms supply and demand to mean the aggregation of *the choices made by all firms and individuals in equilibrium at a given price* on a given market. Thus for a firm, the quantity demanded or supplied at a given price is that which maximizes profits. The equilibrium of each firm does not, of course, imply the equilibrium of the market, since the aggregate of the decisions of all firms need not lead to equality of supply and demand. At any given moment, the decision made by a firm or individual need not be optimal from its point of view at the given price, since economic agents require time to make decisions and to learn. It is assumed that each agent gradually corrects its errors, but in the process the firm or individual will not, by definition, be on its demand or supply curve. We hold that the process by which an economic agent moves towards its own internal equilibrium is an integral part of the process by which the market as a whole comes into equilibrium.

In Marshall's formulation, two equilibria were distinguished, short-run and long-run. A movement along a long-run demand or supply curve manifests itself as a shift in the short-run curve. Market price at any moment may diverge from *both* equilibrium prices. In comparative static analysis all that is shown is that under certain assumptions about the nature of supply and

[1] See, for example, Marshall's well-known analysis of the equilibrating process on the corn market, *Principles of Economics*, 8th ed., pp. 332–34. P. A. Samuelson has shown the fundamental importance of the law of supply and demand in stability analysis; see *Foundations of Economic Analysis*, pp. 263, 269–70.

demand functions, price will tend to move toward both short-run and long-run equilibrium price, given a shift in one or both of these functions. Over short periods of time, in which we are interested, the shift of the short-run demand or supply functions can be taken as exogenous trends, and will be so treated in this paper. Our analysis is, in Marshallian terms, short-run; but it differs from the neoclassical analysis in that we are presenting a model which explains not only the direction of price adjustment (i.e., toward equilibrium) but the rate of adjustment in the face of continued shifts in the short-run functions.

For purposes of comparison we draw the usual price-quantity diagram (see Figure 1). If P_1 is the initial price, we expect the existence of a shortage

FIGURE 1

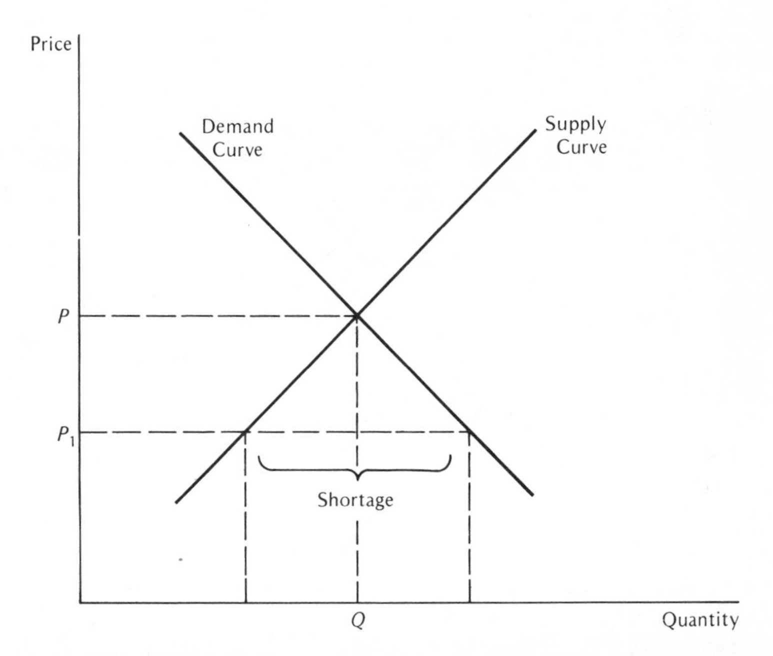

to raise the price gradually to the equilibrium value P. During the process, the shortage decreases to zero. The shortage can persist only if the price is held at some value such as P_1 by an outside force, such as price control. In that case, we have a shortage due to a fundamental imperfection of the market.

Now suppose that we have a market which is initially in equilibrium. For concreteness, we may think of it as the market for engineers and scientists. Suppose further that the price of a commodity that uses engineers in its production has increased. Assume further that each firm producing this commodity was in equilibrium before the increase in the commodity price, that is, that it had as many engineers as it wished to hire at a given salary level. Under the new conditions, the number of engineers that it would pay the firm to hire at the previous salary has gone up, and therefore the market demand has risen. The change from the old situation to the new is illustrated in Figure 2. Here D_1 represents the original demand curve for engineers. Curve D_2 represents the new demand arising from some change in external conditions, in this instance the rise in the price of the commodity in whose production the engineers are engaged. Recall that for present purposes we define demand as the amount which the firm would choose to buy after careful calculation. At any given moment of time, the firm may not be fully aware of what its demand (in our sense) is and seek to hire more or fewer engineers. But we do assume that the firm will gradually become aware of any such errors and correct them.

In Figure 2, P_1 represents the equilibrium price when the demand curve is D_1 Let us assume that in fact P_1 was the price prevailing just before the shift

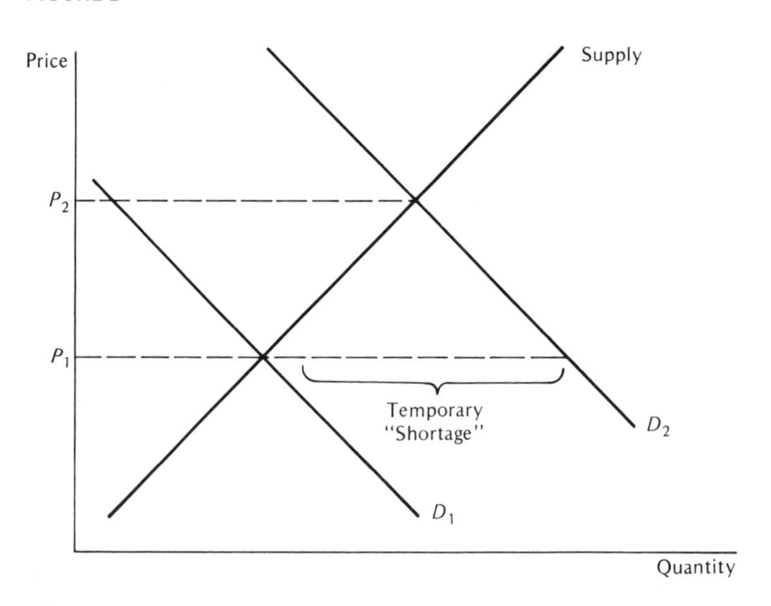

in the demand curve. After the demand curve has shifted to D_2, the price that would bring supply and demand into equilibrium is P_2. But movement to this price or salary level typically will take time.

Consider the situation of a firm just after the shift of the demand curve to D_2. A comparison of Figures 1 and 2 shows a strong analogy, not to say identity. At the moment of the shift, the market is experiencing a shortage, which is in many respects comparable to what it would face under price control. Each firm seeks to hire additional engineers at the price it currently pays, but there are no more engineers available at this price. We do not assume that each firm recognizes fully its demand, that is, how many engineers it would be best to have under the new conditions. All that is required is that each firm realize it wants more engineers than it now has. Then there will be unfilled vacancies so long as the firms do not raise salaries above what they are currently paying.

Is there any evidence of a shortage in the sense just described? In view of all the discussion of the "shortage" problem, it is remarkable how little direct evidence is available. The National Science Foundation in 1953 asked officials in large companies whether or not they were experiencing a shortage of engineers and scientists for research and development purposes, but no clear operational definition of the term "shortage" was supplied to these officials. At least half of the firms reported that they were unable to hire enough research scientists and engineers to meet their needs, although, except for the aircraft industry, there was no industry in which all firms reported such a shortage. Such a situation is to be expected when the demand curve has shifted and the price does not immediately rise to the level that would equate supply and demand.

The Process of Adjustment in the Market

We will trace briefly the sequence of events that will be observed in the market as a result of the shift in the demand curve from D_1 to D_2. At the moment, any individual firm may not have fully calculated how many more engineers it could profitably hire, but we may suppose that it will be aware of wanting more engineers than it now employs. It will begin by seeking to hire more engineers at the going salary but will find that there are none to be had. Its advertised vacancies find no takers; its offers are refused. The firm becomes aware that in order to hire additional engineers it must pay higher salaries, and it will now have to calculate whether or not the additional product derivable from additional engineers will be sufficient to cover the higher level of salaries. In the situation envisaged, the firm will indeed eventually decide to hire some additional engineers at a higher salary, but the decision will take time. First, there must be recognition of the need for higher salaries, then approval must be obtained from various echelons of management, and finally orders must be issued to hire.

Thus the time lag in the firm's reaction is spent partly in learning about the supply conditions in the market and partly in determining the profitability of additional hiring under the new supply conditions. This, however, is only one step in the process of adjustment. First of all, the firm may not yet have fully adjusted to the new demand curve; it has hired some more engineers than before but possibly not as many as would achieve maximum profitability. But, second, even if the firm has hired as many as would be profitable at the new salary level, the market as a whole would still not be in equilibrium, because the firm is now paying a lower salary to its old employees than to the new ones, and there is really more than one price being paid for the identical services rendered by different individuals. The multiplicity of prices is characteristic of disequilibrium situations, but in any well-developed market it cannot persist indefinitely. What happens is that other firms, also experiencing shortages, bid for the services of the engineers belonging to the firm we have been considering. While old employees will probably have some reluctance to move, this reluctance is certainly not absolute and can be overcome by a sufficiently high salary offer. That engineers do change jobs in sufficient numbers to suggest a responsiveness to market forces has been shown by Blank and Stigler.[2] However, we would again expect a lag in information. An employed engineer may not be in touch with current salary offers, and it may take some time before he is aware that the salary he is receiving is below what he might receive elsewhere. We would, however, certainly expect that he will become informed eventually, and that the discrepancy between his actual and his possible salary will tend to be reduced over time. While some individuals will not be tempted to move even in the presence of considerable possible salary increases, many would be willing to do so; either they will in fact move or the hiring firm, to keep them, will raise their salaries to the competitive level. Thus the initial tendency within the firm for new employees to enjoy higher salaries than old ones will gradually be overcome as the salaries of the latter are raised in response to competition.

There is another mechanism which will work to eliminate salary differences within a firm but at the expense of slowing down the firm's willingness to raise salary offers for new personnel. Salary differences within the firm are certain to be a source of morale problems to the extent that they are known, and clearly complete secrecy is out of the question. There will be pressure on the firm to increase the salaries of all its employees (in the same category) to the new higher levels. The lag in adjustment of the salaries of already-employed engineer-scientists is thereby reduced, but on the other hand the firm is more reluctant to increase its salary offers to new employees because it realizes it must incur the increased cost not only for the new employees but also for the old ones. In effect, the additional cost of the salary rise is recognized by the firm to be much greater if it has to extend the increase to all employees.

The total lag in the response of salaries to a shortage (in the sense of an excess of demand over supply) is then compounded out of the time it takes the firm to recognize the existence of a shortage at the current salary level, the time it takes to decide upon the need for higher salaries and the number of vacancies at such salaries, and either the time it takes employees to recognize the salary alternatives available and to act upon this information or the time it takes the firm to equalize salaries without outside offers.

A Model of Dynamic Shortages and Price Rises

While there is, strictly speaking, no one market price during the process of adjusting supply to increased demand, a multiplicity of prices being charac-

[2] David M. Blank and George J. Stigler, *The Demand and Supply of Scientific Personnel* (New York: National Bureau of Economic Research, 1957), pp. 29–30.

teristic, we may focus attention on the average price being paid for engineering services. The preceding discussion makes clear that the average price will tend to rise so long as there is an excess of demand over supply, but it will not rise instantaneously to the level that will bring supply and demand into equality (P_2 in Figure 2). Further, the forces that induce price rises will clearly operate more strongly the greater the excess of demand over supply. Hence, we find it reasonable to accept the usual view that the rate of increase of price per unit of time is greater the greater the excess of demand over supply. As a corollary, price will cease rising when the price is such that demand equals supply. Recall that demand and supply at any given price are defined as the quantities demanded and supplied after complete rational calculation.

Call the ratio of the rate of price rise to the excess of demand over supply the *reaction speed.* Then the amount of shortage will tend to disappear faster the greater the reaction speed and also the greater the elasticity of supply (or demand).

We have thus far been sketching a way of looking at the response of the market to a single shift of the demand curve; we have suggested that the price will tend to move to the new equilibrium but with a lag. This analysis has been preliminary to our main purpose, which is to consider a situation of *continuing* change in demand (or supply). We will suggest that this has been the case for engineer-scientists in the period beginning about 1950. If, for example, the demand curve is rising steadily; then as the market price approaches the equilibrium price, the latter steadily moves away from the former. There will be a chronic shortage in the sense that as long as the rise in demand occurs, buyers at any given moment will desire more of the commodity at the average price being paid than is being offered, and the amount of the shortage will not approach zero. The price will increase steadily and indefinitely but always remain below the price that would clear the market. This condition will continue as long as demand is increasing.

In the market for engineer-scientists or for any other commodity, we expect that a steady upward shift in the demand curve over a period of time will produce a shortage, that is, a situation in which there are unfilled vacancies in positions where salaries are the same as those being currently paid in others of the same type and quality. Such a shortage we will term a *dynamic shortage.* The magnitude of the dynamic shortage depends upon the rate of increase in demand, the reaction speed in the market, and the elasticity of supply and demand. The reaction speed in any particular market depends partly on institutional arrangements, such as the prevalence of long-term contracts, and partly on the rapidity with which information about salaries, vacancies, and availability of personnel becomes generally available throughout the market. In the case of an organized exchange, such as those for securities or certain agricultural products, we should expect the information to be passed on so rapidly that the reaction speed is virtually infinite and dynamic shortages virtually nonexistent. In the following section, we will advance evidence for the hypothesis that the engineer-scientist market for the last seven or eight years has shown a dynamic shortage in the sense just defined.

Dynamic Shortage in the Engineer-Scientist Market

The preceding analysis has been very abstract. Though we have referred to the market for engineer-scientists for the sake of concreteness, actually everything said would be equally applicable to any other market. We want to argue here that because of the character of the engineer-scientist market and the demands made on it over the last few years, the magnitude of the dynamic shortage may well have been sufficient to account for a great proportion of the complaints. It should be made clear that we are not arguing that the market is subject to unusual imperfections. Rather the very way in which the market performs its functions leads to the shortage in this particular period.

A dynamic shortage is a possible explanation of the observed tensions in the engineer-scientist market because (1) there has been a rapid and steady rise in demand, (2) the elasticity of supply is low, especially for short periods, and (3) the reaction speed on the engineer-scientist market may, for several reasons, be expected to be slow. The hypothesis stated in the previous section would imply that under such conditions a dynamic shortage could be expected. And we believe that such a shortage would largely explain such reactions as intensified recruiting and attempts at long-range policy changes observable in the industries affected.

1. The market on which the tensions seem to be focused is not the engineer-scientist market in general but the market for engineers and scientists for research and development purposes. It is a matter of common knowledge that there has been a very rapid increase in demand in this market. The increase in demand is, in turn, to be explained chiefly by the action of the government in contracting for research and development work by private industry. The type of research and development done on military contract is more complicated than the usual industrial work. This would imply that there is some differentiation between the markets for engineer-scientists in military and in other research and development, so that the full force of the increased demand would fall on the former.

2. The elasticity of the supply of engineer-scientists with respect to price changes may be expected to be small but not zero over short periods of time, owing to the length of time it takes to train new personnel. Over longer periods, higher salaries will certainly elicit a greater supply, though again because of the importance of noneconomic factors in choosing a career and because of the uncertainty of rewards in the distant future, the responsiveness of supply will be less than for commodities such as manufactured goods. Hence while it would be totally incorrect to deny the influence of price on supply, the responsiveness is sufficiently low to add to the possibility of a dynamic shortage.

3. There are three good reasons why it might be expected that the speed of reaction in the engineer-scientist market would be slower than that in the markets for other commodities, such as manufactured goods, or even than in other labor markets. They are the prevalence of long-term contracts, the influence of the heterogeneity of the market in slowing the diffusion of information, and the dominance of a relatively small number of firms in research and development.

We have remarked earlier that the market for engineer-scientists is not a single one. The heterogeneity of the market may interfere with the diffusion of information because an individual engineer-scientist may not know to which market he belongs. He may be aware that an associate is getting a higher salary, which may suggest that he ought to look around for another position. But he may very well wonder whether the associate's higher salary is perhaps due to superior ability or to the fact that somewhat different skills are being rewarded more highly at the moment. Because of his doubts, he may be delayed in ascertaining his alternative opportunities. Thus the length of time before he actually does achieve a higher salary, either from another firm or from his own, will be longer, and the reaction speed will be correspondingly less.

One special characteristic of the market for engineers and scientists in research and development is that the typical buyer is large; in particular a single buyer, the government, directly and indirectly accounts for about half of total demand. Up to a certain point, a large firm with large competitors has an incentive to keep salaries down rather than bid engineer-scientists away from competitors. Any one firm in an industry dominated by a few large ones will fear that increasing salaries in order to attract more scientists and engineers may set off competitive bidding that will end up with no substantial change in the distribution of scientists and engineers among firms, but with a considerably higher salary bill.

If nothing else happens, the competition of smaller firms forces the large firms to match their offers. There is no evidence that attempts by large firms to avoid competitive bidding can in the long run prevent the market price from reaching its equilibrium level. But they certainly can slow down the speed with which prices will rise in response to an excess of demand over supply and so, in accordance with the analysis of the preceding section, increase and prolong the dynamic shortage.

Alternate Definitions of a Shortage

It is not our purpose here to present an exhaustive review of alternate concepts of shortage. However, it is appropriate to call attention to the discussion of the alleged shortage of scientists and engineers presented in the recently published, important study of the engineer-scientist market by Blank and Stigler.[3]

[3] Blank and Stigler, *op. cit.*, p. 9; Chap. II, p.2.

After considering several definitions of the term "shortage," the authors settle on the following: "A shortage exists when the number of workers available (the supply) increases less rapidly than the number demanded *at the salaries paid in the recent past.* Then salaries will rise, and activities which were once performed by (say) engineers must now be performed by a class of workers less well trained and less expensive." [4] Blank and Stigler rely primarily on a comparison of the earnings of engineers with the earnings of other professional groups and wage earners in order to test the hypothesis of a shortage of engineers. By definition, a shortage exists if the relative earnings of engineers have risen.

Blank and Stigler acknowledge that there has been considerable talk about a shortage of engineers and scientists, but having concluded that there has not in fact been a "shortage" of the price-rise type of any significance, they make no attempt to explain all the talk except to point to the use of the word "shortage" as embodying some social criterion. It may be their hypothesis that the recent complaints of "shortage" have been based solely on this use of the term.

There are other possible explanations for at least some of the public concern over the "shortage" of scientists and engineers in recent years. It should be emphasized that many of those who have discussed this problem have been using the term "shortage" in a very different sense from that we have employed here. In particular, careful reading of such statements indicates that the speakers have in effect been saying: There are not as many engineers and scientists as this nation should have in order to do all the things that need doing such as maintaining our rapid rate of technological progress, raising our standard of living, keeping us militarily strong, etc. In other words, they are saying that (in the economic sense) demand for technically skilled manpower *ought* to be greater than it is—it is really a shortage of *demand* for scientists and engineers which concerns them. A somewhat different implicit definition of shortage which has been applied asserts that since we are not producing scientists and engineers at as fast a rate as the Soviet Union we have a "shortage." Still another explanation of the complaints may be found if one recalls the servant shortage of World War II days. In that situation, there is no evidence that the market did not respond to changed supply and demand conditions; alternative opportunities for employment developed for those who had previously been servants; the higher wages in these alternate lines of employment lured many to these occupations so that, *at the price they had been paying for household help,* many families found that they could no longer find such people. Rather than admit that they could not pay the higher wages necessary to keep help, many individuals found it more felicitous to speak of a "shortage." There is reason to think that at least some of the complaints of shortage in the scientist-engineer market have the same cause. Indeed, in any market when there is a relatively sudden and dramatic change in either demand or supply

[4] *Ibid.*, p. 24. Italics by Blank and Stigler.

which results in large price increases, we may find complaints of a "shortage" while people get used to the fact that the price has risen significantly.

Conclusion

It is our view that the model of dynamic shortage developed in this paper is useful in helping to understand the behavior of the market for scientists and engineers in the past several years. The very rapid increase in demand in the market during this period has led to "shortage" conditions resulting basically from a failure of the price of such services to adjust upward as rapidly and by as large an amount as warranted by the increasing demand, given the supply schedule of such services. This lag in adjustment, so far as we can see, can be attributed to a significant extent, not to any successful overt attempt to control prices artificially, but to certain inherent characteristics of supply and demand conditions and of the operation of the market. While the relative rigidity of supply in the short run is unpleasant (from the buyers' standpoint), and the price rise required to restore the market to equilibrium may seem to be very great, it is only by permitting the market to react to the rising demand that, in our view, it can allocate engineer-scientists in the short run and call forth the desired increase in supply in the longer run.

54 A price floor on hourly wages has equity and efficiency consequences. Welch finds both effects undesirable.

THE RISING IMPACT OF MINIMUM WAGES

FINIS WELCH
University of California, Los Angeles

The notion that everyone should earn a decent wage is as appealing as the idea that everything good should be cheap. But does it follow that to ensure jobs at high wages it is only necessary to establish a wage floor? In its simplest form, a law setting a minimum hourly wage is a statement to workers that unless they can find jobs at or above the specified minimum they cannot work. It is simultaneously a statement to employers that workers who would be employed at lower wages must be paid the minimum (plus legally required fringe benefits) or they cannot be employed. Employment, per se, is not required; instead, the law establishes the terms of whatever employment occurs. Is it surprising, then, that minimum wage laws reduce employment? Or that they reduce employment most for groups whose wages are lowest?

Economists have long been aware of the likelihood of these effects. Yet, even though we have had a federal minimum wage law for forty years, virtually all of the systematic studies of the law's effects (studies concentrating primarily on teenagers) have been carried out in the past ten years—and most in the past five. Only in this period have data on the law's coverage become available, and their use has made possible more refined estimates and has revealed historical effects even more dramatic than were once supposed. These findings are particularly arresting for what they suggest about the current and future impact of minimum wage regulation.

The Growing Impact

When Congress passed the Fair Labor Standards Act in 1938, it provided for a national minimum wage rate of 25 cents an hour and applied that minimum to an estimated 43 percent of all employees in private nonagricultural work. Forty years later, the minimum has reached $2.65 an hour, a tenfold increase, and coverage has been approximately doubled.

The 1938 act has been amended six times—first in 1950 and most recently

---

Reprinted from Finis Welch, "The Rising Impact of Minimum Wages," *Regulation,* November/December 1978, pp. 28–37.

in 1977. Each amendment raised the basic hourly minimum, and all but those in 1950 and 1956 also provided for subsequent step increases in the rate. In addition, the 1961, 1966, and 1974 amendments broadened the act's coverage, while smoothing the effects of this by setting lower—though gradually rising—minimums for the newly covered sectors. (These new coverage differentials were eliminated in 1977.)

Table 1 gives historical information on federal minimum wage rates and coverage. Note that the table leaves out the years between changes in the basic minimum—which means that the column showing the minimum as a percent of average wages (column three) does not reflect the impact of rising average wages for the times when the nominal rate was not increased. During those times, there would of course have been a decline in the minimum as a percent

Table 1 The Basic Minimum Wage and Aggregate Coverage, 1938–81

Month/Year of Change in Minimum	*Basic Minimum*	*Basic Minimum as a Percent of Average Manufacturing Wage*	*Coverage (Percent of nonsupervisory, private nonagricultural workers covered)*	*Index of Combined Effect of Coverage and Minimum Wage Levels*[a]
10/38	$0.25	41.7	43.4	60.5
10/39	0.30	49.5	47.1	92.5
10/45	0.40	42.1	55.4	78.7
1/50	0.75	54.0	53.4	124.8
3/56	1.00	52.9	53.1	119.1
9/61	1.15	51.2	62.1	130.5
9/63	1.25	52.7	62.1	138.3
2/67	1.40	51.5	75.3	160.1
2/68	1.60	55.6	72.6	179.9
5/74	2.00	47.2	83.7	149.5
1/75	2.10	45.1	83.3	135.8
1/76	2.30	46.0	83.0	140.8
1/78	2.65	48.4[b]	83.8[c]	157.4
1/79	2.90	49.7[b]	83.8[c]	166.0
1/80	3.10	49.9[b]	83.8[c]	167.3
1/81	3.35	51.9[b]	83.8[c]	181.0

[a] The index, whose 1938–76 average equals 100, is proportional to CM^2 where C is the proportionate coverage rate and M is the basic minimum as a percentage of the average manufacturing wage. See Finis Welch, *Minimum Wages: Issues and Evidence* (Washington, D.C.: American Enterprise Institute, 1978), for rationale underlying this construction.

[b] Manufacturing wages are extrapolated based on log-linear trend, 1965–76. During this period wages grew 6.3 percent a year (R^2 for the trend line is 0.989).

[c] The coverage rate given is the one estimated for 1977 by Employment Standards Administration. The 1977 amendment did not change coverage.

Source: Wage and coverage data from unpublished tabulations of Employment Standards Administration, U.S. Department of Labor.

of the average. What is clear is that, up until now, the upward movement in the minimum has been more or less in line with general wage growth.

The most important change in minimum wages has thus been the rise in the proportion of workers covered from 43 percent in 1938 to 84 percent today (column four). While the impact of higher nominal minimums has been lessened by inflation and rising real wages, the increase in coverage has not been offset. This is all the more so because minimum wages were originally applied mostly to high-wage industries (mining, manufacturing, transportation) and then extended to industries with lower wages (services and retail trade). Among other things, the expansion in federal coverage appears to have made state minimum wage laws increasingly redundant. After 1938, many states passed their own laws—usually to cover firms not covered at the federal level—but the effect of these laws has substantially declined in recent years. My estimates show that non-redundant state laws covered 17 percent of private nonagricultural employment in 1960 but only 8 percent in 1976, meaning that the uniformity of minimum wage coverage has risen substantially.

In column five of the table, I offer a simple index of the overall impact of federal minimum wage legislation. This index, which gives the combined effect of coverage and the minimum wage level, is calculated under the assumption that the only effect of a higher minimum is to increase the wages of those who were earning less than the new minimum. It ignores employment reductions in covered sectors and increases in uncovered sectors where displaced workers seek alternative employment—not because these changes do not occur but because the index is designed to measure the *pressure* for them to occur—a measure, so to speak, of the *impetus* for effect.

The index deserves a fairly full explication since it presents a measurement not in general use. It is proportionate to the coverage rate (column four) and to the *square* of the minimum wage measured as a percentage of the average manufacturing wage (column three). The proportionality with coverage reflects an assumption that a doubling of the fraction of workers covered doubles the effect—an obvious point. The second point, the more-than-proportionate effect of the minimum wage rate, is less obvious but can be illustrated with a simple example.

In this example a $1.00 hourly minimum is established and then raised to $2.00. When the minimum is first imposed, only those earning less than $1.00 are affected and, since they would be earning something in any case, their average wage is increased by less than $1.00. As the minimum is raised to $2.00, all those initially affected get an extra increment of a *full* dollar and this alone gives a more than proportionate increase over the initial effect. Further, with the increase to $2.00, those originally earning between $1.00 and $2.00 are added to the pool of candidates for job losses. The index simply assumes that, in relevant ranges, the number of workers who would earn any given wage without the legislation is the same as the number who would receive any other wage. In that case the effect is proportionate to the square of the minimum wage level.

The figures in column five describe an impact (or impetus) that is erratic and growing. Its erratic nature is understated because the table does not show erosion from wage inflation between steps, but is overstated because the table does not show the lower minimums provided for newly covered sectors in the 1961, 1966, and 1974 amendments. Even should the understatement and overstatement not cancel out, what is important is this: if the index is in the ballpark, and if general wage growth continues at its average rate of the last decade (6.3 percent a year), then by 1981 the impact of the hourly minimum will exceed anything we have seen before.

Characteristics of the Low-Wage Labor Market

Until 1973 when the Current Population Survey began collecting wage rate data for a large, nationally representative sample, minimum wage studies were restricted to demographic groups consisting disproportionately of low-wage earners, and virtually all of these studies focused on teenagers. This emphasis has had its cost. Teenagers and low-wage workers have become synonymous in the public mind. We have lost sight of the fact that what happens to teenagers is only illustrative of what happens to low-wage workers and that the low-wage population is dispersed throughout demographic categories. The fact is that, in 1973, only 30 percent of the persons with usual hourly earnings of less than $2.00 were teenagers. In addition, just under half of this population worked part time, a fourth were heads of families, some two-thirds were female, and about one-tenth were sixty-five years of age or more. Finally, almost 50 percent were twenty-five to sixty-four years of age. This last is particularly important, because the characteristics of the low-wage population in general are probably the same as those of workers displaced by minimum wage laws. Programs that are designed to reduce the undesirable side effects of minimum wages but that are targeted only at teenagers will therefore miss most of the affected population.

Based on Current Population Survey data, we also find that 12.5 percent of teenage wage earners received less than the $1.60 minimum in 1973, compared to 3 percent of the young adults and 25.4 percent of the aged. Furthermore, of the low-wage teenagers, 84 percent worked part-time, 70 percent were students (students account for two-thirds of all part-time teenage job holders), and 60 percent were female.

By taking proportions of workers receiving wage rates near or below the minimums in the three years, 1973–75, we can get an idea of the overall size of the population affected, with those not working (that is, those who have lost their jobs *because* of minimum wage legislation) not reflected in the data. From this it is clear that low or near-minimum wage rates are a problem for far more than an irrelevant few. Perhaps 10 to 25 percent of the U.S. labor force is involved.

Some Effects of Minimum Wages: Theory

Simple Effects

If the world were simple, the theory of minimum wage effects would also be simple. For example, if wages were the only form of remuneration, if there were no job amenities or fringe benefits, and if all workers were of one quality, then everyone would get the same wage. A minimum that attempted to raise the wage would reduce employment. If the minimum were imposed on only some firms, their employment would fall and displaced workers would compete for jobs in uncovered sectors and would drive wages in those sectors down as employment rose to accommodate the increased number of applicants.

But workers are of varying productivity, so that wages also vary and a minimum that attempts to raise the wage of those with the lowest productivity should have effects for them similar to those described in the one-quality case. With full coverage, some will get jobs at higher wages and others will lose jobs. Among those who would earn less than the minimum without minimum wages, those who would be closest to it are the ones whose continued employment will cost employers least and they will be most likely to keep their jobs. Within the low-productivity group, the minimum will function much like a tax, from the poor to the poor, but winners will be those who in any case would have fared best. With incomplete coverage, those losing covered-sector jobs can search in the uncovered sector where, as a result of increased competition, wages should fall. If business cycles occur, so that labor demand fluctuates, then employment of those whose productivity is "near," the minimum will also fluctuate. In booms, their productivity will exceed the minimum and they will be hired; and in busts, their productivity will fall short of the minimum and they will be laid off.

Empirical work has addressed only these simple effects: employment reductions in covered sectors, shifts into uncovered sectors, and the heightened vulnerability of low-wage workers to business cycles. Although these studies necessarily gloss over most real-world complexities they largely support the simple theory. Nonetheless, other effects can be explored.

In the public debate there is much confusion between minimum wage effects on employment and on unemployment. These effects are not the same. Moreover, while the implications for employment are straightforward, those for unemployment are not. To see that theory makes no prediction of minimum wage effects on *unemployment* rates, consider the behavior of someone who loses his job as a result of an increase in the minimum. If he searches for a job (and he might, because if he is lucky enough to find one, it will have a higher wage) he is counted as unemployed. If he drops out of the labor force (and he might, because the number of job openings has fallen), he is not counted as unemployed.

The main point is that minimum wages reduce employment of low-wage workers. These reductions flow from two sources—the first being the reactions of consumers as firms try to pass on cost increases in the form of higher prices, and the second being the ways in which firms substitute as they try to avoid the cost increases. These ways include both automation and substitution in favor of high-wage labor.

Indirect Effects

Minimum wage legislation directly influences only one component of what workers receive in return for their services on a job. But fringe benefits (the nonwage components of remuneration) are affected indirectly. These benefits, which range from opportunities for on-the-job training or a pleasant work environment to health and disability benefits, are affected because they can be substituted for wages: employers might for example absorb part of the increased wage costs resulting from an imposed higher minimum by providing fewer fringe benefits. Consider three nonwage benefits for workers: job location, part-time work, and on-the-job training.

Suppose a firm is trying to decide where to locate a new plant. Should it find a site convenient to its workers or to the consumers of its product? If it chooses to locate near its workers, it can take advantage of the added convenience to them by offering a lower wage, but it will have to compensate consumers either by offering its product at a lower price or by transporting the product to them. A minimum wage rate restricts options for trade-offs between convenience to workers and their wages: as wages are forced upward, jobs migrate toward locations less convenient to workers.

Similarly, work interruptions caused by the arrivals and departures of part-time workers are expensive. Yet efforts can be made to accommodate people who prefer part-time work if wages can be reduced accordingly. A wage floor restricts options for this kind of trade-off: as wages are forced upward, employers have fewer incentives to accommodate part-timers.

Formal apprenticeships are rare today, but most careers include learning phases where what is learned is important to the career. Learners may be productive but their productivity is less than it will be when they are more fully trained, and the portion of on-the-job time spent learning instead of producing varies. Since workers can take the benefits of training with them when they leave for other employment, firms may have little incentive to offer training. But, as the case of other kinds of fringe benefits, firms can be bribed through lower wages—that is, they can offer on-the-job training in exchange for lower wages. The worker sacrifices current wages for improved prospects, and the firm gets less current product while paying the lower wages. Again, a wage floor impedes this trade-off; as wages are forced upward, employers have fewer incentives to accommodate learners, so that potential learners must more often choose between jobs offering higher current wages with less future potential and schools where, although learning is work, few have argued that students be paid minimum wages.

Ripple Effects

There is a popular idea that an imposed minimum sets forces in motion that increase wages not only for those who would have earned less than the minimum but also for those who would have earned more—and that those closest to the minimum are affected most. This idea is a restatement of the substitution phenomena mentioned above in the discussion of different qualities of labor—with an added assumption that those having the most similar wage potential are the best substitutes for each other. As minimum wages raise the cost of the lowest wage workers, firms adjust by replacing them with their best substitutes—in this case those whose wage would be just above the minimum.

The nature of the ripples, or derivative effects, extends from the way firms seek to mitigate effects by substituting to the way cost-conscious consumers react. Some industries (retail trade, services, agriculture) depend much more than others on low-wage workers, and minimum wages raise product costs (and the prices consumers pay) in direct proportion to each industry's dependence on low-wage labor. Consumers react by demanding less of the industry's products whose prices are more affected—and vice versa.

Are the ripples smooth? Among those who in any case would earn more than the minimum, do the largest gains go to those receiving the lowest wage? Although the answer is unclear, if cost-saving adjustments *within* firms dominate, the answer could be yes. But the story of cost-saving adjustments by consumers suggests a reverse ripple, so that if these effects dominated the answer would be no.

Whichever way the ripples go, the thing that makes them go is the elimination of jobs for those who would otherwise earn less than the minimum. They are the big losers—though not the only ones. Workers, after all, are consumers too, and when minimum wages raise costs in fast-food outlets, when theater managers respond to higher minimums by substituting chains (even in velvet wrap) for ushers or by making seating catch-as-catch-can, the consumer's enjoyment is affected.

Some Effects of Minimum Wages: Evidence

It would be nice if, after forty years of minimum wage regulation, I could say the evidence on its effects were unambiguous. But to economists the law that employment reductions accompany mandated wage increases is as basic as the law of gravity is to physicists—and, to paraphrase an old friend, "as scientists, economists have as much to gain from showing minimum wages reduce employment as physicists have to gain from showing that apples fall when dropped."

Such a view has obviously restricted the amount of data analysis of minimum wage effects. Nevertheless, because legislators are more likely to ignore or try to repeal economic laws than physical laws, economists have conducted a number of analyses of these effects. What, then, do the data show?

The Run from Cover

The coverage provided in the initial minimum wage act was uneven, ranging from almost all workers in some industries to almost none in others. Since 1938 the proportion of low-wage earners employed in any given industry has fallen as coverage has been extended to that industry. With an increase in minimum wage rates, there is a shift in low-wage (especially teenage) employment from covered to uncovered sectors—a "run from cover."

Today we think of industries such as retail trade and services as teenage-intensive. Moreover, we know that industrial patterns of teenage and adult employment are uneven, and we think of this as normal. But it has not always been so. In 1930, teenagers generally worked where adults did and the age distribution of workers across industries was amazingly even by today's standards. Then, between 1930 and 1940, teenage employment fell from 9.2 to 5.9 percent of the U.S. total. Part of this drop may have resulted from the introduction of the minimum wage rate in 1938, but the Great Depression and increasing school enrollment probably played a larger role. What is particularly intriguing about the 1930-to-1940 change is not that teenage employment fell but that it fell the most in the industries that were newly covered.

In the 1930s, teenage employment dropped more than the national average in every industry with above-average coverage (see Table 2). Correspondingly, in every industry with below-average coverage, the drop in teenage employment was less than the drop in the national average. Overall, teenage employment not only fell, but also shifted from covered to uncovered sectors.

This process continued for many years. Since 1930 over 80 percent of working teenagers have been employed in three industries—manufacturing, trade, and services—and the minimum wage has not changed this. It has only shifted teenagers from the covered to the uncovered sectors and, presumably, driven wages in uncovered sectors down. In 1930 manufacturing was by far the largest teenage employer, accounting for roughly 40 percent of working teenagers, and the figure for adults, 36 to 38 percent, was nearly the same. The initial legislation covered approximately 95 percent of manufacturing workers and, by 1955, the percentage of teenagers working in manufacturing had fallen to half the earlier level while the figure for adults remained roughly constant. After the 1938 act, wholesale and retail trade replaced manufacturing as the leading teenage employer. The shift was largely into retail establishments, where initially only workers in mail-order houses (3 percent of total retail employment) were covered.

The data show that, with the 1961 and 1966 amendments (which broadened coverage first to 30 percent and then to 58 percent of retail trade employees),

Table 2 Minimum Wage Coverage and Changes in Teenage Employment, by Industry, 1930–40

Industry	*Extent of Coverage (percent of all workers covered)* 1940	*Teenagers as Percent of All Workers* 1930	1940	*Relative Change in Teenage Share of Employment, 1930 to 1940*[a]
Coverage above national average:				
Mining	99	5.3	2.3	0.66
Manufacturing	95	9.6	4.8	0.78
Transportation and Communication	88	5.5	2.1	0.78
Finance, Insurance, and Real Estate	74	7.1	2.9	0.64
Coverage below national average:				
Construction	44	3.2	2.5	1.19
Services	19	7.5	6.0	1.23
Wholesale, Retail, and Trade	13	8.8	6.0	1.05
Agriculture, Forestry, and Fishing	—	14.2	10.6	1.16
Governments	—	3.2	3.4	1.63
Miscellaneous	—	11.2	10.5	1.45
Total	56[b]	9.2	5.9	1.00

[a] Calculated by dividing the 1940 share (column 3) by the 1930 share (column 2) and then dividing this ratio by the national averages (5.9/9.2).
[b] These coverage data were issued by the U.S. Department of Labor prior to 1973. Recent revisions place the initial (1938), average coverage rate at 43 percent (see Table 1).

the proportion of employed teenagers working in retail establishments fell. As coverage has expanded, the amount of available teenage employment has shrunk, and as the originally uncovered industries have been included, the initial bulge in those sectors has subsided. With each step in the process, there have been fewer and fewer uncovered jobs for teenagers to turn to for employment.

Employment Effects

If there is a general theme to the empirical literature on the subject, it is that the simple theoretical predictions are confirmed. Almost every serious scholar of minimum wages would argue (on the basis of available evidence) that wage minimums have reduced employment for those who would otherwise earn low wages, particularly teenagers. But because employment of teenagers is affected by other things and because minimum wage laws are complex (and it is not clear how their complexities should be taken into account), the available studies paint a mixed picture: they generally agree that employment has been reduced, but their estimates on the extent of the reduction differ.

Let me briefly summarize eight recent studies. All but the one that James Cunningham and I carried out used U.S. aggregate data beginning in 1954 or later (reflecting the fact that in that year the monthly *Current Population Survey* began to carry information on employment, unemployment, and labor force status disaggregated by age, sex, and color). I will emphasize effects on *employment* because, as Jacob Mincer showed in his article in 1976, no firm theoretical predictions can be made for the effects of minimum wages on measured *unemployment*.

Mincer and Masanori Hashimoto, in their 1970 study for the National Bureau of Economic Research, found statistically significant employment reductions associated with rising wage minimums for white and nonwhite teenagers, for white and nonwhite males aged twenty to twenty-four years, for white males aged sixty-five and over, and for white and non-white females aged twenty and over. Their estimates also suggested (though with less statistical precision) employment reductions for nonwhite males aged sixty-five and over and—surprisingly—for white and nonwhite males aged twenty-five to sixty-four years. It is not surprising that they found reduced employment for low-wage groups. But the fact that they found no corresponding increase—but rather a probable decrease—for males aged twenty-five to sixty-four suggests that the minimum-wage employment lottery is not a zero-sum game. Their evidence is that the minimum wage causes *net losses* in employment.

The Hashimoto-Mincer study is also noteworthy because it found employment reductions to be associated with a reduction in the size of the labor force. In other words, potential workers are evidently more likely to drop out of the labor force than to queue for rationed jobs.

As part of a 1970 Labor Department survey, Hyman Kaitz analyzed employment and unemployment effects separately for males and females, white and nonwhite, for ages sixteen through seventeen and eighteen through nineteen. He reported significant employment reductions for white males aged sixteen through nineteen and for white females aged sixteen through seventeen. The estimates were erratic for other groups and showed numerically large (and marginally significant) employment increases for nonwhite males eighteen and nineteen years old.

It is somewhat surprising that the studies by Kaitz and by Hashimoto and Mincer showed so little agreement for nonwhites. I think the main explanation is that Kaitz used "fine" partitions (by age, race, and sex), while Hashimoto and Mincer used the simple white-nonwhite division for teenagers. The data came from a random sample of the U.S. population, and were subject to sampling error that can be important when data are finely partitioned. For the less noisy data—data that give a clearer signal—the two studies agreed. In fact, when

Kaitz pooled all teenagers into a single composite, his estimated unemployment effect was much larger than the effects. Hashimoto and Mincer reported for whites and nonwhites separately.

In a closely related study using the same data that Kaitz used, I found statistically significant employment reductions for all teenagers aged sixteen through nineteen years, but when fourteen- and fifteen-year-olds (a group presumed more vulnerable) were added, the estimated effect was reduced and statistical significance lost. This is evidence of the nature of these data. If minimum wages affect anyone, it is most likely to be the very young. Noisy data can conceal the effects.

James Ragan used the same sex, race, and age partitions as Kaitz, as well as the same minimum wage variable, but began with 1963, the year when students were first distinguished in the data. Ragan found more precise estimates than Kaitz: higher minimums reduced employment for males in each of eight groups (sixteen and seventeen or eighteen and nineteen years of age, black or white, student or nonstudent)—and in five of the eight by statistically significant amounts. As with the Hashimoto-Mincer results, the bulk of the evidence showed that both employment and labor force participation fall as the minimum wage rate increases.

In his recent study, Edward Gramlich of Brookings found that, between 1948 and 1975, minimum wages had no significant effect on the total number of teenagers employed; but when full- and part-time workers were distinguished (from 1963 on, when separate data are available), he found reductions in full-time work with partially offsetting increases in part-time work. Since part-time workers can earn less than full-time workers, and since the effect of minimum wage rates should be greater in lower-wage sectors, this result may seem perverse.

None of these studies took cognizance of state minimum wage laws, only Gramlich distinguished full- from part-time work, and only Ragan distinguished students. In a study that considered coverage of both state and federal laws and that adjusted for reduced student work hours (students work only slightly more than half as many hours as nonstudents), James Cunningham and I found dramatic effects from minimum wage laws. This study used a larger sample from the 1970 census to distinguish teenage employment by age groups: fourteen and fifteen, sixteen and seventeen, and eighteen and nineteen. We measured the estimated effect of the minimum wage on the costs of hiring eighteen- and nineteen-year-olds. This effect was greatest in states where wages were low, where federal coverage was high, and where state extensions covered many workers at high minimums.

We found that, for an increase in the minimum that raised the costs of hiring eighteen- and nineteen-year-olds by 1 percent, the employment of this group fell by 1.3 percent, while employment of sixteen- and seventeen-year-olds fell by 2.4 percent, and employment of fourteen- and fifteen-year-olds fell by 4 percent. The larger responses for younger workers came from the fact that, without the minimum wage rate, their wages would have been lower than those of the others. Given our estimate that by spring 1970 wage minimums had on the average increased the costs of hiring eighteen- and nineteen-year-olds by 11.3 percent over what those costs would otherwise have been, the inference is that the employment of eighteen- and nineteen-year-olds had been reduced by 15.2 percent as a result of wage minimums, that of sixteen- and seventeen-year-olds by 26.9 percent, and that of fourteen- and fifteen-year-olds by 45.6 percent. These estimates should be viewed as conjectural because of the much smaller effects found in time series studies.

Minimum Wages and Business Cycles

Aggregate U.S. employment steers an unsteady course as the currents of business activity fluctuate and the impact of fluctuating labor demand is felt unevenly among different industries and workers. With some workers more marginal to the work force than others, the figures react as though firms divided laborers into a hard-core and a marginal group. When conditions are steady, both groups are employed and form some sort of normal composite. When demand booms, firms expand first by relying disproportionately on marginal workers and then by gradually enlarging the long-term base as the boom appears to provide a firmer footing for longer-term commitments. When demand busts, marginal workers are the first to go.

Since the minimum wage provides a floor below which wages cannot fall, it contributes to the way workers are distributed between the normal and transitory work forces. There are other reasons for expecting firms to depend more than proportionately on less-skilled workers to absorb the brunt of cyclical variations. But, regardless of what these effects would otherwise be, wage floors destabilize employment of those whose productivity fluctuates about the minimum.

Marvin Kosters and I, in a 1972 study, estimated the effects of the minimum wage on the age, race, and sex composition of aggregate employment during cyclical changes (using quarterly data). Our estimates showed that for the 1954–68 period teenagers constituted, on average, about 6.3 percent of normal employment and 22.1 percent of transitional employment. White adult males were found to be generally more immune to the cycle than any of the other groups considered, and teenagers peculiarly vulnerable: between 1954 and 1968 a teenager was more than four times as likely as an adult to lose his or her job in a cyclical downturn.

We also estimated how minimum wages affected employment over business cycles, stating our results in terms of the minimum wage's effect on an index of "marginality" (or vulnerability to cycles). For example, we estimated that a hike of 1 percent in the minimum reduced the vulnerability of white adult males by 1.5 percent—that is, further insulated them from cyclical variations. Larger effects in the opposite direction were found for teenagers—that is, a minimum wage increase heightened their vulnerability to the cycle.

How important are these estimated effects? Because of expanded coverage, the effective minimum wage rate increased greatly between 1954 and 1968. If the average effective minimum that existed in the years 1954–58 were raised in one step to the average for the 1965–68 period, our estimate is that cyclical vulnerability would have been a third lower for white adult males and more than double for teenagers. Clearly, teenagers have been especially vulnerable to business cycles, and our findings suggested that no small amount of this vulnerability has been the result of minimum wages.

Some Policy Implications

The most obvious result of the interaction between business cycles and wage minimums is the increase in job losses during recessions. In an unsteady world, minimum wage laws have raised the real costs of economic fluctuations. Because hourly minimums are set in nominal terms rather than being indexed to the general price level, inflation reduces their adverse effects on employment; consequently, a lowering in the rate of inflation makes those adverse effects stronger than they would otherwise have been. For example, recall the index presented in Table 1 (column 5), in which the projected minimum wage impact reaches an unprecedented 181 in the year 1981. Should the rate of inflation be reduced by one percentage point a year between now and then, that number would rise to 192.

Economists have used teenagers to study the effects of minimum wages simply because, in the available data for broadly defined demographic classes, teenagers have a higher propotion of low-wage workers than other groups. The bulk of the evidence is that teenage employment has been partly shifted into uncovered sectors—as coverage expansion has been gradually shrinking those sectors and thereby diminishing these secondary opportunities. In covered sectors, teen employment has fallen overall and what has remained has become more vulnerable to business cycles. But in considering the measured effect of minimum wages on teenagers, remember that it *understates* the effect on low-wage workers in general. This is true because some teenagers would earn more than the minimum in any case and because the measured effect for *all* teenagers combines job losses for those with the lowest wage potential with partially offsetting gains for those of greater potential.

As the evidence of adverse effects on teenagers has accrued, support for youth differentials—lower wage minimums for teenagers—has grown. A number of European countries have adopted such programs, as have some U.S. states, and the 1977 minimum wage amendment calls for detailed consideration of a youth differential by a recently established federal commission.

There is, of course, a possibility that enacting a youth differential could have value as a demonstration. We would expect it to show that lower minimums increase employment, just as the lack of a youth differential has had the cruel advantage of making teenagers a good subject for study—guinea pigs for research on the employment effects of minimum wages. If it had not been for this research, the evidence for teenagers would not be available, and there is a real question whether the basic minimum would now be higher than it is.

In addition, if we had a nationwide youth differential, we would be forced to ask about those just above the age break, and we would be forced to ask about those near or past normal retirement who seek supplementary income through part-time work and who would earn wages close to those of teenagers. With a full-fledged "two-tiered" minimum they would have the worse of two worlds. First, they would have to convince employers they were worth the higher minimum and, second, they would have to compete with youths who, because of the differential, could accept lower wages. Should we not then consider differentials for young adults, the aged, the less schooled, and so forth? We have enacted temporary differentials for a limited number of students and for handicapped workers, which is an acknowledgment that lower wages are necessary to give them a competitive edge. The logic for extending these differentials is inexorable. Why not extend a differential to all who would earn less than the minimum? In other words, why have a minimum wage at all?

Against the fact that a youth differential would increase teen employment must be weighed the undesirable side effects on the other low-wage groups. Advocates of youth differentials must have mixed feelings. I do believe, however, that one can make a less ambiguous case for regional differentials than for age differentials. Wages vary among states, and some areas have much higher percentages of low-wage workers than others. In the Welch-Cunningham study, we estimated that a uniform federal minimum had raised costs of employing teenagers by more than twice as much in Arkansas as in Illinois and New Jersey.

Although I have dwelt on the evidence that teenagers are adversely affected by minimum wage rates, the effects are not limited to them. They may be more affected than other specific classes or categories of workers, but the low-wage low-productivity population is widely dispersed and hard to separate into classes or categories. Because of this, remedial measures (like youth differentials) that are aimed at specific classes or categories of workers may not reach most of those affected. And when they do reach one specific group, it is likely that they will exacerbate the plight of others.

In comparison with welfare-related programs that transfer income from the "haves" to the "have-nots," minimum wage laws are perverse: the transfer they make is actually from some have-nots to other have-nots. Of course this country has added (and will continue to add) welfare programs that partially compensate minimum wage losers, spreading the losses more broadly across the population. Perhaps this is as it should be, but let us bear in mind the nature of this transaction. We first impose a law that results in job losses. Then, for those who lose their jobs and qualify for welfare, we give partial compensation. Is it not strange that at a time when a major concern of welfare programs is to increase work incentives we also push a minimum wage program that reduces work?

The establishment of a minimum wage rate was one of our earliest forays into a national welfare program. It was a misguided idea even in 1938, and the world of welfare has changed since then. After forty years of evidence of adverse effects, it would seem that the time for requiring minimum wage rates has passed.

Selected References

Edward M. Gramlich, "Impact of Minimum Wages on Other Wages, Employment, and Family Incomes," in *Brookings Papers on Economic Activity*, 2/1976, pp. 409–451.

Masanori Hashimoto and Jacob Mincer, "Employment and Unemployment Effects of Minimum Wages" (Washington, D.C.: NBER, 1970), mimeo.

Hyman Kaitz, "Experience of the Past: The National Minimum," in Bureau of Labor Statistics, *Youth Unemployment and Minimum Wages*, Bulletin no. 1657 (Washington, D.C.: BLS, 1970).

Marvin Kosters and Finis Welch, "The Effects of Minimum Wages on the Distribution of Changes in Aggregate Employment," in *American Economic Review*, vol. 62 (June 1972), pp. 323–332.

Jacob Mincer, "Unemployment Effects at Minimum Wages," in *Journal of Political Economy*, vol. 84 (August 1976), pp. S87–S104.

James Ragan, "Minimum Wages and the Youth Labor Market," in *Review of Economics and Statistics*, vol. 59 (May 1977), pp. 129–136.

Finis Welch, "Minimum Wage Legislation in the United States," in *Economic Inquiry*, vol. 12 (September 1974), pp. 285–318 and "Reply" in vol. 15 (January 1977), pp. 139–142.

Finis Welch and James Cunningham, "Effects of Minimum Wages on the Level and Age Composition of Youth Employment," in *Review of Economics and Statistics*, vol. 60 (February 1978), pp. 140–145.

Part Ten

Economics was once known as political economy. This name for the subject was more than just a pair of words. It carried with it the implication that the highest aim of those who thought and wrote on political economy was to guide the ship of state along the routes of wisdom. Thus the force of the expression political economy is analysis in the service of policy. For two centuries economists have offered their advice to statesmen who, it must be admitted, have not always followed the advice.

Economics has played still another role in government. For many decades, economists in this and in other countries have participated in the details of the administration of the affairs of governments. Economists have worked on tax systems and tax reforms; they have devised new monetary structures and have helped put them in operation; economists have served as advisers on tariff negotiations and on the settlement of industrial disputes; economists have, in fact, been busy in almost all of the varied activities of governments. Yet in all this, economists have been generally guided more by their knowledge of the facts of specialized fields than by the principles of formal economic analysis. Their suc-

Efficiency in Government

cess as advisers has also depended on their qualities of judgment and on their abilities to see the art of the possible.

Although such work by economists continues to be important, the postwar period has seen formal economic analysis come into use as a way of thinking for improving the efficiency of government. This could have happened before, but it did not. New in the postwar period have been the massive spending of the federal government on applied economic research, the development of and the widespread interest in new and sophisticated techniques of analysis, and the emergence of electronic computers to perform extensive numerical computations. All this has swelled an intense interest in methods of making rational decisions, both in government and in business. Work on the methods has rushed far ahead of their actual use by the men who do, in fact, make decisions. Economists have applied the methods of economic analysis in investigating certain operations of government and in demonstrating how to improve efficiency. The national defense is one great activity of government where applied economic analysis has already contributed to greater economy and efficiency.

55 Every few weeks the newspapers carry another story of the threat of serious water shortages for the whole nation in the not distant future. Predictions of water shortages come from comparisons of the rapidly growing "need" for water with the smaller additional amounts of it that will probably become available. Economists point out, however, that proper pricing policies can prevent shortages. If the demand for water grows, higher prices can allocate the amounts available among users, each of whom can make his own decisions on how much to use.

This selection is a condensation of the first and last chapters of a careful study of the economics, the technology, the law, and the public policy problems of water supply in the United States. The authors are skeptical of the prospects of getting the salt out of sea water at low cost. Their third to last paragraph here might cause some readers to pucker their faces.

THE WATER PROBLEM

JACK HIRSHLEIFER
JAMES C. DEHAVEN
JEROME W. MILLIMAN
The RAND Corporation

It is a commonplace to hear today that the supply of water for households, agriculture, and industry in the United States is a real and growing problem. In one area or another, even in the relatively humid East, it has become periodically necessary to place restrictions upon the use of water. In dry years, reservoirs of some of our largest cities have fallen to dangerously low levels, and over large areas of the nation declining groundwater levels are threatening the structure of local economies based upon water from underground sources. To avert or remedy such conditions, enormously expensive projects have been built or are under consideration for the near future.

Evidently, then, water is a problem which should concern all intelligent citizens. Or should it? Consider a famous example often cited in economic textbooks: the problem of supplying food to the people of New York City. At first glance, it would appear that here is a problem of truly appalling difficulty. Months if not years in advance of consumption, arrangements must be made to place under cultivation a myriad of items, including potatoes in Idaho, watermelons in California, and bananas in Panama, and to

Taken, adapted, and reprinted from *Water Supply: Economics, Technology, and Policy* by Jack Hirshleifer, James C. DeHaven, and Jerome W. Milliman, by permission of The University of Chicago Press, 1960, pp. 1–6, 357–363, 366, 367. Reproduced by special permission of the RAND Corporation.

transport the harvested products at the right time and in the right carriers to the city, where the actual inventories of food supplies might not last a week if replenishment were not forthcoming. And yet, amazingly when one thinks of it, here is a problem which is solved without anyone's devoting any particular thought to it! It is solved, that is, by the decisions of thousands of private individuals typically pursuing each his own private advantage, though subject to a variety of general laws and specific regulations of government.

Food is no less essential than water. Why, then, does New York City have a recurrent water problem but no particular food problem? Or is the water problem simply an illusion, a creation of alarmist publicity? We shall show, indeed, that in some respects it is a false problem—a confusion of thought. Once this confusion is eliminated, we shall see that an important question concerning the wise utilization of water resources does remain. This remaining problem cannot be examined in its true light, however, until we have exorcised the specter, sometimes raised, of our civilization's collapsing for lack of water unless this or that grandiose scheme is adopted.

More Water Available—at a Price

During the last forty years, precipitation over the United States has averaged 30 inches, or a total of 1,564,800 billion gallons per year. According to a recent estimate, water utilization (as of 1955) in the United States for irrigation, industrial, public, and other supplies was at the rate of 87,600 billion gallons per year, a gross utilization of about 5.6 per cent of annual precipitation. In addition, of course, a large quantity of water has been stored up by nature and, to some extent, by man in surface and underground reservoirs. The gross quantity available is, however, not ideally distributed in time and space, and, in addition, much is unavoidably lost. After deducting the loss of water through evaporation from beneficial and nonbeneficial vegetation and from the soil, present gross utilization comprises 20 per cent of the recurring precipitation. For regions less endowed with water, the ratio is substantially higher.

Since, evidently, the gross rate of use of water is steadily rising while precipitation is not, it might appear that we do have, at least on the long view, cause here for real concern. Thus, improperly applying a type of reasoning often employed in engineering problems, one might think: "100 per cent efficiency is not attainable. In fact, frequently one is doing very well to get as high as 50 per cent efficiency, and here we are already at 20 per cent efficiency of utilization nationwide, even higher in some regions. How, then, are we going to meet the increasing demand?" The first point in answer to this chain of argument is that, since the figures in question refer to gross utilization of precipitation, there is no reason why "efficiency" in this sense cannot rise to 110, 200, or 10,000 per cent, even without drawing on the stored water from past ages. Today, even before gross utilization is anywhere near 100 per cent of precipitation, it is already economical to engage in multiple reuse of water supplies. This takes many forms: water in a river may rush through a turbine at a dam, then be diverted to a factory for cooling purposes, returning to the river somewhat warmer than before; it may then enter a public water supply, be used domestically, be returned to the ground via septic tank, and be pumped up hundreds of miles away for irrigation purposes, at which point it might end the ground phase of the hydrologic cycle by evaporating into the atmosphere from a growing plant. Clearly, this process may be expanded, if required, so that every bit of water is made to serve a multiplicity of purposes in the available ground phase of the cycle. The 20 per cent gross utilization figure implies an upper limit upon possible use of existing supplies where no such limit exists.

This point alone suffices to answer many of the arguments often heard about the urgency of the water problem. It is still not the most fundamental point, however. Suppose that, in fact, there were some absolute limit on the total use of water. Even then the "efficiency" of utilization of water supplies could always be increased as demand rises, since more highly valued uses could bid away some of the water from less highly valued uses. Under such circumstances, as pressure of demand upon water supplies increased, the price of water would rise. Water uses which cannot bear the burden of the higher costs would be forced to give up their supplies to those more intensely demanded uses which can. Thus, even should the amount of water available to society as a whole be fixed, the amount available to any given use or user could be increased—at a price.

Water Shortages

What, then, is a water shortage? Certainly, the people of New York City did suffer in the fall of 1949, when lawn-sprinkling and car-washing were forbidden and bathless days gained social acceptance. And, in some smaller communities throughout the country, local interruptions of supply occur which cause inconvenience or even harm. In ordinary parlance, the word "shortage" is sometimes used to indicate absolute stringency of supply ("Water is short in the Sahara Desert") or sometimes any reduction of the supply to which people have been accustomed ("Rainfall is unusually light this year, so water will be short"). For our purposes, however, it will be instructive to use the term somewhat differently.

The reader is invited to cast his mind back to the great "meat shortage" of 1946. Here was a case where the current rate of meat consumption was by all previous standards quite high, yet for the individual housewife meat was always hard to find in the shops. The reason was that a larger quantity of meat was demanded by consumers than producers cared to supply at the then-effective controlled OPA prices. After the removal of controls, meat prices rose sharply, inducing or compelling housewives to shift part of their effective demand to other commodities or to save their money instead, so the quantity of meat demanded in the markets fell until it balanced the supply. On the supply side, the high prices made it unprofitable to hold back cattle from the market and also encouraged an expansion of production which improved the supply situation in following years. This type of "shortage" is neither absolute stringency nor a fall in supply, but rather a situation in which more of a commodity is demanded in the market than is being supplied *at the going price.*

This definition brings to mind an obvious remedy for such shortages—raise the price! And, indeed, it will be shown that this is a solution which will frequently be the most advantageous possible. There are other possibly desirable solutions, however. The limited quantity available may be rationed by coupon or by informal arrangement of the seller, or the supply available may be increased by various government devices, including subsidies to producers. The demand may also be reduced by voluntary co-operation or by legal restrictions on quantities or types of permissible use. Our main point here is to indicate that this type of "economic water shortage" has a relatively simple cause and cure. When we say that the cure is simple, we mean that, from the economic point of view, it is easy to understand and that it could be carried out without great expenditure; from the political point of view, however, there may be most serious difficulties.

By way of contrast, absolute stringency is much harder to overcome. If water is very scarce in a region and cannot even be transported there without enormous cost, the region will simply not support much human habitation unless, indeed, the product yielded there by human effort is sufficiently valuable to yield a surplus over the cost of transporting water there. (It is also possible, of course, that on some extra-economic ground human habitation in such a region will be subsidized by an outside group.) As for a "shortage" in the sense of a fall in supplies as compared with past historical periods, if there is a real permanent decrease in supply (as when overdraft on an underground aquifer gradually reduces the quantity available to draw upon), the community must adjust to higher water costs or to reduced utilization—unless technological advance lowers costs or a source of subsidy can be found. Or, if it is a temporary or cyclical reduction in supply, the community must decide if it wishes to bear the burden of the reduction or alternatively, to pay the cost of providing enough storage to even out such supply fluctuations.

The Alleged "Unique Importance" of Water

Much nonsense has been written on the unique importance of water supply to the nation or to particular regions. Granted that the nation, or any individual thereof, could not survive without water, that does not show uniqueness. No human can survive without food, without oxygen, and without a variety of other supporting environmental conditions, many not even fully known today. Nor could an individual survive very well, at least in the northern part of our country, without clothing, yet somehow we do not have frequent conferences and symposiums of public-spirited bodies on "the clothing problem."

This is not to deny that, as a commodity, water has its special features; for example, its supply is provided by nature partly as a store and partly as a flow, and it is available without cost in some locations but rather expensive to transport to others. Whatever reason we cite, however, the alleged unique *importance* of water disappears upon analysis.

Public Concern in Water Problems

Is there, then, any real water problem at all? Perhaps, if left alone, it might solve itself, like the food problem for New York City, without any need for the average citizen to worry about it. Unfortunately, this is not the case. The first reason is that private enterprise has in the past and will presumably in the future have only a limited role to play in water supply. The public agencies dominating the water-supply field are therefore not subjected to those checks of competition which we ordinarily count on to penalize inefficiency and restrain uneconomic practices in the production and supply of most commodities. The citizen should therefore be concerned as to the functioning of the process of supply and distribution of water by public agencies. In fact, even where water supply is provided privately, the nature of the industry is such that a "natural monopoly" usually exists—it is as inefficient to have competing water-supply systems as to have competing telephone systems. In the presence of these natural monopolies, competition cannot provide protection for the consumer under unrestricted private enterprise, and for this reason private firms supplying commodities under these conditions are generally publicly regulated.

Another fundamental reason for public concern in the field of water resources is the fact that the pervasive interdependence of water uses makes it impracticable or undesirable—or at least such has been the traditional thought—to extend conventional property rights to this field. Thus, if I own land, I can generally use it as I see fit. But, if a river flows across my land, I cannot generally use the stream without consideration for the rights of downstream property-owners. Similarly, since the beginning of our nation, navigable streams have been under the control of the federal government and could not become private property.

We may conclude by mentioning briefly two other commonly cited reasons for public interest in water problems. The first is that the best use of the nation's water resources seems, at times, to require projects of such enormous cost that only governments can amass the huge quantities of capital required. There may be something in this, but we do not believe it deserves much emphasis; the business corporation is a very efficient device for amassing large quantities of private capital wherever the returns seem sufficiently promising. Of rather more weight is the consideration that it may be impracticable to charge the beneficiaries of the development of water resources in any adequate way; to the extent that this is the case, private enterprise might require government subsidy in any event.

Finally, another justification frequently given for government intervention in this field is the need to develop resources in one particular region, where the reason given for doing so is outside the scope of market calculations—for example, to mitigate poverty in the Tennessee Valley or to populate the West. Generally speaking, these are more or less disguised pleas for special subsidies, which must be examined individually on their merits. We need only point out here that the process of development is not costless, and subsidized development of one region will (in the absence of general depression) absorb resources which could have been used to maintain or develop, without subsidy, the productivity of another.

Some Controversial Conclusions and their Implications

Water-supply problems should and will receive increasing attention in the future because water is becoming relatively less abundant in comparison with other resources. It is in transition from an almost free good in the humid areas (or a very cheap good in the most arid) to a more expensive commodity. Consequently, competition among uses and users is becoming more intense. In addition, the costs are increasing in terms of other resources and services foregone to obtain additional supplies of water. The absolute magnitudes of the investments required to obtain these increased supplies are also of substantial importance in respect to the total wealth both of the nation and of local regions proposing these supply increments.

Economic Efficiency and Welfare

The correct application of economic principles will produce the greatest efficiency in water-supply procurement and utilization *in relation to, and in competition with, all the other desires of the community.* Perhaps we have not stressed strongly enough the implication of economically efficient decisions for the long-term welfare of the local areas involved and for the nation as a whole. Critics of economic analysis may have partially succeeded in creating the impression that economic criteria for decision-making are abstruse theoretical postulates invented and circulated only by academic professional economists or, at best, that economic analysis is suitable only for application to idealized situations that have little relation to the real world.

Some cynics plausibly argue, for example, that the United States is a wealthy nation and can well afford the luxury of overinvesting in waterworks. The construction of huge dams and lengthy aqueducts to make the desert bloom even as the rose might then be an example of a "monument syndrome." The people like to see these constructed as demonstrations of our engineering skills and national wealth. They vote for politicians who push the construction of these works, thereby demonstrating their tastes and preferences in this regard. These preferences may therefore be considered a mark of the citizen-voters' non-pecuniary valuation of these works.

There are several important things wrong with this argument. In the first place, such works are not presented to the voters for consideration as national or regional monuments. Rather, they are promoted as financially attractive and necessary investments to increase the wealth and development of the nation or of local regions. The voters are therefore misinformed about the issues on which they express their preference, so that their choices are no firm indications of non-pecuniary values. Second, as we have pointed out, the political decision process for allocation of resources is highly imperfect, so that even if voters were perfectly informed the actual choices made may, for example, be influenced by such factors as a coalition of minorities against the general interest ("logrolling").

Overinvestment and Pricing Decisions

Perhaps our most controversial substantive conclusion justified by a wide variety of evidence from our separate case studies and from our survey of federal and local experience in water-supply decisions, is that in this country major water investments are typically undertaken prematurely and on an overambitious scale. Consequently, at any given time there exists overinvestment in water supply.

Overinvestment for any particular area is indicated when facilities stand idle or else are put to makeshift uses, either to avoid the appearance of idleness or to minimize the losses due to past mistakes. Or uneconomic overinvestment may be indicated not by idle facilities but by relatively low return earned on capital invested in water supply. Here the water is actually being put to use, but the price charged is so low that the revenue to the water enterprise is small in relation to cost. There is overinvestment because the same capital investment could have been put to work producing goods and commodities valued more highly on the margin by consumers; consumers' marginal values in use for water are low in comparison with what could have been obtained had the dollars been spent elsewhere. Specifically, our two major area studies both revealed the highly premature nature of the decision to build the Cannonsville Project in the one case and the proposal for construction of the Feather River Project in the other. Or, looking at return to capital, we have seen that, for public water-supply systems in general, this is of the order of 2 per cent—an astonishingly low figure.

Our own emphasis throughout has been upon errors of fact or of reasoning which have played a role in bringing about the pattern of overinvestment. Perhaps the most important of these might be simple oversight: that when the total of water use begins to approach system capacity, administrators simply do not think of attempting to make better use of existing supplies as an alternative to initiating new construction. The possibility of adjusting prices does not often occur to those responsible, even though studies have shown that demand is responsive to price and that the widely divergent price levels and price structures existing in different cities suggest that a schedule presently in effect in a particular city is not necessarily the only one possible or even the best available in the circumstances. Of course, rationing water use by raising prices across the board, or by eliminating discrimination benefiting certain classes of use, has its cost, but it is a cost which should be properly analyzed against the alternative of new construction.

Equally ignored, at times, are possibilities for avoiding or deferring expensive new construction by taking better care of existing supplies or by seeking out possibly unconventional but cheaper sources. Thus we have seen in the New York case that the major construction decision ignored the promise of the extremely large saving that could be made simply by detecting and correcting leaks in the city's own distribution system. And, in California, the responsible authorities have shown little interest in such technological possibilities as evaporation control on reservoirs or in economic solutions involving reallocation of water from agricultural uses as urban demand rises.

The typical pattern of overinvestment is related in various ways to our argument that water prices are too low. What we mean by this latter statement is that raising prices will in general be the major alternative to building new water supplies; in that sense we have clearly overbuilt and correspondingly underpriced, so as to receive inadequate return on capital invested in water-supply developments. On the other hand, once a water-supply system finds itself in an overbuilt situation, it *will* typically be justifiable to charge quite a low price rather than have the installation lie idle (i.e., marginal costs are quite low for dam-aqueduct systems operating well below capacity). Thus the Metropolitan Water District of Southern California—given the initial error of premature construction—was correct in charging prices far below average cost. And in New York City, once Cannonsville begins to operate, it will probably be justifiable to reduce water prices (to those consumers who are metered) rather than have that enormous capacity lie idle.

Our second important conclusion about prices concerns the importance of the peak-load problem in the case of water supply. The cost of special metering is such, however, that very elaborate schemes of differential peak and slack prices are not justified. Introduction of a peak-*season* price (in the summer, normally), on the other hand, will not require any special metering and seems clearly indicated as an alternative to expensive new construction when it is only the peak-season loads that press on system capacity.

Centralized or Decentralized Water-Supply Decisions?

The authors have a certain "old-fashioned" sympathy with the principle of decentralization of authority in respect to economic decisions in general and to water-supply decisions in particular. Other things being equal, we prefer local to state authority, state to federal—and private decision-making (the extreme of decentralization) to any of these. Our fundamental reason for this preference is the belief that the cause of human liberty is best served by a minimum of government compulsion and that, if compulsion is necessary, local and decentralized authority is more acceptable than dictation from a remote centralized source of power. This is an "extramarket value" for which we at least would be willing to make some sacrifices in terms of loss of economic efficiency. Despite all this, we have tried to leave this consideration out of our basic analysis, which assumes neutrality on the question of the proper locus of decision except insofar as questions of economic efficiency are involved. Even on grounds of efficiency, however, we have some faith that the more nearly the costs and benefits of water projects are brought home to those who make the decisions, the more correct those decisions are likely to be—a consideration which argues for decentralization in practice.

The interrelated nature of water-supply decisions ideally requires, on grounds of economic efficiency, some departure from complete laissez-faire. There is in principle an argument for centralized regulation whenever private and social benefits or costs diverge ("technological spillover effects" of private decisions exist), and they do to an important extent in water-supply decisions; for example, pollution of a stream by its use for waste disposal may cause great loss to downstream users. In the common-pool situation we have shown that unregulated pumping will lead to excessive withdrawals in terms of the net social balance of benefits and costs, so that there is a prima facie case for government intervention to remedy this deficiency. We cannot leave the subject without noting, however, that the record of governmental intervention in the resource field does not demonstrate that it will actually improve matters over the admittedly inefficient unregulated result. To cite only one instance, the sound argument for intervention in the common-pool situation has been used, in the case of petroleum, as an excuse to form state-directed cartels designed to restrict output and raise prices to consumers. We do have hope, however, that, with a clearer understanding of the justifications for and the desirable limitations upon governmental intervention and control in the sphere of water supply, the record of regulation in the future may be better than in the past.

One reason often given why water projects must be planned and constructed by state or federal governments instead of by local or private agencies is that the costs are now too great for the local or private agencies to bear. However, the private corporation has proved to be an efficient institution for the accumulation of large amounts of capital for investment in productive development of natural resources—witness the utility corporations, pipelines, television, and other instances too numerous to mention. The relative magnitude of the cost of the next increment of water supply is certainly no greater now in comparison with the total resources of local regions and cities than it was years ago when the then small city of Los Angeles built the aqueduct to Owens Valley, or when New York reached to the Catskills, or when the Metropolitan Water District of Southern California was organized on a regional basis to tap the distant Colorado River. The large investment barrier to local development is a bogy often raised by those who hope to secure taxpayers' contributions to defray at least some of the costs of providing water. Or, to put it another way, costs do seem high in relation to resources when what is under consideration is an uneconomic project.

It is, nevertheless, possible to plan for, construct, and operate water projects at the central state or federal level in an efficient manner—and, whatever the locus of decision, we think that it is desirable to achieve economic efficiency. Our extensive discussion of principles of project analysis is most applicable, in fact, to the decisions of centralized decision-making agencies, since the market will tend to regulate the projects of private agencies. The economic principles we have presented are generally independent of the agency by which they are to be applied—private individuals or local, regional, or national bodies. If properly evaluated, the same alternative water project would be chosen as best by local individuals (if the rules protect against spillover effects) or by a central decision-making group. The chief analytical problem for centralized decisions is the difficulty of securing the relevant information at a level remote from the actual effects of the project in question and where the costs are to be borne by others than those to whom the benefits accrue. The crucial defect of private and local decision-making—the spillover effects—we have shown to be at least partly remediable through a more appropriate definition of property rights to coincide with the span of the decisions involved.

Technological Prospects

We have stressed the importance of considering a wide range of technical and economic alternatives in planning for increased water supply if maximum efficiency is to be realized. This is not the usual procedure whether the plans are made at the local, state, or federal level. There is a great tendency to consider dam and aqueduct construction as the only solution for obtaining a net increase in supply. Perhaps this is because civil engineers are usually employed in planning water developments, and aqueduct and dam construction is one of their specialities. Perhaps this narrowness of outlook is a reflection of the "monument syndrome." Commemorative bronze plaques can be prominently displayed on a dam, but not on repaired leaks or on an improved schedule of prices.

The relative costs of all the alternatives should be determined, too. We have attempted to present the most acceptable ways for determining these costs, both by describing the principles involved and by illustrating their use through specific practical examples. Often these costs are difficult to estimate because of uncertainty in the basic information required as inputs. Even so, the discipline of going through the appropriate cost determinations provides insights not otherwise possible. Although the costs so determined may be but rough first approximations, they can provide a better basis for decision-making than "hunches" or generalized rules of thumb. The increased use of meters may or may not be a better alternative than a new imported supply, etc., depending upon each local situation and time.

Aside from the historical tendency to overemphasize long-distance importation as the source of increased water supply, we believe that among other technical alternatives the possibilities for sea-water conversion are overblown. There should be no objection to a modest research and development program exploring the potentialities of producing fresh water from the sea. However, nothing so far in the laboratory gives any indication of promising a source of supply by conversion for municipal, and certainly not for irrigation, use at costs that approach those of many other technical and economic alternatives. Sea-water conversion processes are handicapped by high capital costs or by high power costs, or both. None of the presently conceived processes is likely to be chosen as a source of water in any significant amount for any purpose within the United States for many years to come—if the users must pay the costs of the water produced. Of course, there is always the possibility that installations will be subsidized by the government.

In contrast, we feel more optimistic about the future costs and returns of some of the possibilities for water-conservation techniques. Monomolecular film control of evaporation is progressing rapidly and will probably be widely used to produce the next increments of supply, especially in the more arid regions. The elimination of non-beneficial vegetation growing in and surrounding reservoirs, along streams, and on watersheds also holds promise for reducing the large water losses attributable to transpiration. Seepage losses from reservoirs and transmission canals appear to be large. At present, only expensive lining techniques are available to reduce these losses. Little research appears to be directed toward studying inexpensive soil treatments to reduce seepage, especially in reservoirs, but it seems possible that such treatments could be developed. The creation of artificial aquifers for storage purposes, as in the Netherlands, is an especially interesting development in additional entrapment and storage of runoff water for areas near the sea.

The most interesting technological possibility not now being utilized is purposeful reclamation of sewage water. We use the word "purposeful" because reclamation is effectively occurring today in many river supply systems where one city's water intake may be a little below another city's sewage outfall. And, in rural areas, there ordinarily is hydrologic connection between wells and septic tanks. Despite the prevalence of unintended reclamation, and despite the favorable costs of such supplies (a reclamation plant will cost little more than the sewage-treatment plants often required anyway), we are inclined to be conservative here. At least until the mechanism of propagation of virus disease is better understood, we believe it to be a wise precaution to prevent direct human consumption of such supplies unless arrangements can be made to pass the water some distance through the ground before being used. Nevertheless we feel safe in asserting that sewage reclamation is an important source of supply for the future, as expanding population and industry compete more and more avidly for the limited supply of suitable natural water.

The "Water-Is-Different" Philosophy

We cannot close without mentioning once again that peculiar, metaphysical line of reasoning which seems to pervade public thinking about water: the "water-is-different" or the "magic-of-water" philosophy. Even businessmen, engineers, and lawyers who are familiar with water supply often demonstrate this quirk. We frequently hear or read of their saying things like "We must not allow the waste of a single drop of our precious water to the sea" or "It is proper that a wasting resource, petroleum, pay for the renewal of a renewable resource, water." In the context in which such statements are made they can sound convincing—as though the speaker were firmly against sin. The reader of this book will, of course, immediately recognize the implications of such statements. The first says that, on the margin, water is more valuable than any combination of other resources necessary to recover it. The second implies that it is proper for users of petroleum products, primarily motorists and electric-power consumers, to subsidize water-users, primarily irrigation agriculture.

This attitude might be only amusing if it did not lead to some political actions having very serious implications; in particular, it has led to the near-universal view that private ownership is unseemly or dangerous for a type of property so uniquely the common concern of all.

56 During the 1960's cost-benefit, or cost-effectiveness, studies became the vogue in many agencies of the federal government. In fact, in 1965 the White House ordered governmental units to conduct such studies. But they have many pitfalls. Professor Dunn analyzes one of these, in pointing to the difficulties of using market prices as measures of the real social cost of resources in a fully employed economy.

A PROBLEM OF BIAS IN BENEFIT-COST ANALYSIS: CONSUMER SURPLUS RECONSIDERED

ROBERT M. DUNN, JR.
The George Washington University

One of the major problems of the application of economics to public policy has been the development of an objective criterion for the allocation of scarce resources between the private and public sectors, that is, for deciding whether or not particular government projects are in the public interest. Benefit-cost accounting is an apparently simple and straightforward answer to this problem. Assuming that a project's costs are largely current, as in a public works proposal, and that the benefits flow through time, the benefits are discounted by a market rate of interest, a present value is reached for aggregate returns, and a ratio of these benefits to costs is estimated. If this ratio exceeds unity, benefits exceed costs and the project is to be undertaken. The intent of this system is to compare the value produced by using scarce resources in a public project with the value which those resources would produce in any alternative private use, on the assumption that their cost represents this latter value. This paper* will argue that this assumption is incorrect, and that the current market value of the resources to be used in a project may not be an accurate measure of their cost to society.

The accepted version of benefit-cost analysis accepts the benefits of a project with negligible marginal cost as being the total area under an imagined demand line. "To ascertain whether a navigation system should be

* The author would like to acknowledge the helpful comments of L. G. Hines and G. L. McDowell who read earlier drafts of the paper.

Taken and adapted from Robert M. Dunn, Jr., "A Problem of Bias in Benefit-Cost Anlaysis: Consumer Surplus Reconsidered," *Southern Economic Journal*, Vol. XXXIII, No. 3, January 1967, pp. 337–342.

constructed, it must be shown that the total benefit exceeds total cost. In order to approximate *total revenue that a perfect system of price discrimination could produce*, the benefit accruing for different categories of shippers can be measured by the savings and transportation charges that will be realized to the waterway"[1] (my italics).

"An estimation of the value of collective goods—principally flood protection, within the context of multiple river development—needs to reflect the *sum which beneficiaries would be willing to pay for such protection* if they were given the choice . . . they would be willing to spend no more than the cost that they would be prepared to incur for repairing flood damages and avoiding the consequences associated with flooding. This would indicate the economic value of flood protection"[2] (my italics).

The benefit total for the project is quite rationally the sum of what the individuals would have been *willing* to pay for protection, rather than the price times quantity estimate of what it might have cost in a private market for insurance. The total area under the imagined demand curve is explicitly included. A study by Roland McKean makes the same point in a discussion of public investment in a canal project.

"In accordance with the arguments above, the investment should be regarded as an all-or-none proposition and the benefits should be the sum of the maximum amounts that users would be willing to pay—*discriminatory* amounts"[3] (my italics).

The point of this paper is that the principle that is so wisely applied to measuring benefits is not carried over to the measurement of costs, and hence a bias is created. The usual theory assumes that the opportunity costs of resources are accurately measured by their market prices, an assertion which can be true only if the demand curve for the alternative private output is horizontal.

"The social cost of the capital raised from foregone investment is clear; the investment would have yielded a certain rate of return to the community which would have increased the future flow of national income. The social cost, therefore, is equal to the foregone rate of return on private investment."[4]

The current federal government guide for river basin expenditures also makes this point quite clear.

"When goods and services are utilized for any purpose, the economic effect of that action is to preclude their use for other projects. The economic cost of using goods and services for project purposes is, in effect, the benefits foregone; i.e., the value which would have resulted from alternative

[1] Otto Eckstein, *Water Resource Development* (Cambridge, Mass., Harvard University Press, 1958), p. 30.

[2] J. V. Krutilla, and Otto Eckstein, "Welfare Aspects of Benefit-Cost Analysis," *Journal of Political Economy*, June 1961, p. 73.

[3] Roland McKean, *Efficiency in Government Through Systems Analysis* (New York: John Wiley and Sons, 1958), p. 173.

[4] Krutilla and Eckstein, *op. cit.*, p. 79.

uses. Under the usual conditions of relatively full employment there are other uses for the goods and services used in river basin projects." [5]

Thus far the argument is clearly accurate. This paper's argument is with the sentence which follows the above.

"In such cases, it may be reasonably assumed that the goods and services used for the project purposes are diverted from uses in which their consumptive or productive value would be approximately equal to the prices paid for them." [6]

Although the measurement of benefits from a proposed public project quite rationally includes all of the area under the demand curve which is estimated for its services, the alternative private utilization of these resources is measured as only its cash income. If the private project were to have operated in an imperfect market, it would have faced a sloping demand line and hence would have produced benefits (consumer surplus) in excess of its total revenues.

If the curves in Figure 1 are taken to represent a potential public project, and then an alternative private one, this point becomes apparent.[7]

If the project described by Figure 1 lines were publicly financed, the standard benefit-cost approach would use the total area *AOD* as a measure of its returns, since with marginal cost pricing the price will be zero. Private calculations of return would include only the area *BCEO*, since here pricing is such that marginal cost equals marginal revenue.[8] The triangle *CED* is a benefit which the private firm would produce, and which would be realized by society, but which cannot be included in the firm's calculations because it is not appropriable. To the extent that benefit-cost accounting fails to include this area in its calculations of the opportunity cost of the replaced private investment, a bias is created. In this case a benefit cost ratio is produced for the public project which is well in excess of the true ratio of benefits to costs of the public operation of the project. The true ratio is—area *ADO*:area *BCDO*, while the usual practices suggest—area *ADO*:area *BCEO*. This bias can be avoided, if the private project which is to be replaced is known, by the subtraction of an estimate of its total consumer surplus from the total benefits of the public project before the ratio is constructed. Calculation of the cost part of the ratio on the basis of the returns to a perfectly discriminating monopolist in the alternative private project would accomplish the same purpose.

Thus far it has been implicitly assumed that the public project will re-

[5] Subcommittee on Evaluation Standards, *Proposed Practices for Economic Analysis of River Basin Projects*, Inter-Agency Committee on Water Resources, Washington, D.C., 1958, pp. 8–9.

[6] *Ibid.*, pp. 8–9.

[7] The project is assumed to have a zero marginal cost in order to simplify the graph. The argument is unchanged if a positive marginal cost is assumed, but the diagram is unnecessarily complicated.

[8] The lack of the triangle *ABC* is a reason for making the project public. Marginal cost pricing requires production of *AO* at a zero price, and hence public operation with a subsidy. The average cost curve is defined as including a normal return to invested private capital.

place one private project of equal size. But if the withdrawal of resources from the private sector reduces the size of a number of private projects, through a rise in interest rates and the prices of other inputs (which results in increases in the average and marginal cost curves), the bias is reduced in importance.

FIGURE 1

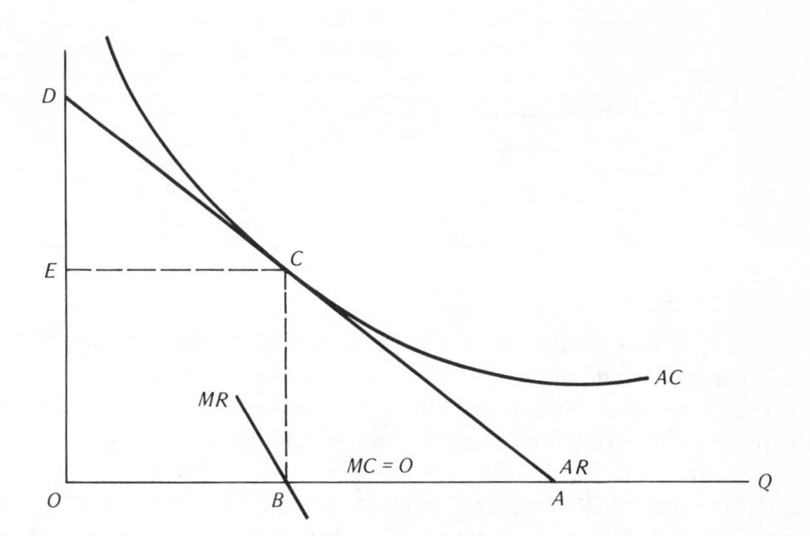

The consumer surplus loss on each private project becomes the small triangle 'a' in Figure 2 and the total loss becomes the sum of the areas of a series of such triangles. This sum is far less than triangle *CED* in Figure 1.[9] If the affected private businesses are in imperfect markets, the bias can be seen to be one half of the total reduction in their output times the average price rise associated with the reduction.[10]

[9] It can be shown by elementary goemetry that if two projects of equal size are equally affected, the bias is reduced by one half. In addition to the bias under discussion, there is a potentially larger one in the form of profits in excess of a normal interest rate. The output foregone in the firm represented in Figure 2 is valued for purposes of benefit cost analysis as the average cost of producing it, that is rectangle *ABCD*. In fact the lost value to society is rectangle *ABEF*, a much larger amount. The bias created by the assumption of no excess profits, which is implicit in benefit cost analysis, is, however, a separate topic and will be left for the present.

[10] If *A* is taken to be the number of private projects equally affected, and *B* to be the output reduction per project, and *C* the average price rise associated with the output reduction for each project, and e the average angle from the horizontal of the demand lines of the affected projects between the point at which they were operating and that at which they finally operate, the bias area, which is the total loss of consumer surplus resulting from the project, is equal to $ABC/2$ which is in turn equal to $AB^2 \tan e/2$. With e, and hence $\tan e$, given, and *AB* constant (the total private output reduction resulting from a public project should not be affected by variation of the number of private firms involved, unless significant economies or diseconomies of scale in the private sector are assumed), the whole expression clearly goes to zero as *A* approaches infinity and *B* zero. There is no bias if an infinite number of firms are infinitesimally affected by the public project. Without the assumption that the output reductions for the private projects are equal, the bias becomes larger and far more complex in definition.

FIGURE 2

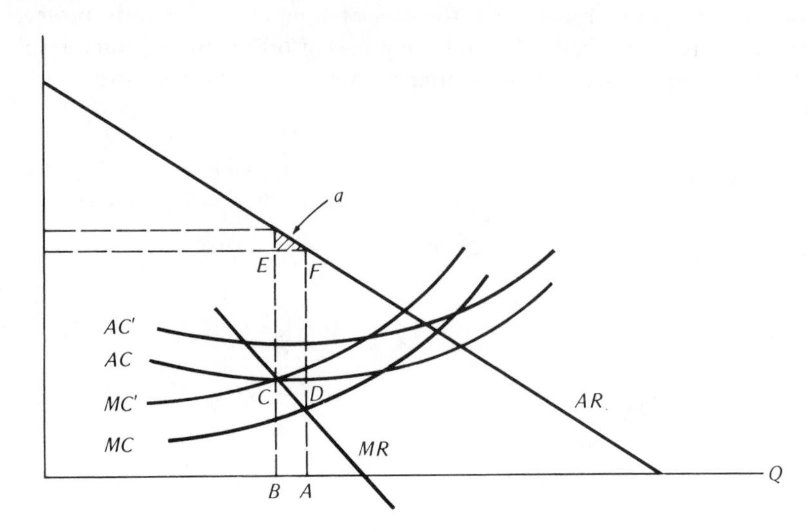

The bias is then directly related to the extent of the imperfections of the private markets and inversely related to the number of projects affected: In the case of an infinite number of businesses infinitesimally affected, the bias disappears with a large number of triangles of no area.

A description of this bias for cases in which the markets for goods using the same inputs as the public project are perfectly competitive is slightly more involved. Superficially it would appear that it disappears because there is no obvious 'consumer surplus' associated with individual firms in such markets. The problem, however, also exists for competitive markets; if the effect of a public project's removal of resources from the private sector is to raise costs facing competitive equilibrium results in higher prices and reduced output.

FIGURE 3

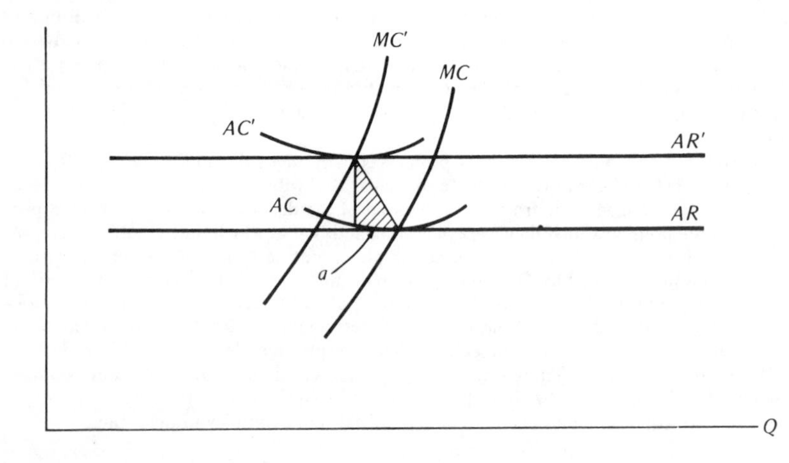

An area of consumer surplus, small triangle 'a' in Figure 3, is lost for each firm in the process. The size of this area obviously depends on the slope of the *industry* demand curve, and the total bias area is again the sum of a series of such triangles, and is inversely related to the number of firms affected. The point of interest here is that benefits to society which are called 'consumer surplus' exist in both monopolistic and competitive industries. The fact that the individual firm in a competitive market faces a horizontal demand curve merely confuses the issue somewhat, since the industry demand schedule is actually more relevant in this case.

One major limitation on this paper's concept of a bias remains, and must be stressed; if the economy in question is so large, and the resources withdrawn from its private sector so widely used, that no significant effect on individual firms occurs, there is no bias. Returning to Figure 2, if an infinite number of firms are infinitesimally affected, the number of triangles 'a' increases, but their total area disappears. As footnote 9 implies, a doubling of the number of projects equally affected reduces the bias by one half. The expression for the bias area in footnote 10 clearly goes to zero as the number of affected businesses approaches infinity and the average reduction of output per firm and increase in price approach zero. This restriction on the original point brings into question its practical importance. It is obviously of little relevance to the American economy. If the United States were fully employed, the withdrawal from the private sector of the resources necessary for one public works project would have a minor effect on the costs facing private investments. The bias problem would be relevant only for consideration of a massive public program, such as a war, during a period of full employment, or a project which used highly specialized resources.

In an underdeveloped country, however, the situation changes; capital and other factor markets are often extremely narrow. Any sizable flotation of bonds is almost certain to have significant effects on interest rates (or merely the availability of capital if non-price rationing exists) and hence on the optimum scale of the relatively small number of private projects currently being financed. Industrial markets in such countries are often narrow and far from perfectly competitive. The demand curve facing a prospective entrant is likely to be far from horizontal, and hence the consumer surplus associated with the beginning, or any major change in the scale, of an industrial firm is significant. The conditions for a serious bias are perfectly met, particularly if markets are further narrowed by high tariffs. The use of the generally-accepted tools of benefit cost analysis in such economies is almost certain to produce serious resource misallocations, in that public projects will be undertaken which actually cost more than they produce.

POSTSCRIPT

In addition to the bias described above as growing out of an aspect of consumer surplus, there are at least two other difficulties in using market factor prices for benefit-cost analysis; a loss of producer surplus occurs in the markets for alternative outputs when factors are withdrawn which is analogous to the loss of consumer surplus discussed above, and a further bias in the same direction results from the difference between factor marginal revenue product and the value of marginal physical product in imperfect output markets. These two additional sources of bias are discussed and mathematically combined with the problem of consumer surplus in "Cost Bias in Benefit-Cost Analysis: A Comment" by W. J. Stober, R. B. Ekelund, Jr., and L. H. Falk in *The Southern Economic Journal* of April 1968. Their conclusions suggest that the total bias in using market prices for inputs is somewhat larger than that attributed to consumer surplus above, and that one portion of this bias (that resulting from the difference between factor marginal revenue product and the value of marginal physical product in imperfect output markets) does not disappear as the number of affected firms approaches infinity.

57 This selection is from a book published in 1960 and addressed mainly to military officers. Many of the methods of analysis recommended here have already been put into practice. Notice how the authors stress optimum allocation as opposed to setting up "requirements" and "priorities." This is analogous to stressing the demand for water as opposed to the need for it.

ECONOMIC ANALYSIS FOR THE NATIONAL DEFENSE

CHARLES J. HITCH
University of California, Berkeley

ROLAND N. McKEAN
The RAND Corporation

The essence of economic choice in military planning is not quantitative analysis: calculation may or may not be necessary or useful, depending upon the problem and what is known about it. The essential thing is the comparison of all the relevant alternatives from the point of view of the objectives each can accomplish and the costs which it involves; and the selection of the best (or a "good") alternative through the use of appropriate economic criteria.

The Elements of an Economic Analysis

The elements of a military problem of economic choice, whether its solution requires advanced mathematics, high-speed computing equipment, or just straight hard thinking are therefore the following:

1. An objective or objectives. What military (or other national) aim or aims are we trying to accomplish with the forces, equipments, projects, or tactics that the analysis is designed to compare? Choice of objectives is fundamental: if it is wrongly made, the whole analysis is addressed to the wrong question.

2. Alternatives. By what alternative forces, equipments, projects, tactics, and so on, may the objective be accomplished? The alternatives are frequently referred to as *systems* because each combines all the elements—men, machines, and the tactics of their employment—needed to accom-

---

Reprinted by permission of the publishers from *The Economics of Defense in the Nuclear Age* by Charles J. Hitch and Roland N. McKean, Cambridge, Mass.: Harvard University Press, 1960, pp. 118–125, 163–167. Reproduced by special permission of The RAND Corporation.

plish the objective. System A may differ from System B in only one respect (for example, in number of bombs per bomber), or in several (number of bombs per bomber, number of strikes, and so on), but both are complete systems, however many elements they have in common. The great problem in choosing alternatives to compare is to be sure that all the good alternatives have been included. Frequently we lack the imagination to do this at the beginning of an analysis; we think of better alternatives (that is, invent new systems) as the analysis proceeds and we learn more about the problem. The invention of new and better systems in this fashion is indeed one of the principal payoffs from this kind of analysis.

3. Costs or resources used. Each alternative method of accomplishing the objective, or in other words each system, involves the incurring of certain costs or the using up of certain resources (these are different phrases to describe the same phenomena). Costs are the negative values in the analysis (as the objectives are positive values). The resources required may be general (as is commonly the case in problems of long-range planning), or highly specific (as in most tactical problems), or mixed.

4. A model or models. Models are abstract representations of reality which help us to perceive significant relations in the real world, to manipulate them, and thereby predict others. They may take any of numerous forms. Some are small-scale physical representations of reality, like model aircraft in a wind tunnel. Many are simply representations on paper—like mathematical models. Or, finally, they may be simple sets of relationships that are sketched out in the mind and not formally put down on paper. In no case are models photographic reproductions of reality; if they were, they would be so complicated that they would be of no use to us. They have to abstract from a great deal of the real world—focusing upon what is relevant for the problem at hand, ignoring what is irrelevant. Whether or not one model is better than another depends not on its complexity, or its appearance of reality, but solely on whether it gives better predictions (and thereby helps us to make better decisions).

5. A criterion. By "criterion" we mean the test by which we choose one alternative or system rather than another. The choice of an appropriate economic criterion is frequently the central problem in designing a systems analysis. In principle, the criterion we want is clear enough: the optimal system is the one which yields the greatest excess of positive values (objectives) over negative values (resources used up, or costs). But as we have already seen, this clear-cut ideal solution is seldom a practical possibility in military problems.[1] Objectives and costs usually have no common measure: there is no generally acceptable way to subtract dollars spent or aircraft lost from enemy targets destroyed. Moreover, as in two of the cases above, there may be multiple objectives or multiple costs that are incommensurable. So in most military analyses, we have to be satisfied with some approximation to the ideal criterion that will enable us to say, not that some system A is opti-

[1] In private industry this "ideal" criterion is the famliar one of profit maximization.

mal, but that it is better than some other proposed systems B, C, and so on. In many cases, we will have to be content with calculating efficient rather than optimal systems, relying on the intuitive judgment of well-informed people (of whom the anlayst may be one) to select one of the efficient systems in the neighborhood of the optimum.

It cannot be stated too frequently or emphasized enough that economic choice is *a way of looking at problems* and does not necessarily depend upon the use of any analytic aids or computational devices. Some analytic aids (mathematical models) and computing machinery are quite likely to be useful in analyzing complex military problems, but there are many military problems in which they have not proved particularly useful where, nevertheless, it is rewarding to array the alternatives and think through their implications in terms of objectives and costs. Where mathematical models and computations are useful, they are in no sense alternatives to or rivals of good intuitive judgment; they supplement and complement it. Judgment is always of critical importance in designing the analysis, choosing the alternatives to be compared, and selecting the criterion. Except where there is a completely satisfactory one-dimensional measurable objective (a rare circumstance), judgment must supplement the quantitative analysis before a choice can be recommended.

The Requirements Approach

In the absence of systematic analysis in terms of objectives and costs, a procedure that might be called the "requirements approach" is commonly used in the military departments and throughout much of the government. Staff officers inspect a problem, say, the defense of the continental United States or the design of the next generation of heavy bombers, draft a plan which seems to solve the problem, and determine requirements from the plan. Then feasibility is checked: Can the "required" performance characteristics, such as some designated speed and range, be achieved? Can the necessary budget be obtained? Does the nation have the necessary resources in total? If the program passes the feasibility tests, it is adopted; if it fails, some adjustments have to be made. But the question: What are the payoffs *and the costs* of alternative programs? may not be explicitly asked during the process of setting the requirement or deciding upon the budget. In fact, officials have on occasion boasted that their stated "requirements" have been based on need alone.

This, of course, is an illusion. Some notion of cost (money, resources, time), however imprecise, is implicit in the recognition of any limitation. Military departments frequently determine "requirements" which are from 10 to 25 per cent higher than the available budget, but never ten times as high, and seldom twice as high. But this notion of cost merely rules out grossly infeasible programs. It does not help in making optimal or efficient choices.

For that purpose it is essential that alternative ways of achieving military objectives be costed, and that choices be made on the basis of payoff and cost. How *are* choices made by military planners prior to any costing of alternatives? We have never heard any satisfying explanation. The derivation of requirements by any process that fails to cost alternatives can result in good solutions only by accident. Probably military planners sometimes weigh relative costs in some crude manner, at least subconsciously, even when they deny they do; or they make choices on the basis of considerations which ought to be secondary or tertiary, such as the preservation of an existing command structure, or the matching of a reported foreign accomplishment.

The defects of the requirements approach can be seen clearly if we think of applying it to our problems as a consumer. Suppose the consumer mulls over his transportation problem and decides, "on the basis of need alone," that he requires a new Cadillac. It is "the best" car he knows, and besides Jones drives one. So he buys a Cadillac, ignoring cost and ignoring therefore the sacrifices he is making in other directions by buying "the best." There are numerous alternative ways of solving the consumer's transportation problem (as there are always numerous ways of solving a military problem), and a little costing of alternatives prior to purchase might have revealed that the purchase of "the best" instrument is not *necessarily* an optimal choice. Perhaps if the consumer had purchased a Pontiac or a secondhand Cadillac he would have saved enough to maintain and operate it and take an occasional trip. Or if he had purchased a Chevrolet he could have afforded to keep his old car and become head of a two-car family. One of these alternatives, properly costed and compared, might have promised a far greater amount of utility for the consumer than the purchase of a new Cadillac "on the basis of need alone." Or the exercise might have reassured the consumer that the new Cadillac was indeed optimal. While expensive unit equipment is not necessarily optimal, in some cases it can be proved to be.

The Priorities Approach

Another procedure that seems to have a great deal of appeal, in both military planning and other governmental activities, is the "priorities approach." To facilitate a decision about how to spend a specified budget, the desirable items are ranked according to the urgency with which they are needed. The result is a list of things that might be bought, the ones that are more important being near the top and the ones that are less important being near the bottom. Lists that rank several hundred weapons and items have sometimes been generated in the military services.

At first blush, this appears to be a commendable and systematic way to tackle the problem. When one reflects a bit, however, the usefulness and significance of such a list begins to evaporate. Consider the following items ranked according to their (hypothetical) priorities: (1) Missile X, (2) Radar device Y, (3) Cargo aircraft Z. How do you use such a ranking? Does it mean that the entire budget should be spent on the first item? Probably not, for it is usually foolish to allocate all of a budget to a single weapon or object. Besides, if a budget is to be so allocated, the ranking of the items below the first one has no significance.

Does the ranking mean that the money should go to the first item until no additional amount is needed, then to the second item until no further amount is needed, and so on? Hardly, because there could be some need for more of Missile X almost without limit. Even if only a limited amount of Missile X was available, to keep buying right out to this limit would usually be a foolish rule. After quite a few Missile X's were purchased, the next dollar could better be spent on some other item. Even using lifeboats for women and children first is foolish if a sailor or doctor on each lifeboat can save many lives.

Perhaps a priority list means that we should spend more money on the higher-priority items than on those having a lower priority. But this makes little sense, since some of the items high on the list, for example, the radar device, may cost little per unit and call at most for a relatively small amount of money; while some lower-ranking purchases, such as the cargo aircraft, may call for comparatively large sums if they are to be purchased at all. In any event, the priorities reveal nothing about how much more should be spent on particular items.

Just how anyone can use such a list is not clear. Suppose a consumer lists possible items for his monthly budget in the order of their priority and he feels that in some sense they rank as follows: (1) groceries, (2) gas and oil, (3) cigarettes, (4) repairs to house, (5) liquor, and (6) steam baths. This does not mean that he will spend all of his funds on groceries, nor does it mean that he will spend nothing on liquor or steam baths. His problem is really to allocate his budget among these different objects. He would like to choose the allocation such that an extra dollar on cigarettes is just as important to him as an extra dollar on groceries. At the margin, therefore, the objects of expenditure would be equally important (except for those that are not purchased at all).

The notion of priority stems from the very sensible proposition that one should do "first things first." It makes sense, or at least the top priority does, when one considers the use of a small increment of resources or time. If one thinks about the use of an extra dollar or of the next half-hour of his time, it is sensible to ask, "What is the most urgent—the first-priority—item?" If one is deciding what to do with a budget or with the next eight hours, however, he ordinarily faces a problem of *allocation*, not of setting priorities. A list of priorities does not face the problem or help solve it.

Thus in formulating defense policy and choosing weapon systems, we have to decide how much effort or how many resources should go to each item. The "priorities approach" does not solve the allocation problem and can even trap us into adopting foolish policies.

Some Misunderstandings

There is some resistance to the use of economic analysis in military problems that is based on misunderstanding.

An economically efficient solution to military problems does not imply a cheap force or a small military budget. It simply implies that whatever the military budget (or other limitation, for example, on personnel), the greatest military capabilities are developed. Since military capabilities are plural and not easily commensurate, an efficient military establishment, in the technical sense, would merely be one in which no single capability—antisubmarine, ground warfare, offensive air, and so on—could be increased without decreasing another. An optimal establishment would in addition have the right "balance" among capabilities—a harder problem for analysis.

From the point of view of the nation, of the military establishment as a whole, and of the Treasury Department, the achievement of efficiency and the approach to an optimal solution can be a common objective. There is a conflict of interest between the Treasury, the Bureau of the Budget, and economy-minded Congressmen on the one hand, and the military services on the other when the level of the budget is in question. The military services always (and properly) want more; the economizers always (and also properly) offer resistance, or try to impose reductions. But once the budget has been determined, there is no longer conflict of interest.

In fact, the choices that maximize military capability for a given budget are the same choices that minimize the cost of attaining that capability. The capability-maximizing criterion (given budget) and cost-minimizing criterion (given capability) are logically equivalent and therefore lead to the same choices and the same programs (for any given scale of operations, as determined by either budget or capability). If an Atlas missile system maximizes our strategic air power for a given SAC budget, it also minimizes the cost of providing that much strategic air power.

Some officers object to economic analysis because they think it implies cheap equipment, or the continued use of obsolescent equipment. This is by no means the case except, properly, where the use of cheap or old equipment results in lower system cost. New equipment does tend, on a unit basis, to be more expensive than old; but this does not mean that its use is uneconomic, any more than the use of modern more expensive equipment is necessarily uneconomic in industry. What counts, in the military as in industry, is not the unit cost of procurement, but the total system cost—the cost of procuring and maintaining and operating the whole system in which the new equipment is embedded—of achieving an appropriate capability or objective. This may be greater or less with new, more "expensive," higher performance equipment. The problem of the relative worths and costs of quality and quantity is, in the military as in private industry, an economic problem, amenable to economic calculus.

Another misunderstanding is reflected in the question, "What do dollars matter when national survival is at stake?" They matter precisely because they represent (however imperfectly in some circumstances) generalized national resources at the disposal of the military. Unless they are economically used, resources will be wasted, and the nation will have less military capability and a smaller chance of survival. If any one dimension of military power is wastefully planned, that is, at greater than minimum cost, some other dimension will, with a given total military budget, have fewer resources at its disposal and necessarily less capability. Of course waste can be compensated, within limits, by voting higher military budgets at the expense of nonmilitary objectives, but legislatures are understandably less than willing to raise budgets for this purpose. If they vote a higher budget, they want the still greater military capability that an economic use of the higher budget would make possible.

In a free enterprise economy, we have a price mechanism and a system of incentives which, imperfectly but pervasively, enforce some measure of consistency between the lower level criteria used by individuals and firms in making their economic decisions and certain higher level criteria appropriate to the economy. A whole branch of economic theory, rather unfortunately labeled "welfare economics," is concerned with relations between high and low economic criteria. Under certain circumstances (the most important being absence of monopoly, free movement of factors of production, "full employment," and no external economies or diseconomies), the maximization of their own preference functions by individuals and of their own profits by firms will lead to an "efficient" use of resources in the economy—in the precisely defined senses that it will be impossible to produce more of any one good or service without producing less of some other *and* that it will be impossible to improve the satisfaction of any one individual without reducing that of another.[2] Since, in general, firms do try to maximize profits and individuals do try to maximize preference functions, there will be a tendency for resources to be efficiently used in the economy to the extent that the assumed circumstances are approximated.

This is an interesting and, within limits, a useful conclusion. It might be regarded as equally plausible, or even more plausible, that the higher level economic criterion would require firms to minimize cost per unit of output (the ratio of cost to output) or to maximize productivity per head or per man-hour (the ratio of output to some one input) instead of maximizing profits (receipts minus costs). In fact, both these criteria have been widely used—in some cases appropriately, in others not—as indexes of efficiency in comparisons between firms and countries. But it can be demonstrated that

[2] Of course efficiency in this sense does not imply an "optimal" distribution of income from anyone's point of view or an "optimal" rate of growth. Efficiency is not a sufficient condition for an optimum, but it does enable us to identify improvements in many situations.

maximizing either of the ratios by firms in choosing methods of production, scale of operations, and so on, would result in an inefficient use of resources in the economy.

Some Criterion Errors

In the military (and indeed in the government generally), there is no comparable mechanism that tends to insure consistency between high level and low level criteria.[3] Since piecemeal analysis and therefore the use of low level criteria cannot be avoided, the prevention of even gross errors in the selection of criteria requires hard thought. In a very general sense, all criterion errors involve inconsistency between the tests that are selected in analyzing lower level problems and the tests that are applicable at higher levels. However, some of the mistakes that occur most frequently have special characteristics and can be put into categories.

Maximizing Gain While Minimizing Cost

The consequences of an action fall into two types—(1) those positive gains which we like to increase, or the achievement of objectives, and (2) those negative effects which we like to decrease, or the incurrence of costs. Neither type by itself can serve as an adequate criterion: the maximizing of gains without regard to cost or resource limitation is hardly a helpful test, and the minimizing of cost regardless of other consequences of the alternative actions is nonsense. Hence, both gains and costs must appear in criteria but, as will be seen, they can make their appearance in various ways.

One ubiquitous source of confusion is the attempt to maximize gain while minimizing cost or, as a variant, the attempt to maximize two types of gain at once. Such efforts are made, or at least talked about, in connection with all manner of problems. It is sometimes said, for example, that we should choose new weapons on a "maximum effectiveness at minimum cost" basis.

Actually, of course, it is impossible to choose that policy which simultaneously maximizes gain and minimizes cost, because there is no such policy. To be sure, in a comparison of policies *A* and *B*, it may turn out occasionally that *A* yields greater gain, yet costs less, than *B*. But *A* will not also yield more and cost less than all other policies *C* through *Z*; and *A* will therefore not maximize yield while minimizing cost. Maximum gain is infinitely large, and minimum cost is zero. Seek the policy which has that outcome, and you will not find it.

[3] There are administrative devices—committees, special staffs at higher levels, etc.—which attempt, through cooperation and "coordination," to mitigate the consequences of the absence of such a mechanism.

Overlooking Absolute Size of Gain or Cost

One common procedure is to pick that policy which has the highest ratio of "effectiveness," or achievement-of-objective, to cost. In that case, the maximizing of this ratio is the criterion. Note that the terms "effectiveness" and "achievement of objectives" mean positive gains, or the achievement of tasks that is desirable to carry out. To examine this criterion, let us look at the comparison of alternative military weapons. These could be anything from various antitank weapons to different bombers, but suppose it is the latter. Let the ability to destroy targets, in the relevant circumstances, be the measure of effectiveness. Suppose next that a B-29 system, already on hand and relatively easy to maintain, would be able to destroy 10 targets and would entail extra costs of $1 billion—a ratio of 10 to 1—while System X would destroy 200 targets and cost $50 billion—a ratio of 4 to 1. Does it follow that we should choose the B-29 system, the one with the higher ratio? The answer is surely No, for it might merely be a system that would invite and lose a war inexpensively. To maximize the ratio of effectiveness to cost may be a plausible criterion at first glance, but it allows the absolute magnitude of the achievement or the cost to roam at will. Surely it would be a mistake to tempt the decision-maker to ignore the absolute amount of damage that the bombing system could do.

Of course, if the ratios did not alter with changes in the scale of achievement (or cost), the higher ratio would indicate the preferred system, no matter what the scale. That is, if the ratio of achievement to cost were 10 to 1 for the B-29 system and 4 to 1 for System X at *all* levels of achievement, then the B-29 system would be "dominant." For it would destroy 500 targets at the $50 billion level of cost, clearly a better performance than that of System X. But to assume that such ratios are constant is inadmissible some of the time and hazardous the rest.

It might be observed that ratios are sometimes handy devices for ranking a list of possible actions when (1) the scale of activity is fixed, and (2) the actions are not interdependent. Thus the rate of return on stocks and bonds (the ratio of annual net return to the cost of the investment) is a convenient aid in ranking securities. Then, *with a fixed investment fund*, the set of securities that yields the greatest return for that fund can be quickly determined. Note, however, the limited conditions under which this procedure can be used.